Exploring Chemical Elements and Their Compounds

David L. Heiserman

WITHDRAWN

TAB Books

Division of McGraw-Hill

New York San Francisco Washington, D.C. Auckland Bogotá
Caracas Lisbon London Madrid Mexico City Milan
Montreal New Delhi San Juan Singapore
Sydney Tokyo Toronto

pbk   10 11 12 13 14 15 16 DOC/DOC 9 9
hc   6 7 8 9 10 11 12 13 14 DOC/DOC 9 9 8 7

Library of Congress Cataloging-in-Publication Data

Heiserman, David L., 1940-
   Exploring chemical elements and their compounds / by David L.
Heiserman.
     p. cm.
   Includes index.
   ISBN 0-8306-3018-X (h)   ISBN 0-8306-3015-5 (p)
   1. Chemical elements. I. Title.
QD466.H38 1991
546—dc20   91-17687
                                        CIP

Acquisitions Editor: Roland S. Phelps
Book Editor: Barbara Ann Ettinger
Director of Production: Katherine G. Brown
Book Design: Jaclyn J. Boone
Managing Editor: Sandra L. Johnson
Cover Design: Holberg Design, York, Pa.

EL1
3760

Contents

Introduction

As a high school chemistry student contemplating a science fair project, I came across a book in our public library that described chemical elements and their compounds. The book was very technical and very, very thick, as I remember it. I understood very little of the material it contained, but I was quite taken with descriptions of colors, textures, and especially the endless variety of chemical reactions. That mental snapshot of the past turned out to be the seed for writing a book on the same topic, but one that is less technical, not quite as thick, and much easier to understand.

Chemistry—the way it is taught and implemented professionally—has changed a great deal since my first exposure to it 35 years ago. Yes, there are more elements and entire families of radioactive isotopes that were unknown a generation ago, but changes of that kind are trivial when compared with the basic transformation of how chemists regard atomic structures, molecules, and reactions. It is not enough simply to update the numbers and add new figures and tables; a book of this type must also reflect the spirit of modern chemistry. (Please excuse my occasional lapses into subjective descriptions of chemical substances and reactions—these are all part of the excitement of chemistry past, present, and future I am trying to share with you.)

This book is organized according to the atomic numbers assigned to the elements. Hydrogen, being element number 1, is the first; and a summary of the new superheavy elements, beginning with element number 108, appears at the end of the book. Discussions of each element are broken down into smaller sections that include a technical summary of basic physical properties, a brief history of the element, a more detailed description of its chemical and physical properties, production methods, a summary of some of the important and interesting compounds, and a list of known isotopes. The crystal structure diagram found beneath an element's name is the most common crystal structure for that particular element.

Unfortunately, a single book cannot be all things to all people. In this instance, I have no room to explain the rudiments of chemistry that are required for a full appreciation of the discussions. For example, you might not understand the difference between atomic numbers and atomic weights or allotropes and isotopes; and you might not know how to interpret symbolic representations of chemical reactions. This doesn't mean you are stupid or out of touch with the world. It simply means you have to make the effort to find another book that explains such matters in more detail than I can here. Check your public library for elementary chemistry textbooks, especially in a department that specializes in books for people of junior-high age.

This book is dedicated to the very special kind of people who will pioneer the chemistry of tomorrow: people like the lad who discovered bromine during his summer vacation between high school and college, and people like Madame Curie, whose personal laboratory notebooks are still too radioactive to handle safely. All historical anecdotes come from *Discovery of the Elements* by M.E. Weeks and H.J. Leichester (7th edition, 1968).

I would also like to thank Fred Glasser for proofreading much of the manuscript and providing valuable technical advice and insight, and my wife Judy for her continuing support and encouragement.

Element 1: Hydrogen

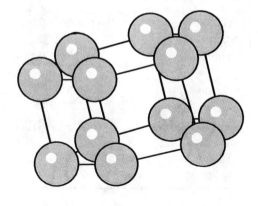

Name	Hydrogen
Symbol	H
Atomic Number	1
Atomic Weight	1.00794
Melting Point	-255.34°C
Boiling Point	-252.87°C
Density	0.08988 g/l
	(gas, 0°C, 1 atm)
Specific Gravity	70.8 (liquid, -253°C)
	70.6 (solid, -262°C)
Oxidation States	-1, +1
Electron Config.	$1s^1$

- Name pronounced as **Hi-dreh-jen**
- Name taken from the Greek *hydro* + *genes*, "water generator"
- Isolated and identified as an element by Henry Cavendish in 1766
- Colorless, odorless, tasteless gas
- Lightest and simplest chemical element
- Most abundant element in the cosmos

The hydrogen atom is the simplest atom that can possibly exist. Its most common isotope is composed of a single proton and an electron. If you take away either of these parts, you no longer have an atom at all.

As shown in Fig. 1-1, the hydrogen atom is the most abundant in the cosmos. There is relatively little hydrogen gas in the earth's atmosphere, but there are plenty of hydrogen atoms showing up in hydrogen compounds—ordinary water, for instance. Then consider that every molecule of water in all the seas, lakes, and streams includes two hydrogen atoms. Figure 1-2 shows that hydrogen makes the list of the ten most abundant elements on the earth.

Nearly two-thirds of the hydrogen that is commercially produced today is used in the Haber process for manufacturing ammonia. The food industry also consumes a lot of hydrogen for hydrogenating simple vegetable oils. The end products including margarine, cooking oil, and salad dressings, are much healthier for you than their counterparts traditionally produced from animal fats. Finally, a small amount of elemental hydrogen is used in liquid form as a rocket fuel.

Historical background

The existence of hydrogen was apparently well established by the time Robert Boyle published a work in 1671 entitled *New Experiments Touching the Relation Betwixt Flame and Air*. In this paper, Boyle describes how you can generate hydrogen gas by simply adding a

Element	Abundance (Si = 1)
Hydrogen	40,000
Helium	3,100
Oxygen	22
Neon	8.6
Nitrogen	6.6
Carbon	3.5
Silicon	1
Magnesium	0.91
Iron	0.60
Sulfur	0.38

Element	Concentration (ppm)
Oxygen	464,000
Silicon	282,000
Aluminum	83,200
Iron	56,300
Calcium	41,500
Sodium	23,600
Magnesium	23,300
Potassium	20,900
Titanium	5700
Hydrogen	1400

1-1 Hydrogen is the most abundant element in the cosmos, with 40,000 atoms per atom of silicon.

1-2 Hydrogen barely makes it onto the list of the ten most abundant elements in the earth's crust.

dilute acid to iron filings in a test tube. He suggests using mars (iron) and either a saline spirit (hydrochloric acid) or oil of vitriol (sulfuric acid). The scientist notes how ". . . the mixture grew very hot, and belched up copious and stinking fumes . . ." He then further notes, "But whencesoever this stinking smoke proceeded, so inflammable it was, that on the approach of a lighted candle to it, it would readily enough take fire and burn with a bluish and somewhat greenish flame at the mouth of the vial . . . with more strength that one would easily suspect." Through the subsequent centuries, this hydrogen-generating experiment has been repeated countless times in countless elementary chemistry classes throughout the world.

A chemistry textbook published in 1716 describes Boyle's experiment in terms of how the "liquor heats and boils considerably" and how a lighted candle causes the vapor to "immediately take fire and at the same time produce a violent, shrill fulmination." But like so many enthusiastic experimenters, the author carried his thinking a bit too far, attempting in this case to cite the experiment as one demonstrating the cause of thunder and lightning in the atmosphere.

A few years later, a Russian scientist named M. V. Lomonsov stated that the inflammable mixture emerging from the mouth of the test tube was "nothing less than phlogiston, evolved by the friction of the solvent with the molecules of the metal and carried along by the escaping air with the finer particles of the spirit that evolved." At least the language was beginning to sound somewhat more scientific by this time, although Lomonsov somewhat overestimated the importance of his observation by ascribing the effect to the theoretically important, but elusive, phlogiston.

Henry Cavendish (1731 – 1810) is credited with isolating and identifying hydrogen gas as a true chemical element—an "inflammable air from the metals." Although he wrongly believed the metal, and not the acid, was the source of hydrogen gas, his contribution to the first part of the table of elements stands firm.

Chemical properties of hydrogen

Hydrogen is chemically unique in a number of ways. Among these unique features is its ability to form compounds by giving up an electron or acquiring one. Elements that give up electrons to form compounds are considered *electropositive* and appear at the left side of the periodic chart of the elements. On the other hand, elements that gain electrons to form compounds are called *electronegative* elements, and appear near the righthand side of the periodic chart. Hydrogen is the one and only element that can do both; it can be placed in Group IA (electropositive) or Group VIIA (electronegative). No other element has an ambiguous position on the periodic chart. Most periodic charts show hydrogen in its IA position. A few, such as the one in Fig. 1-3, show it in the VIIA position as well.

	IA	IIA	IIIB	IVB	VB	VIB	VIIB	← VIII	VIII	VIII →	IB	IIB	IIIA	IVA	VA	VIA	VIIA	0
1	1 H																1 H	2 He
2	3 Li	4 Be											5 B	6 C	7 N	8 O	9 F	10 Ne
3	11 Na	12 Mg											13 Al	14 Si	15 P	16 S	17 Cl	18 Ar
4	19 K	20 Ca	21 Sc	22 Ti	23 V	24 Cr	25 Mn	26 Fe	27 Co	28 Ni	29 Cu	30 Zn	31 Ga	32 Ge	33 As	34 Se	35 Br	36 Kr
5	37 Rb	38 Sr	39 Y	40 Zr	41 Nb	42 Mo	43 Tc	44 Ru	45 Rh	46 Pd	47 Ag	48 Cd	49 In	50 Sn	51 Sb	52 Te	53 I	54 Xe
6	55 Cs	56 Ba	57 La	72 Hf	73 Ta	74 W	75 Re	76 Os	77 Ir	78 Pt	79 Au	80 Hg	81 Tl	82 Pb	83 Bi	84 Po	85 At	86 Rn
7	87 Fr	88 Ra	89 Ac	104 Rf	105 Ha	106 Unh	107 Uns											

6	58 Ce	59 Pr	60 Nd	61 Pm	62 Sm	63 Eu	64 Gd	65 Tb	66 Dy	67 Ho	68 Er	69 Tm	70 Yb	71 Lu
7	90 Th	91 Pa	92 U	93 Np	94 Pu	95 Am	96 Cm	97 Bk	98 Cf	99 Es	100 Fm	101 Md	102 No	103 Lr

1-3 Only hydrogen has properties that permit it to be located at two different positions on the periodic table—at the tops of Group IA and Group VIIA.

Hydrogen tends to be *diatomic*. This means the molecules are composed of two atoms; therefore, the gas is represented symbolically as H_2.

There are two types of H_2 molecules, *ortho*-hydrogen and *para*-hydrogen. In the ortho-hydrogen molecule, the two protons spin in the same plane; in the para-hydrogen molecule, the spins are in opposite planes. This affects the magnetic properties and electronic band spectra of the molecules. In ordinary hydrogen gas and normal environmental temperatures, the ratio of ortho- to para-hydrogen is 3:1. The portions are roughly equivalent at $-200\,^{\circ}C$, and the amount of para-hydrogen approaches 100% as the temperature nears absolute zero.

Laboratory and commercial production

The simplest procedure for generating hydrogen gas in the laboratory is identical to the one used by the early investigators: a reaction between an acid and an active metal. Today the usual combinations are dilute sulfuric acid and zinc metal:

$$Zn + H_2SO_4 \rightarrow H_2 + ZnSO_4$$
(zinc metal + sulfuric acid → hydrogen gas + zinc sulfate)

or dilute hydrochloric acid and zinc metal:

$$Zn + 2HCl \rightarrow H_2 + ZnCl_2$$
(zinc metal + hydrochloric acid → hydrogen gas + zinc chloride)

The zinc used in such reactions is often impure, thus creating a gas having trace impurities such as the hydrides arsine (AsH_3) and phosphine (PH_3). Hydrogen has a low solubility in water and most oxidizing agents, so it is possible to remove a good share of any impurities by bubbling the gas through an aqueous solution of potassium permanganate.

Hydrogen is also produced quite easily in relatively small amounts by electrolyzing an aqueous solution of potassium hydroxide (KOH) or sodium chloride (NaCl). As shown in Fig. 1-4, hydrogen gas is generated at the cathode and oxygen at the anode. The reactions are:

$$2H_2O + 2e^- \rightarrow H_2 + 2OH^- \text{ (cathode reaction)}$$
$$2H_2O \rightarrow O_2 + 4H^+ + 4e^- \text{ (anode reaction)}$$
$$2H_2O \rightarrow 2H_2 + O_2 \text{ (cell reaction)}$$

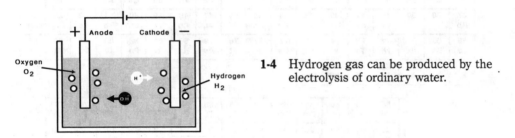

1-4 Hydrogen gas can be produced by the electrolysis of ordinary water.

A salt such as sodium hydroxide or sodium chloride must be added to the water; however, you can see from the equations that these additives are not part of the main reaction. Their role is to neutralize the unbalanced electrical charges that would otherwise occur at the electrodes—a situation that would quickly block the electrolytic action.

The two methods just described for producing hydrogen gas are not practical for the quantities demanded by today's chemical industry, especially manufacturers of ammonia and ammonia products (see Element 7: Nitrogen). Large quantities of hydrogen can be produced at a reasonably low cost by extracting it from methane gas or passing water vapor over carbon.

Methane gas (CH_4), commonly called *natural gas*, is found in abundance around oil wells and in subterranean pockets scattered virtually everywhere on earth. At temperatures in the range of 650 °C to 900 °C, methane reacts with high-pressure steam to produce carbon monoxide and hydrogen gas:

$$CH_4 + H_2O \rightarrow CO + 3H_2$$
(methane + water + heat → carbon monoxide + hydrogen gas)

With further heating, the carbon monoxide reacts with the steam to yield carbon dioxide and still more hydrogen gas:

$$CO + H_2O \rightarrow CO_2 + H_2$$
(carbon monoxide + water + heat → carbon dioxide + hydrogen gas)

Just as methane and superheated steam yield carbon monoxide and hydrogen gas, so can superheated steam in contact with carbon. The carbon in this case is usually supplied by ordinary coal. The hydrogen is taken from the water molecules as shown in this reaction:

$$C + H_2O \rightarrow CO + H_2$$
(carbon + water + heat → carbon monoxide + hydrogen gas)

This reaction is known as the *water gas reaction*. The resulting *water gas* is often piped directly to the user.

Some compounds of hydrogen

The hydrogen atom is the most abundant in the known universe, and hydrogen compounds are the most abundant of all compounds on the earth. All biological matter—from the simplest components of the DNA molecule to the complex structure of human brain tissue—includes compounds of hydrogen. Even if these biochemicals are omitted from the list, most hydrogen-carbon (hydrocarbon) molecules remain in the world of organic chemistry. If organic compounds are omitted, we are still left with an extensive list of inorganic compounds. There are certainly too many to list here.

The following summary of common hydrogen compounds features two major categories: inorganic acids and hydrides.

Common inorganic acids

Boric acid, H_3BO_3, is a weak acid that generally has the form of a soft, smooth, white solid. It is commonly used in cosmetics and pharmaceuticals.

Your refrigerator might hold some containers of *carbonic acid*, H_2CO_3. Modern-day, cosmopolitan humans actually consume a great deal of carbonic acid in the form of carbonated soft drinks. This acid is produced by dissolving carbon dioxide gas (CO_2) in water, usually at normal room temperature and at a relatively high gas pressure. Although the acid level is moderate in carbonated drinks, there is a sufficient amount of carbonic acid to corrode a common nail that is immersed in it.

Hydrochloric acid, HCl, is sometimes called *hydrogen chloride* or *muriatic acid*. HCl is a common acid for laboratory, commercial, industrial, and pharmaceutical applications. Most hydrochloric acid is now produced as a byproduct of modern plastics industries that use organic chloride chemicals. It can be produced in small, extremely pure amounts by triggering an explosive reaction between hydrogen and chlorine gasses.

Hydrochloric acid also occurs in nature—right in your own stomach. Contrary to popular belief, this "stomach acid" doesn't eat away at the food you consume; rather, it triggers production of an enzyme that digests protein.

Hydrosulfuric acid, H_2S, (perhaps better known as *hydrogen sulfide*) is best known for its distinctive "rotten egg" odor. There is nothing funny about smelling this gas, however; it is lethal to humans in concentrations of 100 parts-per-million of air. It is actually deadlier than the most infamous gassy poison, hydrogen cyanide. It is commercially produced, largely for laboratory applications, by a reaction between any metallic sulfide and another acid. Consider the reaction between ferrous sulfide and hydrochloric acid:

$$FeS + 2HCl \rightarrow H_2S + FeCl_2$$
(ferrous sulfide + hydrochloric acid → hydrogen sulfide + ferrous chloride)

Besides being a popular laboratory acid, *nitric acid* (HNO_3) has widespread commercial applications as a nitrating agent in chemical fertilizers and explosives. The following reaction shows how nitric acid and ammonia combine to produce ammonium nitrate, one of industry's most commonly used nitrates:

$$NH_3 + HNO_3 \rightarrow NH_4NO_3$$
(ammonia + nitric acid → ammonium nitrate)

Nitric acid, itself, is commercially produced by the *Ostwald process* whereby ammonia and oxygen are ultimately transformed into nitric acid and water:

$$NH_3 + 2O_2 \rightarrow HNO_3 + H_2O$$
(ammonia + oxygen gas → nitric acid + water)

Phosphoric acid, H_3PO_4, is also known as *orthophosphoric acid*. This is a solid in its purest form, but is better known in dilute, aqueous (water) solution. Like nitric acid, phosphoric acid is widely used in the production of fertilizers—phosphated fertilizers in this case. This acid is produced in commercial quantities by calcium phosphate.

Sulfuric acid, H_2SO_4, is the principal acid in industry as well as the laboratory. It is less expensive than the other strong acids, it is quite stable at room temperature, and it can be shipped and stored in high concentrations. Most commercial-grade sulfuric acid is used in the manufacture of fertilizers.

Sulfurous acid, H_2SO_3, is easily produced by dissolving sulfur dioxide gas (SO_2) in ordinary water. Sulfur dioxide is also easy to produce—simply burn some sulfur or sulfur compounds. Once you know how sulfur dioxide is produced, you can easily understand the origin of so-called "acid rain." Coal, especially that from the eastern United States, contains a significant amount of sulfur. When it is burned in large quantities at coal-burning electric power plants, a great deal of sulfur dioxide is released into the surrounding atmosphere. This SO_2 then combines with moisture in the air to produce an acidic vapor that can condense and fall to earth as acid rain.

Hydrides

Hydrides are compounds composed of two different elements, one of them being hydrogen. The following summary is brief and hardly begins to indicate the extent of the world of hydrides. For instance, there are thousands of carbon-hydrogen hydrides. *Methane* (CH_4), for one, is the elemental building block for the entire world of hydrocarbon chemistry. This colorless, odorless gas is also the primary constituent of ordinary natural gas, sometimes called *swamp gas*. (This name comes from the fact that methane is a natural byproduct of decaying vegetation.) As a popular household, commercial, and industrial heating fuel, natural gas is a significant economic commodity. As described earlier in this chapter, methane is also the primary ingredient in the commercial production of hydrogen.

A close cousin of methane is *ethane*, C_2H_6. It is also a colorless, odorless gas. Ethane is a common ingredient in natural gas, so much of it is used as a heating fuel. It is also used in the petrochemical industry as a base for many kinds of plastics.

Butane gas, C_4H_{10}, is also colorless, odorless, and highly volatile. This hydrocarbon has two forms, or *isomers*. In the instance where the four carbon atoms are connected in a straight chain, the gas is called *n-butane*, or *normal-butane*. Its isomer, one where the same four carbon atoms comprise a branched chain, is called *isobutane*.

Ammonia, NH_3, is a colorless gas that has a distinctive choking odor. It is widely used as a solvent, a refrigerant, and a source of nitrates for chemical fertilizers.

Phosphine, PH_3, is an extremely poisonous gas that has a choking, garlic odor. Current applications include manufacturing processes for certain classes of plastics and flame-resistant cotton fabrics.

Isotopes of hydrogen

The table in Fig. 1-5 shows the basic data for the three isotopes of hydrogen. Figure 1-6 illustrates them schematically. The most abundant, by far, is hydrogen-1, or *protium*. Some hydrogen-2, also known as *deuterium* and *heavy hydrogen*, exists in nature in recoverable amounts. Radioactive hydrogen-3, or *tritium*, is found only in trace amounts.

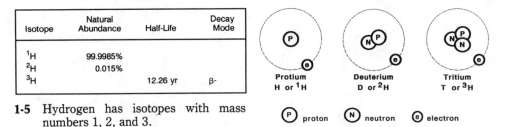

Isotope	Natural Abundance	Half-Life	Decay Mode
^{1}H	99.9985%		
^{2}H	0.015%		
^{3}H		12.26 yr	β-

1-5 Hydrogen has isotopes with mass numbers 1, 2, and 3.

Protium — H or ^{1}H; Deuterium — D or ^{2}H; Tritium — T or ^{3}H

(P) proton (N) neutron (e) electron

1-6 The isotopes of hydrogen differ in their numbers of neutrons and protons.

Today, deuterium gas is prepared by the fractional distillation of liquid hydrogen. As liquid hydrogen warms to the vaporization point, the common hydrogen isotope boils off first, leaving behind a residue that is rich in heavy hydrogen. This isotope is often given a special chemical symbol, *D*, to distinguish it from ordinary hydrogen.

The most common compound of deuterium is its oxide form: deuterium oxide (D_2O), better known as *heavy water*. This name is appropriate because the deuterium atom is twice as heavy as the more common protium atom. This means that water made up mostly of deuterium weighs more than ordinary water. Ordinary water contains nearly 7000 molecules of H_2O to every one of D_2O.

Heavy water can be prepared by means of a prolonged electrolysis of water. Whenever you electrolyze water, the system generates oxygen gas, O_2, at the anode and hydrogen gas, H_2, at the cathode. The deuterium in the system tends to remain behind, however. Therefore, as the electrolysis progresses, the concentration of heavy water in the system increases. At the beginning of the process, most of the water has the usual H_2O form. As the process continues, increasing amounts of H_2O are replaced with HDO—a water molecule consisting of a protium, a deuterium, and an oxygen. At the conclusion of the process, all hydrogen-1 atoms are replaced with D atoms and the water is pure heavy water, D_2O.

Approximately 100,000 gallons of water have to be carefully electrolyzed in this fashion to produce a single gallon of pure heavy water. Considering the cost of the electrical energy involved in such a process, it is little wonder heavy water is generally regarded as a scarce commodity.

Heavy water gained some notoriety, both in fact and fiction, shortly after World War II. This deuterium-rich water happens to be a suitable and convenient moderator in nuclear reactors. The Allied and Axis powers were both experimenting with nuclear energy, but, as the stories go, the Allies were first to produce the required moderator—heavy water—in the necessary quantities. So Axis spies and other types of high-technology villains attempted to steal the secrets of heavy-water production in various, usually sinister, ways.

The double-neutron isotope, *tritium* or *hydrogen-3*, is extremely rare in nature. It occurs in ordinary water, but only in portions of one atom for every 10^{18} atoms of hydrogen-1. It is nevertheless given its own chemical symbol, T, to distinguish it from the two other isotopes of hydrogen, H and D.

Tritium is more effectively produced by nuclear reactions than by separation from water by electrolysis. Tritium was first observed after bombarding deuterium atoms with high-energy deuterium nuclei (the neutron and proton from a deuterium atom—a *deuteron*). The most effective procedure, however, is to bombard lithium-6 with neutrons. The reaction yields tritium and an alpha particle, or helium atom:

$$^6\text{Li} + {}^1n \rightarrow {}^3\text{T} + {}^4\text{He}$$

Element 2: Helium

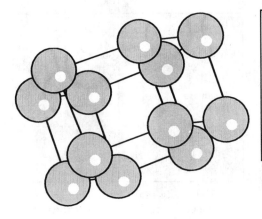

Name	Helium
Symbol	He
Atomic Number	2
Atomic Weight	4.0026
Melting Point	< -272.2°C (26 atm)
Boiling Point	-268.934°C
Density	0.1785 g/l
	(gas, 0°C, 1 atm)
Oxidation State	0
Electron Config.	$1s^2$

- Name pronounced as **HEE-li-em**
- Name taken from the Greek *helios*, "sun"
- Discovered independently by Pierre Janssen and Joseph Norman Lockyer in 1868
- Inert, colorless, odorless, tasteless gas
- Second only to hydrogen in abundance in the cosmos

Helium is the gas of choice for toy balloons, an element discovered in the sun before it was found on earth, an inert atmosphere for high-technology welding and metal-cutting operations, and a harmless gas that makes you talk like Donald Duck. Versatile and harmless, plentiful and inexpensive, stuff for fun and for serious work—this all characterizes the element helium.

There is plenty of helium in the universe. In fact, Fig. 2-1 shows that helium ranks second only to hydrogen in terms of abundance throughout the cosmos. Figure 2-2, however, shows that helium is not as common in the earth's atmosphere as it is in outer space. The relative scarcity of helium in our atmosphere, coupled with the fact that it does not react with other elements, accounts for the reason why the gas was discovered in space before it was discovered on earth.

Historical background

The existence of helium was not even suspected until the second half of the nineteenth century; even then, its presence in our atmosphere remained questionable for another quarter century. The story begins in India in the year 1868. Generally, this was near the beginning of the explosion of new knowledge brought about by the invention of spectroscopic processes, and specifically it was the occasion of a total solar eclipse. Pierre-Jules-César Janssen (1824–1907), a French astronomer, packed up his spectroscopic instruments and sailed to India in order to do a spectral analysis of the sun's chromosphere during a total eclipse.

Janssen saw the lines he expected during the eclipse, but he also found a stranger—a yellow line very close to the familiar sodium line. Close—even very close—doesn't count in spectroscopy. Janssen had discovered a spectral line that no one had noticed before; when he returned to France, he found he could not reproduce the new line with the spectrum from

Element	Abundance (Si = 1)
Hydrogen	40,000
Helium	3,100
Oxygen	22
Neon	8.6
Nitrogen	6.6
Carbon	3.5
Silicon	1
Magnesium	0.91
Iron	0.60
Sulfur	0.38

Gas (Sea level)	Content by volume	
	(percent)	(ppm)
Nitrogen, N_2	78.09	—
Oxygen, O_2	20.95	—
Argon, Ar	0.93	—
Carbon Dioxide, CO_2	0.03	—
Neon, Ne	—	18.18
Helium, He	—	5.24
Krypton, Kr	—	1.14
Methane, CH_4	—	2
Nitrous oxide, N_2O	—	0.5
Hydrogen, H_2	—	.05
Xenon, Xe	—	.087

2-1 Helium is the second most abundant element in the known universe, with 3,100 atoms for each atom of silicon.

2-2 Helium is ranked sixth on the abundance chart for gasses in the earth's atmosphere.

any known element. This was sufficient evidence to prove the existence of an unknown element. Janssen called it *helium* after the Greek *helios*, or "sun."

Clearly, helium existed on the sun. But did it exist anywhere on earth? Janssen's announcement of his discovery set off excited searches for earth-bound helium and helium compounds. Nothing conclusive developed in this regard until 1890, when an American chemist, William F. Hillebrand, noticed an inert gas coming from a sample of uraninite he washed in acid. He thought that the gas was nitrogen, and he published a paper outlining his finding. An Englishman, Sir William Ramsay (1852 – 1916), disagreed with Hillebrand's conclusions and repeated the experiment, using a close relative of uraninite called *cleveite*.

Ramsay found nitrogen in the gasses evolved by the acid treatment of cleveite, and he found some argon as well. But he could not account for a third gas that showed some peculiar spectral lines. Because Ramsay's spectroscope was not a very good one, he could not confirm or deny the presence of helium. So he sent samples to two renowned spectrographers, Sir William Crookes and solar astronomer Sir Norman Lockyer. These were good choices because Crookes had already demonstrated his prowess with the spectroscope when he used it in his discovery of thallium (*see* Element 81: Thallium), and Lockyer had been studying helium lines from the sun for nearly twenty years. Lockyer gets credit for confirming the discovery. By 1895, investigators were finding helium in the atmosphere.

Chemical properties of helium

Helium heads the list of Group 0 elements along the right-hand edge of the periodic chart— a group more commonly called the *noble gasses*. These gasses are most noted for their relative inactivity.

Helium and the other noble gasses were once considered totally inert; that is, it was thought they could not react with any element to produce compounds. There was good theoretical and practical evidence to support this earlier view. First, from a theoretical viewpoint, all electron orbits for the noble gasses are completely filled. This means the atoms are extremely stable and neither give up nor gain electrons under normal circumstances. From a practical point of view, no one had found a noble-gas compound until 1962.

Nowadays it is possible to prepare stable compounds of the three heavier noble gasses: krypton (Kr), xenon (Xe), and radon (Rn). The lighter noble gasses—helium (He), neon (Ne), and argon (Ar)—still pose a problem with regard to making stable compounds. Researchers, however, have seen evidence of an unstable ion that combines one of the lighter noble gasses with an atom of hydrogen. In the case of helium, this ion is HeH^+.

Helium is the only element that cannot be converted to a solid by lowering its temperature. At ordinary atmospheric pressure, helium is believed to remain a liquid at absolute zero. As shown in Fig. 2-3, however, the critical temperature is a bit above absolute zero. Helium can thus be solidified by means of a combination of low temperature and high pressure.

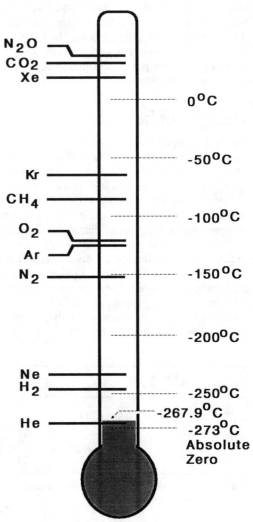

2-3 The critical temperature of helium is very close to absolute zero, making production by liquification of air impractical.

Helium gas is also noted for having an unusually high rate of expansion with heating. And, although helium is almost twice as dense as hydrogen, it has nearly 98% of hydrogen's lifting power. This lifting power, combined with the fact that it is non-flammable, makes helium the preferred gas for dirigibles, or blimps, as well as for toy balloons.

Commercial production of helium

It is possible to obtain pure helium gas directly from the atmosphere. The general procedure in this instance is to liquify ordinary air to a temperature somewhat lower than the critical temperature of hydrogen. Helium, having the lowest boiling point of the atmospheric gasses, is the only one that remains in a gaseous state at that temperature. The gas that is bled off is thus fairly pure helium.

Commercial volumes of helium gas are extracted from raw natural gas, however. This gas, mostly methane, is drawn from natural underground deposits, cleaned up, and sold to commercial, industrial, and residential markets as a heating fuel. Raw natural gas is rich in methane gas, but raw gas also contains significant proportions of nitrogen and helium. The helium is recovered from this mixture by liquifying the gasses. As the temperature drops, the methane liquifies first, followed by the nitrogen. Once those two gasses are liquified and removed from the system, nothing remains but fairly pure helium. This helium can then be further purified by passing it through activated charcoal at a temperature slightly below the boiling point of nitrogen.

Isotopes of helium

Figure 2-4 shows the five isotopes of helium. The most common is helium-4: two protons and two neutrons in the nucleus. Some helium-3 exists in nature, as does an immeasurably small quantity of helium-5. Helium-6 and -8 are both radioactive isotopes, decaying by beta (electron) emission to lithium-6 and -8, respectively.

Beta emission is usually shown symbolically as $\beta-$. Whenever an atom emits a beta particle, a neutron in the nucleus is transformed into a proton. There is no loss of mass, however. So beta emission raises the atomic number by 1, but leaves the mass number unchanged. This is why $\beta-$ emission converts helium-6 (atomic number 2, atomic mass 6) to lithium-6 metal (atomic number 3, atomic mass 6).

While on the subjects of helium and atomic radiation, you should realize that the nucleus of an atom of helium-4 is considered to be an alpha particle, α. An alpha particle, in other words, is an atom of common helium that has its orbital electrons stripped away as shown in Fig. 2-5. The mass of an alpha particle is 4 and the number of protons is 2 (which is another way of saying the electrical charge is $+2$).

Isotope	Natural Abundance	Half-Life	Decay Mode
^{3}He	0.014%		
^{4}He	99.9986%		
^{5}He			
^{6}He		8.808 sec	β-
^{8}He		0.122 sec	β-

2-4 Helium has isotopes with atomic weights between 3 and 8.

P-proton
N-neutron
e-electron

Helium atom

Alpha particle (helium nucleus)

2-5 An alpha particle is a helium atom that has its electrons stripped away, leaving a mass number of 4 and a charge of $+2$.

Element 3: Lithium

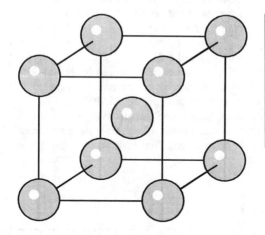

Name	Lithium
Symbol	Li
Atomic Number	3
Atomic Weight	6.941
Melting Point	180.54°C
Boiling Point	1342°C
Specific Gravity	0.534 (20°C)
Oxidation State	+1
Electron Config.	(He) $2s^1$

- Name pronounced as **LITH-i-em**
- Name taken from the Greek *lithos*, "stone"
- Discovered by Johan August Arfwedson in 1817
- Soft, silvery-white metal
- Lightest and simplest of all solid elements

Lithium is the lightest of all metals. In its vaporized state, it is the third-lightest of all known substances—only hydrogen and helium are lighter. Solid metallic lithium weighs about the same as a piece of ordinary dry wood of the same volume, and this metal does in fact float on water.

I do not recommend, however, that you try floating your only sample of metallic lithium on water. Lithium reacts rather vigorously with water to form hydrogen gas and lithium hydroxide. Lithium does not survive long in water. Lithium also reacts readily with oxygen in the atmosphere. Upon contact with air, especially moist air, this soft, lightweight, silvery-white metal quickly becomes encrusted with a dull, grayish coating of lithium oxide.

Because lithium metal reacts so readily with water and air, it cannot exist in nature in its pure form. Lithium is thus refined from minerals and ores that contain lithium compounds that do not react so readily with any of the normal conditions of nature. Also because of its affinity for moisture and air, lithium metal must be packed, shipped, and stored in an oxygen- and water-free environment. This is usually accomplished by packing the metal in a container of oil, kerosene, naptha, or other anhydrous (moisture-free), non-reactive liquid.

Lithium, in its mineral form, accounts for only 0.0007% of the earth's crust. Its compounds are used in certain kinds of glass and porcelain products. More recently, lithium has become a vital component in dry-cell batteries and nuclear reactors.

Historical background

The road to the discovery of lithium began with a rather routine study of a newly found mineral called *petalite*. In the autumn of 1817, Johan August Arfwedson (1792 – 1841) was just completing a thorough analysis of manganese oxides when he turned his attention to rocks of petalite taken from a mine on the Swedish island of Utö.

During the course of his careful chemical analysis, Arfwedson identified silica and alumina, but after counting them out of the analysis, he could not account for 4% of the ingredients. He repeated the analysis, taking into account a bit of barium sulfate. He removed every known element and compound from the samples, burned out the ammonium salts and was still left with a residue that appeared to be some sort of sulfate.

Arfwedson focused his attention on the mysterious residue; by a process of elimination, determined that ". . . it contained a definite fixed alkali, whose nature had not previously been known." We now know that petalite is lithium aluminum silicate, $LiAl(Si_2O_5)_2$.

Arfwedson and his mentor, Jöns Jacob Berzelius, announced the discovery of lithium in late 1817. A few months later, Arfwedson found lithium in two other minerals, *spodumene* and *lepidolite*, but he was not the first to isolate the pure metal. That task was accomplished independently by W. T. Brande and Sir Humphry Davy.

Chemical properties of lithium

Lithium heads the list of Group IA metals known as *alkali metals*. This group includes some other metals with familiar-sounding names and a few that are relatively obscure to the everyday world: sodium (Na), potassium (K), rubidium (Rb), cesium (Cs), and francium (Fr). One of the distinguishing characteristics of these metals is their great affinity for forming strong hydroxides—compounds once classified as alkalis.

Lithium, the leading member of this group, is one of the most reactive of all known metals, and it is a strong reducing agent. Like the other alkali metals, lithium reduces water to yield a hydroxide and liberate hydrogen gas and heat. The general reaction is:

$$2Li + 2H_2O \rightarrow 2LiOH + H_2$$
(lithium metal + water → lithium hydroxide + hydrogen gas + heat)

And in ordinary air, lithium reacts with oxygen to produce lithium oxide:

$$4Li + O_2 \rightarrow 2Li_2O$$
(lithium metal + oxygen gas → lithium oxide)

Production of lithium metal

Lithium metal is produced on a commercial scale by the electrolysis of molten lithium chloride (LiCl). The basic process begins by heating a mixture of lithium chloride and potassium chloride (KCl). This particular combination of chlorides turns out to be an *eutectic* system—in other words, the melting point of the mixture is below that of either of the two compounds. Lithium chloride, for example, normally melts at 605 °C and potassium chloride at 770 °C. Using the proportions required for industrial production of lithium metal, the mixture melts completely at about 400 °C.

The electrolysis setup is shown schematically in Fig. 3-1. The positive electrode (anode) is made of graphite; the negative electrode (cathode) is made of steel. When electrical energy is applied to the electrodes, lithium metal forms at the steel cathode. Chlorine ions are attracted to the anode. The reactions are:

$$Li^+ + e^- \rightarrow Li \text{ (cathode reaction)}$$
$$2Cl^- \rightarrow Cl_2 + 2e^- \text{ (anode reaction)}$$
$$LiCl \rightarrow Li + Cl_2 \text{ (cell reaction)}$$
(lithium chloride + electrolysis $\rightarrow$ lithium metal + chlorine gas)

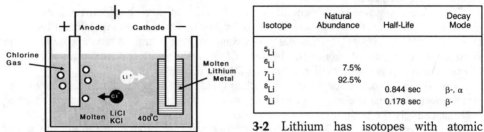

Isotope	Natural Abundance	Half-Life	Decay Mode
^5Li			
^6Li	7.5%		
^7Li	92.5%		
^8Li		0.844 sec	β-, α
^9Li		0.178 sec	β-

3-2 Lithium has isotopes with atomic weights between 5 and 9.

3-1 Lithium can be produced by the electrolysis of its chloride.

Molten lithium metal gathers around the steel cathode. When a sufficient amount is collected, it is dipped out and poured into molds. The temperature of the lithium metal is now falling rapidly from 400 °C in the electrolyte to 108 °C—the melting point of the metal. As the metal cools, impurities, such as traces of the electrolyte and compounds of gasses that happen to be in the surrounding atmosphere, solidify and separate from the lithium. Subsequent melting-and-skimming operations further refine the metal.

Lithium metal must be kept in a dry, oxygen-free environment throughout the production process. This requirement adds significantly to the cost of this metal.

Some compounds of lithium

Lithium has a single oxidation state of $+1$. This means the metallic ion combines with anions of -1 oxidation state as shown here:

Lithium chloride, LiCl

$$Li^+ + Cl^- \rightarrow LiCl$$

Lithium hydroxide, LiOH

$$Li^+ + OH^- \rightarrow LiOH$$

and with -2 anions as:

Lithium oxide, Li_2O

$$2Li^+ + O^{2-} \rightarrow Li_2O$$

Lithium sulfate, Li_2SO_4

$$2Li^+ + (SO_4)^{2-} \rightarrow Li_2SO_4$$

Lithium carbonate, Li_2CO_3

$$2Li^+ + (CO_3)^{2-} \rightarrow Li_2CO_3$$

Lithium occurs naturally in minerals classified as aluminosilicates such as lepidolite and spodumene. In the chemical world, they are known as $KLi[A1(OH,F_2)A1](SiO_3)_3$ and

LiAlSi$_2$O$_6$, respectively. These minerals are the starting point for producing commercially valuable lithium compounds and, ultimately, pure lithium metal for special laboratory and high-technology applications.

Lithium chloride, LiCl, is an important compound for the electrolytic production of lithium metal as well as other lithium compounds. It is also used as a flux for welding operations and a dehumidifying agent. It is a white, cubical-crystal substance that resembles ordinary table salt, sodium chloride.

There are two processes in general use for obtaining lithium chloride from lithium aluminosilicate minerals. One is to pass vapors of hydrochloric acid over lepidolite at temperatures of 900 °C to 1000 °C. In this nasty environment, the lithium atoms are more apt to combine with the chloride ions from the hot HCl vapor than with the aluminum and silicon atoms. The result is the formation of molten lithium chloride.

The second process for producing lithium chloride uses chlorine gas, instead of hydrochloric acid, as the source of chloride ions. Spodumene, lepidolite, or a mixture of both, can supply the lithium ion in this instance.

Lithium carbonate, Li$_2$CO$_3$, is another starting point for producing lithium metal and other compounds. It is derived from spodumene by first treating the mineral with sulfuric acid, then neutralizing the acid with calcium carbonate, and finally adding sodium carbonate. Lithium carbonate is also sold as a prescription drug for the treatment of chronic emotional depression.

Lithium hydroxide, LiOH, is a water-soluable white solid. It is produced by allowing lithium oxide (Li$_2$O) to react with water:

$$Li_2O + H_2O \rightarrow 2LiOH$$
(lithium oxide + water → lithium hydroxide)

Lithium oxide, Li$_2$O, is a white solid that is easily formed by allowing lithium metal to come into contact with oxygen, including oxygen in the surrounding atmosphere. The reaction is:

$$4Li + O_2 \rightarrow 2Li_2O$$
(lithium + oxygen → lithium oxide)

Lithium metal and hydrogen combine at very high temperatures to produce a compound that is properly known as *lithium hydride*, LiH. It appears to be a simple, white crystalline substance with a tinge of blue. It is highly flammable, but with care, it can be safely packaged, transported, and stored for long periods of time. This simple compound has been called "instant hydrogen." Just add some water and presto! . . . generous quantities of hydrogen gas:

$$LiH + H_2O \rightarrow LiOH + H_2$$
(lithium hydride + water → lithium hydroxide + hydrogen gas)

Lithium aluminum hydride, LiAlH$_1$, is a reducing agent commonly used in organic reactions. It is produced by a reaction between lithium hydride and aluminum chloride.

Isotopes of lithium

There are five known isotopes of lithium. Two of them, lithium-6 and lithium-7, are stable and found in nature. However, notice in Fig. 3-2 on p. 15, that lithium-7 is by far the more abundant. Lithium-5 is stable, but artificial; lithium-8 and lithium-9 are both radioactive isotopes having very short half-lives.

Element 4: Beryllium

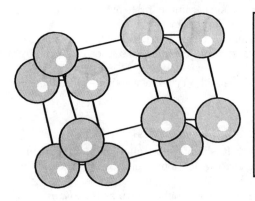

Name	Beryllium
Symbol	Be
Atomic Number	4
Atomic Weight	9.01218
Melting Point	1278°C
Boiling Point	2970°C
Specific Gravity	1.85 (20°C)
Oxidation State	+2
Electron Config.	(He) $2s^2$

- Name pronounced as **beh-RIL-i-em**
- Name from the Greek *beryllos*, "beryl" (a mineral)
- Once known as *glucinum*, sweet tasting
- Oxide form discovered in beryl and emeralds by Louis-Nicolas Vauquelin in 1798; isolated independently by Friedrich Wölhler and A. Bussy in 1828
- Hard, brittle, steel-gray metal

Beryllium is named for its principal natural source, the mineral beryl. The element was first discovered and isolated from samples of beryl, and commercial tonnage of the metal as well as its industrially important compounds are extracted from the same mineral. *Beryl* was not the first choice of a name for this lightweight metallic element. Beryllium is also known as *glucinum*, or "sweet." The reason is that beryllium metal and many of its compounds have a sugary taste. It is not a good idea to go around tasting beryllium, however, because it is a deadly poison. Exposure to its dust particles has been identified as the source of a painful disease known as berylliosis.

Beryl is even better known as the foundation material for the popular emerald gemstone. Emerald is a form of beryl, and beryl is a beryllium ore. So it follows that beryllium is the primary constituent of emeralds.

Most beryllium is used in the manufacture of components for the nuclear power industry. Some is alloyed with copper to produce an industrial-strength metal known as beryllium bronze.

Historical background

Until 1798, it was not understood that emerald and beryl were the same mineral. From the time of the early Egyptian dynasties, emeralds were considered gemstones, and beryl was regarded as a semiprecious material for elegant carvings and engravings. Until the 18th century, no one had even guessed that emerald and beryl were the same mineral. In 1798, Abbé Haüy proved that the crystal structure and density of beryl and emerald were identical. Later that same year, Louis-Nicolas Vauquelin (1763 – 1829) discovered that a single element was common to emerald and beryl.

The new element, element 4, was first named *glucina* because of the sugary taste it imparts to many of its compounds. Shortly after Vauquelin announced his discovery, chemists all over Europe began looking for glucium compounds and attempted to isolate the metal itself. Efforts to isolate the metal were unsuccessful at first, but it was found that emerald is a high-grade beryl that contains some chromium.

The breakthrough in isolating the new element came about in 1828. Known as beryllium by this time, Friedrich Wölhler and A. Bussy both managed to reduce the metal from its chloride.

The electrolytic reducing process—one that is still very popular today—was announced by one P. Lebeau in 1898.

Properties of beryllium

Beryllium metal is hard, brittle, and steely gray. It is lighter than aluminum, but resembles it in many other ways. For example, an oxide coating develops rapidly on the metallic surfaces, thus preventing further oxidation.

Beryllium heads the list of Group IIA elements commonly known as the *alkaline-earth metals*: magnesium (Mg), calcium (Ca), strontium (Sr), barium (Ba), and radium (Ra). The common name for this group is derived from theories and beliefs that prevailed prior to the early 1800s. Until that time, any element that did not obviously look, feel, and behave like a metal, and could not be dissolved in water was considered an *earth* element (from the ancient concept of the elements being earth, fire, and air). Any earth element that behaved like a common alkali, such as soda and potash, was considered an alkaline-earth metal. These views have since been abandoned in favor of more correct, precise, and comprehensive perspectives; nevertheless, the tradition remains alive in the common name of the Group IIA elements.

Production of beryllium

There are two principal procedures for producing beryllium metal on a commercial scale; one uses a chemical reducing procedure and the other an electrolytic process. In the first instance, beryllium oxide that is extracted from beryl is treated with an ammonium fluoride and some lead compounds to remove traces of impurities and yield beryllium fluoride. The beryllium in the fluoride is then reduced with magnesium at about 900 °C to extract pebbles of beryllium metal.

In the electrolytic procedure, the electrolyte is a mixture of molten beryllium chloride and sodium chloride (NaCl). The sodium chloride is added in order to make the mixture electrically conductive—a condition that is vital for electrolysis to occur. The temperature is maintained at a level necessary for keeping the electrolyte in a molten state, but far below the melting point of beryllium metal. Thus, the beryllium does not collect at the cathode as the cations do in most electrolytic processes. Rather, the beryllium is recovered as flakes of the metal when the electrolysis is completed.

Some compounds of beryllium

The oxidation state of beryllium is $+2$. This means it combines with anions of oxidation state -1 in this way:

Beryllium fluoride, BeF_2

$$Be^{2+} + 2F^- \rightarrow BeF_2$$

Beryllium nitrate, $Be(NO_3)_2$

$$Be^{2+} + 2(NO_3)^- \rightarrow Be(NO_3)_2$$

and with -2 anions as:

Beryllium oxide, BeO

$$Be^{2+} + O^{2-} \rightarrow BeO$$

Beryllium carbonate, $BeCO_3$

$$Be^{2+} + (CO_3)^{2-} \rightarrow BeCO_3$$

Beryllium oxide is the only compound of beryllium that has significant commercial value in its own right. This oxide is found in beryl, a mineral technically known as beryllium aluminum silicate, $3BeO \cdot Al_2O_3 \cdot 6SiO_2$.

The production process for high-purity beryllium oxide begins with finely ground beryl that is mixed with sodium fluoferrate, packed into blocks, and heated to about 750 °C. The result is oxides of silicon, iron, and aluminum, and sodium beryllium fluoride:

$$3BeO \cdot Al_2O_3 \cdot 6SiO_2 + 2Na_3FeF_6 \rightarrow 6SiO_2 + Fe_2O_3 + Al_2O_3 + 3Na_2BeF_4$$
(aluminum silicate + sodium fluoferrate → silicon(IV) oxide + iron(III) oxide
+ aluminum(III) oxide + sodium beryllium fluoride)

The sodium beryllium fluoride is filtered out of the mixture then treated with sodium hydroxide to produce beryllium hydroxide and sodium fluoride (NaF):

$$3Na_2BeF_4 + NaOH \rightarrow Be(OH)_2 + 4NaF$$
(sodium beryllium fluoride + sodium hydroxide → beryllium hydroxide + sodium fluoride)

Finally, the beryllium hydroxide is baked at 800 °C to produce beryllium oxide (BeO) and water.

Isotopes of beryllium

Figure 4-1 lists all of the known isotopes of beryllium. Beryllium-9 is the one that occurs in nature. The remainder are radioactive and artificially produced.

4-1 Beryllium has isotopes with atomic weights between 6 and 11.

Isotope	Natural Abundance	Half-Life	Decay Mode
^6Be			
^7Be		53.92 day	ec
^8Be		0.067 sec	α
^9Be	100%		
^{10}Be		1.6×10^6 yr	β-
^{11}Be		13.8 sec	β-, α

Element 5: Boron

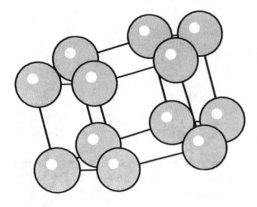

Name	Boron
Symbol	B
Atomic Number	5
Atomic Weight	10.81
Melting Point	2079°C
Sublimation Point	2550°C
Specific Gravity	2.34 (20°C)
Oxidation State	+3
Electron Config.	$1s^2\,2s^2\,2p^1$

- Name pronounced as **BO-ron**
- Name from the Arabic and Persian words for borax
- Compounds of boron were known in ancient times; the element was isolated in 1808 by Joseph-Louis Gay-Lussac and Louis-Jaques Thénard, and independently by Sir Humphry Davy
- Hard, brittle, lustrous black semimetal

Boron has proven to be a tricky element—tricky when you consider the relative simplicity of its atom. One would think that an element that is so simple and so readily available would be quite well understood, but it is not. For reasons that are not entirely clear, boron is described in much the same terms as some of the newer and more esoteric elements.

This is not to suggest that boron and its compounds are so strange that no one has figured out a way to use them: common applications only begin with products such as boric acid and gasoline additives. But so much about it seems strange—the vast range of organic complexes that can be formed with boron, nitrogen, oxygen, carbon and hydrogen, for example.

Boron exists in the earth's crust with an average proportion of only 10 parts-per-million. This means boron is on the same scale of abundance as lead. Most natural boron is compounded with sodium, hydrogen, and water to form the mineral *borax*.

Historical background

Few people throughout the history of the chemical elements regarded borax as an element, even though no one could figure out what its essential components were. Around the middle part of the 1700s, a knowledgeable chemist wrote, "Though Borax is of great use in many chymical operations, especially in the fusion of metals, . . . yet till of late years Chymists were quite ignorant of its nature, and they still are of its origin."

By 1799, it was established that common "sedative salt" is actually boric acid. This discovery proved to be the key to unlocking the long-standing mystery about the composition of borax. In 1808, two Frenchmen, Joseph-Louis Gay-Lussac and Louis-Jaques

Thénard, and an Englishman, Sir Humphry Davy, managed to isolate the new element from boric acid. The Frenchmen called the new element *bore* and Davy called it *Boracium*.

These first samples were produced by decomposing boric acid with potassium:

$$H_3BO_3 + 3K \rightarrow B + 3KOH$$
(boric acid + potassium metal → born + potassium hydroxide)

Properties of boron

Boron is generally described as a shiny black, extremely hard crystal. In this purified form, it is nearly as hard as diamond, but it is too brittle to be useful as an industrial cutting material.

Boron heads the list of Group IIIA elements. It is a semimetal, or metalloid. In many ways it resembles a common metal such as aluminum, but in other ways it behaves as a nonmetal such as carbon. At high temperatures, for example, it is a very good electrical conductor, thus showing a characteristic of a metal. At room temperature and below, however, it behaves as an electrical insulator.

An amorphous form of boron is a dark brown powder.

Production of boron

Boron can be reduced from boron oxide by heating it with magnesium:

$$B_2O_3 + 3Mg \rightarrow 3MgO + 2B$$
(boron oxide + magnesium → magnesium oxide + boron)

Where borax is easily obtained, boron can be produced by heating it with carbon:

$$Na_2B_4O_7 + 7C \rightarrow 4B + 2Na + 7CO$$
(borax + carbon → boron + sodium metal + carbon monoxide gas)

High-purity boron, on the order of 99.99%, can be produced by the electrolysis of a molten mixture of potassium fluroborate and potassium chloride.

Some compounds and the isotopes of boron

Boron has an oxidation state of $+3$. This means it combines with anions having an oxidation state of -1 in this fashion:

Boron chloride, BCl_3

$$B^{3+} + 3Cl^- \rightarrow BCl_3$$

with -2 anions as:

Boron oxide, B_2O_3

$$2B^{3+} + 3O^{2-} \rightarrow B_2O_3$$

Boron sulfide, B_2S_3

$$2B^{3+} + 3S^{2-} \rightarrow B_2S_3$$

and with -3 anions as:

Boron nitride, BN

$$B^{3+} + N^{3-} \rightarrow BN$$

The two most common compounds of boron are *boric acid* (H_3BO_3) and *borax* ($Na_2B_4O_7$ • $10H_2O$). Boric acid is known as an antiseptic and borax as a cleaning agent and water softener.

Borax is readily available from large, concentrated deposits. Boric acid is prepared by heating a mixture of borax and hydrochloric acid:

$$Na_2B_4O_7 + 2HCl + 5H_2O \rightarrow 2NaCl + 4H_3BO_3$$

(borax + hydrochloric acid + water → sodium chloride + boric acid)

Boron carbide, B_4C, is second only to diamond in hardness. It is produced at high temperature and pressure by an otherwise simple reaction between boric acid and carbon.

Figure 5-1 is the list of known isotopes of boron. Notice that most of the boron in nature is boron-11; about one-fifth is boron-10. The remaining isotopes are radioactive and produced artificially.

Isotope	Natural Abundance	Half-Life	Decay Mode
^8B		0.772 sec	β+, α
^9B		0.85 sec	α
^{10}B	19.8%		
^{11}B	80.2%		
^{12}B		0.0202 sec	β-
^{13}B		0.0173 sec	β-, α

5-1 Boron has isotopes with atomic weights between 8 and 13.

Element 6: Carbon

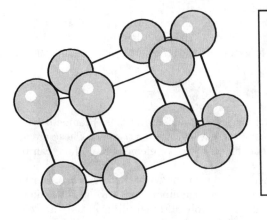

Name	Carbon
Symbol	C
Atomic Number	6
Atomic Weight	12.011
Melting Point	3550°C
Boiling Point	4827°C
Specific Gravity	1.9 (amorphous)
	2.25 (graphite)
	3.52 (diamond)
Oxidation States	+2, +4, -4
Electron Config.	(He) $2s^2\ 2p^2$

- Name pronounced as **KAR-ben**
- Name from the Latin *carbo*, "charcoal"
- Carbon, in all forms except the radioactive isotopes, have been known from ancient times
- Allotropic forms include graphite and diamond

Carbon is not the most common element in the earth's crust. In fact, it is not even among the top ten. There is more of the less-familiar element, titanium, in the earth than carbon. The earth is indeed a strange place, then, because carbon is the sixth most-abundant atom in the cosmos (see Fig. 6-1). It is the most abundant element we usually regard as being a solid, but the higher concentrations must be somewhere else in the cosmos.

Element	Abundance (Si = 1)
Hydrogen	40,000
Helium	3,100
Oxygen	22
Neon	8.6
Nitrogen	6.6
Carbon	3.5
Silicon	1
Magnesium	0.91
Iron	0.60
Sulfur	0.38

6-1 Carbon is one of the most abundant elements in the cosmos, having 3.5 atoms per atom of silicon.

Gas (Sea level)	Content by volume	
	(percent)	(ppm)
Nitrogen, N_2	78.09	—
Oxygen, O_2	20.95	—
Argon, Ar	0.93	—
Carbon Dioxide, CO_2	0.03	—
Neon, Ne	—	18.18
Helium, He	—	5.24
Krypton, Kr	—	1.14
Methane, CH_4	—	2
Nitrous oxide, N_2O	—	0.5
Hydrogen, H_2	—	.05
Xenon, Xe	—	.087

6-2 Two carbon compounds, carbon dioxide and methane, are among the gasses commonly found in the earth's atmosphere.

23

There are a couple of carbon-containing gasses in the earth's atmosphere. Figure 6-2 shows they are carbon dioxide and methane (also known as *natural gas*). Although the portions tend to get lost among the vast quantities of nitrogen and oxygen, the carbon gasses can be concentrated and applied in many useful ways.

Carbon's most critical role on earth is its place in life forms, both plant and animal life. Every living cell is built from molecules that include carbon and hydrogen atoms. Every organic molecule—from human brain cells to gasoline—are structures that include carbon atoms.

Historical background

Applications of charcoal, coal, and soot reach back into prehistoric times. Diamonds have been known as precious gems from the times of the earliest written records. These are all forms of natural carbon. There is no way that the discovery of element 6, carbon, can be attributed to an individual.

The history of carbon is largely concerned with the chemistry of the late 1700s. During this time, several renowned chemists were able to show that amorphous carbon (also known as soot, or lampblack), graphite, and diamond were simply different forms of the same element.

Properties of carbon

Carbon heads the list of Group-IVA elements. Carbon combines very slowly with oxygen at room temperatures. At moderately high temperatures, however, carbon combines with oxygen quite readily. It can even be said that carbon becomes "oxygen hungry" at red-hot temperatures. Most metals can be reduced from their oxides simply by heating them in the presence of carbon. Iron, for example, is reduced from iron oxide by heating it in the presence of a form of carbon known as *coke*.

Carbon has three well-known allotropic forms: amorphous, graphite, and diamond. Unlike the allotropic forms of most other elements, the transition from one form of carbon to another is not a simple matter of changing its temperature. The allotropes of carbon are originally formed under certain conditions of raw materials, pressure, temperature, and time. Once the allotropic form is set, it is extremely difficult to force the transition to a different form.

Production of carbon

Most elemental carbon is taken directly from the earth, mostly in the form of coal, but also as natural graphite and diamonds. These natural forms are not suitable for all of the modern applications of carbon, so there have to be commercial procedures for producing the alternative forms. The production method that is used in any given instance depends largely upon the type of carbon product that is desired.

Coke, for example, is a graphite product that is about 94% carbon. Large amounts must be produced each year to meet the demands of metal refineries. It is produced by heating soft coal in an oven that has no access to outside air. This burns off most of the impurities, leaving a fairly pure form of carbon. The product is crushed into pieces between one and four inches in diameter.

Powdered carbon, or *lampblack*, is used in the printing industry and can be pressed into shapes. The carbon rods commonly used in dry-cell batteries are made in this way. Lampblack is produced by burning methane gas in a special room that has no access to outside oxygen and has water-cooled metallic walls. As the oxygen-starved yellow flame burns, it produces a dense black soot that collects on the surfaces of the room. This powder is scraped from the walls and shoveled into shipping containers.

The natural supply of graphite cannot meet its commercial demand as a lubricant, so it has to be produced synthetically on a fairly large scale. Most graphite is obtained from petroleum coke—the black tar that remains after all of the useful fuels and organic lubricants have been distilled from crude oil. This tar is treated in an oxygen-free oven to burn off any remaining organic matter and more volatile impurities such as sulfur. The material that remains in the oven contains a very high percentage of graphite.

The demand for industrial-grade diamonds exceeds the natural supply, so most of these lower-grade diamonds are produced synthetically these days. The general idea is to force an allotropic transition from the graphite to the diamond form of carbon. This is done by subjecting high-grade graphite to extremely high temperature and mechanical pressure over a period of several days or weeks.

Some compounds of carbon

Carbon monoxide, CO, is best known as a toxic gas that is generated by the incomplete combustion of hydrocarbon fuels, including natural gas and gasoline. Improperly vented gas heaters and confined automobile exhaust fumes are responsible for hundreds of accidental deaths in the United States each year.

Carbon monoxide can be prepared on a laboratory scale by a reaction between formic acid and concentrated sulfuric acid. The result is carbon monoxide gas and dilute sulfuric acid:

$$HCOOH + H_2SO_4 \rightarrow CO + H_2SO_4 \cdot H_2O$$
(formic acid + sulfuric acid → carbon monoxide + dilute sulfuric acid)

You can substitute most other organic acids for formic acid, but the gas will be a mixture of CO and carbon dioxide (CO_2).

Carbon monoxide is prepared on a commercial scale by passing superheated water vapor at $600\,°C - 1000\,°C$ over carbon. The result is a mixture of carbon monoxide and hydrogen gas. The tricky part of this operation is making certain the temperature remains above $500\,°C$. The process is endothermic. In other words, the reaction absorbs heat energy and tends to cool its own environment; if the temperature is allowed to fall below $500\,°C$, the reaction yields carbon dioxide (CO_2) instead of carbon monoxide. This procedure is also used for producing large amounts of hydrogen gas. The resulting mixture is called *water gas*.

Carbon tetrachloride, CCl_4, a popular drycleaning agent, is prepared on a commercial scale by a reaction between carbon disulfide and chlorine gas:

$$CS_2 + 3Cl_2 \rightarrow CCl_4 + S_2Cl_2$$
(carbon disulfide + chlorine → carbon tetrachloride + sulfur chloride)

Antimony(III) chloride or iodine is used as a catalyst. The carbon tetrachloride is separated from the sulfur chloride by fractional distillation.

Trichlorofluoromethane, CCl_3F, is more commonly known as Freon-11. This halogenated compound of carbon is a popular refrigerant and an important compound used in the producton of Freon-12, or dichlorofluoromethane. CCl_3F is commercially produced by reacting carbon tetrachloride with hydrogen fluoride:

$$CCl_4 + HF \rightarrow CCl_3F + HCl$$

(carbon tetrachloride + hydrogen fluoride → trichlorofluoromethane + hydrochloric acid)

This reaction requires a catalyst, antimony tetrachlorofluoride ($SbCl_4F$).

Dichlorofluoromethane, CCl_2F_2, is also known as Freon-12—a very popular refrigerant. CCl_2F_2 is commercially produced by reacting tichlorofluoromethane (CCl_3F), or Freon-11, with hydrogen fluoride (HF):

$$CCl_3F + HF \rightarrow CCl_2F_2 + HCl$$

(trichlorofluoromethane + hydrogen fluoride
→ dichlorofluoromethane + hydrochloric acid)

This reaction also uses antimony tetrachlorofluoride as a catalyst.

Isotopes of carbon

Figure 6-3 lists all the known isotopes of carbon. Nearly all carbon found in nature is carbon-12. A bit over one percent is carbon-13. The remaining isotopes are radioactive and, except for carbon-14, have very short half-lives.

Isotope	Natural Abundance	Half-Life	Decay Mode
^9C		127 ms	β+, α
^{10}C		19.3 sec	β+
^{11}C		20.3 min	β+
^{12}C	98.90%		
^{13}C	1.10%		
^{14}C		5730 yr	β-
^{15}C		2.45 sec	β-

6-3 Carbon has isotopes with atomic weights between 9 and 15.

Radioactive carbon-14 is a well-known tool for determining the age of geological specimens and archeological artifacts. The procedure, known as *carbon-14 dating* or *radiocarbon dating*, is reasonably accurate for setting the age of objects between 500 and 50,000 years old.

Carbon-14 dating is used mainly for determining the age of objects that had once been living—fossilized plants and animals, for example. A great variety of carbon compounds cycle through all living things, and some of this carbon is radioactive carbon-14. When the creature or plant dies, the ingestion and cycling operations cease, and no fresh carbon-14 is introduced. Whatever amount of carbon-14 happens to be in the object at the time of its death begins to decay. Carbon-14 decays to nitrogen-14 at a fixed rate (half-life), so the older a specimen is, the lower its concentration of carbon-14. The concentration can be measured easily with a Geiger counter.

Element 7: Nitrogen

Name	Nitrogen
Symbol	N
Atomic Number	7
Atomic Weight	14.0067
Melting Point	-209.86°C
Boiling Point	-195.8°C
Density	1.2506 g/l
Specific Gravity	(gas, 0°C, 1 atm)
	0.808 (liquid, -195.8°C)
	1.026 (solid, -252°C)
Oxidation States	+1, -1, +2, -2, +3,
	-3, +4, +5
Electron Config.	(He) $2s^2 2p^3$

- Name pronounced **NYE-treh-gen**
- Name taken from the Greek *nitron* + *genes*, "soda forming"
- Discovered by Daniel Rutherford in 1772; also discovered independently by Joseph Priestley, Henry Cavendish, Carl Wilhelm Scheele
- Colorless, odorless, tasteless, and generally inert gas

Nitrogen is one of the most abundant elements in the cosmos, as Fig. 7-1 shows. Figure 7-2 shows that nitrogen is by far the most abundant gas in the earth's atmosphere. Every breath you take is nearly 80% nitrogen.

Element	Abundance (Si = 1)
Hydrogen	40,000
Helium	3,100
Oxygen	22
Neon	8.6
Nitrogen	6.6
Carbon	3.5
Silicon	1
Magnesium	0.91
Iron	0.60
Sulfur	0.38

Gas (Sea level)	Content by volume	
	(percent)	(ppm)
Nitrogen, N_2	78.09	—
Oxygen, O_2	20.95	—
Argon, Ar	0.93	—
Carbon Dioxide, CO_2	0.03	—
Neon, Ne	—	18.18
Helium, He	—	5.24
Krypton, Kr	—	1.14
Methane, CH_4	—	2
Nitrous oxide, N_2O	—	0.5
Hydrogen, H_2	—	.05
Xenon, Xe	—	.087

7-1 Nitrogen is one of the most abundant elements in the cosmos, having 6.6 atoms per atom of silicon.

7-2 Nitrous oxide, sometimes called laughing gas, is found among the gasses in the earth's atmosphere.

Close to 25 million tons of nitrogen are recovered commercially each year from liquified air. The atmosphere, made up of some 4000 trillion tons of nitrogen, is an inexhaustable source of the element.

Most commercially produced nitrogen is used in the Haber process for making ammonia, although a great deal is also converted to nitric acid—a primary component in explosives. About a third of the commercially produced nitrogen is used in an oilfield operation called *enhanced oil recovery*, whereby the compressed gas is used to force oil from its underground deposits. It would appear to be far more convenient and less expensive to use ordinary air for this process, but ordinary air is made up of a mixture of gasses, many of which can react with the oil to produce undesirable byproducts. Nitrogen gas, on the other hand, is notably unreactive. A significant amount of nitrogen is also used in industrial soldering and welding operations where it is important to keep other atmospheric gasses away from the high-temperature part of the work.

Historical background

The existence of nitrogen came as something of a surprise when Daniel Rutherford (1749 – 1819) announced the results of his famous experiment in 1772. Chemists of the time already knew that the atmosphere was composed of at least two gasses—one that supported life and flame, and one that did not. They had found that sealing a mouse in a bell jar until the critter suffocated caused the volume of air to be reduced by $1/16$. The oxygen was gone; that was proven by the fact that a second mouse died almost immmediately in the air. That is how Rutherford started his experiment.

His next step was to remove the "fixed air" by allowing it to react with caustic potash (potassium hydroxide). The volume of air was thus reduced by an additional $1/11$. The volume of air that remained could not support life nor flame, and it seemed to be unresponsive to any known chemical or chemical treatment. Rutherford called the gas *noxious air*.

The question of whether or not nitrogen is a true element was still an issue in 1848 when David Low, in *Simple Bodies of Chemistry*, suggested that nitrogen had to be a compound consisting of carbon and oxygen. His reasoning was quite Aristotilian, to say the least: Ammonia is derived from the organic kingdom; everything derived from the organic kingdom is composed of carbon; nitrogen is derived from ammonia, therefore, nitrogen has to include a carbon, and probably oxygen as well.

Properties of nitrogen

Nitrogen heads the Group-VA elements. In its gaseous form, nitrogen is colorless, odorless, and tasteless. As a liquid, it is also colorless and odorless, resembling ordinary water in appearance, density, and viscosity.

Nitrogen is a fairly inert gas, although it does form a few extremely important compounds which, oddly enough, tend to be very active. This can be explained by the fact that nitrogen gas is comprised of two nitrogen molecules that have a very strong binding energy. Of the common gasses, only the molecules of carbon dioxide are more difficult to separate than the two atoms of nitrogen. But once the gas molecules are pulled apart, the individual atoms become very reactive.

Preparation of nitrogen

Small amounts of nitrogen, usually for student experiments, can be prepared by combining and gently warming a mixture of ammonium and nitrate salts. Using ammonium chloride (sal ammoniac) and sodium nitrite, for example, the reaction is:

$$NH_4Cl + NaNO_2 \rightarrow N_2 + NaCL + H_2O$$
(ammonium chloride + sodium nitrite → nitrogen gas + sodium chloride + water)

Gasses such as nitrogen are recovered from liquified air by means of a process known as *fractional distillation*. Gasses are liquified by combining high pressure and low temperature. Figure 7-3 shows the critical temperatures of the atmospheric gasses; the critical temperature is the highest temperature at which the gas will liquify, regardless of the pressure. You can see on this scale that each gas has a different temperature at which it changes state between a liquid and a gas. In the process of fractional distillation, the mixture is first liquified, then it is allowed to warm gradually. As this warming takes place, the gasses boil off separately and in a sequence represented by the upward direction on the critical-temperature scale.

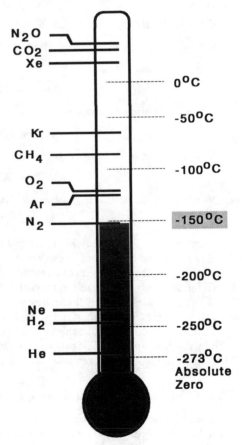

7-3 The relatively low critical temperature of nitrogen gas makes it the coldest element in commercially produced liquid air.

In the commercial operations for producing nitrogen, ordinary air is liquified under the pressure-temperature conditions required for liquifying the nitrogen. Under these conditions, nitrogen and all the gasses above it on the critical-temperature scale are in their liquid state (*see* Fig. 7-3). The three elements below nitrogen on the temperature scale, neon, hydrogen, and helium, remain in their gaseous state.

When it comes to sorting out the nitrogen, the first step is to draw off the elements that are still in their gaseous states. The next step is to increase the temperature (or decrease the pressure) just enough to allow the nitrogen to change from a liquid to a gas. The gas that is drawn off at this point is pure nitrogen that is placed in steel containers for storage and shipment.

Some compounds of nitrogen

Very few elements exhibit such a wide range of both positive and negative oxidation states. The positive oxidation states are exemplified by the element's oxides:

Nitrogen(I) oxide, or *nitrous oxide*, N_2O

$$2N^+ + O^{2-} \rightarrow N_2O$$

Nitrogen(II) oxide, or *nitric oxide*, NO

$$N^{2+} + O^2 \rightarrow NO$$

Nitrogen(III) oxide, or *dinitrogen trioxide*, N_2O_3

$$2N^{3+} + 3O^{2-} \rightarrow N_2O_3$$

Nitrogen(IV) oxide, or *nitrogen peroxide*, NO_2

$$N^{4+} + 2O^{2-} \rightarrow NO_2$$

Nitrogen(V) oxide, or *nitrogen pentoxide*, N_2O_5

$$2N^{5+} + 5O^{5-} \rightarrow N_2O_5$$

Nitrogen(VI) oxide, or *nitrogen trioxide*, NO_3

$$N^{6+} + 3O^{2-} \rightarrow NO_3$$

Ammonia, NH_3, is the major commercial nitrogen compound. It is popularly known as a cleaning agent and refrigerant. However, most of it is used in the production of fertilizers, nitric acid, and other nitrogen compounds.

Water and ammonia share a remarkable number of physical and chemical characteristics. The similarities do not include their smell; ammonia has an acrid, burning smell that is difficult to tolerate and potentially harmful to moist mouth, nose, throat, and lung tissue.

Virtually all ammonia—the millions of tons produced worldwide each year—is manufactured by the *Haber process*. The process is conceptually simple and inexpensive. It combines the basic elements of hydrogen and nitrogen:

$$3H_2 + N_2 \rightarrow 2NH_3$$
(hydrogen gas + nitrogen gas → ammonia)

The trick to making this reaction practical is to use an iron catalyst, pressures on the order of 1000 atmospheres, and a temperature in the range of 500 °C.

Nitric acid, HNO_3, is one of the most common reagents in any chemical laboratory. It is also one of the most valuable commercial chemicals, with large annual tonnages being used in the fertilizer and explosives industries.

Fresh nitric acid is a clear, watery liquid that combines readily with water. Exposed to sunlight, however, it eventually decomposes to form a useless, yellow or brownish-colored liquid. The reaction to sunlight can be described this way:

$$4HNO_3 \rightarrow 4NO_2 + 2H_2O + O_2$$
(nitric acid → nitrogen peroxide + water + oxygen)

The oldest method for producing nitric acid was described by J.R. Glauber in 1648—heat a mixture of sodium nitrate and concentrated sulfuric acid:

$$NaNO_3 + H_2SO_4 \rightarrow HNO_3 + NaHSO_4$$
(sodium nitrate + sulfuric acid → nitric acid + sodium hydrogen sulfate)

The more modern production method is somewhat more complicated, but it yields larger quantities at a lower cost. Called the *Ostwald process*, it begins by producing ammonia from elemental hydrogen and nitrogen by the Haber process described earlier in this chapter. The second step is to oxidize the ammonia in the presence of a platinum-gauze catalyst:

$$4NH_3 + 5O_2 \rightarrow 4NO + 6H_2O$$
(ammonia + oxygen → nitric oxide + water)

The nitric oxide reacts readily with atmospheric oxygen to produce nitrogen dioxide:

$$2NO + O_2 \rightarrow 2NO_2$$
(nitric oxide + oxygen → nitrogen dioxide)

Finally, the nitrogen dioxide reacts with water to form nitric acid:

$$3NO_2 + H_2O \rightarrow 2HNO_3 + NO$$
(nitrogen dioxide + water → nitric acid + nitric oxide)

The nitric oxide that is given off by the final reaction can be recycled back to the first step.

Concentrated nitric acid is actually just 69% acid and 31% water. *Fuming nitric acid* is a popular rocket fuel that is made up of a mixture of concentrated nitric acid and dissolved nitrogen oxides.

Nitrous oxide, N_2O, is the most stable and useful of the various oxides of nitrogen. It is often used as a mild anesthetic better known as laughing gas. This gas is produced by gently heating ammonium nitrate:

$$NH_4NO_3 \rightarrow N_2O + 2H_2O$$
(ammonium nitrate → nitrous oxide + water)

Isotopes of nitrogen

Figure 7-4 lists the known isotopes of nitrogen. All but a trace of natural nitrogen is nitrogen-14. The remaining amount of natural nitrogen is nitrogen-15. All other isotopes are radioactive and artificial.

7-4 Nitrogen has isotopes with atomic weights between 12 and 19.

Isotope	Natural Abundance	Half-Life	Decay Mode
^{12}N		11 ms	β+, α
^{13}N		9.97 min	β+
^{14}N	99.63%		
^{15}N	0.37%		
^{16}N		7.13 sec	β-, α
^{17}N		4.17 sec	β-, n
^{18}N		0.63 sec	β-
^{19}N		0.42 sec	β-

Element 8: Oxygen

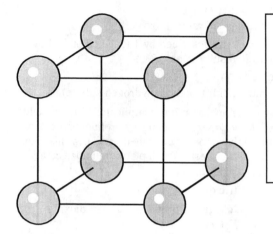

Name	Oxygen
Symbol	O
Atomic Number	8
Atomic Weight	15.9994
Melting Point	-218.4°C
Boiling Point	-182.962°C
Density	1.429 g/l
	(gas, 0°C, 1 atm)
Specific Gravity	1.14 (liquid, -182.96°C)
Oxidation State	-2
Electron Config.	(He) $2s^2\,2p^4$

- Name pronounced as **OK-si-jen**
- Name taken from the Greek *oxys* + *genes*, "acid former"
- Discovered around 1772 by Carl Wilhelm Scheele and independently by Joseph Priestly in 1774. Antoine Lavoisier identified oxygen as a true element and gave it its present-day name between the years 1775 and 1777
- Colorless, odorless, tasteless gas; pale blue liquid

Oxygen is absolutely vital for sustaining life as we know it. Figure 8-1 shows that the oxygen atom is one of the most abundant atomic species in the cosmos. Does this suggest that familiar life forms could exist elsewhere besides *Terra Firma*? Maybe so, maybe not. The earth is certainly blessed with a concentration of oxygen. Figure 8-2 shows that oxygen is the most common element in the earth's crust. Figure 8-3 shows that diatomic oxygen gas comprises more than 20% of the atmosphere.

The most important application of oxygen comes to all of us free of charge—as free as the air we breathe, so to speak. Commercially speaking, the United States annually produces some 15-million tons of liquid oxygen for applications in industry, aerospace, the military, and medicine. Oxygen is important to life, and it is big business.

Historical background

It was once believed that air was an elemental substance; today we know that it is not. Air is composed of a number of different elemental gasses. The famous Italian artist, scientist, and inventor, Leonardo da Vinci (1452 – 1519) goes on record as the first to suggest responsibly that air is composed of at least two different gasses. Furthermore, he found that one of the gasses supported both flame and life: "Where flame cannot live no animal that draws breath can live."

Between 1630 and 1756, chemists repeatedly demonstrated that metals that normally gained weight when heated in the atmosphere did not gain weight when heated in the absence of air. (Today we know that metals oxidize when heated in air, and that the oxides of

Element	Abundance (Si = 1)
Hydrogen	40,000
Helium	3,100
Oxygen	22
Neon	8.6
Nitrogen	6.6
Carbon	3.5
Silicon	1
Magnesium	0.91
Iron	0.60
Sulfur	0.38

8-1 Oxygen is one of the most abundant elements in the cosmos, having 22 atoms per atom of silicon.

Element	Concentration (ppm)
Oxygen	464,000
Silicon	282,000
Aluminum	83,200
Iron	56,300
Calcium	41,500
Sodium	23,600
Magnesium	23,300
Potassium	20,900
Titanium	5700
Hydrogen	1400

8-2 Oxygen is the most abundant element in the earth's crust.

8-3 Oxygen gas accounts for nearly 21 percent of the earth's atmosphere.

Gas (Sea level)	Content by volume	
	(percent)	(ppm)
Nitrogen, N_2	78.09	—
Oxygen, O_2	20.95	—
Argon, Ar	0.93	—
Carbon Dioxide, CO_2	0.03	—
Neon, Ne	—	18.18
Helium, He	—	5.24
Krypton, Kr	—	1.14
Methane, CH_4	—	2
Nitrous oxide, N_2O	—	0.5
Hydrogen, H_2	—	.05
Xenon, Xe	—	.087

a metal are heavier than the metal itself.) Why did it take more than a hundred years of experimentation, demonstration, and hard work to learn about the simple oxidation of metals in air? Because chemists were still fighting against the old *phlogiston* theory; and when you are working against a faulty basic theory, your experimental results tend to complicate matters, rather than explain them.

Old manuscripts preserved in the archives of European science indicate that several chemists unwittingly produced oxygen in the years between 1756 and 1772. Then in 1772, the famous Swedish scientist, Carl Wilhelm Scheele (1742–1786), published a book that described how air is composed of two different gasses, and that one of them supported fire and the other did not. He called them "fire air" and "vitated air." Before the book appeared in England, Joseph Priestly (1733–1804) announced he had produced the special gas by heating oxides of mercury and lead.

Although Scheele and Priestly share the honors for being the first to isolate "fire air," Antoine Lavoisier was the one who recognized it as a true element and gave it its present name.

Properties of oxygen

Oxygen is usually described as a colorless, odorless, tasteless gas that is essential to living organisms. Given the proper conditions for the reactions, oxygen reacts with virtually every known element to produce oxides.

Oxygen heads up the Group-VIA elements on the periodic table. The other members of this oxygen group are sulfur (S), selenium (Se), tellurium (Te), and polonium (Po). All except polonium are relatively plentiful in nature.

There are two allotropes of oxygen, one composed of two oxygen molecules (O_2) and the other composed of three (O_3). The latter is known as *ozone*. Ozone is a very strong oxidizing agent that is capable of adding an oxygen molecule to stable ions, thus changing sulfides to sulfates, dioxides to trioxides, and so on. This property makes it useful as a disinfectant and bleaching agent. It is also used in the treatment of sewage and the manufacture of chemicals.

Ozone occurs naturally in the earth's upper atmosphere where it serves as an effective shield against harmful radiation from the sun. Commercial amounts are prepared by passing oxygen (O_2) through an electric spark. The pungent odor often detected around electrical equipment is often that of ozone.

Laboratory and commercial production of oxygen

Small amounts of oxygen can be generated in the laboratory by heating potassium chlorate ($KClO_3$) with a manganese dioxide (MnO_2) catalyst. Potassium chlorate is "anxious" to give up its oxygen atoms to form potassium chloride (KCl) and oxygen. Heating alone does not release the oxygen very effectively nor does mixing the potassium chlorate with manganese dioxide. If you heat a mixture of the two chemicals, however, you get plenty of free oxygen. The manganese dioxide in this case is not consumed by the reaction. It is a true catalyst, and this particular reaction is a classic in elementary chemistry classes because it clearly demonstrates a catalytic reaction.

Small amounts of oxygen can also be obtained by electrolyzing water—actually a mixture of water and a good electrolyte such as sodium sulfate (Na_2SO_4), or Glauber's salt. The sodium sulfate does not participate directly in the reaction, so the scheme will not produce sodium, sodium hydroxide, nor any sulfates. Rather, the sodium sulfate (or similar salt) improves performance by neutralizing the ionic charges throughout the bath.

Oxygen is produced on a commercial scale by the fractional distillation of liquid air. Figure 8-4 shows that the critical temperature of oxygen is −118°C. Since liquid air is held at about 198°C, fractional distillation produces nitrogen (N_2) first at −147°C, followed by argon (Ar), and oxygen (*see* Element 7: Nitrogen for more details about the fractional distillation of liquid air).

Most commercially produced oxygen is consumed by the steel industry. Pure oxygen is blown over the molten steel where it converts excess carbon to carbon-dioxide gas and oxidizes other impurities so they can later be removed with the slag.

Some compounds of oxygen

The ten most common compounds in the earth's crust are all oxides. *Silicon dioxide*, SiO_2, accounts for nearly half the matter; about one-third is *magnesium oxide* (MgO), and a bit less

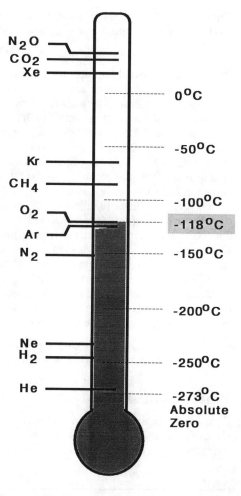

N_2O	
CO_2	
Xe	
	0°C
	-50°C
Kr	
CH_4	
	-100°C
O_2	-118°C
Ar	
N_2	-150°C
	-200°C
Ne	
H_2	-250°C
He	-273°C Absolute Zero

8-4 The critical temperature of oxygen places it in a position where it will boil away from liquid air before nitrogen, but after carbon dioxide.

than a fourth is *iron(II) oxide* (FeO). A few more examples include *aluminum oxide* (Al_2O_3), *calcium oxide* (CaO), and *iron(III) oxide* (Fe_2O_3).

The active Group-IA metals all react vigorously with oxygen at normal room temperature and atmospheric pressure. With oxygen's −2 oxidation state and the Group-IA's +1 oxidation state, the general expression for these reactions is:

$$4M + O_2 \rightarrow 2M_2O$$

where M is any one of Group-IA metals lithium (Li), sodium (Na), potassium (K), rubidium (Rb), cesium (Cs), and francium (Fr).

Reactions between oxygen and the Group-IIA metals are not quite as vigorous, but their +2 oxidation states are responsible for oxides that form this way:

$$2M + O_2 \rightarrow 2MO$$

where M is any one of Group-IIA metals beryllium (Be), magnesium (Mg), calcium (Ca), strontium (Sr), barium (Ba), and radium (Ra).

The lanthanides, or rare-earth metals, form an important group of oxides. In fact, most of the lanthanides exist in nature as their oxides, and some are even given special names.

Since most of the rare-earth metals have an oxidation state of $+3$, the oxides are put together in this fashion:

$$4M + 3O_2 \rightarrow 2M_2O_3$$

where M is any one of the rare-earth elements—scandium (Sc), yttrium (Y), and lanthanum (La, or element 57) through lutetium (Lu, or element 71). The oxides of these metals tend to have special names such as *scandia, yttria,* and *lanthana.*

Oxides of the less-active metals such as aluminum, tin, and lead do not have such simple and predictable formulations, or *stoichiometries.* In some cases, such as lead, a particular oxide might exhibit a metallic oxidation state that is not a small whole-number value. In other instances, notably vanadium and manganese, the great number of different oxidation states complicates the picture. The oxidation of iron, although it is the very familiar phenomenon known as rusting, is far more complex at the molecular level than it might appear.

Oxygen combines readily with most nonmetals to form some of the most familiar oxides: *carbon dioxide* (CO_2), *nitrous oxide* (N_2O), and *sulfur dioxide* (SO_2). Oxygen also combines with some of the nonmetals to yield important *radicals,* or ions made up of two or more atoms that behave as a single-element ion. Common examples are the hydroxyl ion (OH^-), carbonate ion (CO_3^{2-}), sulfate ion (SO_4^{2-}), and the phosphate ion (PO_4^{-3}).

Even the so-called inert elements in Group 0 are not totally immune to oxidation. Although such reactions are unknown in nature, they can be forced to take place under laboratory conditions. *Xenon trioxide,* XeO_3, is one example. It can be produced by a reaction between xenon hexafluoride and water:

$$XeF_6 + 3H_2O \rightarrow XeO_3 + 6HF$$
(xenon hexafluoride + water $\rightarrow$ xenon trioxide + hydrofluoric acid)

Isotopes of oxygen

Figure 8-5 lists all of the known isotopes of oxygen. Oxygen-16 accounts for all but a trace of atmospheric oxygen. The little bit that is not oxygen-16 is a mixture of oxygen-17 and -18. The other isotopes are produced artificially and are radioactive.

Isotope	Natural Abundance	Half-Life	Decay Mode
^{13}O		8.9 ms	$\beta+$, p
^{14}O		70.6 sec	$\beta+$
^{15}O		122 sec	$\beta+$
^{16}O	99.762%		
^{17}O	0.038%		
^{18}O	0.200%		
^{19}O		26.9 sec	$\beta-$
^{20}O		13.5 sec	$\beta-$
^{21}O		3.14 sec	$\beta-$

8-5 Oxygen has isotopes with atomic weights between 13 and 21.

Element 9: Fluorine

Name	Fluorine
Symbol	F
Atomic Number	9
Atomic Weight	18.9984
Melting Point	-219.62°C
Boiling Point	-188°C
Density	1.696 g/l (gas, 0°C)
Oxidation State	-1
Electron Config.	(He) $2s^2 2p^5$

- Name pronounced as **FLU-eh-reen** or **FLU-eh-rin**
- Name taken from the Latin *fluere*, "flow"
- Existence predicted early in the 17th century; isolated by Henri Moissan in 1886
- Greenish-yellow, pungent, corrosive gas
- Extremely reactive

Fluorine is an element of extremes. For instance, it is the most powerful oxidizer of all known substances; this means that no other chemical substance can release fluorine from any of its compounds. Fluorine, in fact, is an extremely active, gassy element that combines spontaneously and explosively with hydrogen to produce hydrogen fluoride—an acid commonly used for etching glass. It is so active that it cannot exist very long in nature without compounding with other elements. For this reason, elemental fluorine gas does not exist in nature.

Fluorine is now added to the drinking water in most metropolitan regions of the United States. Mixed in a proportion of about one part-per-million of water, the fluorine retards the occurrence of cavities in teeth. Compounds of fluorine are also added to toothpastes to aid in the reduction of cavities.

The principal minerals of fluorine are *fluorite* (CaF_2, often called *fluorospar*) and *cryolite*, Na_3AlF_6.

Historical background

Fluorine and its compounds did not play a significant role in the early history of civilization. The earliest hints of fluorine appeared around 1670 in a set of instructions for etching glass. The formula for producing the etching material included a mineral called Bohemian emerald which we know today as green fluospar, of *fluorite* (calcium fluoride, CaF_2).

By the late 1700s, some of the finest chemistry minds of the age were trying to unravel the mystery of an acid that could etch glass. The fact that high-grade fluorspar glowed in the dark when slightly heated simply added to the aura of mystery.

Fluorine gas and hydrofluoric acid do not exist in nature in amounts that can affect the human senses. Chemists were thus unaware of the hazards of working directly with concentrated doses of these materials. As a result, the early history of their efforts is highlighted with tragic stories of serious injuries and even deaths. It was about this time that one Paul Schultzenberger stated that the new element would be the most reactive of all.

Those who tried isolating the element by the electrolysis of hydrofluoric acid simply ended up with fluorochlorides and oxyfluorides. George Gore managed to obtain a little bit of fluorine in 1869, but his electrolysis apparatus exploded when the fluorine came into contact with hydrogen gas from the opposite electrode:

$$H_2 + F_2 \rightarrow 2HF$$
(hydrogen gas + fluorine gas → hydrogen fluoride)

We now realize that the reaction between hydrogen and fluorine is second in violence only to that of hydrogen and oxygen. The hydrogen-fluorine reaction is especially dangerous, however, because it occurs spontaneously at room temperature (the hydrogen-oxygen reaction has to be started with a flame or electric spark).

Ferdinand Frederic Henri Moissan (1852 – 1907) finally managed a task that was becoming seemingly impossible. He used the electrolysis principle, but with some significant refinements. First, he used a mixture of potassium fluoride and hydrofluoric acid. Second, he made certain the gasses evolved from the electrodes would not come into contact with one another. And third, he constructed the whole apparatus from platinum. The work was completed successfully in 1886.

Moissan's brilliant work put the capstone on nearly two centuries of agony. Maybe his efforts seem mundane from our sophisticated, provincial 21st-century perspective. But the world of his time certainly appreciated his accomplishment, rewarding this college dropout with the Nobel Prize for chemistry in 1906.

Properties of fluorine

Fluorine heads the list of Group-VIIA elements that are commonly known as the *halogens*. The remainder of the group is made up of chlorine (Cl), bromine (Br), iodine (I), and astatine (At). All halogens, with the notable exception of astatine, occur in nature. Notice that the names of the halogens all end in *-ine*.

The halogens are all very active, nonmetallic elements that readily combine with most metals to account for a large family of metallic salts. In such instances, the halogens are represented by ions having a charge of -1.

Fluorine can oxidize any metal, reacting with it to form some common fluorides. The oxidation state is -1, so most of the metallic fluorides are fairly simple. Like the other halides, fluorine is diatomic; that is, elemental fluorine is made up of two atoms of the gas, F_2.

Production of fluorine

Fluorine is such a strong oxidizing agent that electrolysis is the only practical method for commercial production. Basically, the procedure is the electrolysis of hydrofluoric acid or potassium acid fluoride. In both cases, fluorine gathers around the anode and hydrogen around the cathode. Since hydrogen and fluorine explode when mixed, the electrolysis arrangement must be carefully designed to keep the two gasses separated.

Hydrofluoric acid, HF, is a poor conductor of electricity, so when producing fluorine gas from HF, it is necessary to mix in a conductive material such as potassium fluoride, KF.

Hydrofluoric acid is a liquid that dissolves potassium fluoride quite readily to make an electrically conductive mixture. Figure 9-1 shows the basic setup for producing elemental fluorine gas.

The problem of making the electrolyte conductive can be avoided by using a conductive compound of fluorine in the first place. A popular candidate in this instance is potassium acid fluoride, KHF_2. This is a crystalline substance, however, that must be heated to a molten state before electrolysis can effectively take place.

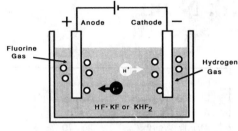

Isotope	Natural Abundance	Half-Life	Decay Mode
^{17}F		64.7 sec	β +
^{18}F		109.8 min	β +, ec
^{19}F	100%		
^{20}F		11.0 sec	β-
^{21}F		4.33 sec	β-
^{22}F		4.23 sec	β-
^{23}F		2.2 sec	β-

9-1 Fluorine can be produced by the electrolysis of a mixture of hydrofluoric acid and potassium fluoride, or by the electrolysis of potassium acid fluoride.

9-2 Fluorine has isotopes with atomic numbers between 17 and 23.

Some compounds and the isotopes of fluorine

Hydrofluoric acid, also known as *hydrogen fluoride* is commercially prepared by distilling a mixture of powdered calcium fluoride (fluorspar) and concentrated sulfuric acid:

$$CaF_2 + H_2SO_4 \rightarrow 2HF + CaSO_4$$
(calcium fluoride + sulfuric acid → hydrogen fluoride + calcium sulfate)

Since the boiling point of HF is just slightly below normal room temperature, it is technically simple to provide the product in gas or liquid forms. As described earlier, the commercial process for producing fluorine gas uses HF in its liquid form.

Potassium fluoride, KF, is used in the manufacture of fluorine gas, but only as an electrolyte. KF is, itself, prepared on a commercial scale by evaporating it from a mixture of common potash (potassium carbonate, K_2CO_3) and liquid hydrogen fluoride:

$$K_2CO_3 + 2HF \rightarrow KF + H_2CO_3$$
(potassium carbonate + hydrogen fluoride → potassium fluoride + carbonic acid)

Sodium fluoride (NaF), *stannous(II) fluoride* (SnF_2, also known as fluoristan), and *sodium monofluorophosphate* (Na_2PO_3F) are all active ingredients in fluoride toothpastes.

Fluorine has most recently had an impact on the plastics and other major industries built around organic chemicals. The most notable molecules of this type are the *fluorocarbons*, complex molecules that use combinations of carbon and fluorine atoms.

Isotopes of fluorine

Figure 9-2 shows the known isotopes of fluorine. All natural fluorine is fluorine-19. The rest are radioactive and artificially produced.

Element 10: Neon

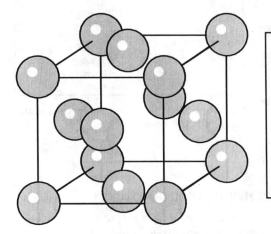

Name	Neon
Symbol	Ne
Atomic Number	10
Atomic Weight	20.179
Melting Point	-248.67°C
Boiling Point	-246.048°C
Density	0.89990
	(gas, 0°C, 1 atm)
Oxidation State	0
Electron Config.	$1s^2\,2s^2\,2p^6$

- Name pronounced as **NEE-on**
- Name taken from the Greek *neos*, "new"
- Discovered by Sir William Ramsay and Morris W. Travers in 1898
- Colorless, odorless, tasteless gas

Neon is most popularly known for its commercial application in neon lights. This gas can be confined in a glass tube that is outfitted with an electrical connection at each end. When a sufficiently high voltage is applied to the electrodes,the gas glows with an even intensity throughout the length of the tube. Unlike ordinary incandescent lamps, neon tubes can be bent and twisted into an infinite variety of meaningful and interesting shapes without degrading the quality of the light.

Figure 10-1 shows that neon is among the more common gasses in the earth's atmosphere. This should come as no surprise considering, as shown in Fig. 10-2, that neon is the fourth most abundant element in the known universe.

Historical background

Sir William Ramsay and Morris W. Travers were still rejoicing over their discovery of krypton gas in May of 1898 when they unveiled yet another one, neon. Ramsay believed he had unlocked a pattern of elements on the periodic table. Once a pattern is suggested, one knows what to look for, and when one knows what to look for, one certainly has a better chance of finding it.

Ramsay and Travers had looked for a heavy inert gas in the cold mix of gasses and liquids that remained as residue in a liquid-air machine after drawing off helium and argon. They found krypton. (*See* Element 36: Krypton, for more details about the discovery of this element.) What the investigators did not realize at the time was that they were drawing off neon with the helium and argon.

Having found the next-heavier element and seeing the pattern of atomic weights, they were certain a new gas existed between helium and argon. So they cranked up the liquid-air

Gas (Sea level)	Content by volume	
	(percent)	(ppm)
Nitrogen, N_2	78.09	—
Oxygen, O_2	20.95	—
Argon, Ar	0.93	—
Carbon Dioxide, CO_2	0.03	—
Neon, Ne	—	18.18
Helium, He	—	5.24
Krypton, Kr	—	1.14
Methane, CH_4	—	2
Nitrous oxide, N_2O	—	0.5
Hydrogen, H_2	—	.05
Xenon, Xe	—	.087

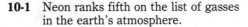

10-1 Neon ranks fifth on the list of gasses in the earth's atmosphere.

Element	Abundance (Si = 1)
Hydrogen	40,000
Helium	3,100
Oxygen	22
Neon	8.6
Nitrogen	6.6
Carbon	3.5
Silicon	1
Magnesium	0.91
Iron	0.60
Sulfur	0.38

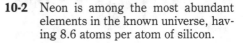

10-2 Neon is among the most abundant elements in the known universe, having 8.6 atoms per atom of silicon.

machine again, improved the sensitivity of their fractional distillation procedure, and found the new gas. When subjected to an electric arc, this new gas emitted a brilliant red glow that we now recognize as characteristic of neon signs.

This took place in June, 1898, but Ramsay and Travers were not done yet. They would discover xenon less than a month later.

Chemical properties of neon

Neon is classified as a *noble gas*, a group of gasses that are noted for being relatively inert. Neon is located in Group 0 on the periodic chart, between helium (He) and argon (Ar). Because their electron orbits are completely filled, the noble gasses are very stable and do not form compounds with other elements under normal conditions. In fact, it is this level of stability that other elements attempt to achieve when they combine to form compounds.

We have known since the early 1960s that the noble gasses, including neon, are not totally inert as was once thought. The three heavier noble gasses, krypton (Kr), xenon (Xe), and radon (Rn), can form a few stable compounds. there are no known stable compounds for helium (He), neon, and argon (Ar); however, ionized versions of these atoms can combine with a proton, or hydrogen ion, to form a two-element ion. Electrical discharges in confined mixtures of helium and neon, for example, have been found to produce the ion NeH^+.

Neon is monatomic. Unlike some of the other gasses, including oxygen, nitrogen, and hydrogen, a molecule of neon gas is made up of one atom. Whereas an oxygen molecule is portrayed as a diatomic molecule, O_2, the symbol for a neon gas molecule is simply Ne.

Production of neon

The liquification of air is a large-scale commercial process today, providing the primary source of liquid oxygen (O_2) and nitrogen (N_2). As shown in Fig. 10-3, these two gasses liquify at temperatures that are well above the boiling point of neon, however. This means neon, as well as a few other gasses, remain as gassy residues in air-liquification processes. Commercial neon is thus produced as a secondary product at liquid nitrogen/oxygen plants.

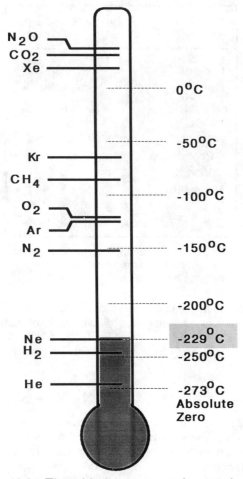

N$_2$O
CO$_2$
Xe

0°C

-50°C

Kr

CH$_4$

O$_2$

-100°C

Ar

N$_2$ — -150°C

-200°C

Ne — -229°C
H$_2$ — -250°C

He — -273°C
Absolute
Zero

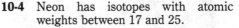

Isotope	Natural Abundance	Half-Life	Decay Mode
^{17}Ne		109 ms	β+, p
^{18}Ne		1.67 sec	β+
^{19}Ne		17.22 sec	β+
^{20}Ne	90.51%		
^{21}Ne	0.21%		
^{22}Ne	9.22%		
^{23}Ne		37.2 sec	β-
^{24}Ne		3.38 min	β-
^{25}Ne		0.61 sec	β-

10-4 Neon has isotopes with atomic weights between 17 and 25.

10-3 The critical temperature for neon is nearly as low as those of hydrogen and helium.

Neon is included in the cold gas that remains after removing the liquid products from conventional liquid-air distillation processes. The leftover gas is about 75% neon, a little over 24% helium, and a trace of hydrogen. Both impurities are removed by passing the chilled gas through activated charcoal.

Isotopes of neon

Figure 10-4 lists the isotopes of neon. Just over 90% of the neon in the earth's atmosphere is neon-20. Nearly 10% is neon-22, however; and you can see there is a trace of neon-21 in the atmosphere. None of the naturally occurring species of neon is radioactive. The six remaining species on the list are radioactive and artificially produced.

Element 11: Sodium

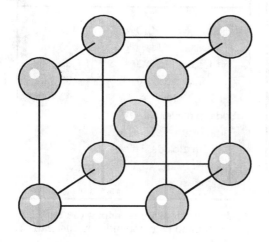

Name	Sodium
Symbol	Na
Atomic Number	11
Atomic Weight	22.9898
Melting Point	97.81°C
Boiling Point	882.9°C
Specific Gravity	0.97 (20°C)
Oxidation State	+1
Electron Config.	(Ne) $3s^1$

- Name pronounced as **SO-di-em**
- Name taken from the Medieval Latin *sodanum*, "headache remedy"
- Chemical symbol, Na, taken from the Latin *natrium*, "sodium carbonate"
- Isolated and identified as an element by Sir Humphry Davy in 1807
- Soft, silvery-white metal
- Burns in air with a brilliant white flame

Sodium metal is a soft metal that is so lightweight it can float on water. This metal cannot be found in nature in its pure form, though, because even the tiniest amount of air or moisture immediately converts the metal to one of its compounds. It is so reactive that the pure metal has to be stored in containers filled with a non-reactive liquid such as kerosene.

Figure 11-1 shows that sodium is one of the top ten elements in the earth's crust; even so, it exists only in forms where it is compounded with other elements. Notice in Fig. 11-2, for example, that sodium oxide is ranked sixth among the most abundant compounds on earth. There is plenty of sodium in seawater, too. In this case, it is mostly in the form of sodium chloride, or ordinary salt.

Sodium is highly reactive and plentiful. It follows, then, that there would be a lot of different inorganic sodium compounds in addition to the sodium oxide and chloride just mentioned—on the order of 500 of them.

Historical background

The early history of sodium is interwoven with the story of potassium. Until the 1700s, most chemists could not see any difference between mineral alkali (sodium carbonate) and vegetable alkali (potassium carbonate). The fact that the sources of the two alkalis were totally different didn't seem to bother anyone prior to that time.

By 1702, chemists were beginning to recognize some differences in the crystalline forms of "artificial" and "natural" alkalis. Crystals of the so-called artificial alkalis were

Element	Concentration (ppm)
Oxygen	464,000
Silicon	282,000
Aluminum	83,200
Iron	56,300
Calcium	41,500
Sodium	23,600
Magnesium	23,300
Potassium	20,900
Titanium	5700
Hydrogen	1400

Compound	Weight (ppm)
Silicon dioxide, SiO_2	428,600
Magnesium oxide, MgO	350,700
Ferrous oxide, FeO	89,700
Aluminum oxide, Al_2O_3	69,900
Calcium Oxide, CaO	43,700
Sodium oxide, Na_2O	4500
Ferric oxide, Fe_2O_3	3600
Titanium dioxide, TiO_2	3300
Chromic oxide, Cr_2O_3	1800
Manganese oxide, MnO	1400

11-1 Sodium is among the ten most abundant elements in the earth's crust.

11-2 Sodium oxide is among the ten most common compounds in the earth's crust.

prepared by leeching water through wood ashes. Crystals of the natural alkalis were found scattered about on the ground and in shallow mines.

In 1736, Henri-Louis Duhamel du Monceau (1700–1782) clearly showed that mineral, or natural, alkali, ordinary table salt, Glauber's salt, and borax included a common constituent. He also concluded that mineral alkali was the basis of sea salt.

By 1758, chemists were getting close to isolating sodium metal. Because of the explosive manner in which sodium reacts to oxygen and moisture in the air, early endeavors to isolate the metal usually included some thinly disguised excitement about how the substances detonated, flashed, cumbusted, and otherwise made life a bit more interesting around the old laboratory.

It was up to Sir Humphry Davy and his marvelous electrolysis equipment to isolate sodium metal successfully in 1807. He inserted electrodes into a bath of molten sodium hydroxide and found molten sodium metal forming around the cathode.

Some properties of sodium

Sodium is a very soft, silvery-white metal. It looks very much like aluminum, but is much softer; it is so soft, in fact, that it can be easily cut with a knife. However, few people have a chance to see and work with pure sodium metal on a regular basis. The compounds are all over the place, but the metal itself has virtually no practical application and does not adapt readily to normal environmental conditions.

Sodium reacts vigorously with atmospheric oxygen, for example, to produce sodium peroxide:

$$2Na + O_2 \rightarrow Na_2O_2$$
(sodium metal + oxygen → sodium peroxide)

It reacts violently with water to produce hydrogen and sodium hydroxide:

$$2Na + 2H_2O \rightarrow H_2 + 2NaOH$$
(sodium metal + water → hydrogen gas + sodium hydroxide)

Sodium belongs to the alkali metals of Group IA on the periodic table of elements. Hydrogen (H) is grouped with these metals and they have a number of features in common—except one very important feature: hydrogen is a gas. The Group IA metals are known as alkali metals because they form very strong and caustic (or alkaline) compounds with the OH^- ion. Common household lye, for example, is potassium or sodium hydroxide. Lithium hydroxide is even nastier, and far too dangerous for household use.

Sodium alloys with three other metals in its group to form an important and unusual series of eutectic metals. Recall that an alloy is a mixture of two or more metals. An eutectic system is a mixture of substances whose melting point is lower than that of any of the individual parts. Figure 11-3 shows the melting points for the pure metals sodium, potassium and cesium. Notice that the lowest melting point of the three is well above 0 °C. The four alloys, however, have melting points at −4.5° or below. The Na-K-Cs eutectic alloy has the lowest melting point of any metal ever isolated.

Sodium and its salts impart a yellow color to a flame test.

Element	Melting Point
Sodium (Na)	97.81°C
Potassium (K)	63.25°C
Cesium (Cs)	38.89°C

Alloy	Melting Point
Sodium-Potassium, Na-K	-10°C
Sodium-Rubidium, Na-Rb	-4.5°C
Sodium-Cesium, Na-Cs	-30°C
Sodium-Potassium-Cesium, Na-K-Cs	-78°C

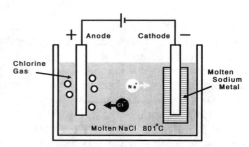
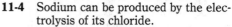

11-3 Sodium is an important ingredient in eutectic alloys—mixtures that have melting points lower than those of the individual elements.

11-4 Sodium can be produced by the electrolysis of its chloride.

Production of sodium metal

Sodium is produced commercially by the same procedure Sir Humphry Davy used for isolating the first samples of the pure metal nearly two centuries ago. The procedure is based on the electrolysis of absolutely moisture-free, molten sodium chloride (NaCl). Figure 11-4 illustrates the basic setup. The reactions are:

$$2Cl^- \rightarrow Cl_2 + 2e^- \text{ (anode reaction)}$$
$$Na^+ + e^- \rightarrow Na \text{ (cathode reaction)}$$
$$2NaCl \rightarrow Cl_2 + 2Na \text{ (cell reaction)}$$
$$\text{(sodium chloride + electrolysis} \rightarrow \text{chlorine gas + sodium metal)}$$

Electrolyzing molten sodium chloride produces chlorine gas at the anode and sodium metal at the cathode. The reaction is conducted at a temperature somewhat above the melting point of NaCl (801 °C). Clearly, the sodium metal, with its melting point of a mere 98 °C, will be in a molten state.

The equipment actually used for producing sodium metal on a commercial scale is only slightly modified from the basic electrolysis arrangement. The commercial version, called a *Downs cell*, has more convenient and effective provisions for draining off the molten sodium.

Some compounds of sodium

Sodium has a single oxidation state of $+1$. The most stable metal ion is Na^+, so it combines with anions having an oxidation state of -1 in this way:

Sodium chloride, NaCl

$$Na^+ + Cl^- \rightarrow NaCl$$

Sodium hydroxide, NaOH

$$Na^+ + OH^- \rightarrow NaOH$$

It combines with anions of -2 as:

Sodium monoxide, Na_2O

$$2Na^+ + O^{2-} \rightarrow Na_2O$$

Sodium sulfate, Na_2SO_4

$$2Na^+ + (SO_4)^{2-} \rightarrow Na_2SO_4$$

The most commonly known compound of sodium is *sodium chloride* (NaCl), better known as ordinary table salt. Sodium chloride can be obtained directly from salt deposits in the earth or recovered from evaporated brine and seawater. Sodium chloride is also readily formed when hot sodium metal and chlorine gas come into contact with one another.

Sodium chloride might be the best-known of all sodium compounds, but *sodium oxide* (Na_2O) is the most abundant in the earth's crust. Notice that sodium oxide appears on the list of top-ten compounds in Fig. 11-2 on p. 44 while sodium chloride does not. Sodium oxide is the main ingredient in natural soda compounds and shows up in commercially important sodium compounds such as washing soda and baking soda.

Sodium hydroxide, NaOH, is one of the most popular compounds in the chemical industry. The only common household application is as a drain cleaner. It is produced on a commercial scale by electrolyzing an aqueous solution of sodium chloride, usually seawater or brine from salt mines. The basic cell reaction is:

$$2NaCl + 2H_2O \rightarrow Cl_2 + H_2 + 2NaOH$$
(aqueous sodium chloride + electrolysis → chlorine gas
+ hydrogen gas + sodium hydroxide)

Chlorine gas appears at the anode and hydrogen gas at the cathode. The sodium hydroxide, however, remains in solution. The reaction yields generous amounts of pure chlorine and hydrogen gas that can be sold as elemental gasses or combined to produce commercially valuable amounts of hydrochloric acid (HCl). The problem here is one of getting the sodium hydroxide out of the solution; this becomes important when you realize that the OH^- and Cl^- ions react to yield the hypochlorite ion, OCl^-, which is a contaminant.

One solution to the problem is to use a design called a *diaphragm cell*. An asbestos filter, or diaphragm, separates the ions around the cathode from those around the anode. OH^- ions generated at the cathode combine with Na^+ ions attracted to the cathode to form adqueous NaOH, which is allowed to drip away from the electrolysis assembly. Once the NaOH has been removed from the electrolytic tank, it can be further concentrated by a simple evaporation process.

A second solution—one that is more appropriate for producing high-purity NaOH—uses a *mercury cell* design. Here, the cathode is made of mercury; sodium ions attracted to this cathode combine with the mercury to produce an amalgam that is forced out of the electrolysis bath and into a water-vapor chamber. In this chamber, the sodium in the amalgam reacts with the water to form hydrogen gas and pure NaOH.

Both of these designs for producing commercial yields of sodium hydroxide are continuous processes. That is, the brine is fed into one end of the system continuously, and the end products of hydrogen, chlorine gas, and dilute sodium hydroxide emerge continuously from the other.

Baking soda, sodium bicarbonate or *sodium hydrogen carbonate* ($NaHCO_3$, is another common sodium compound. It is used as a leavening in bakery products in stomach antiacids and as a fire-extinguishing agent. This compound occurs naturally.

Sodium carbonate, Na_2CO_3, is commonly used as a cleaning agent and bleach. It is ranked eleventh in the United States chemical industry as far as annual tonnage produced. It is produced by means of a two-step Solvay process. In the first step, ammonia and carbon dioxide are bubbled through an aqueous solution of sodium chloride. This produces sodium bicarbonate and, as a by-product, ammonium chloride:

$$NH_3 + CO_2 + NaCl + H_2O \rightarrow NaHCO_3 + NH_4Cl$$
(ammonia + carbon dioxide + sodium chloride + water
$\rightarrow$ sodium bicarbonate + ammonium chloride)

The second step in the Solvay process is to heat the sodium bicarbonate to produce sodium carbonate and, as byproducts, carbon dioxide gas and water vapor:

$$NaHCO_3 \rightarrow Na_2CO_3 + CO_2 + H_2O$$
(sodium bicarbonate + heat $\rightarrow$ sodium carbonate + carbon dioxide + water)

Although *sodium cyanide*, NaCN, is not well-known outside the walls of the steel industry, large amounts of this highly toxic compound are used each year to case-harden steel. It is produced by heating *sodium amide* with carbon:

$$NaNH_2 + C \rightarrow NaCN + H_2$$
(sodium amide + carbon $\rightarrow$ sodium cyanide + hydrogen gas)

The sodium amide is, itself, produced by bubbling ammonia gas through molten sodium.

Sodium nitrate ($NaNO_3$), or soda nitre, is a common component in fertilizers and explosives. Like most of the other common sodium salts, sodium nitrate is found in large natural deposits. The richest source is Chilean saltpeter. This compound can also be produced in the laboratory by reacting nitric acid and soda ash, or sodium carbonate.

Sodium sulfate has two common different names, depending upon its water content. Anhydrous (water-free) sodium sulfate, Na_2SO_4, is sometimes called salt cake. When water molecules are present in a ratio of 10:1, the formula becomes $Na_2SO_4 \cdot 10H_2O$. This is sodium sulfate decahydrate, or Glauber's salt. In either case, it can be produced a couple of ways. The first process combines sodium chloride and sulfuric acid:

$$2NaCl + H_2SO_4 \rightarrow Na_2SO_4 + 2HCl$$
(sodium chloride + sulfuric acid $\rightarrow$ sodium sulfate + hydrochloric acid)

The second process uses sodium bicarbonate and sulfuric acid:

$$NaHCO_3 + H_2SO_4 \rightarrow Na_2SO_4 + H_2O + CO_2$$
(sodium bicarbonate + sulfuric acid $\rightarrow$ sodium sulfate + water + carbon dioxide)

Sodium thiosulfate, NaS_2O_3, is commonly used as a fixing agent in photographic processes. Photographers know it better as *hypo*, or sodium hyposulfite.

Isotopes of sodium

Figure 11-5 shows that there are isotopes of sodium. All of the naturally occurring sodium is in the form of stable, or nonradioactive, sodium-23. The remaining isotopes are radioactive, none having a half-life longer than about $2^1/_2$ years.

Isotope	Natural Abundance	Half-Life	Decay Mode
^{19}Na		0.31 sec	β+, p
^{20}Na		0.446 sec	β+, α
^{21}Na		22.5 sec	β+
^{22}Na		2.605 yr	β+, ec
^{23}Na	100%		
^{24m}Na		20.2 ms	β-
^{24}Na		14.97 hr	β-
^{25}Na		59.3 sec	β-
^{26}Na		1.07 sec	β-
^{27}Na		0.29 sec	β-
^{28}Na		30 ms	β-
^{29}Na		43 ms	β-, n
^{30}Na		53 ms	β-
^{31}Na		17 ms	β-, n

11-5 Sodium has isotopes with atomic weights between 19 and 31.

Element 12: Magnesium

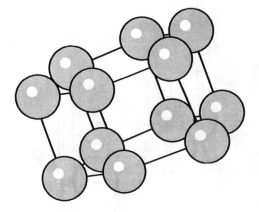

Name	Magnesium
Symbol	Mg
Atomic Number	12
Atomic Weight	24.305
Melting Point	648.8°C
Boiling Point	1090°C
Specific Gravity	1.74 (20°C)
Oxidation State	+2
Electron Config.	(Ne) $3s^2$

- Name pronounced **mag-NEE-zhi-em**
- Named for ancient Magnesia in the district of Thessaly, Greece
- Isolated by Sir Humphry Davy in 1808
- Lightweight, malleable, silvery-white metal

The crust of the earth and, indeed, the universe, itself, is laced with a generous proportion of magnesium. According to the abundance table in Fig. 12-1, magnesium is the eighth most abundant element in the known universe. There is almost as much magnesium as iron and sulfur put together. If you analyze the content of the earth's crust (as in Fig. 12-2), magnesium is the seventh most abundant element. Magnesium really takes over the show when

Element	Abundance (Si = 1)
Hydrogen	40,000
Helium	3,100
Oxygen	22
Neon	8.6
Nitrogen	6.6
Carbon	3.5
Silicon	1
Magnesium	0.91
Iron	0.60
Sulfur	0.38

Element	Concentration (ppm)
Oxygen	464,000
Silicon	282,000
Aluminum	83,200
Iron	56,300
Calcium	41,500
Sodium	23,600
Magnesium	23,300
Potassium	20,900
Titanium	5700
Hydrogen	1400

12-1 Magnesium ranks eighth on the list of ten most abundant elements in the known universe.

12-2 Magnesium is among the ten most abundant elements in the earth's crust.

you consider how much of its main compound, magnesium oxide, is on the earth. Figure 12-3 shows that more than a third of the material on the earth's surface is comprised of MgO-bearing minerals. In this respect, magnesium oxide is second only to silicon dioxide, or ordinary beach sand.

Compound	Weight (ppm)
Silicon dioxide, SiO_2	428,600
Magnesium oxide, MgO	350,700
Ferrous oxide, FeO	89,700
Aluminum oxide, Al_2O_3	69,900
Calcium Oxide, CaO	43,700
Sodium oxide, Na_2O	4500
Ferric oxide, Fe_2O_3	3600
Titanium dioxide, TiO_2	3300
Chromic oxide, Cr_2O_3	1800
Manganese oxide, MnO	1400

12-3 Magnesium oxide is among the ten most common compounds in the earth's crust.

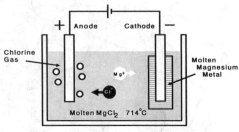
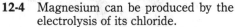

12-4 Magnesium can be produced by the electrolysis of its chloride.

Magnesium is a chemically active metal. As such, it is often used for reducing other metals from their salts and oxides. Finely ground or powdered magnesium burns easily in air, producing a brilliant white light.

Magnesium is the lightest metal that can be used for everyday construction purposes. It resembles the next-heavier metal, aluminum, in this respect. Magnesium is flammable at temperatures characteristic of burning gasoline and other petrochemicals, so its application as a structural metal is limited. Magnesium is an important alloying agent for improving the working characteristics of aluminum and zinc; it makes them easier to roll, extrude, weld, and machine. Magnesium is also an important catalyst in organic reactions and a metal that is essential to good health.

Historical background

The history of magnesium begins in 1618 when a farmer's cows refused to drink water from a certain mineral well in Epsom, England. Once the farmer tasted the bitterness of the water, he could not blame the cows for not drinking it; but he also found that the water had some positive healing effects on scratches and rashes on his skin.

There was no TV, no radio, no *U.S.A. Today* in those days, so ad campaigns got off to a slow start. Nevertheless, the well at Epsom eventually became a world-wide commercial success. The well at Epsom could not supply the demand, so entrepreneurs began working the "bitter salts" out of wells in Limington and Portsea Island. Then, as now, the product was called Epsom salt, regardless of its origin.

By 1755, chemists were beginning to take a serious look at the Epsom salt and its "earth" which was being called *magnesia alba*. It soon became clear that Epsom salt is a sulfate and magnesia is an oxide of the same basic element. Sir Humphry Davy flipped the switch on his electrolysis equipment once again in 1855. This time the electrodes were inserted into a mixture of magnesia (magnesium oxide) and mercuric oxide. A magnesium amalgam—an alloy of magnesium and mercury—formed at the cathode. Heating the amalgam released the mercury as a vapor, leaving behind magnesium metal.

Davy wanted to call the new element *magnium*, because he thought (and rightly so) that the name *magnesium* would be too easily confused with the name of another element, manganese. Tradition prevailed over common sense, however, and every beginning chemistry student since that time has struggled with the magnesium/manganese problem.

Properties of magnesium

Magnesium belongs to the set of Group-IIA metals known as the alkaline-earth metals. This means they have a number of significant properties in common. They are all very metallic in nature, for example. They are silvery white, fairly hard, and good conductors of electricity. They all have much higher melting temperatures than their alkali-metal counterparts in Group IA.

Magnesium is perhaps better known for its high level of reactivity. It combines with most nonmetals and is frequently used as an oxidizer to displace other metal ions from their compounds. Magnesium also serves as a catalyst in a few important inorganic reactions and in a rather large number of biochemical processes.

Finely ground magnesium readily burns in air, giving off a brilliant blue-white light. Magnesium was the primary ingredient in photographic flash bulbs.

Production of magnesium metal

The world's oceans are a source of magnesium that can be regarded as inexhaustible; each cubic mile of ordinary seawater contains about 12 billion pounds of magnesium. Most processes for producing magnesium metal and commercial magnesium compounds thus involve extracting magnesium from seawater. Sources of magnesium are not strictly limited to seawater, however. It can be recovered from brines that are often found near salt deposits and, in some instances, oil-well operations. Sometimes it is more practical to recover magnesium from minerals such as dolomite ($CaCO_3 \cdot MgCO_3$) and carnallite ($KCl \cdot MgCl_2 \cdot 6H_2O$), especially where seawater is not conveniently available.

Unforunately, magnesium metal cannot be removed directly from seawater and brines. Most procedures lead to a step where magnesium chloride ($MgCL_2$) is electrolyzed to yield magnesium metal and chlorine gas. An alternative approach, called the Pigeon process, removes magnesium metal from dolomite by means of chemical, rather than electrolytic, reduction.

The electrolytic process

Magnesium chloride, the essential electrolyte in the electrolytic process, is not available in nature in sufficient quantities. It has to be produced from available raw materials; seawater and oyster shells, or seawater and dolomite. Where oyster shells are readily available, they are ground to a powder and baked in an oven to produce calcium hydroxide, $Ca(OH)_2$. When mixed with seawater, the OH^- ions bond with Mg^+ in the water to produce magnesium hydroxide, $Mg(OH)_2$—an insoluable solid that is better known as milk of magnesia. As the reaction progresses, increasing amounts of this white substance settle to the bottom of the vat. The precipitate is finally drawn from the settling vat and treated with hydrochloric acid to produce magnesium chloride. The general reaction is:

$$Mg(OH)_2 + HCl \rightarrow MgCl_2 + 2H_2O$$

(magnesium hydroxide + hydrochloric acid → magnesium chloride + water)

Where oyster shells are not available, dolomite ($CaCO_3 \cdot MgCO_3$) is a suitable substitute. In this case, the dolomite is first heated to convert the carbonates to oxides, calcium oxide (CaO) and magnesium oxide (MgO). The solid oxides are then mixed with seawater or brine, and magnesium hydroxide collects at the bottom of the container. This precipitate is then treated with hydrochloric acid to yield magnesium chloride as described for the oyster-shell process.

Figure 12-4 illustrates the electrolysis portion of the operation where molten magnesium chloride, whether derived from oyster shells or dolomite, is converted to magnesium metal and chlorine gas. Molten magnesium chloride is a fairly good electrical conductor, and the melting point is, conveniently, a bit less than 100 °C above that of magnesium metal. Therefore, there is no need for adding secondary compounds to improve the conductivity of the melt nor to adjust the melting points. Molten magnesium metal collects at the cathode, and chlorine gas bubbles off at the anode. The chlorine gas is usually saved and used for producing the hydrochloric acid that is used in the earlier phase of the production procedure.

The Pidgeon process

The Pidgeon process (named for the World War II Canadian inventor, L.M. Pidgeon) does away with the need for locating magnesium refineries near sources of brine and seawater. The raw materials in this case are ferrosilicon and dolomite.

The dolomite ($CaCO_3 \cdot MgCO_3$) is crushed and baked to produce a mixture of calcium and magnesium oxides. Ferrosilicon, a mixture of iron- and silicon-bearing minerals, is combined with the two oxides, and the mix is pressed into briquets.

The briquets are fired in a vacuum retort at about 1200 °C. The silicon reduces the magnesium in the magnesium oxide; the metal then vaporizes from the briquets and condenses in the cooler part of the retort as pure molten metal. The residue from this process is a mixture of iron and calcium silicate, $CaSiO_4$.

Some compounds of magnesium

The most stable oxidation state of magnesium is +2. The most common ion is thus Mg^{2+}. The chloride has this general form:

Magnesium chloride, $MgCl_2$

$$Mg^{2+} + 2Cl^- \rightarrow MgCl_2$$

The all-important oxide is put together this way:

Magnesium oxide, MgO

$$Mg^{2+} + O^{2-} \rightarrow MgO$$

Magnesium chloride is the principal magnesium compound in seawater and magnesium oxide occupies 35% of the earth's crust. The chloride is obtained directly from seawater and is chiefly used in the manufacture of magnesium metal.

The Mg^{2+} ion combines with anions of higher oxidation states to form compounds such as:

Magnesium phosophate, $Mg_3(PO_4)_2$

Magnesium silicide, Mg_2Si (sometimes called dimagnesium silicide)

$$2Mg^{2+} + Si^4 \rightarrow Mg_2Si$$

Magnesium carbonate, $MgCO_3$, occurs in nature as magnesite and dolomite. This white crystalline compound is used in the manufacture of paints and inks. As an additive to table salt, magnesium carbonate prevents caking due to the absorption of atmospheric moisture.

Magnesium fluoride, MgF_2 is recovered from natural sellaite. In its pure form, magnesium fluoride is a white, fluorescent, crystalline substance that has a tinge of violet. It is commonly used as a thin-film coating on optical glass to reduce glare and reflection.

Isotopes of magnesium

Figure 12-5 shows the known isotopes of magnesium. Nearly all naturally occurring magnesium on the earth is magnesium-24. About 20% of the mix is a fairly even combination of magnesium-25 and -26. The rest of the isotopes are radioactive and artificially produced.

12-5 Magnesium has isotopes with atomic weights between 20 and 31.

Isotope	Natural Abundance	Half-Life	Decay Mode
^{20}Mg		0.1 sec	β+, p
^{21}Mg		122 ms	β+, p
^{22}Mg		3.86 sec	β+
^{23}Mg		11.32 sec	β+
^{24}Mg	78.9%		
^{25}Mg	10.00%		
^{26}Mg	11.01%		
^{27}Mg		9.45 min	β-
^{28}Mg		21.0 hr	β-
^{29}Mg		1.3 sec	β-
^{30}Mg		0.33 sec	β-
^{31}Mg		0.25 sec	β-

Element 13: Aluminum

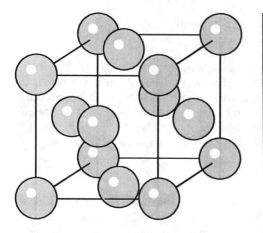

Name	Aluminum
Symbol	Al
Atomic Number	13
Atomic Weight	26.9815
Melting Point	660.37°C
Boiling Point	2467°C
Specific Gravity	2.699 (20°C)
Oxidation State	+3
Electron Config.	(Ne) $3s^2\ 3p^1$

- Name pronounced as **ah-LOO-men-em**, sometimes as **al-yoo-MIN-i-em**
- Name taken from the Latin *alumen, aluminis* "alum"
- Existence proposed by Antoine Lavoisier in 1787, named by Sir Humphry Davy in 1807, and finally isolated by Hans Christian Orsted in 1825
- Soft, lightweight, silvery-white metal

Aluminum is the most abundant metal on the surface of the earth; Fig. 13-1 shows that it is exceeded in abundance only by the nonmetals oxygen and silicon. Even so, its existence remained a secret until the late 1700s. The early civilizations were aware of two important compounds of aluminum: alum and aluminum oxide. Figure 13-2 shows that aluminum oxide, historically known as *alumina*, is the fourth most abundant compound in the earth's crust.

Historical background

The discovery of aluminum metal was a three-step process that involved three different scientists and covered a period of 38 years. The sequence began in 1787 when Antoine Lavoisier stated his conviction that common alum was a compound of at least one metallic element.

By the beginning of the 1800s, chemists generally understood that an unknown metal was common to alum and alumina; it was, therefore, obvious to Sir Humphry Davy that this metal, when actually proven to exist, should be given an alum or alumina-like name. He suggested the name, *alumium*; but when the metal was finally isolated, he agreed to the suggestion that the name be changed to *aluminum*.

The final part of the story began in 1807 when Hans Christian Orsted found an effective way to get a reaction between aluminum chloride and an alloy of potassium and mercury (an *amalgam*). This reaction yielded iron chloride and an amalgam of aluminum. Heating the amalgam at low air pressure allowed the mercury to boil away, leaving behind flecks of a silvery-white metal—aluminum.

Element	Concentration (ppm)
Oxygen	464,000
Silicon	282,000
Aluminum	83,200
Iron	56,300
Calcium	41,500
Sodium	23,600
Magnesium	23,300
Potassium	20,900
Titanium	5700
Hydrogen	1400

Compound	Weight (ppm)
Silicon dioxide, SiO_2	428,600
Magnesium oxide, MgO	350,700
Ferrous oxide, FeO	89,700
Aluminum oxide, Al_2O_3	69,900
Calcium Oxide, CaO	43,700
Sodium oxide, Na_2O	4500
Ferric oxide, Fe_2O_3	3600
Titanium dioxide, TiO_2	3300
Chromic oxide, Cr_2O_3	1800
Manganese oxide, MnO	1400

13-1 Aluminum ranks third on the list of ten most abundant elements in the earth's crust.

13-2 Aluminum oxide is among the ten most common compounds in the earth's crust.

Properties of aluminum

In its purest form, aluminum is a bluish-white metal which is highly malleable and ductile. It is commercially notable as a lightweight construction material and as a good conductor of heat and electricity. Pure aluminum is, in fact, too soft for construction applications; however, adding small amounts of silicon and iron (less than 1%) hardens and strengthens it.

It is said that aluminum resists oxidation. This is quite true, but only in the sense that the metal is actually protected by a thin film of corrosion-resistant aluminum oxide that forms the moment the pure metal is cut. Without its ever-present oxide coating, aluminum would be quickly destroyed by atmospheric gasses and moisture. Even the protective oxide coating cannot protect aluminum metal forever, thus accounting for the fact that the metal does not exist in nature in its elemental state.

Aluminum belongs to the boron group, Group IIIA, on the periodic table. Like its companions in this group—boron, gallium, and indium for example—aluminum's principal oxidation state is +3.

Production of aluminum

All but a tiny fraction of the vast annual tonnage of aluminum is produced by the *Hall process*. This is basically a simple electrolytic process that has been up-scaled to operate efficiently at high production levels. The electrolyte is aluminum oxide, Al_2O_3, readily obtained from natural bauxite.

Figure 13-3 illustrates the Hall process schematically. The electrolyte is listed as aluminum oxide, but minerals *cryolyte* and *fluorite* are mixed with it. These minerals act as fluxes, thereby reducing the melting temperature of the electrolyte without affecting the chemical reactions in any other way. The fundamental reaction for the Hall process is:

$$2Al_3O_2 \rightarrow 4Al + 3O_2$$
(aluminum oxide + electrolysis → aluminum + oxygen)

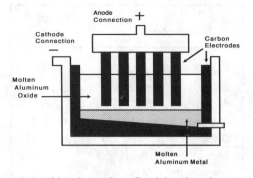

13-3 Aluminum is refined by the electrolytic Hall process.

Isotope	Natural Abundance	Half-Life	Decay Mode
^{22}Al		70 ms	β+
^{23}Al		0.47 sec	β+
^{24}Al		2.07 sec	β+
^{25}Al		7.17 sec	β+
^{26m}Al		6.34 sec	β+
^{26}Al		7.2x10^5 yr	β+, ec
^{27}Al	100%		
^{28}Al		2.25 min	β-
^{29}Al		6.5 min	β-
^{30}Al		3.69 sec	β-
^{31}Al		0.64sec	β-

13-4 Aluminum has isotopes with atomic weights between 22 and 31.

As this reaction progresses, aluminum metal forms at the cathode. The cathode in this instance is actually a carbon liner for the container; as the aluminum forms on the surfaces, gravity pulls it to the bottom where it is readily drained out and formed into ingots.

Aluminum can also be produced by the electrolysis of aluminum chloride. In this case, common aluminum oxide is first converted to aluminum chloride by heating it with chlorine gas:

$$2Al_2O_3 + 6Cl_2 \rightarrow 4AlCl_3 + 3O_2$$
(aluminum oxide + chlorine → aluminum chloride + oxygen)

Then the aluminum chloride is electrolyzed in a liquid state to yield aluminum metal at the cathode and chlorine gas at the anode. The metal is recovered from the electrolyte and molded into ingots; the chlorine is saved and used again in the first reaction in this process.

Some compounds of aluminum

Aluminum has a single oxidation state of +3, so it tends to form compounds looking like these:

Aluminum fluoride, AlF_3

$$Al^{3+} + 3F \rightarrow AlF_3$$

Aluminum sulfide, Al_2S_3

$$2Al^{3+} + 3S^2 \rightarrow Al_2S_3$$

Aluminum phosphate, $AlPO_4$

$$Al^{3+} + PO_4{}^{3-} \rightarrow AlPO_4$$

Aluminum carbide, Al_4C_3

Aluminum chloride, $AlCl_3$, is a white crystalline substance that fumes in moist air and reacts explosively in water to form aluminum oxide and hydrochloric acid:

$$2AlCl_3 + 3H_2O \rightarrow Al_2O_3 + 6HCl$$
(aluminum chloride + water → aluminum oxide + hydrochloric acid)

$AlCl_3$ is commercially produced by the direct action of the two elements:

$$2Al + 3Cl_2 \rightarrow 2AlCl_3$$
(aluminum metal + chlorine gas → aluminum chloride)

Aluminum chloride is an important catalyst in the synthesis of many organic compounds.

Aluminum sulfate, $Al_2(SO_4)_3$, is used in the production of paper and paper products, and it is widely applied at sewage treatment facilities. In its anhydrous form (no water molecules attached to it), it is a colorless crystalline substance. When hydrated, such as in $Al_2(SO_4)_3 \cdot 18H_2O$, it is a white powder.

Aluminum sulfate is commercially produced by treating bauxite (raw aluminum oxide) with sulfuric acid:

$$Al_2O_3 + 3H_2SO_4 \rightarrow Al_2(SO_4)_3 + 3H_2O$$
(aluminum oxide + sulfuric acid → aluminum sulfate + water)

Aluminum sulfate combines with sulfates of the Group IA metals to form double sulfates that are commonly known as *alums*. The common styptic pencil is made up of an alum. This substance constricts severed blood capillaries, thus making it a handy device on those days when you have to shave with a shaky hand. This particular product is a potassium alum properly called potassium aluminum sulfate, $KAl(SO_4)_2 \cdot 12H_2O$. It is produced on a commercial scale by reacting aluminum sulfate with potassium sulfate:

$$Al_2(SO_4)_3 + K_2SO_4 \rightarrow 2KAl(SO_4)_2$$
(aluminum sulfate + potassium sulfate → potassium aluminum sulfate)

Aluminum hydroxide, $Al(OH)_3$, is commonly used in ceramics and rubber materials. The formula suggests that it might be produced by reacting an aluminum salt with an alkali such as sodium hydroxide. This is indeed the case. For example:

$$AlCl_3 + 3NaOH \rightarrow Al(OH)_3 + 3NaCl$$
(aluminum chloride + sodium hydroxide → aluminum hydroxide + sodium chloride)

There is an alternative approach to obtaining aluminum hydroxide, and it is an approach that only requires you to juggle some formulas on paper. You have already seen that most aluminum compounds come from bauxite and that bauxite is basically aluminum oxide. It is basically hydrated aluminum oxide, $Al_2O_3 \cdot 3H_2O$. Notice that there is a total of six oxygens and six hydrogens in that formula. If you gather them as $(OH)_6$, the formula can be rewritten as $Al_2(OH)_6$ that can be reduced to $Al(OH)_3$. Therefore, hydrated aluminum oxide is also aluminum hydroxide.

Isotopes of aluminum

Figure 13-4 on p. 56 lists all of the known isotopes of aluminum. All naturally occurring aluminum is aluminum-27. The remaining isotopes are artificial and radioactive.

Element 14: Silicon

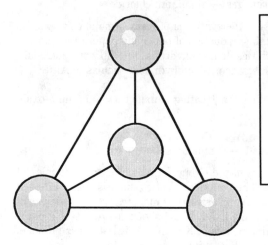

Name	Silicon
Symbol	Si
Atomic Number	14
Atomic Weight	28.0855
Melting Point	1410°C
Boiling Point	2355°C
Specific Gravity	2.33 (25°C)
Oxidation States	+2, +4, -4
Electron Config.	(Ne) $3s^2\,3p^2$

- Name pronounced as **SIL-i-ken**
- Name taken from the Latin *silex, silicus*, "flint"
- Isolated and identified by Jöns Jacob Berzelius in 1824
- Amorphous form is a brown powder; crystalline form has a gray metallic appearance

Casually thinking about silicon might bring up two thoughts: warm sandy beaches and electronic semiconductors, or maybe the cooler beaches of northern California and the nearby Silicon Valley. Perhaps some people think of window glass—that is made of silicon, too.

The cosmic abundance table in Fig. 14-1 shows silicon in seventh place. It is also significant to note that silicon has been chosen as the atom by which the abundances of all other elements are reckoned. The table thus indicates that there is 3.5 times as much carbon as silicon in the known cosmos. On the other hand, there is 0.91 times as much magnesium as silicon.

Figure 14-2 shows that silicon stands in second place, behind oxygen, on the list of the ten most abundant elements in the earth's crust. On the average, 282 thousand out of one million atoms of the earth's crust are silicon atoms. That is better than one out of four.

Silicon steals the show, however, when you look at the abundances of various compounds that make up the earth's crust. Figure 14-3 shows that silicon dioxide, or common beach sand, accounts for nearly half of it.

Historical background

Heating silica to produce glasslike materials, usually decorative items, dates back as far as 1500 B.C. By the end of our own 18th century, chemists understood that there was some sort of common link between sand, quartz, and silica. Until 1824, however, no one was convinced that the common link was an unknown element.

The renowned Sir Humphry Davy failed to isolate the new element, first by means of his electrolysis apparatus then by passing potassium vapor over firey hot silica. This was one of the few times that Davy missed out on isolating a new element he was pursuing.

Element	Abundance (Si = 1)
Hydrogen	40,000
Helium	3,100
Oxygen	22
Neon	8.6
Nitrogen	6.6
Carbon	3.5
Silicon	1
Magnesium	0.91
Iron	0.60
Sulfur	0.38

14-1 Silicon ranks seventh on the list of ten most abundant elements in the known cosmos, and it is the standard by which amounts of all the other elements are measured.

Element	Concentration (ppm)
Oxygen	464,000
Silicon	282,000
Aluminum	83,200
Iron	56,300
Calcium	41,500
Sodium	23,600
Magnesium	23,300
Potassium	20,900
Titanium	5700
Hydrogen	1400

14-2 Silicon is second only to oxygen as far as amounts of the elements in the earth's crust are concerned.

Compound	Weight (ppm)
Silicon dioxide, SiO_2	428,600
Magnesium oxide, MgO	350,700
Ferrous oxide, FeO	89,700
Aluminum oxide, Al_2O_3	69,900
Calcium Oxide, CaO	43,700
Sodium oxide, Na_2O	4500
Ferric oxide, Fe_2O_3	3600
Titanium dioxide, TiO_2	3300
Chromic oxide, Cr_2O_3	1800
Manganese oxide, MnO	1400

14-3 Silicon dioxide, the main ingredient in common beach sand, is the most abundant compound in the earth's crust.

Isotope	Natural Abundance	Half-Life	Decay Mode
^{24}Si		0.1 ms	β+, p
^{25}Si		220 ms	β+, p
^{26}Si		2.2 sec	β+
^{27}Si		4.14 sec	β+
^{28}Si	92.23%		
^{29}Si	4.67%		
^{30}Si	3.10%		
^{31}Si		2.62 hr	β-
^{32}Si		100 yr	β-
^{33}Si		6.2 sec	β-
^{34}Si		2.8 sec	β-

14-4 Silicon has isotopes with atomic weights between 24 and 34.

Jöns Jacob Berzelius (1779 – 1848) managed to isolate and identify a fairly high-quality sample of silicon in 1824. He began with a reaction that other investigators had described a few years earlier—heating chips of potassium metal in a container of silica:

$$SiF_4 + 4K \rightarrow 4KF + Si$$
(silicon tetrafluoride + potassium → potassium fluoride + silicon)

The mixture of KF and Si, however, has to be separated chemically. At room temperature, silicon does not react with water, but potassium fluoride does:

$$KF + H_2O \leftrightarrow HF + KOH$$
(potassium fluoride + water ↔ hydrofluoric acid + potassium hydroxide)

The second step is the most difficult and tedious; with care and patience, Berzelius managed to wash away the byproducts, leaving behind bits of silicon.

Properties and production of silicon

Silicon is characterized as a crystalline semimetal, or metalloid. There are actually two allotropic forms, however; a dark brown, powdery amorphous form and the gray, metallic-looking crystalline form. The amorphous form is best known for its presence in ordinary beach sand. The crystalline form is best known for its impact upon modern civilization—as the foundation material for electronic semiconductor components.

In spite of the widespread existence of silicon dioxide, silicon is relatively inert. Hydrofluoric acid is the only acid that corrodes silicon, for example; many other reactions take place only at very high temperatures. Silicon does react with the halogens and some of the alkalis, however.

Commercial production of silicon depends on a reaction between sand, or silicon dioxide, and carbon at temperatures on the order of 2200 °C:

$$SiO_2 + 2C \rightarrow 2CO + Si$$
(silicon dioxide + carbon → carbon monoxide + silicon)

$$SiF_4 + 4K \rightarrow 4KF + Si$$
(silicon tetrafluoride + potassium → potassium fluoride + silicon)

Some compounds and the isotopes of silicon

A useful compound of silicon is popularly known as *water glass*. This is a thick, clear liquid that is used for making soaps and adhesives, and for preserving eggs. Water glass is technically known as *sodium silicate*, Na_2SiO_3. Glass is a common silicon product; water glass is a silicon product that happens to dissolve in water. It is produced by reacting silicon dioxide with sodium hydroxide at a high temperature:

$$SiO_2 + 2NaOH \rightarrow H_2O + Na_2SiO_3$$
(silicon dioxide + sodium hydroxide → water + sodium silicate)

Silicon carbide, SiC, is a tough, abrasive substance that is used mostly for grinding metals. It is a dark, bluish-black crystal that is usually produced by heating sand and coke (carbon) together at a high temperature.

Silicon tetrachloride, $SiCl_4$ is used by the military for generating smoke screens from dense clouds of white vapor. It is produced commercially by reacting the two basic elements at a high temperature:

$$Si + 2Cl_2 \rightarrow SiCl_4$$
(silicon + chlorine gas → silicon tetrachloride)

Silicon tetrafluoride, SiF_4, is a colorless, choking gas that is mainly used in the production of other fluorosilicates. It is produced by a reaction between sand and hydrofluoric acid:

$$SiO_2 + 4HF \rightarrow SiF_4 + H_2O$$
(silicon dioxide + hydrofluoric acid → silicon tetrafluoride + water)

Figure 14-4 on p. 59 lists the isotopes of silicon, including their percent of natural abundance as well as the half-lives and decay modes for the radioactive species. You can see that most naturally occurring silicon is silicon-28. There is a little bit of silicon-29 and -30 mixed in. The remaining isotopes are artificially produced and are radioactive.

Element 15: Phosphorus

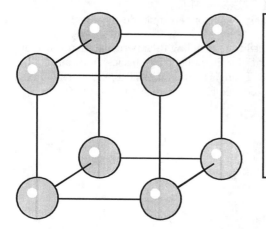

Name	Phosphorus
Symbol	P
Atomic Number	15
Atomic Weight	30.9738
Melting Point	44.1°C (white)
Boiling Point	280°C (white)
Specific Gravity	1.82 (20°C)
Oxidation States	+3, -3, +5
Electron Config.	(Ne) $3s^2\ 3p^3$

- Name pronounced as **FOS-fer-es**
- Name taken from the greek word *phosphoros*, "bringer of light"
- Isolated by Hennig Brand in 1669
- The most common white form is a waxy, phosphorescent solid

If you are ever asked to associate three different things with the element phosphorus, you will be doing well to name the following: phosphorescence, fireworks, and fertilizers. The most common form of phosphorus, as well as some of its compounds, are noted for their peculiar ability to glow in the dark. Other kinds of phosphorus are used in fireworks, safety matches, and incendiary weapons. Most phosphorus produced today, however, is used in the production of all kinds of fertilizers. From very humble and primitive beginnings, the science and technology of phosphorus has evolved into a major commercial force.

Historical background

Compounds of phosphorus have been known since ancient times. Most evidence is taken from accounts of materials that would phosphoresce, or glow in the dark. The element was finally isolated by Hennig Brand, a 17th-century alchemist and physician. Today, phosphorus is recovered from phosphate rock, $Ca_3(PO_4)_2$; Brand used a seemingly bizarre approach that can be justified only on the grounds that it works. It is anyone's guess how Brand came up with his procedure.

The following account of Brand's procedure for producing phosphorus is taken from W. Derham's 1726 edition of *Philosophical Experiments and Observations of the Late Eminent Dr. Robert Hookes, F.R.S. and Geom Prof. Gresh and Other Eminent Virtuosos in His Time* and was presented in Weeks and Leicester's *Discovery of the Elements* (1968).

> Take a quantity of Urine (not less for one Experiment than 50 or 60 Pails full); let it lie steeping in one or more Tubs, . . . till it putrify and breed Worms, as it will do in 13 or 14 days. Then, in a large Kettle, set some of it to boil on a strong Fire, and, as

it consumes and evaporates, pour in more, and so on, till, at last, the whole Quantity be reduced to a Paste . . . and this may be done in two or three Days, if the Fire be well tended, but else it may be doing a Fortnight or more. Then take the said paste, or Coal; powder it, and add thereto some fair Water, about 15 Fingers high . . .; and boil them together for 1/4 of an Hour. Then strain the Liquor and all through a Woolen Cloth . . . the Liquor that passes must be taken and boil'd till it come to a Salt, which it will be in a few Hours. Then take off the Caput Mortuum (which you have at any Apothecary's, being the Remainder of Aqua Fortis [nitric acid] from Vitriol and Salt of Niter) and add a Pound thereof to half a Pound of the said Salt, both of them being first finely pulverized. And then for 24 Hours steep'd in the most rectify'd Spirit of Wine, two or three Fingers hight, so as it will become a Kind of Pap.

Then evaporate all in warm Sand, and there will remain a red, or reddish, Salt. Take this Salt, put it into a Retort, and, for the first Hour, begin with a small Fire; more the next, a greater the 3d, and more the 4th; and then continue it, as high as you can, for 24 Hours. Sometimes by the Force of the Fire, 24 Hours proves enough; for when you see the Recipient white, and shining with Fire, and that there are no more Flashes, or, as it were, Blasts of Wind, coming from Time to Time from the Retort, then the Work is finished. And you may, with Feather, gather the Fire together, or scrape it off with a Knife, where it sticks.

Durham later describes how he saw phosphorus used as the lead of a pencil that produced letters that glowed in the dark. And speaking of the dangers of handling phosphorus, ". . . he had once wrapp'd up a Knob [of white phosphorus] in Wax, at Hanover, and it being in his Pocket, and he busy near the Fire, the very Heat set it in Flame, and burn'd all his Cloaths, and his Fingers also, for though he rubbed them in the Dirt, nothing would quench it, unless he had Water; he was ill for 15 Days, and the Skin came off . . . ."

Properties of phosphorus

Phosphorus belongs to the nitrogen group, Group VA, on the periodic table of the elements. It is a nonmetal, or metalloid, having properties closer to those of Sulfur (S) and arsenic (As) than to silicon (Si) and nitrogen in the same portion of the table.

Phosphorus has ten known allotropic forms. This is an unusually large number of allotropes for any element, but the picture can be greatly simplified by placing each of them into one of three general categories: white, red, and black phosphorus.

White phosphorus is a white, waxy substance that usually takes on a slightly yellow tinge due to the presence of impurities. There are two major allotropic forms of white phosphorus. The alpha form has a cubic crystalline structure and is stable down to $-78\,°C$ where it turns into the beta form. The beta form is somewhat more dense and has a hexagonal crystalline structure.

Red phosphorus is formed by exposing white phosphorus to sunlight or heating it at about 250°C. Black phosphorus is also produced by heating white phosphorus, but in the presence of a mercury catalyst and a seed crystal of black phosphorus.

White phosphorus is by far the most volatile and explosive of the three basic allotropic forms. It is also the most useful in the production of other compounds of phosphorus. Red phosphorus is, itself, a fairly stable form, but the heat from simple friction is enough to convert it to explosive white phosphorus. This feature is used to great advantage in the manufacture of safety matches. Black phosphorus is the least reactive and has the least commercial value.

Production of phosphorus

Pure metallic phosphorus is no longer obtained by the messy and tedious process that characterized its discovery. Rather, it is obtained from a heated mixture of phosphate rock, coke, and silica. At about 1450 °C, the reaction is:

$$Ca_3(PO_4)_2 + 5C + 3SiO_2 \rightarrow 2P + 5CO + 3CaSiO_3$$
(calcium phosphate + carbon + silicon dioxide → phosphorus
+ carbon monoxide + calcium silicate)

Some compounds of phosphorus

Phosphoric acid, H_3PO_4, is used in soft drinks, solvents, and fertilizers. All commercially useful phosphates, compounds that include the PO_4^{3-} ion, can be produced from this acid.

Phosphoric acid, itself, is derived from natural calcium phosphate rock with the help of sulfuric acid:

$$Ca_3(PO_4)_2 + 3H_2SO_4 \rightarrow 3CaSO_4 + 2H_3PO_4$$
(calcium phosphate + sulfuric acid → calcium sulfate + phosphoric acid)

One application of phosphoric acid is in the preparation of superphosphate fertilizers. A common mineral called *apatite*, $Ca_5(PO_4)_3(OH,F,Cl)$, can be treated with dilute phosphoric acid to produce a triple superphosphate fertilizer, $Ca(H_2PO_4)_2$:

$$Ca_5(PO_4)_3(OH,F,Cl) + 7H_3PO_4 + H_2O \rightarrow 5Ca(H_2PO_4)_2 \cdot H_2O + H(OH,F,Cl)$$
(apatite + phosphoric acid + water → "triple superphosphate" + an H^+ byproduct)

Metal phosphates can be formed by a reaction between the metal and phosphoric acid or a metal salt and *trisodium phosphate*. An example of the latter is:

$$3ZnCl_2 + 2Na_3PO_4 \rightarrow Zn_3(PO_4)_2 + 6NaCl$$
(zinc chloride + trisodium phosphate → zinc phosphate + sodium chloride)

In this case, zinc chloride is the metal salt and zinc phosphate is the desired product.

The oxides of phosphorus are *phosphorus(III) oxide* and *phosphorus(V) oxide*—P_4O_6 and P_4O_{10}, respectively.

Isotopes of phosphorus

Figure 15-1 lists the known isotopes of phosphorus. Note that all naturally occurring phosphorus is phosphorus-31. The remaining isotopes are both radioactive and man-made. Since phosphorus is a vital element in plant and animal life, radioactive isotopes of phosphorus are used as tracers in biological research and medical diagnosis.

Isotope	Natural Abundance	Half-Life	Decay Mode
^{26}P		20 ms	β+, p
^{28}P		270 ms	β+
^{29}P		4.14 sec	β+
^{30}P		2.50 min	β+
^{31}P	100%		
^{32}P		14.28 day	β-
^{33}P		25.3 day	β-
^{34}P		12.4 sec	β-
^{35}P		47 sec	β-
^{36}P		5.9 sec	β-

15-1 Phosphorus has isotopes with atomic weights between 26 and 36.

Element 16: Sulfur

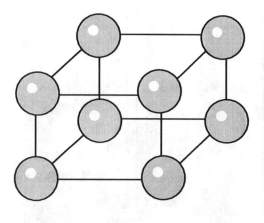

Name	Sulfur
Symbol	S
Atomic Number	16
Atomic Weight	32.06
Melting Point	112.8°C Note 1
	119.0°C Note 2
Boiling Point	444.6°C
Specific Gravity	2.07 (20°C) Note1
	1.957 (20°C) Note 2
Oxidation States	-2, +4, +6
Electron Config.	(Ne) $3s^2 3p^4$

Note 1: Rhombic form
Note 2: Monoclinic form

- Name pronounced as **SUL-fer**
- Name taken from Latin *sulphur*, "sulfur"
- Known in ancient times, classified as an element by Antoine Lavoisier in 1777
- Tasteless, odorless, light-yellow, brittle solid

If you have ever attempted to fumigate your home with a product that generates sulfur fumes, you are engaging in an application of sulfur that dates back to the time of the ancient Greeks. With the invention of gunpowder, the historical demand for sulfur experienced a great boost.

Sulfur is of ancient origin, and no single person can take credit for discovering it. The closest we can come to honoring anyone with regard to this ancient element is to state that Antoine Lavoisier convinced his contemporaries that sulfur was a true chemical element. Many others around the year 1777 thought sulfur was a mixture of other elements.

Figure 16-1 shows that sulfur is the tenth most abundant atom in the cosmos. The average amount of sulfur on the earth is not as significant, however. Sulfur fails to make the top-ten abundance lists for elements and their compounds.

Properties of sulfur

Sulfur, even in its pure elemental form, is a rather common substance. It is generally characterized as a pale yellow, brittle solid that has no taste. It is not supposed to have an odor, either; but common experience suggests otherwise. Actually, pure sulfur has no odor; the distinctive, biting aroma is really that of sulfur dioxide which forms in small amounts when sulfur comes into contact with oxygen and moisture in the air.

Like ordinary water, sulfur is a commonplace substance that exhibits a confusing array of unusual characteristics. Even though sulfur has been studied and used since ancient times, there are still experts in the world who are devoting their professional lives to the study of this element.

Sulfur is a nonmetal. It is one of the oxygen elements in Group VIA on the periodic table.

Element	Abundance (Si = 1)
Hydrogen	40,000
Helium	3,100
Oxygen	22
Neon	8.6
Nitrogen	6.6
Carbon	3.5
Silicon	1
Magnesium	0.91
Iron	0.60
Sulfur	0.38

16-1 Sulfur just makes it onto the list of ten most abundant elements in the known cosmos.

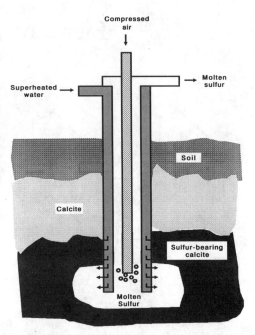

16-2 Sulfur is recovered from underground deposits by the Frasch process.

Sulfur exists in three allotropic forms: *orthorhombic, monoclinic,* and *amorphous.* As their names suggest, orthorhombic and monoclinic sulfur are crystalline forms. The orthorhombic form is the most common because it is the most stable. Monoclinic sulfur is stable only between 96 °C and 119 °C; it forms naturally as molten sulfur and gradually cools through that temperature range. Below 90 °C, monoclinic sulfur quickly returns to the orthorhombic form.

Amorphous, or plastic, sulfur is formed by rapidly cooling molten sulfur by dribbling molten sulfur into cold water, for example. Amorphous sulfur has no crystalline form; in fact it is a soft, elastic material. It is difficult to maintain sulfur in its amorphous form because it gradually reverts to the more stable orthorhombic form.

Commercial production of sulfur

Sulfur is one of the four major raw commodities of the chemical industry, sharing the limelight with coal, limestone, and salt. Production, delivery, and trading volumes of these commodities are used as indicators of the economic health of the chemical industry and, to a smaller extent, the economic health of the nation.

Most commercially available sulfur is used in the manufacture of sulfuric acid, a valuable component in fertilizers and automobile batteries. The remainder is used in insecticides, dyes, and industrially useful sulfur compounds.

Most sulfur is recovered in a pure, elemental form directly from underground deposits of sulfur-bearing calcite and calcium sulfate. These deposits usually exist over large subterranean salt deposits. A significant amount, a bit less than 25%, is recovered from gaseous byproducts of petroleum-refining and ore-processing industries.

An ancient production method called for burning large piles of sulfurous rock, or brimstone, to release molten sulfur and recover it before it all burned. There are obvious environmental hazards associated with this approach and, even so, the level of impurities remains so high that the product is virtually useless by today's more demanding standards.

Figure 16-2 illustrates the *Frasch process* for recovering raw sulfur deposits located between 200 and 2000 feet underground. This process accounts for about three-fourths of the American production of the element.

The apparatus for the process includes three concentric pipes. The outer pipe has a diameter of about six inches, the middle about three inches and the inner about one inch. This assembly fits into a shaft that is drilled into a known sulfur pocket. Water that is superheated to about 160 °C is injected into the space between the outer and middle pipes. A screen near the bottom of the assembly allows the water to contact the sulfur and sulfur-bearing rock. Sulfur melts at about 112 °C, so the sulfur liquifies and flows to the bottom of the pocket.

Air is forced downward into the inner pipe, thus raising the air pressure in the sulfur pocket and forcing hot, foaming sulfur up through the space between the inner and middle pipe. As the molten sulfur emerges from the top of the assembly, it is piped to vats or storage areas where it cools to a yellow, resinous solid that is better than 99% pure.

The Frasch process, first implemented around 1900, revolutionized sulfur production and economy. It not only allows the recovery of millions of tons of sulfur each year at a low cost, but it also purifies the sulfur.

Common compounds of sulfur

Hydrogen sulfide, H_2S, is a gas that is especially known for smelling like rotten eggs. Everyone in the halls of a typical high school know the day when the chemistry classes are studying sulfur compounds.

Hydrogen sulfide is most commonly produced by reacting iron sulfide with hydrochloric acid:

$$FeS + 2HCl \rightarrow H_2S + FeCl_2$$
(iron sulfide + hydrochloric acid → hydrogen sulfide + ferrous chloride)

Sulfur dioxide SO_2, has an unusually wide range of applications, including a bleaching agent, solvent, disinfectant, and refrigerant. Most of the commercially produced product is used in the production of sulfuric acid. Sulfur dioxide is produced in commercial quantities by simply burning sulfur in air. Assuming a sufficient amount of oxygen is present in the air, the reaction can be portrayed rather simply:

$$S + O_2 \rightarrow SO_2$$
(elemental sulfur + oxygen gas → sulfur dioxide gas)

Sulfur dioxide can also be produced by roasting metal sulfides in air:

$$2ZnS + 3O_2 \rightarrow 2ZnO_2 + 2SO_2$$
(zinc sulfide + oxygen → zinc oxide + sulfur dioxide)

SO_2 can also be produced by a reaction between a metal sulfite and a strong acid:

$$Na_2SO_3 + 2HCl \rightarrow 2NaCl + H_2O + SO_2$$
(sodium sulfite + hydrochloric acid → sodium chloride + water + sulfur dioxide)

Sulfur dioxide combines readily with water to form a weak acid, *sulfurous acid* H_2SO_3.

Sulfurous acid is produced commercially simply by dissolving sulfur dioxide in water:

$$SO_2 + H_2O \rightarrow H_2SO_3$$
(sulfur dioxide + water → sulfurous acid)

This acid is produced in nature whenever the stack fumes of coal-burning industries combine with atmospheric moisture. Most coal, especially that mined in the eastern half of the United States, contains a high percentage of sulfur and sulfur compounds. When this coal is burned in the presence of oxygen, sulfur dioxide escapes through the stack into the air where it combines with outdoor moisture to produce sulfurous acid rain.

Sulfuric acid, H_2SO_4, leads all other chemicals in annual tonnage produced. In the United States alone, production exceeds 40-million tons per year. Most of it is used in the manufacture of fertilizers, explosives, pigments, and dyes, It is a strong acid which can oxidize most metals. Curiously enough, however, concentrated sulfuric acid does not react with steel, making it the only commercially valuable acid that can be easily transported in concentrated form in steel containers. This otherwise nasty acid does not corrode iron and its alloys.

Sulfuric acid also has the ability to extract hydrogen and oxygen from organic compounds to transform them to simple water and carbon. The classic demonstration of this feature involves adding some concentrated sulfuric acid to a bit of ordinary sugar ($C_{12}H_{22}O_{11}$). The $-H_{22}O_{11}$ portion of the molecule is almost instantly drawn away as water vapor (H_2O), leaving behind a black, sponge-like mass of carbon.

Concentrated sulfuric acid is produced in ton quantities by means of an interesting multiple-step contact process.

- *Step 1*: Burn elemental sulfur in air to produce sulfur dioxide:

$$S + O_2 \rightarrow SO_2$$
(sulfur + oxygen → sulfur dioxide)

- *Step 2*: Heat the sulfur dioxide in the presence of oxygen and a catalyst of vanadium pentoxide (*see* Element 23: Vanadium) to produce sulfur trioxide:

$$2SO_2 + O_2 \rightarrow 2SO_3$$
(sulfur dioxide + oxygen gas + heated vanadium pentoxide → sulfur trioxide)

- *Step 3*: Bubble the sulfur trioxide through concentrated sulfuric acid to produce disulfuric acid:

$$SO_3 + H_2SO_4 \rightarrow H_2S_2SO_7$$
(sulfur trioxide + sulfuric acid → disulfuric acid)

- *Step 4*: Add water to the disulfuric acid to produce twice as much sulfuric acid as used in the previous step:

$$H_2S_2O_7 + H_2O \rightarrow 2H_2SO_4$$
(disulfuric acid + water → sulfuric acid)

Sulfuric acid is often used in the production of other acids. It reacts with sodium chloride (table salt) to yield hydrochloric acid:

$$2NaCl + H_2SO_4 \rightarrow Na_2SO_4 + 2HCl$$
(sodium chloride + sulfuric acid → sodium sulfate + hydrochloric acid)

Sulfuric acid reacts with sodium nitrate (soda niter) to yield nitric acid:

$$2NaNO_3 + H_2SO_4 \rightarrow Na_2SO_4 + 2HNO_3$$
(sodium nitrate + sulfuric acid → sodium sulfate + nitric acid)

Sulfate ions ($SO_4{}^{2-}$) combine with many different metallic atoms to form some common compounds: *copper sulfate* ($CuSO_4$), *magnesium sulfate* ($MgSO_4$) and *sodium sulfate* (Na_2SO_4). Two common sulfates that are better known by their mineral names of *gypsum* (*calcium sulfate*, $CaSO_4$) and *barite* (*barium sulfate*, $BaSO_4$).

Sulfides comprise a number of popular, naturally occurring minerals as well. These include *pyrite* (*iron disulfide*, FeS_2), *galena* (*lead sulfide*, PbS), *cinnabar* (*mercury sulfide*, HgS) and *sphalerite* (*zinc sulfide*, ZnS). Any of these can be produced in the laboratory by heating a mixture of the metal and sulfur.

Isotopes of sulfur

Figure 16-3 lists the eleven known isotopes of sulfur. Except for trace amounts of sulfur-33 and -36, naturally occurring sulfur is a mixture of isotopes sulfer-32 and -34. The other isotopes are created artificially and are radioactive. None of them has any special commercial or laboratory significance.

16-3 Sulfur has isotopes with atomic weights between 29 and 39.

Isotope	Natural Abundance	Half-Life	Decay Mode
^{29}S		0.19 sec	β+, p
^{30}S		1.18 sec	β+
^{31}S		2.55 sec	β+
^{32}S	95.02%		
^{33}S	0.75%		
^{34}S	4.21%		
^{35}S		87.2 day	β-
^{36}S	0.02%		
^{37}S		5.05 min	β-
^{38}S		2.84 hr	β-
^{39}S		11.5 sec	β-

Element 17: Chlorine

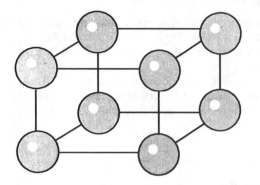

Name	Chlorine
Symbol	Cl
Atomic Number	17
Atomic Weight	35.453
Melting Point	-100.98°C
Boiling Point	-34°C
Density	3.214 g/l (0°C , 1 atm)
Oxidation State	-1
Electron Config	(Ne) $3s^2\ 3p^5$

- Name pronounced as **KLOR-een** or **KLOR-in**
- Name taken from the Greek work *chloros*, "greenish yellow"
- Prepared by Carl Wilhelm Scheele in 1774; shown to be an element by Sir Humphry Davy in 1810
- Greenish-yellow, disagreeable gas

Chlorine is best known to the general public as the smell of household bleach or a swimming pool. In a concentrated form, chlorine is more than something with an antiseptic smell—it is a deadly gas. In fact, it was one of the most common weapons in the gas warfare of World War I.

Today chlorine is a common bleaching agent and antiseptic. It is also the backbone of many plastics and chemical industries. Few other elements combine so readily with so many different elemental metals.

Historical background

During the late 1700s, a German chemist named Carl Wilhelm Scheele (1742 – 1786) moved to Sweden to complete his study of the mineral *pyrolusite*. Pyrolusite is manganese dioxide; it is the principal ore for producing manganese metal, and there is no chlorine content. Scheele, however, decided to soak some powered pryolusite in a liquid that was known in his day as *muriatic acid*. Much to his surprise, there was some bubbling and a terrible, biting smell that reminded him of warm aqua regia. He figured that the pyrolusite was "dephlosgisticating the muratic acid"—or whatever. Basically, Scheele thought he was observing an interesting side effect, and not the outright production of an unknown element.

A few years later, Sir Humphry Davy was finding himself in the middle of a controversy about the true source of hydrogen gas that is evolved whenever an active metal, such as potassium, was placed into muriatic acid. Davy believed the acid was the source of hydrogen (which it is), while his opponents thought the metal was the source of hydrogen. As the arguments raged, the opponents' views became increasingly complicated as they attempted to fit additional findings into a preconceived theory. In 1810, Davy finally decided to end the matter by suggesting that a new and very simple element was behind the apparent complication. Having made this suggestion, the findings neatly fell into place and the apparent complications vanished.

Properties of chlorine

Chlorine is a member of the Group-VIIA, or halogen, elements. Notice that the names of all the halogens end with -ine: fluorine (F), bromine (Br), iodine (I), and astatine (At).

Being a halogen means that chlorine is a very reactive ion, forming -1 bonds with nearly all metals. For example, the best known compound of chlorine, sodium chloride (NaCl), combines the chlorine ion with the metallic element, sodium. Like the other halogens, elemental chlorine forms a diatomic molecule, or halide, that can be represented as Cl_2.

Chlorine is a nonmetal that exists as a greenish-yellow, highly corrosive gas at room temperature. It is essential that you avoid inhaling even the smallest dose of concentrated chlorine gas. If you want to get some appreciation of its suffocating odor, you can experience it at safe concentrations around large swimming pools and in areas where someone is using chlorine bleach.

Production of chlorine

Small amounts of chlorine gas can be produced in the laboratory by oxidizing the Cl^- ion in acidic solution; or to put it more simply, by mixing together some hydrochloric acid (HCl) and manganese dioxide (MnO_2). The hydrochloric acid provides the Cl^- ion as well as the acid environment, and manganese dioxide is, indeed, a strong oxidizing agent. This is the same general formulation used in the earliest studies of chlorine gas:

$$MnO_2 + 4HCl \rightarrow MnCl_2 + 2H_2O + Cl_2$$
(manganese dioxide + hydrochloric acid → manganese chloride + water + chlorine gas)

Chlorine gas can also be produced by the electrolysis of sodium chloride (NaCl) which is, of course, ordinary table salt. Figure 17-1 shows a basic electrolysis arrangement for a saturated solution of NaCl—saltwater. The reaction is not as simple as one might suspect at first glance because the electrolysis affects both the NaCl and H_2O molecules:

$$2Cl^- \rightarrow Cl_2 + 2e^- \text{ (anode reaction)}$$
$$2H_2O + 2e^- \rightarrow H2 + 2OH^- \text{ (cathode reaction)}$$
$$2NaCl + 2H_2O \rightarrow Cl_2 + H_2 + 2NaOH \text{ (cell reaction)}$$

Basically, chlorine gas appears at the anode and hydrogen gas at the cathode. You do not see the sodium ion appearing in either of the half-cell reactions; it is a *spectator ion* because water is far more easily reduced than sodium. The spectator ion, Na^+, is nevertheless a significant ingredient in the overall cell reaction, combining with the hydroxide ion (OH^-) to produce sodium hydroxide (NaOH) in the solution.

The vast amounts of chlorine required for the plastics industries and municipal water-treatment plants are produced by the electrolysis of aqueous sodium chloride, ordinary sea-water, or brine from salt mines. The industrial processes for producing significant quantities of chlorine by electrolysis would be quite simple if chlorine gas were the only product that was desired. The commercial demand for sodium hydroxide is equally strong, however, and it would be a shame to throw away all the sodium hydroxide that results from generating chlorine gas by electrolysis. Recovering the sodium hydroxide from a chlorine-gas operation requires special equipment designs—designs and procedures that are somewhat more complicated than a basic electrolysis setup. The equipment is thus tailored to

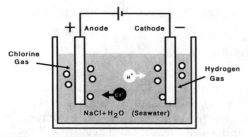

17-1 Chlorine can be recovered in large amounts by the electrolysis of NaCl as found in ordinary seawater.

Isotope	Natural Abundance	Half-Life	Decay Mode
^{31}Cl		0.15 sec	β+
^{32}Cl		297 ms	β+, p
^{33}Cl		2.51 sec	β+
^{34m}Cl		32.2 min	β+
^{34}Cl		1.53 sec	β+
^{35}Cl	75.77%		
^{36}Cl		3x10^5 yr	β-
^{37}Cl	24.23%		
^{38m}Cl		0.70 sec	i.t.
^{38}Cl		37.2 min	β-
^{39}Cl		55.7 min	β-
^{40}Cl		1.35 min	β-
^{41}Cl		34 sec	β-

17-2 Chlorine has isotopes with atomic weights between 31 and 41.

deal with the problems of recovering NaOH and chlorine is regarded as a valuable bypro- duct (*see* Element 11: Sodium for more information about the commercial production of sodium hydroxide and chlorine gas).

Some compounds of chlorine

Chlorine combines with nearly all the elements. It forms ionic bonds with the metals and molecular bonds with the semimetals and nonmetals.

Metallic compounds

Virtually every metal on the periodic table of the elements forms an ionic bond with chlo- rine. Chlorine is represented in these instances by its Cl⁻ ion, and it combines with virtually every oxidation state the metals have. It is little wonder there are so many different chloride salts.

The Group-IA metals, for example, form simple, one-for-one ionic bonds to form some of the most familiar salts: *lithium chloride* (LiCl), *potassium chloride* (KCl), and the most common salt of all, *sodium chloride* (NaCl).

The Group-IIA metals have 2+ ions, so they bond with chlorine to form salts such as *magnesium chloride* ($MgCl_2$) and *calcium chloride* ($CaCl_2$). The metals in Groups IIIB and IVB tend to have 3+ and 4+ ions, so their chlorides can be represented by *lantanum chlo- ride* ($LaCl_3$) and *zirconium tetrachloride* ($ZrCl_4$)

Matters become more interesting in Groups VB through IB where the metals tend to have several stable oxidation states. Manganese, for example, readily forms two different chlorides: *manganese(II) chloride*, $MnCl_2$ (also known as manganese dichloride and the min- eral *seacchite*), and *manganese(III) chloride*, $MnCl_3$ (also known as manganese trichloride).

Vanadium forms three different chlorides: *vanadium(II) chloride*, VCl_2 (also called vana- dium dichloride); *vanadium(III) chloride*, VCl_3 (also known as vanadium trichloride); and *vanadium(IV) chloride*, VCl_4 (also called vanadium tetrachloride).

Most of the chloride salts are produced by a reaction between chloride gas and the metal or by the reaction between the metal or its oxide with hydrochloric acid. An example of a direct combination of the two elements is:

$$2Li + Cl_2 \rightarrow 2LiCl$$
(lithium metal + chlorine gas → lithium chloride)

The classic example of producing a chloride with reaction between a metal and hydrochloric acid is:

$$Zn + 2HCl \rightarrow ZnCl_2 + H_2$$
(zinc metal + hydrochloric acid → zinc chloride + hydrogen gas)

To see how a chloride salt is produced by the reaction between a metal oxide and hydrochloric acid, consider:

$$MgO + 2HCl \leftrightarrow MgCl_2 + H_2O$$
(magnesium oxide + hydrochloric acid ↔ magnesium chloride + water)

Oxides of chlorine

Chlorine combines with oxygen to form a set of four different oxides: Cl_2O, ClO_2, Cl_2O_6 and Cl_2O_7.

Dichlorine monoxide, Cl_2O, is a reddish-yellow gas that liquifies at $-20\,°C$ to form a reddish-brown liquid. It is produced by a reaction between chlorine gas and mercury(II) oxide:

$$2Cl_2 + HgO \leftrightarrow HgCl_2 + Cl_2O$$
(chlorine gas + mercury(II) oxide ↔ mercury(II) chloride + dichlorine monoxide)

Chlorine dioxide, ClO_2, is an explosive, orange-yellow gas. It is so unstable that it can be safely stored only after diluting it with an inert gas such as argon. Nevertheless, chlorine dioxide is used as a commercial bleaching agent and in the manufacture of other chlorites. The simplest method of preparation is to combine sodium chlorate, sulfur dioxide, and sulfuric acid:

$$2NaClO_3 + SO_2 + H_2SO_4 \rightarrow ClO_2 + 2NaHSO_4$$
(sodium chlorate + sulfur dioxide + sulfuric acid → chlorine dioxide + sodium hydrogen sulfate)

Dichlorine hexoxide, Cl_2O_6, is a red liquid that readily decomposes to chlorine and chlorine dioxide at room temperature. It can be prepared by the reaction between chlorine dioxide and ozone:

$$2ClO_2 + 2O_3 \rightarrow Cl_2O_6 + 2O_2$$
(chlorine dioxide + ozone → dichlorine hexoxide + oxygen)

Dichlorine heptoxide, Cl_2O_7, is a colorless liquid and a very strong oxidizer. It is the anhydrous version of perchloric acid, $HClO_4$; it is perchloric acid with the H_2O removed.

HCl, the hydrogen compound of chlorine

Hydrogen and chlorine gasses combine explosively to produce *hydrogen chloride*, HCl. This is a colorless gas that has a very biting, irritating odor. It dissolves readily in water to produce the familiar strong acid, hydrochloric acid.

Hydorchloric acid is one of the leading industrial acids (behind sulfuric acid). It is used as a solvent in a great variety of industries and as a key ingredient in the production of modern plastics. The chemical industry, itself, uses a great deal of hydrochloric acid for producing other chlorides.

Concentrated hydrochloric acid is about 40% HCl and 60% water. It can be produced on a commercial scale by a direct combination of the two gasses:

$$H_2 + Cl_2 \rightarrow 2HCl$$
(hydrogen gas + chlorine gas → hydrogen chloride)

or by a reaction between an active-metal chloride and sulfuric acid:

$$NaCl + H_2SO_4 \rightarrow NaHSO_4 + HCl$$
(sodium chloride + sulfuric acid → sodium hydrogen sulfate + hydrogen chloride)

Isotopes of chlorine

Figure 17-2 on p. 72 lists the isotopes of chlorine. Natural chlorine is a combination of chlorine-35 and -37. The remainder are radioactive, with chlorine-36 having the longest half-life—some 300,000 years.

Element 18: Argon

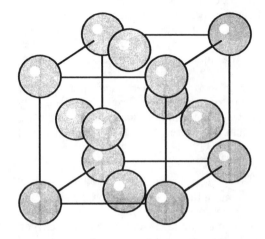

Name	Argon
Symbol	Ar
Atomic Number	18
Atomic Weight	39.948
Melting Point	-189.2°C
Boiling Point	-185.7°C
Density	1.784 g/l (0°C , 1 atm)
Oxidation State	0
Electron Config.	$1s^2\,2s^2\,2p^6\,3s^2\,3p^6$

- Name pronounced as AR-gon
- Name from the Green *argos*, "inactive"
- Henry Cavendish suggested the existence of an inert gas in the atmosphere in 1785; Lord Rayleigh and Sir William Ramsay isolated argon and identified it as an element in 1894
- Colorless, odorless, tasteless, noble gas

Figure 18-1 shows that argon gas comprises about 1% of the earth's atmosphere. This places argon third on the abundance list of atmospheric gasses, far behind oxygen, but well ahead of some of the more commonly known gasses such as carbon dioxide, helium, methane, and hydrogen.

18-1 Argon ranks third on the list of gasses in the earth's atmosphere.

Gas (Sea level)	Content by volume	
	(percent)	(ppm)
Nitrogen, N_2	78.09	—
Oxygen, O_2	20.95	—
Argon, Ar	0.93	—
Carbon Dioxide, CO_2	0.03	—
Neon, Ne	—	18.18
Helium, He	—	5.24
Krypton, Kr	—	1.14
Methane, CH_4	—	2
Nitrous oxide, N_2O	—	0.5
Hydrogen, H_2	—	.05
Xenon, Xe	—	.087

Since 1914, argon has been used for filling incandescent light bulbs. This inert gas does not play a direct role in the function of such lamps; it simply replaces the air inside the bulb—oxygen-bearing air that can corrode the hot filament. As light bulb production increased through the decades, so did the demand for argon gas. Since argon is a byproduct of large-scale commercial oxygen and nitrogen distillation, there has never been a shortage of argon. In fact, there were significant surpluses in the early 1970s. Chemical engineers consequently found it desirable to rework industrial applications to use argon in place of helium.

Argon is used wherever there is a need for an inert atmosphere—inside an ordinary light bulb, for example. Crystals for the semiconductor industries are grown in a chemically inert argon atmosphere. It is possible to use arc-welding techniques for welding aluminum, stainless steel, and certain other exotic metals, but only where active atmospheric gasses in the region of the arc are replaced with argon.

Historical background

Just as Daniel Rutherford had discovered nitrogen more than a century before by absorbing all the oxygen from a sample of air and analyzing the residue, Sir William Ramsay (1852 – 1916) thought it might be a good idea to take a look at a sample of air after removing oxygen and nitrogen. After removing those two gasses, he took special care to remove all traces of carbon dioxide, dust, and moisture. The remaining gas amounted to about 1.23% of the original volume. This was an encouraging figure because Daniel Rutherford, upon announcing his discovery of nitrogen, predicted there was an additional gas that would occupy about 0.8%. (As shown in Fig. 18-1, the actual figure is now known to be 0.93%.)

Ramsay was convinced that he was working with a second form of nitrogen, something analogous to the ozone form of oxygen. Ramsay and Sir William Crookes both ran spectroscopic tests on the samples and found lines not belonging to any known gas. Ramsay, along with his mentor and coworker, Lord Rayleigh, found a place for a new gas on the periodic table. The atomic weight of the samples matched the weight predicted by its position on the periodic table; in 1894, they conceded that they had discovered a new chemical element. The duo astonished their Oxford fellows by announcing the new element was the first in a series of inert gasses.

Properties of argon

Argon is a member of the Group-0 elements. Until the late 1960s, this group was often called the *inert gasses* because it was believed they could not possibly combine with any other element to form compounds. Today we know that the so-called inert gasses can indeed combine with other elements. Admittedly, it is difficult to create these compounds; most of them are highly unstable and some barely qualify as being compounds at all. None of them has any practical application. In the world of theoretical chemistry where truth and knowledge are more important than an improved shoe polish, the notion that the noble gasses can combine with other elements is one of the most satisfying discoveries of this generation.

Finding that the inert gasses are no longer inert has forced some changes in chemical nomenclature. First, these are now *noble* gasses instead of inert gasses. This has not been a difficult change in nomenclature because the terms were used interchangeably before *inert* fell from grace. Changing the notation on periodic tables is taking a bit longer, though. Notice, for example, that the noble gasses on most periodic tables are still designated to Group-0. These were formerly known as the Group-0 gasses because of their unique oxidation state of zero. This is still the most stable oxidation state for noble gasses, but we now know that others exist. Some newer periodic charts call this group VIIIA instead of 0.

Production of argon

Argon gas is captured and separated for commercial and laboratory applications by fractional distillation of liquid air. Actually, argon has long been considered a byproduct of commercial nitrogen and oxygen production. Nitrogen and oxygen have long enjoyed vast commercial markets in industry, science, and medicine. The most economical and reliable was to produce them by distilling them from liquified air.

As shown in Fig. 18-2, argon liquifies at a temperature between that of oxygen and nitrogen, so any facility that produces liquid nitrogen and oxygen gets crude argon as well. Crude argon is a mixture that is rich in argon, but contains measurable amounts of krypton and xenon. Crude argon can be further refined for applications requiring higher levels of purity.

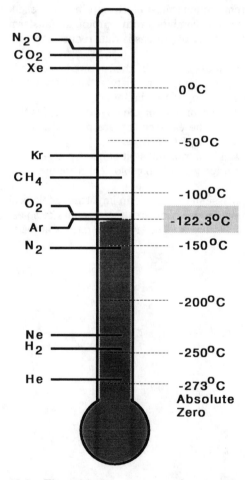

Isotope	Natural Abundance	Half-Life	Decay Mode
^{32}Ar		0.1 sec	β+, p
^{33}Ar		17 ms	β+
^{34}Ar		.844 sec	β+
^{35}Ar		1.77 sec	β+
^{36}Ar	0.337%		
^{37}Ar		3.8 day	ec
^{38}Ar	0.063%		
^{39}Ar		269 yr	β-
^{40}Ar	99.60%		
^{41}Ar		1.83 hr	β-
^{42}Ar		33 yr	β-
^{43}Ar		5.4 min	β-
^{44}Ar		1.9 min	β-
^{45}Ar		21 sec	β-
^{46}Ar			

18-3 Argon has isotopes with atomic weights between 32 and 46.

18-2 The critical temperature for argon is between that of oxygen and nitrogen, making it a natural byproduct of commercial liquid oxygen and nitrogen operations.

Isotopes of argon

Argon gas is formed in deposits of potassium-bearing minerals and compounds by a radioactive-decay process known as electron-capture decay. The parent isotope in this case is naturally occurring radioactive potassium-40. This isotope decays to stable, nonradioactive argon gas.

Electron-capture, or K-shell, decay produces a stable isotope by reducing the number of protons in the nucleus of the atom. The mass number (the sum of the number of protons and neutrons in the nucleus) remains unchanged, but the atomic number (number of protons) is reduced by one. The process is accompanied by the loss of one electron and emission of one neutrino. Tables of isotopes, such as the one for argon in Fig. 18-3 on p. 77, indicate electron-capture decay as an *ec* mode of decay.

This ec process generally begins when an atom responds to the need for nuclear stability by forcing one of its own electrons to fall from the innermost electron orbit, or K-shell, into the nucleus. Once there, the electron immediately combines with a proton to transform the two entities into a single neutron. The total number of protons is thus reduced by one, while the number of neutrons is increased by one.

Nuclear stability is not complete, however, until the gap left by the captured electron is filled by an electron from a higher level. This happens almost immediately; the electron that falls into the gap emits energy in the form of a neutrino, or X-radiation.

When potassium-40 decays into argon-40, the accounting for the operation begins this way: 19 protons, 21 neutrons, 19 electrons. When the electron-capture process is completed, the totals look like this: 18 protons, 22 neutrons, 18 electrons.

Radioactive potassium is thus converted to stable argon, and a bit of energy is given off in the process. In nature, the result is pockets of argon gas within geological structures containing significant amounts of potassium minerals.

Incidentally, the conversion of radioactive potassium to argon is an important geological dating tool. This tool, known as potassium-argon dating, compares the amounts of potassium-40 and argon-40 to determine the age of rock samples. The larger the ratio of argon to potassium-40, the older the samples must be.

Element 19: Potassium

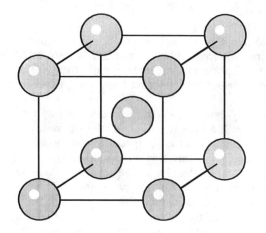

Name	Potassium
Symbol	K
Atomic Number	19
Atomic Weight	39.0983
Melting Point	63.25°C
Boiling Point	759.9°C
Specific Gravity	0.862 (20°C)
Oxidation State	+1
Electron Config.	(Ar) $4s^1$

- Name pronounced as **pe-TASS-i-em**
- Name from the English *pot ash*
- Chemical symbol, K, from the Latin *kalium*, "alkali"
- Discovered and isolated by Sir Humphry Davy in 1807
- Soft, waxy, silver-white metal

Figure 19-1 shows that the element potassium is ranked eighth in abundance of elements in the earth's crust. Like other highly active metals such as calcium and lithium, potassium does not exist naturally in its pure metallic state. This is because it readily forms compounds with common natural elements such as air and water. In fact, potassium catches fire spontaneously upon contact with water, generating corrosive potassium hydroxide and giving off explosive hydrogen gas.

19-1 Potassium is among the ten most abundant elements in the earth's crust.

Element	Concentration (ppm)
Oxygen	464,000
Silicon	282,000
Aluminum	83,200
Iron	56,300
Calcium	41,500
Sodium	23,600
Magnesium	23,300
Potassium	20,900
Titanium	5700
Hydrogen	1400

Potassium ions are vital to life processes, particularly the function of nerve and muscle tissues.

Historical background

The early history of potassium is identical to that of sodium. The reason is that, until the 1700s, most chemists did not recognize any real difference between mineral and vegetable alkalis (now known to be sodium carbonate and potassium carbonate, respectively). The fact that one comes directly from deposits in the earth and the other from wood ashes did not seem to make any difference to them.

As chemistry matured into the 18th century, however, chemists began noticing that crystals of the so-called "artificial" and "natural" alkalis were quite different from one another. Those produced by leeching water through wood ashes (potassium compounds) were quite different from those found ready-formed in nature (sodium compounds).

During the early 1700s, researchers focused their attention on the similarities among vegetable alkali, saltpeter, salt of tartar, and cream of tartar. An unknown metallic element, potassium, as common to all these studies, but no one could prove it yet.

By the end of the 1700s, chemists had finally found that nitrogen was present in several alkalis, but was not an essential ingredient. This led to the conclusion that saltpeter (the form now known to be potassium nitrate) was not an element in its own right, but a compound consisting of nitrogen and an unknown substance common to the natural alkali from wood ashes (now known to be potassium hydroxide). At the turn of the century, a few chemists began looking for a way to isolate the new element.

It was up to Sir Humphry Davy in 1807 to prove the usefulness of his electrolysis apparatus by being the first to isolate potassium metal. Quite simply, he applied the electrodes to a bath of molten potassium hydroxide and sorted out the liquid potassium metal that collected around the cathode. A few months later, Davy used the same procedure to isolate sodium metal.

Properties of potassium

Pure potassium metal is so soft that many who have worked with it refer to it as a waxy substance. Few people have had such an opportunity, however, because potassium is highly unstable in the normal human environment. It reacts with the oxygen in dry air to produce the *potassium superoxide*, KO_2. If there is any moisture in that air, or if the sample of potassium comes into direct contact with water, you get *potassium hydroxide*, (KOH) and hydrogen gas:

$$2K + 2H_2O \rightarrow 2KOH + H_2$$
(potassium + water → potassium hydroxide + hydrogen gas)

This reaction is *exothermic*; that is, it generates heat—enough heat in this case to ignite the hydrogen gas.

Potassium belongs to Group IA on the periodic chart. With the notable exception of hydrogen (H), the elements in this group are all highly reactive metals that cannot exist in the elemental forms in nature. These metals are commonly called the alkali metals, due to the fact they all form such strong, caustic (alkaline) hydroxides. Household lye, for example, is made up of sodium hydroxide, potassium hydroxide, or a mixture of the two.

Potassium and its salts impart a violet color to a flame test.

Production of potassium

Potassium metal is not in great commercial demand, so two fairly simple refining processes are adequate. In one instance, vaporized potassium chloride (KCl) is combined with hot sodium vapor (Na) that is obtained from molten sodium chloride (NaCl), as shown in Fig. 19-2. The hot gasses combine in a chamber filled with stainless steel rings. The sodium vapor reduces the potassium, generating a sodium chloride slag that is returned to the source of molten NaCl. At the same time, the potassium vapor is drawn out of the chamber where it condenses to liquid potassium, then to the solid metallic form. Both ingredients in this process, potassium chloride and sodium chloride, are abundantly available in nature.

Potassium metal can also be recovered from potassium chloride or potassium fluoride in a cell that is specially designed to eliminate the buildup of explosive gasses that are often associated with potassium reactions. Figure 19-3 is a simplified schematic of the electrolysis setup. The reactions are:

$$2Cl^- \rightarrow Cl_2 + 2e^- \text{ (anode reaction)}$$
$$K^+ + e^- \rightarrow K \text{ (cathode reaction)}$$
$$2KCl \rightarrow Cl_2 + 2K \text{ (cell reaction)}$$
$$\text{(potassium chloride + electrolysis} \rightarrow \text{chlorine gas + potassium metal)}$$

The electrolysis of fused (molten) potassium chloride produces chlorine gas at the anode and potassium metal at the cathode. A temperature of at least 770 °C is required for melting the potassium chloride—the electrolyte. Potassium melts at a mere 63.25 °C, so it is obviously going to be in its liquid state.

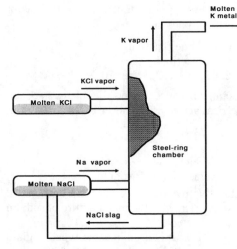

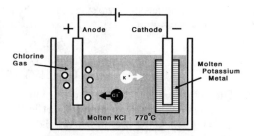

19-3 Potassium can be produced by the electrolysis of its chloride.

19-2 Commercial quantities of potassium are produced by the reaction between hot potassium chloride (KCl) and sodium (Na) vapors in a special retort.

Common compounds of potassium

Potassium has a single oxidation state of $+1$, and its most stable ion is K^+, so it combines with anions having an oxidation state of -1 in this way:

Potassium chloride, KCl

$$K^+ + Cl^- \rightarrow KCl$$

Potassium hydroxide, KOH

$$K^+ + OH^- \rightarrow KOH$$

It combines with anions of -2 as:

Potassium monoxide, K_2O

$$2K^+ + O^{2-} \rightarrow K_2O$$

Potassium sulfate, K_2SO_4

$$2K^+ + (SO_4)^{2-} \rightarrow K_2SO_4$$

Potassium chloride, KCl, is the most abundant of potassium compounds. In the mineral world, natural potassium chloride is known as *sylvite*. Potassium chloride is perhaps best know as a no-sodium table salt substitute. It is also an ingredient in many chemical fertilizers and is used in the manufacture of other chemicals. KCl occurs naturally in the group of salts derived from seawater and subterranean brine deposits. It is also available from the mineral, *carnallite* ($KCl \cdot MgCl_2 \cdot 6H_2O$).

Potassium hydroxide, KOH, is often called *caustic potash*, or lye. Most of the product is used in the manufacture of soaps and detergents. It is a good drain cleaner because it combines with animal grease (presumably one of the causes of a plugged drain) to form water-soluable soaps.

Today, potassium hydroxide is produced on a commercial scale by the electrolysis of aqueous potassium chloride. The reactions at the electrodes are:

$$2e^- + 2H_2O \rightarrow H_2 + 2OH^- \text{ (cathode reaction)}$$
$$2Cl^- \rightarrow Cl_2 + 2e^- \text{ (anode reaction)}$$
$$2Cl^- + 2H_2O \rightarrow H_2 + Cl_2 + 2OH^- \text{ (net cell reaction)}$$

The potassium K^+, does not appear in these reactions because it plays the role of a spectator ion—one that plays no direct part in the electrical activity. It is nevertheless present in the solution, so the overall reaction is:

$$2KCl + 2H_2O \rightarrow H_2 + Cl_2 + 2KOH$$
(potassium chloride + water + electrolysis $\rightarrow$
hydrogen gas + chlorine gas + potassium hydroxide)

The special equipment required for implementing this reaction on a safe and economical commercial scale is described in more detail in connection with the manufacture of sodium hydroxide (*see* Element 11: Sodium).

Potassium carbonate ($KHCO_3$) is often called *pearl ash*. It is used in some types of glass products and soaps. It was originally formed in nature from burned vegetation. Today, it is produced on a commercial scale as a byproduct of the Haber-Bosch process for manufacturing ammonia (*see* Element 7: Nitrogen). It can be prepared in a simple laboratory setting by a reaction between a solution of potassium hydroxide and carbon dioxide:

$$KOH + CO_2 \text{ } KHCO_3$$
(potassium hydroxide + carbon dioxide $\rightarrow$ potassium carbonate)

The manufacture of *potassium superoxide*, KO_2, consumes more elemental potassium metal than all other applications combined. This compound is formed by burning potassium metal in dry air. Potassium superoxide is used in respiratory equipment because it efficiently generates fresh oxygen while removing carbon dioxide. This chemical, in effect, is the opposite of the human respiratory system, where oxygen is inhaled and carbon dioxide exhaled.

Potassium nitrate (KNO_3), better known as *nitre* and *saltpeter*, occurs in nature and is a valuable component in chemical fertilizers and pyrotechnic devices (notably match heads). It is easily prepared in the laboratory by the reaction between nitric acid and potassium hydroxide:

$$HNO_3 + KOH \rightarrow KNO_3 + H_2O$$

(nitric acid + potassium hydroxide → potassium nitrate + water)

It can also be prepared by the fractional crystallization of an aqueous solution of sodium nitrate and potassium hydroxide. The molecular equation for this double replacement reaction is:

$$NaNO_3 + KOH \rightarrow KNO_3 + NaOH$$

(sodium nitrate + potassium hydroxide → potassium nitrate + sodium hydroxide)

A number of different potassium compounds are used in photography processes. Some of these are *potassium bromide* (KBr), *potassium dichromate* ($K_2 Dr_2O_7$), *potassium ferricyanide* ($K_3Fe(CN)_6$), and *potassium oxalate* ($K_2C_2O_4 \cdot H_2O$).

Want to kill some crabgrass in your lawn? Try mixing up a batch of potassium cyanate, KOCN. You can make it by mixing urea ($CO(NH_2)_2$) and potassium carbonate.

Isotopes of potassium

Figure 19-4 lists the isotopes of potassium. More than 99% of naturally occurring potassium is a mixture of potassium-39 and -41. There are trace amounts of radioactive potassium-40 in nature. This radioactive isotope has an incredibly long half-life of 9,000,000,000 years.

The remainder of the potassium isotopes are radioactive and synthetic.

19-4 Potassium has isotopes with atomic weights between 35 and 51.

Isotope	Natural Abundance	Half-Life	Decay Mode
^{35}K		0.19 sec	β+
^{36}K		0.342 sec	β+, p
^{37}K		1.23 sec	β+
^{38m}K		0.926 sec	β+
^{38}K		7.63 min	β+
^{39}K	93.2581%		
^{40}K	0.0117%	1.25×10^9 yr	β-
^{41}K	6.7302%		
^{42}K		12.36 hr	β-
^{43}K		22.3 hr	β-
^{44}K		22.1 min	β-
^{45}K		17.3 min	β-
^{46}K		107 sec	β-
^{47}K		17.5 sec	β-
^{48}K		69 sec	β-
^{49}K		1.3 sec	β-
^{50}K		0.7 sec	β-
^{51}K		0.38 sec	β-

Element 20: Calcium

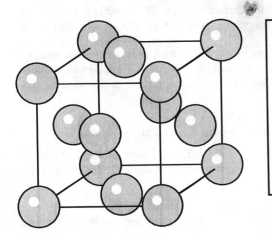

Name	Calcium
Symbol	Ca
Atomic Number	20
Atomic Weight	40.08
Melting Point	839°C
Boiling Point	1484°C
Specific Gravity	1.54 (20°C)
Oxidation State	+2
Electron Config.	(Ar) $4s^2$

- Name pronounced as **KAL-si-em**
- Name from the Latin *calx*, ancient name for lime
- Ancients were familiar with the most common calcium compounds, limestone and gypsum; identified as a metallic element by Sir Humphry Davy in 1808
- Fairly hard, silvery-white metal

People are generally not aware of the presence of calcium in their lives, but it is definitely present. Calcium compounds are present in a variety of commonplace items, from blackboard chalk to teeth and bones. Figure 20-1 shows that calcium is the fifth most abundant element in the earth's crust. None of it exists as calcium metal, however.

Few people have actually seen a piece of elemental calcium. Those who have seen it describe calcium as a hard, silvery-white metal. It is an unstable metal that readily combines with natural substances, such as water and air, to form common compounds that do not resemble a metal in any fashion. Figure 20-2 shows that one of the compounds of calcium, calcium oxide or CaO, is one of the most abundant compounds on earth.

Although there is virtually no commercial demand for calcium metal, two of its naturally occurring compounds, lime and gypsum, are in great demand by a number of different industries.

About 2% of the human body is composed of calcium in one form or another. The primary dietary source of calcium is milk and related dairy products.

Historical background

Calcium, as a chemical element, was virtually unknown until the 19th century. However, limestone and gypsum, the principal minerals of calcium, have been applied, studied, and understood from ancient times. For example, some ancient Egyptian tombs are lined with a form of gypsum plaster which is essentially the same as the drywall product developed for modern-day building construction. The early Greeks and Romans used baked lime and gypsum in various plasters for construction purposes as well as for the base material for casting statuettes. A medical book written about 975 A.D. describes the procedure for using plaster

Element	Concentration (ppm)
Oxygen	464,000
Silicon	282,000
Aluminum	83,200
Iron	56,300
Calcium	41,500
Sodium	23,600
Magnesium	23,300
Potassium	20,900
Titanium	5700
Hydrogen	1400

Compound	Weight (ppm)
Silicon dioxide, SiO_2	428,600
Magnesium oxide, MgO	350,700
Ferrous oxide, FeO	89,700
Aluminum oxide, Al_2O_3	69,900
Calcium Oxide, CaO	43,700
Sodium oxide, Na_2O	4500
Ferric oxide, Fe_2O_3	3600
Titanium dioxide, TiO_2	3300
Chromic oxide, Cr_2O_3	1800
Manganese oxide, MnO	1400

20-1 Calcium is among the ten most abundant elements in the earth's crust.

20-2 Calcium oxide is among the ten most common compounds in the earth's crust.

of paris (dehydrated gypsum) as a bandage for setting broken bones. The procedure has changed little since that time.

By the end of the 1700s, chemists were beginning to suspect that limestone and gypsum shared a common chemical element of some metallic nature. Various attempts at isolating the metal from its compounds failed. The methods they had recently used with success for isolating potassium and sodium metals simply did not work for the new metal.

Sir Humphry Davy came to the rescue in 1808 when he electrolyzed minute, impure bits of calcium metal from a mixture of lime and mercuric oxide. Technical grade calcium metal could not be prepared until the early 1900s, however.

Properties of calcium

Calcium is the most familiar member of the Group IIA elements, or *alkaline-earth* metals. Prior to the 1800s, chemists did not regard these elements—magnesium (Mg) and calcium, for instance—as metals. The elements form hydroxides quite readily, so they were classified as alkaline substances. Furthermore, they were derived from common ores taken from the earth; therefore, it seemed proper to refer to them as earth elements. We now know that the Group-IIA elements are metals, but the older nomenclature remains.

Calcium has a lustrous, slightly grayish appearance when it is first cut. Surfaces exposed to the air tarnish to show a duller finish. The metal is a good conductor of electricity, although there is no practical application for this property.

Like the other metals on the left-hand side of the periodic table, calcium is a very active metal. It combines slowly with dry air to produce a protective coating of an oxide and a nitride:

$$2Ca + O_2 \rightarrow 2CaO$$
(calcium metal + atmospheric oxygen → calcium oxide)

$$3Ca + N_2 \rightarrow Ca_3N_2$$
(calcium metal + atmospheric nitrogen → calcium nitride)

This accounts for the tarnish that soon dulls an otherwise shiny surface on the metal. The compounds in this instance are quite effective at preventing further corrosion of the metal.

Calcium metal does not combine with water explosively as do many of the highly reactive metals, but it does bubble off hydrogen gas and produce calcium hydroxide:

$$Ca + 2H_2O \rightarrow Ca(OH)_2 + H_2$$
(calcium metal + water → calcium hydroxide + hydrogen gas)

Production of calcium

Commercial demands for calcium metal are quite small. Until recently, the world demand could be satisfied by an electrolysis technique similar to the one employed by Sir Humphry Davy in the 19th century. Rather than using a mixture of lime and mercuric oxide, the more modern version uses molten, dehydrated calcium chloride ($CaCl_2$). Figure 20-3 shows the arrangement of components for the electrolytic procedure. The reactions are:

$$2Cl^- \rightarrow Cl_2 + 2e^- \text{ (anode reactions)}$$
$$Ca^{2+} + 2e^- \rightarrow Ca \text{ (cathode reaction)}$$
$$CaCl_2 \rightarrow Ca + Cl_2 \text{ (cell reaction)}$$
(calcium chloride + electrolysis → calcium metal + chlorine gas)

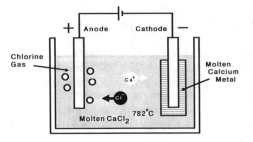

20-3 Calcium can be produced by the electrolysis of its chloride.

Isotope	Natural Abundance	Half-Life	Decay Mode
^{36}Ca		0.1 sec	β+, n
^{37}Ca		175 ms	β+, n
^{38}Ca		0.45 sec	β+
^{39}Ca		0.86 sec	β+
^{40}Ca	96.941%		
^{41}Ca		1×10^5 yr	ec
^{42}Ca	0.647%		
^{43}Ca	0.135%		
^{44}Ca	2.086%		
^{45}Ca		163.8 day	β-
^{46}Ca	0.004%		
^{47}Ca		4.536 day	β-
^{48}Ca	0.187%		
^{49}Ca		8.72 min	β-
^{50}Ca		14 sec	β-
^{51}Ca		10 sec	β-

20-4 Calcium has isotopes with atomic weights between 36 and 51.

This electrolysis procedure eventually proved too difficult and expensive for today's market for calcium metal. A more recent technique uses aluminum metal to displace calcium from lime (calcium carbonate) in hot, low-pressure retorts. The reaction is:

$$2Al + 3CaCO_3 \rightarrow 3Ca + Al_2(CO_3)_3$$
(aluminum + calcium carbonate → calcium + aluminum carbonate)

Common compounds of calcium

Calcium has an oxidation state of $+2$, so the most common ion of the metal is Ca^{2+}. The compounds of calcium with ions having an oxidation state of -1 have this form:

Calcium chloride, $CaCl_2$

$$Ca^{2+} + 2Cl^- \rightarrow CaCl_2$$

Calcium hydroxide, $Ca(OH)_2$ (also called slaked lime)

$$Ca^{2+} + 2OH^- \rightarrow Ca(OH)_2$$

Some calcium compounds with ions of -2 are:

Calcium oxide, CaO (better known as lime)

$$Ca^{2+} + O^{2-} \rightarrow CaO$$

Calcium carbonate, $CaCO_3$ (better known as limestone)

$$Ca^{2+} + CO_3{}^{2-} \rightarrow CaCO_3$$

Calcium sulfate, $CaSO_4$ (better known as gypsum and plaster of paris)

$$Ca^{2+} + SO_4{}^{2-} \rightarrow CaSO_4$$

A calcium compound with an ion of -3 is of special importance to all animal life. This is the primary inorganic substance in bones and teeth, *calcium phosphate*, $Ca_3(PO_4)_2$:

$$3Ca^{2+} + 2PO_4{}^{3-} \rightarrow Ca_3(PO_4)_2$$

Calcium fluoride, CaF_2, is a colorless crystal that is found in nature as the mineral *fluorite*. Another Ca^{2+} compound is *calcium hydride*, CaH_2. It looks and feels like ordinary table salt, but when poured into water, it belches forth quantities of hydrogen gas:

$$CaH_2 + 2H_2O \rightarrow Ca(OH)_2 + 2H_2$$
(calcium hydride + water $\rightarrow$ calcium hydroxide + hydrogen)

Calcium nitrate, $Ca(NO_3)_2$, is a natural fertilizer, but can be produced in commercial quantities by reaction of nitric acid and lime.

Dicalcium silicate (Ca_2SiO_4) and *tricalcium silicate* (Ca_3SiO_5) are principal ingredients in portland cement. *Calcium metasilicate*, $CaSiO_3$, occurs in nature as *wollastonite*.

Isotopes of calcium

Figure 20-4 on p. 86 lists the isotopes of calcium. Natural calcium is distributed among six different stable isotopes; the largest share—by far—is calcium-40.

Element 21: Scandium

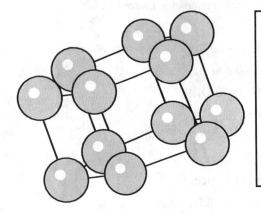

Name	Scandium
Symbol	Sc
Atomic Number	21
Atomic Weight	44.9559
Melting Point	1541°C
Boiling Point	2836°C
Specific Gravity	2.989 (25°C)
Oxidation State	+3
Electron Config.	(Ar) $3d^1\,4s^2$

- Name pronounced as **SKAN-di-em**
- Name from the Latin *Scandia*, Scandinavia
- Predicted by Mendeleyev in 1871; confirmed as an element by Lars Fredrik Nilson in 1879
- Fairly soft, silvery-white metal

Scandium metal is of special interest to the aerospace industries, mainly because of the metal's light weight, resistance to corrosion, and high melting point. It is little wonder, then, that the first pound of 99% scandium ever produced was refined under a contract with the United States Air Force.

It was originally thought that scandium was the rarest of elements, but investigators later found it to be widely distributed on the earth and among the stars, including our own sun. Figure 21-1 shows that natural scandium can be found in a proportion of 5 parts per million in the earth's crust. This puts scandium in the same category of abundance as some of the better known elements such as cobalt and lithium.

Historical background

The existence of scandium was predicted theoretically by Mendeleyev in 1871. He suggested it would resemble boron, so he gave the undiscovered metal the name *ekaboron* and suggested the chemical symbol, Eb. Furthermore, Mendeleyev predicted Eb would have an atomic weight of 44 (atomic weight of Sc is 44.9), its oxide would have a specific gravity of 3.5 (the scandium oxide has a specific gravity of 3.86), the carbonate would be insoluble in water (the Sc carbonate is indeed insoluble), and the element would not be discovered spectroscopically (and it wasn't). There were other predictions as well about Mendeleyev's ekaboron that fit the specifications for scandium when it was finally found.

Mendeleyev did not have to consult a crystal ball nor get some mystical peek into the future in order to suggest the existence of a new chemical element and predict its properties. He did something that is rarely regarded as expedient these days—hard work and serious creative thinking.

Rank (Rare Earths)	Rare-Earth Element	Abundance (ppm)
1	Cerium, Ce	46.0
2	Yttrium, Y	28.0
3	Neodymium, Nd	24.0
4	Lanthanum, La	18.0
5	Samarium, Sm	6.5
6	Gadolinium, Gd	6.4
7	Praseodymium, Pr	5.5
8	Scandium, Sc	5.0
9	Dysprosium, Dy	4.5
10	Ytterbium, Yb	2.7
11	Erbium, Er	2.5
12	Holmium, Ho	1.2
13	Europium, Eu	1.1
14	Terbium, Tb	0.9
15	Lutetium, Lu	0.8
16	Thulium, Tm	0.2
17	Promethium, Pm	0.0

21-1 Scandium is ranked eighth on the abundance chart for rare earths found in the earth's crust.

Isotope	Natural Abundance	Half-Life	Decay Mode
^{40}Sc		182 ms	β+
^{41}Sc		596 ms	β+
^{42m}Sc		61.6 sec	β+
^{42}Sc		680 ms	β+
^{43}Sc		3.89 hr	β+, ec
^{44m}Sc		58.6 hr	i.t., ec
^{44}Sc		3.93 hr	β+, ec
^{45}Sc	100%		
^{46m}Sc		8.7 sec	i.t.
^{46}Sc		83.8 day	β-
^{47}Sc		3.42 day	β-
^{48}Sc		43.7 hr	β-
^{49}Sc		57.3 min	β-
^{50}Sc		1.71 min	β-
^{51}Sc		12.4 sec	β-

21-2 Scandium has isotopes with atomic weights between 40 and 51.

It was Lars Fredrik Nilson (1840 – 1899) who verified Mendeleyev's predictions by finding ekaboron in samples of the mineral *euxenite*. This discovery, however, was accidental.

During the late 1860s, Nilson and a coworker named Pettersson were involved in a study of gadolinite and euxenite. They hoped to recover quantities of some of the newly discovered rare-earth metals that would be sufficient for making careful measurements of their properties—atomic weight, melting and boiling points, and electrical conductivity. While using a routine procedure to isolate very pure ytterbia (ytterbium oxide) for these studies, they found traces of an unknown substance which turned out to be scandium oxide.

Nilson gets credit for the discovery of a new element and, therefore, the privilege of naming it after his homeland, Scandinavia. Per Theodor Cleve found the oxide at about the same time, and pointed out that the new element was Mendeleyev's ekaboron.

Properties of scandium

Scandium is a very lightweight, silvery white metal that is fairly soft. It tarnishes slightly in air, taking on a yellow-pink hue. Scandium heads up Group IIIB on the periodic table of the elements; more importantly, it heads the list of 17 elements known as the *rare-earth elements*. (This name for the group is no longer appropriate because most of them are available in far greater quantities than originally supposed. Tradition prevails, however!) Other rare earths belong to the lantranide series of elements, atomic numbers 57 through 71.

The rare-earth elements are all metals. They are all sufficiently reactive that none exists in nature as the elemental metal. With the notable exception of Scandium, rare-earth ores are found in mixtures of four, five, or more. The rare earths are so similar that the processes for separating them were not well developed until recently.

Production of scandium

Most commercial-grade scandium is obtained from the byproducts of uranium refining operations, although a rare Norwegian mineral, *thortveitite*, contains as much as 34% scandium oxide (Sc_2O_3). Like most rare-earth metals, scandium is separated from other rare earths by an ion-exchange displacement process. The result is trivalent (oxidation state $+3$) scandium which is allowed to react with monovalent anions (oxidation state -1) to yield tolerably pure binary compounds such as scandium fluoride (ScF_3) and scandium chloride ($ScCl_3$).

Metallic scandium can be produced by the electrolysis of a molten, eutectic mixture of potassium chloride, lithium chloride, and scandium chloride. Eutectic mixtures are often chosen for the electrolysis of metals because they have a melting point that is lower than the melting point of any of the compounds individually.

Scandium metal is also produced by reducing scandium fluoride with calcium metal:

$$3Ca + 2ScF_3 \rightarrow 2Sc + 3CaF_2$$
(calcium metal + scandium fluoride → scandium metal + calcium fluoride)

The same kind of reaction is possible with lithium metal and scandium chloride:

$$3Li + ScCl_3 \rightarrow Sc + 3LiCl$$
(lithium metal + scandium chloride → scandium metal + lithium chloride)

In either case, the scandium halide and active metal are loaded into a tantalum crucible and fired in a helium atmosphere. As the reaction progresses, the molten scandium, halide compounds, and excess active metal separate due to differences in density. When this layered mixture is allowed to cool, the scandium is simply cut away from the impurities. The operation can be repeated as often as necessary to achieve the desired level of purity.

Some compounds of scandium

Researchers have studied only a very few compounds of scandium. The 1987–1988 edition of the *CRC Handbook of Chemistry and Physics* lists only ten of them. All are white or colorless.

Scandium has an oxidation state of $+3$ which means its metallic ion is Sc^{3+}. It thus combines with anions having -1 oxidation states as:

Scandium chloride, $ScCl_3$

$$Sc^{3+} + 3Cl^- \rightarrow ScCl_3$$

Scandium hydroxide, $Sc(OH)_3$

$$Sc^{3+} + 3OH^- \rightarrow Sc(OH)_3$$

With anions of -2, scandium forms compounds such as:

Scandium oxide, Sc_2O_3 (also called *scandia*)

$$2Sc^{3+} + 3O^{2-} \rightarrow Sc_2O_3$$

Scandium sulfate, $Sc_2(SO_4)_3$

$$2Sc^{3+} + 3SO_4^{2-} \rightarrow Sc_2(SO_4)_3$$

Most of the compounds are used in the production of scandium metal or other scandium compounds. Some scandium oxide is currently used in the manufacture of high-intensity electric lamps. *Scandium iodide*, ScI_3, is used in lamps that produce light having color values that closely match those of natural sunlight.

Isotopes of scandium

Figure 21-2 on p. 89 lists all the known isotopes of scandium. Notice that all naturally occurring scandium is scandium-45. Radioactive scandium-46 is sometimes used as a tracer agent in large oil refining operations.

Element 22: Titanium

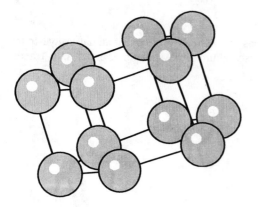

Name	Titanium
Symbol	Ti
Atomic Number	22
Atomic Weight	47.88
Melting Point	1660°C
Boiling Point	3287°C
Specific Gravity	4.5 (20°C)
Oxidation States	+2, +3, +4
Electron Config.	(Ar) $3d^2\ 4s^2$

- Name pronounced as **tie-TAY-ni-em**
- Named for the mythological Greek Titans
- Discovered by William Gregor in 1791 and independently by Martin Heinrich Klaproth in 1795; isolated and purified by Matthew A. Hunter in 1910
- Shiny, dark-gray metal

Titanium is closely associated with strong, corrosion-resistant metals that find esoteric applications in the military and aerospace industries. Although it is indeed a valuable metal, it is neither esoteric nor particularly hard to find. Figure 22-1 shows that titanium metal ranks ninth on the list of most abundant elements in the earth's crust. Most of this is in the form of titanium dioxide which, as shown in Fig. 22-2, is the eighth most abundant compound on earth.

Its primary use is as a strengthening material for structural metals. Titanium pins are used in skeletal surgery because this metal does not react with flesh and bone.

Historical background

Titanium was unknowingly discovered by Reverend William Gregor (1761 – 1817) in 1791. Although serving as pastor of English rectories in Deptford and Bratton Clovelly, Gregor was educated in mathematics and the classics, and he was recognized for his talent as a musician and painter of landscapes. His passion, however, was mineralogy. During the course of his life, Rev. Gregor published high-quality, professionally recognized papers on the analysis of bismuth carbonate, topaz (an aluminum silicate), wavellite (an aluminum phosphate), and lead arsenate. When a certain hard, black, sandy mineral found in his own neighborhood caught his fancy, Gregor took the first steps toward putting his name into the history books of science.

Describing the mineral, Gregor wrote, "The sand is black, and in external appearance resembles gunpowder." His analysis showed 46% magnetite (Fe_3O_4), thus accounting for its attraction to a magnet. There was a bit of silica and a few other substances in small quantities. The important ingredient was a reddish brown powder that occupied 45% of the sample. Gregor's notes show that dissolving this powder in sulfuric acid produced a yellow

Element	Concentration (ppm)
Oxygen	464,000
Silicon	282,000
Aluminum	83,200
Iron	56,300
Calcium	41,500
Sodium	23,600
Magnesium	23,300
Potassium	20,900
Titanium	5700
Hydrogen	1400

Compound	Weight (ppm)
Silicon dioxide, SiO_2	428,600
Magnesium oxide, MgO	350,700
Ferrous oxide, FeO	89,700
Aluminum oxide, Al_2O_3	69,900
Calcium Oxide, CaO	43,700
Sodium oxide, Na_2O	4500
Ferric oxide, Fe_2O_3	3600
Titanium dioxide, TiO_2	3300
Chromic oxide, Cr_2O_3	1800
Manganese oxide, MnO	1400

22-1 Titanium is one of the most common elements in the earth's crust.

22-2 Titanium dioxide ranks fourth on the top-ten abundance chart for compounds in the earth's crust.

substance which turned to purple when combined with zinc. Since this scenario did not fit into any known category of mineral, Gregor rightly assumed he had discovered a new mineral. He named the new mineral *menachanite* in honor of the neighborhood where he found it, Menachan in Cornwall.

It was Martin Heinrich Klaproth, however, who recognized the presence of a new chemical element in Gregor's menachanite.

Properties of titanium

Titanium heads the list of Group-IVB elements, the so-called titanium group of metals. Other members of this group are zirconium (Zr), hafnium (Hf), and rutherfordium (Rf).

Titanium is heavier than aluminum, but not quite as heavy as iron. It can be highly polished, and is relatively immune to tarnishing under normal environmental conditions. For a metal, it is not a very good conductor; it is also paramagnetic—it shows little response to magnetic fields.

Titanium has two temperature-dependent crystal forms, or allotropes. The alpha form has a hexagonal structure and exists up to about 800 °C. Above 800 °C, titanium takes on its cubic beta form.

Production of titanium

Titanium is found in several minerals including *ilmenite* ($FeTiO_3$) and *rutile* (TiO_2). Rutile, chemically known as titanium dioxide, is the preferred ore for most refinery operations. A common two-step operation begins by heating the oxide ore in the presence of carbon and chlorine gas to produce titanium tetrachloride and carbon dioxide:

$$TiO_2 + C + 2Cl_2 \rightarrow TiCl_4 + CO_2$$

(titanium dioxide + carbon + chlorine → titanium tetrachloride + carbon dioxide)

The second step calls for heating the titanium tetrachloride with magnesium in an atmosphere of argon:

$$TiCl_4 + 2Mg \rightarrow Ti + 2MgCl_2$$

(titanium tetrachloride + magnesium → titanium metal + magnesium chloride).

The temperature is finally raised to about 1000 °C to burn off excess magnesium and magnesium chloride.

Small quantities of titanium metal can be produced in the laboratory by heating titanium tetraiodide (TiL_4) in a vacuum.

Compounds of titanium

The three oxidation states for titanium are $+2$, $+3$, and $+4$. This means titanium ions can be expressed as Ti^{+2}, Ti^{+3}, and Ti^{+4}, and that leads to compounds such as:

Titanium(II) chloride, $TiCl_2$ (also called titanium dichloride)

$$Ti^{+2} + 2Cl^- \rightarrow TiCl_2$$

Titanium(III) chloride, $TiCl_3$ (also called titanium trichloride)

$$Ti^{+3} + 3Cl^- \rightarrow TiCl_3$$

Titanium(IV) chloride, $TiCl_4$ (also called titanium tetrachloride)

$$Ti^{+4} + 4Cl^- \rightarrow TiCl_4$$

Titanium(II) oxide, TiO (also called titanium monoxide)

$$Ti^{+2} + O^{-2} \rightarrow TiO$$

Titanium(III) oxide, Ti_2O_3 (also called titanium sesquioxide)

$$2Ti^{+3} + 3O^{-2} \rightarrow Ti_2O_3$$

Titanium(IV) oxide, TiO_2 (also called titanium dioxide and even better known as the mineral, *rutile*)

$$Ti^{+4} + 2O^{-2} \rightarrow TiO_2$$

Titanium(III) nitride, TiN

$$Ti^{+3} + N^{-3} \rightarrow TiN$$

Titanium(IV) carbide, TiC

$$Ti^{+4} + C^{-4} \rightarrow TiC$$

Titanium dioxide (TiO_2) is an intensely white powder that is often used as a paint pigment—titanium white. For commercial applications, titanium dioxide is derived from one of the titanium-bearing minerals.

Titanium tetrachloride ($TiCl_4$) generates a dense white vapor when it reacts with moist air. It is used as a liquid smoke-producing product for skywriting and military smoke-screen devices. The reaction is:

$$TiCl_4 + 2H_2O \rightarrow TiO_2 + 4HCl$$

(titanium tetrachloride + moisture → titanium dioxide + hydrochloric acid)

Isotopes of titanium

Figure 22-3 shows the current list of titanium isotopes. Titanium-48 accounts for most of the element as it exists in nature. None of the radioactive isotopes has any clearly defined application.

22-3 Titanium has isotopes with atomic weights between 41 and 53.

Isotope	Natural Abundance	Half-Life	Decay Mode
^{41}Ti		80 ms	β+, p
^{42}Ti		200 ms	β+
^{43}Ti		490 ms	β+
^{44}Ti		47 yr	ec
^{45}Ti		3.078 hr	β+, ec
^{46}Ti	8.0%		
^{47}Ti	7.3%		
^{48}Ti	73.8%		
^{49}Ti	5.5%		
^{50}Ti	5.4%		
^{51}Ti		5.76 min	β-
^{52}Ti		1.7 min	β-
^{53}Ti		33 sec	β-

Element 23: Vanadium

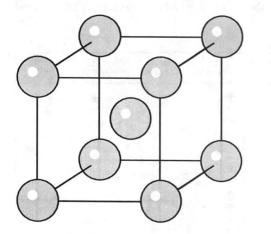

Name	Vanadium
Symbol	V
Atomic Number	23
Atomic Weight	50.9415
Melting Point	1890°C
Boiling Point	3380°C
Specific Gravity	6.11 (20°C)
Oxidation States	+2, +3, +4, +5
Electron Config.	(Ar) $3d^3 4s^2$

- Name pronounced as **veh-NAY-di-em**
- Name for the Scandinavian goddess, *Vanadis*
- Discovered by Andrés Manuel del Rio in 1801; rediscovered independently by Nils Gabriel Sefstrôm in 1830; isolated by Henry Enfield Roscoe in 1867
- Soft, ductile, silvery-white metal

Vanadium belongs to a trio of metals: titanium (Ti), vanadium (V), and chromium (Cr); they are quite similar in many respects. They are aligned side-by-side on the periodic table of elements. Their similarities are especially notable with regard to their relative abundances, physical characteristics, and commercial applications.

About 80% of the vanadium metal produced today is alloyed with iron to produce *ferrovanadium*, an especially strong, shock- and corrosion-resistant material. Vanadium steel is used mainly in the manufacture of cutting tools and springs. The metal itself is sometimes used for making special tubing and plumbing components for the chemical industries.

Historical background

In 1801, a professor of mineralogy in Mexico City found traces of a previously unknown element in samples of brown lead from a mine near Hidalgo in northern Mexico. The properties were similar to those of chromium and uranium. Furthermore, the salts that this Professor del Rio (1764–1849) prepared from the new element were every bit as colorful as those obtained from chromium. So he named the element *panchromium*, meaning "akin to chromium." He later observed that most of the salts turned red upon heating or reaction with an acid, so he renamed the element *erythronium*, "red." (*See* Element 24: Chromium.)

Circumstances, personalities, and human error combined to shake del Rio's confidence in his discovery. Things began to turn sour when the parcel post system of the time failed him. His samples of brown lead ore were sent to the *Institut de France* in Paris for analysis and confirmation. A brief explanation accompanying the samples was ambiguous, pointing out the similarity between the new element and chromium. A complete analysis and description of his laboratory were lost in a shipwreck. So the *Institut* saw nothing but a jar of brown lead and a brief note explaining how much the new stuff resembled chromium.

Failing to receive an enthusiastic response from Paris, de Rio himself lost confidence in the significance of his discovery. To compound the problems, a second sample sent to the *Museum fur Naturkunde* in Berlin was mislabeled *lead chromate* when it arrived. The label was later corrected to read *vanadium lead ore*.

Andrés Manuel del Rio gave up. He conceded that his work simply showed that he had been working with ordinary compounds of chromium. The academic world was ready to accept his apology for being so silly and unprofessional. One has to wonder how many brilliant discoveries have been lost because of discouragement in the face of adverse circumstances or because of concession to the opinions of peers and those who imagine themselves to be peers.

The Swedish physician and chemist, Nils Gabriel Sefström (1787 – 1845), rediscovered vanadium in iron samples from the Taberg mines in Sweden. Even back in 1830, things were made easier in one's career by taking advantage of the "good-ol'-boy" network. Sefström was on good terms with the most prestigious chemists of the day—Freidrich Wöhler and J.J. Berzelius, for example. Matters progressed smoothly, even to the communication of Sefström's charming story about the new element's namesake, the beautiful goddess, Vanadis.

Wöhler later located del Rio's samples of brown lead in Berlin, and subsequently confirmed that the professor from Mexico had indeed discovered vanadium. The compound was later classified as the mineral *vanadinite*.

The existence of the element was confirmed on the basis of its oxide and other compounds. No one managed to obtain samples of pure vanadium metal until 1867, when Sir Henry Enfield Roscoe (1833 – 1915) managed to reduce vanadium chloride with hydrogen gas:

$$2VCl_3 + 3H_2 \rightarrow 2V + 6HCl$$
(vanadium chloride + hydrogen → vanadium + hydrochloric acid)

Properties of vanadium

Vanadium is described as a silvery-white or grayish-colored metal. It is fairly lightweight—somewhat heavier than aluminum, but lighter than iron. It is malleable and ductile, and resistant to corrosion by moisture, air, and even most acids and alkalis at room temperature. Its properties become less desirable at elevated temperatures, however, where vanadium readily combines with atmospheric oxygen and nitrogen.

Vanadium has an unusually large number of different oxidation states and it combines with nearly all nonmetals. These facts account for the large number of compounds of vanadium.

Iron and vanadium work well together and can be alloyed in any desired proportion. Ferrovanadium, for example, is an alloy of iron and a few other metals, plus 1% to 6% vanadium.

Production of vanadium

The fact that vanadium can combine with nearly all nonmetals in the environment accounts for its presence in no less than 56 different minerals. Recoverable amounts of vanadium can also be found in phosphate rock and some varieties of iron ores. Vanadium is most economically recovered from a selection of minerals such as *vanadinite* ($Pb_5(VO_4)_3Cl$) and *carnotite* ($K_2(UO_2)_2(VO_4) \cdot 3H_2O$). The first steps in the refining process are to grind the ore and heat it with carbon and chlorine. The desired product is vanadium trichloride, VCl_3, which is fairly easy to separate from the other compounds produced by the reaction.

The second step calls for heating the chloride with magnesium in an atmosphere of argon:

$$2VCl_3 + 3Mg \rightarrow 2V + 3MgCl_2$$

(vanadium trichloride + magnesium → vanadium metal + magnesium chloride)

Finally, the temperature is raised to about 1000 °C in order to burn off the magnesium chloride and excess magnesium metal.

Small quantities of vanadium metal can be produced in the laboratory by heating vanadium dichloride with hydrogen:

$$VCl_2 + H_2 \rightarrow 2HCl + V$$

(vanadium dichloride + hydrogen → hydrochloric acid + vanadium metal)

Some compounds and the isotopes of vanadium

Vanadium has four oxidation states: +2, +3, +4, and +5. The ions of vanadium can be shown as V^{+2}, V^{+3}, V^{+4}, and V^{+5}. The oxides have these forms:

Vanadium(II) oxide, VO

$$V^{+2} + O^{+2} \rightarrow VO$$

Vanadium(III) oxide, V_2O_3

$$2V^{+3} + 3O^{+2} \rightarrow V_2O_3$$

Vanadium(IV) oxide, VO_2

$$V^{+4} + 2O^{+2} \rightarrow VO^2$$

Vanadium(V) oxide, V_2O_5

$$2V^{+5} + 5O^{+2} \rightarrow V_2O_5$$

The halides take these forms:

Vanadium(II) chloride, VCl_2

$$V^{+2} + 2Cl^{-1} \rightarrow VCl_2$$

Vanadium(III) chloride, VCl_3

$$V^{+3} + 3Cl^{-1} \rightarrow VCl_3$$

Vanadium (IV) chloride, VCl_4

$$V^{+4} + 4Cl^{-1} \rightarrow VCl_4$$

Vanadium(V) fluoride, VF_5

$$V^{+5} + 5F^{-1} \rightarrow VF_5$$

Vanadium oxide or *vanadium pentoxide*, is a popular starting point for the production of other vanadium compounds. It is also used in the production of glassware and as a catalyst in other chemical reactions. This yellowish-red crystal is commonly derived as a byproduct of certain smelting operations and from the stack fumes of petroleum refineries.

Like the compounds of vanadium's sister metal, chromium, many of its compounds are noted for their brilliant and varied colors.

Figure 23-1 shows that most vanadium that occurs in nature is vanadium-51. A small fraction is radioactive vanadium-50. The remaining isotopic species are both artificial and radioactive.

23-1 Vanadium has isotopes with atomic weights between 44 and 55.

Isotope	Natural Abundance	Half-Life	Decay Mode
^{44}V		90 ms	$\beta+$, α
^{46}V		422 ms	$\beta+$
^{47}V		31.3 min	$\beta+$, ec
^{48}V		15.98 day	$\beta+$
^{49}V		331 day hr	ec
^{50}V	0.25%	3.9×10^7 yr	$\beta-$, ec
^{51}V	99.75%		
^{52}V		3.96 min	$\beta-$
^{53}V		1.61 min	$\beta-$
^{54}V		49.8 sec	$\beta-$
^{55}V		6.5 sec	$\beta-$

Element 24: Chromium

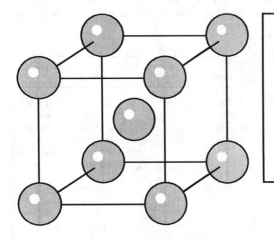

Name	Chromium
Symbol	Cr
Atomic Number	24
Atomic Weight	51.996
Melting Point	1857°C
Boiling Point	2672°C
Specific Gravity	7.19 (20°C)
Oxidation States	+2, +3, +6
Electron Config.	(Ar) $3d^5 \, 4s^1$

- Name pronounced as **KROH-mi-em**
- Name taken from the greek work *chroma*, "color"—a name suggesting the wide variety of intense colors that characterize chromium compounds
- Discovered by Louis-Nicholas Vauquelin in 1797 and isolated a year later
- Very hard, crystalline, steel-gray metal

A chromium ore, sometimes called Siberian red lead, was a popular pigment for brilliant red oil paints in the 18th century. Other compounds produce pigments of other popular colors, including chrome oxide green and lead chromate yellow.

Chromium is also a vital metal alloying agent. Chromium is present in spring steels, in corrosion-resistant steels such as nickel-chromium, and in stainless steel. Iron-nickel-chromium alloys of various percentages yield an incredible variety of the most important metals in modern technology. In addition, chromium issued in the chrome plating that imparts an extraordinarily shiny and corrosion-resistant surface to metals that are otherwise quite ordinary.

Chrome oxide, the popular green pigment, appears in Fig. 24-1 as the ninth most abundant compound in the earth's crust. The green color is not always apparent, however, because the chrome oxide minerals are discolored by the presence of other elements.

Historical background

The story of chromium begins with the analysis of a curious red lead found in Siberia. The samples were soon identified as the mineral *crocoite*, but the story did not end there because no one had yet done a complete analysis of this mineral.

The first serious and competent analysis of Siberian red lead showed that it did indeed contain significant amounts of lead. There was something else, however; something that analytic chemist Johann Gottlob Lehmann (1719 – 1767), described as "a lead mineralized with selenitic spar and iron particles."

Compound	Weight (ppm)
Silicon dioxide, SiO_2	428,600
Magnesium oxide, MgO	350,700
Ferrous oxide, FeO	89,700
Aluminum oxide, Al_2O_3	69,900
Calcium Oxide, CaO	43,700
Sodium oxide, Na_2O	4500
Ferric oxide, Fe_2O_3	3600
Titanium dioxide, TiO_2	3300
Chromic oxide, Cr_2O_3	1800
Manganese oxide, MnO	1400

24-1 Chromic oxide is among the ten most abundant compounds in the earth's crust.

Isotope	Natural Abundance	Half-Life	Decay Mode
^{45}Cr		50 ms	β+, p
^{46}Cr		260 ms	β+
^{47}Cr		460 ms	β+
^{48}Cr		21.6 hr	ec
^{49}Cr		42.1 min	β+, ec
^{50}Cr	4.35%		
^{51}Cr		27.7 day	ec
^{52}Cr	83.79%		
^{53}Cr	9.50%		
^{54}Cr	2.36%		
^{55}Cr		3.5 min	β-
^{56}Cr		5.9 min	β-
^{57}Cr		21 sec	β-

24-2 Chromium has isotopes with atomic weights between 45 and 57.

It was Louis-Nicholas Vauquelin (1763–1829) who first identified the oxide of chromium and subsequently isolated the pure metal. This all took place in 1797–98. Vauquelin's procedure began with crocoite, Siberian red lead. He precipitated the lead by allowing a finely powdered sample of the mineral to react with hydrochloric acid. This left behind a chromium oxide. His intent was to prove the existence of the new metal by producing its family of oxides and, subsequently, its salts. He was convinced that no one could isolate the pure metal, itself, on the basis of the knowledge and techniques of the time. While heating the chromium oxide in a charcoal oven one day, Vauquelin was surprised and delighted to find fine needles of a gray metal he determined to be elemental chromium.

Properties of chromium

Chromium heads the list of Group VIB elements on the periodic table. It shares a number of characteristics, including practical applications, with the two preceding metals in the series, vanadium (V) and titanium (Ti). Pure chromium metal has a blue-white color. It is hard, brittle, and corrosion-resistant at normal environmental temperatures.

There are two known allotropes of chromium. The most common—the one that is stable at room temperature—has a body-centered cubic crystalline structure. The second, or beta, form is stable above 1850 °C. It has a close-packed, hexagonal structure.

Production of chromium

Although chromium was originally discovered in crocoite, most chromium today is obtained from *chromite*, $FeCr_2O_4$. Chromium could have been discovered in chromite, but chemists were taking a close look at crocoite in the 18th century because of its striking red color. Chromite, on the other hand, is a rather ordinary black mineral that no one really noticed until more recent times.

The basic commercial procedure for refining chromium is to reduce the metal from its oxide by heating the ore in the presence of silicon or aluminum. The result is a ferrosilicon or ferroaluminum compound and chromium metal. The metal can be further purified by an electrolysis procedure.

Some compounds of chromium

Chromium has three oxidation states: $+2$, $+3$, and $+6$. The chromium ions are Cr^{+2} Cr^{+3}, and Cr^{+6}. This means the oxides have these general forms:

Chromium(II) oxide, CrO

$$Cr^{+2} + O^{-2} \rightarrow CrO$$

Chromium(III) oxide, Cr_2O_3

$$2Cr^{+3} + 3O^{-2} \rightarrow Cr_2O_3$$

Chromium(VI) oxide, CrO_3

$$Cr^{+6} + 3O^{-2} \rightarrow CrO_3$$

The halides form some ionic compounds with chromium. For example:

Chromium(II) chloride, $CrCl_2$

$$Cr^{+2} + 2Cl^{-1} \rightarrow CrCl_2$$

Chromium(III) fluoride, CrF_3

$$Cr^{+3} + 3F^{-1} \rightarrow CrF_3$$

Lead chromate, $PbCrO_4$, is the basis for the *chrome yellow* pigment. It is usually obtained from the mineral crocoite; however, it can be produced in the laboratory by a reaction between lead compound and *sodium chromate,* $NaCrO_4$.

Chromic oxide is best known for its role in a pigment known as *chrome green,* or chrome oxide green. Using the more modern Stock nomenclature, this popular pigment is called *chromium(III) oxide,* Cr_2O_3. It is found in nature as the ninth most abundant compound in the earth's crust, but it can be synthesized in the laboratory by reducing *sodium dichromate* $Na_2Cr_2O_7$.

Figure 24-2 on p. 101 lists all the known isotopes of chromium. Naturally occurring chromium is a mixture of four different isotopes, none of which is radioactive. All of the synthetic, or man-made, isotopes are radioactive. There are no significant applications of the radioactive isotopes.

Element 25: Manganese

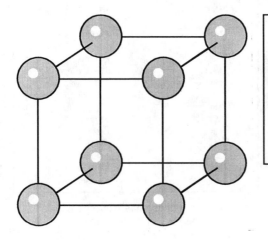

Name	Manganese
Symbol	Mn
Atomic Number	25
Atomic Weight	54.9380
Melting Point	1244°C
Boiling Point	1962°C
Specific Gravity	7.44 (20°C)
Oxidation States	+2, +3, +4, +7
Electron Config.	(Ar) $3d^5\,4s^2$

- Name pronounced as **MAN-ge-nees**
- Name from the Latin *magnes*, "magnet"
- Recognized as an element by Carl Wilhelm Scheele in 1774; isolated later that year by Johan Gottlieb Gahn
- Hard, brittle, gray-white metal

Figure 25-1 shows that manganese oxide just makes the list of ten most abundant compounds in the earth's crust. It is the main source of manganese metal and the starting point for the manufacture of most other compounds of manganese.

Manganese is best known for the role it plays in steel alloys. Manganese enhances ability to form and hot-work steel, and it increases the resistance to impact. The steel used in railroad tracks contains as much as 1.2%. manganese. In biological systems, manganese is crucial to the effectiveness of vitamin B_1.

Historical background

The suggestion that manganese might be a basic chemical element was part of a most remarkable dissertation presented to the Stockholm Academy by Carl Wilhelm Scheele in 1774. The dissertation not only spelled out the chemical nature of manganese for the first time, but also suggested the existence of chlorine, oxygen, and barium. That is four new elements described in a single paper!

Scheele was not able to isolate manganese himself, but he effectively argued against the popular notion that a certain black mineral, sometimes called manganese, was nothing more than lime or magnesia alba. Scheele was convinced that this mineral was a calx of a new element.

It was up to the renowned master of the blowpipe, Johan Gottlieb Gahn (1745–1818), to produce the first bits of the new element. In 1774, Gahn pulverized some *pyrolusite* and fired it in a charcoal container. (Pyrolusite is a mineral now known to be manganese dioxide, MnO_2.) When the oven cooled and Gahn removed the cover, he found a small button of grayish manganese.

Compound	Weight (ppm)
Silicon dioxide, SiO_2	428,600
Magnesium oxide, MgO	350,700
Ferrous oxide, FeO	89,700
Aluminum oxide, Al_2O_3	69,900
Calcium Oxide, CaO	43,700
Sodium oxide, Na_2O	4500
Ferric oxide, Fe_2O_3	3600
Titanium dioxide, TiO_2	3300
Chromic oxide, Cr_2O_3	1800
Manganese oxide, MnO	1400

Isotope	Natural Abundance	Half-Life	Decay Mode
^{49}Mn		380 ms	β+
^{50m}Mn		1.7 min	β+
^{50}Mn		283 ms	β+
^{51}Mn		46.2 min	β+, ec
^{52m}Mn		21.1 min	β+, i.t.
^{52}Mn		5.59 day	β+, ec
^{53}Mn		3.7×10^6 yr	ec
^{54}Mn		312 day	ec
^{55}Mn	100%		
^{56}Mn		2.579 hr	β-
^{57}Mn		1.45 min	β-
^{58}Mn		65 sec	β-
^{59}Mn		4.6 sec	β-
^{60}Mn		1.8 sec	β-
^{62}Mn		0.9 sec	β-

25-1 Manganese oxide is among the ten most abundant compounds in the earth's crust.

25-2 Manganese has isotopes with atomic weights between 49 and 62.

Properties of manganese

Manganese is the first of the Group-VB elements on the periodic table. Pure manganese metal is hard and brittle; it looks and feels a lot like iron. It is fairly reactive, behaving much like iron in this respect as well. It even "rusts" like iron in moist air.

There are four solid allotropes of manganese, α through β. The α (alpha) and β (beta) forms exist at temperatures below 1000 °C and thus represent the element as it is most commonly known. The β state occurs at temperatures between 700 °C and 1000 °C, but can be retained at room temperatures by extremely rapid cooling, or *quenching*.

The γ (gamma) allotrope can exist for extended periods of time at temperatures between 1000 °C and 1100 °C. However, it is also produced at lower temperatures when manganese is subjected to electrolytic operations. As soon as the electrolysis is stopped, the sample quickly reverts to the α allotrope.

The δ (delta) allotrope exists only at temperatures above 1100 °C.

Production of manganese

Manganese metal is produced by reducing the metal from its most common oxide and mineral form, *pyrolucite*, or manganese dioxide (MnO_2). Mines in the Soviet Union, India, and South Africa produce ores containing as much as 40% manganese. Manganese is obtained from the ore by reducing the metal with aluminum or by means of a special electrolytic process.

In the chemical reduction process, the ore is ground, mixed with powdered aluminum, and ignited in a furnace. The result is manganese metal and a slag composed of aluminum and iron oxides. (Iron is the primary impurity in manganese ore.)

The electrolytic process produces a higher grade of manganese. Like the reduction process, this one begins with manganese dioxide, but the ore is first treated with sulfuric acid to produce manganese sulfate—the electrolyte for this process:

$$2MnO_2 + 2H_2SO_4 \rightarrow 2MnSO_4 + O_2 + 2H_2O$$
(manganese dioxide + sulfuric acid → manganese sulfate + oxygen + water)

The electrolytic cell uses a lead-alloy anode and a steel-alloy cathode. As the reaction progresses, manganese collects at the cathode. The purity is at least 99.9%. The reaction also generates sulfuric acid, which can be recycled and used in the first step where it is used for producing manganese sulfate from manganese dioxide.

Some compounds and the isotopes of manganese

Manganese has four oxidation states: $+2$, $+3$, $+4$, and $+7$. The oxides thus have the following forms.

Manganese(II) oxide, MnO (also called manganese monoxide)

$$Mn^{2+} + O^{2-} \rightarrow MnO$$

Manganese(III) oxide, Mn_2O_3 (also called manganese sesquioxide)

$$2Mn^{3+} + 3O^{2-} \rightarrow Mn_2O_3$$

Manganese(IV) oxide, MnO_2 (also called manganese dioxide)

$$Mn^{4+} + 2O^{2-} \rightarrow MnO_2$$

Manganese(VII) oxide, Mn_2O_7 (also called manganese heptoxide)

$$2Mn^{7+} + 7O^{2-} \rightarrow Mn_2O_7$$

Most other compounds use only the Mn^{2+} and Mn^{3+} states, however, so the halides look like this:

Manganese(II) chloride, MnCl

$$Mn^{2+} + Cl^{2-} \rightarrow MnCl$$

Manganese(III) fluoride, MnF_2 (also called manganese trifluoride)

$$Mn^{3+} + 3F^- \rightarrow MnF_3$$

Since manganese is a highly reactive metal it follows that it should be rich in compounds; this is indeed the case. Manganese dioxide (MnO_2), for example, is the most plentiful of all compounds of manganese. It is abundant in nature, but better known in that instance as the mineral pyrolucite. This grayish-colored powder can be prepared in the laboratory by heating *manganese nitrate*, $Mn(NO_3)_2$, or a mixture of *manganese carbonate* ($MnCO_3$) and potassium chlorate.

Manganese dioxide is not soluble in water, but reacts with concentrated acids to yield manganese salts and water. It reacts with hydrochloric acid, for example:

$$MnO_2 + 4HCl \rightarrow MnCl_2 + Cl_2 + 2H_2O$$
(manganese dioxide + hydrochloric acid → manganese dichloride + chlorine gas + water)

Potassium manganate is an important intermediate compound, one that is used in the manufacture of other compounds. It is, itself, produced by a reaction between manganese dioxide and potassium hydroxide in the presence of oxygen:

$$2MnO_2 + 4KOH + O_2 \rightarrow 2K_2MnO_4 + 2H_2O$$

(manganese dioxide + potassium hydroxide + oxygen → potassium manganate + water)

Potassium permanganate ($KMnO_4$) is a powerful oxidizing agent that is used as a bleaching agent, deodorizer, and analytical reagent in inorganic and organic chemistry. This deep purple, crystalline substance is, oddly enough, used as a decolorizer as well. It can be produced by simply allowing potassium manganate to react with water:

$$3K_2MnO_4 + 2H_2O \rightarrow KMnO_4 + MnO_2 + 4KOH$$
(potassium manganate + water → potassium permanganate
+ manganese dioxide + potassium hydroxide)

Figure 25-2 on p. 104 lists the isotopes of manganese. Notice that all naturally occurring manganese is manganese-55. All others are artificial and radioactive.

Element 26: Iron

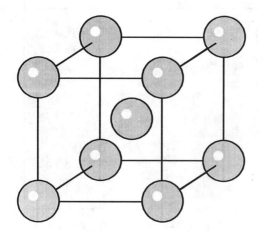

Name	Iron
Symbol	Fe
Atomic Number	26
Atomic Weight	55.847
Melting Point	1535°C
Boiling Point	2750°C
Specific Gravity	7.873 (20°C)
Oxidation States	+2, +3
Electron Config.	(Ar) $3d^6 4s^2$

- Name pronounced as **EYE-ern**
- Name from the Anglo-Saxon, *iron*
- Chemical symbol, Fe, from the Latin **ferrum**, "iron"
- Identified and used since prehistoric times
- Malleable, ductile, silvery-white metal

Iron is a common element. Figure 26-1 shows that it ranks among the ten most abundant atoms in the cosmos. Iron is also one of the most familiar elements on the earth. You can see in Fig. 26-2 that iron is ranked fourth on the abundance chart for elements in the earth's crust. And finally, Fig. 26-3 shows that two of the most common compounds in the earth's crust are iron compounds.

Iron is the most plentiful, least expensive, and most useful of all metals. Molten iron can dissolve carbon, thus producing an alloy better known as steel. Steel is the most common structural metal—from simple nuts and bolts to the framework of tall skyscrapers.

Iron is of ancient origin. The oldest iron artifacts, a few bits of smelted iron, have been dated at 3000 years B.C. The Egyptians knew how to mine, refine, and work iron. There are numerous references to iron mines, furnaces, and iron objects in the Old Testament. Unfortunately, iron objects, themselves, corrode rather readily, so evidence for ancient applications of iron is written, rather than direct, evidence. We cannot know the name of the person who was the first to refine iron, because his name is lost in the mists of prehistory.

Properties of iron

Iron is generally described as a moderately heavy, hard, malleable, and ductile metal. In its pure form, it has a silvery-white color. One of the most distinctive features is its ability to take and retain a magnetic field. Iron is one of the Group-VII transition metals. These metals have two incomplete electron shells.

Iron has four allotropic forms. The alpha form is the most familiar because it is the one that exists at room temperature. As the temperature rises above 770 °C, the beta form

Element	Abundance (Si = 1)
Hydrogen	40,000
Helium	3,100
Oxygen	22
Neon	8.6
Nitrogen	6.6
Carbon	3.5
Silicon	1
Magnesium	0.91
Iron	0.60
Sulfur	0.38

26-1 Iron is one of the most abundant elements in the known cosmos, having 0.6 atoms per atom of silicon.

Element	Concentration (ppm)
Oxygen	464,000
Silicon	282,000
Aluminum	83,200
Iron	56,300
Calcium	41,500
Sodium	23,600
Magnesium	23,300
Potassium	20,900
Titanium	5700
Hydrogen	1400

26-2 Iron ranks fourth among elements found in the earth's crust.

Compound	Weight (ppm)
Silicon dioxide, SiO_2	428,600
Magnesium oxide, MgO	350,700
Ferrous oxide, FeO	89,700
Aluminum oxide, Al_2O_3	69,900
Calcium Oxide, CaO	43,700
Sodium oxide, Na_2O	4500
Ferric oxide, Fe_2O_3	3600
Titanium dioxide, TiO_2	3300
Chromic oxide, Cr_2O_3	1800
Manganese oxide, MnO	1400

26-3 Two oxides of iron, ferrous and ferric, are among the ten most abundant compounds in the earth's crust.

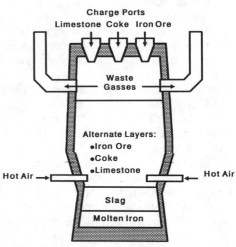

26-4 Commercial tonnage of iron is refined in blast furnaces.

emerges. The most critical feature of this particular transition is that the iron loses its magnetic properties. Transitions to the gamma and delta forms take place at 928 °C and 1530 °C, respectively.

Production of iron

Commercial tonnage of iron is obtained from ores such as *hematite* (Fe_2O_3) and *magnetite* (Fe_3O_4). Both are oxides that can be broken down into iron and oxygen by heating them properly. The heating is usually done in a blast furnace.

Figure 26-4 is a cutaway diagram of a typical blast furnace. The coke, lime, and iron ore are fed into the furnace through charge ports. These ingredients are not mixed, but rather fed into the furnace in turn—ore, coke, lime; ore, coke, lime; and so on.

Hot gasses forced, or blasted, into the bottom of the furnace raise the temperature to the point where the coke glows with a red heat and the iron is reduced from its oxides and liquified by the great heat. The molten iron dribbles down through the layers of coke, lime, and ore, eventually finding its way to the bottom of the furnace where it is drained out from time to time.

Furnaces of this type can be operated continuously. As the ingredients are used up, more can be added through the charge ports.

Steel—the iron-carbon alloy

No discussion of iron is complete without some mention of its most popular alloy, steel. Steel is basically an alloy of iron and carbon. Carbon dissolves readily in molten iron, and commercial steels use carbon in proportions anywhere between 0.3 and 1.5%.

Most steel is produced in an oxygen furnace, although electric furnaces are becoming more popular. Figure 26-5 illustrates a basic oxygen furnace. The container is charged with raw iron and scrap steel, then heated with natural gas. As the temperature rises, coke is added in order to supply the necessary amount of carbon. A water-cooled oxygen tube, or lance, is lowered into the furnace, and oxygen is blown into the melt at velocities exceeding the speed of sound. This creates the very high temperatures required for creating the steel.

The higher the percentage of carbon, the harder the steel becomes. Once a steel is produced, it can be modified by annealing, quench hardening, and tempering. When steel is heated to a red-hot temperature then allowed to cool slowly, it takes on the properties of a softer steel. This is the annealing process.

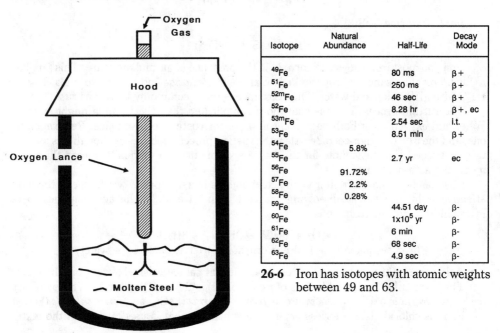

Isotope	Natural Abundance	Half-Life	Decay Mode
^{49}Fe		80 ms	β+
^{51}Fe		250 ms	β+
^{52m}Fe		46 sec	β+
^{52}Fe		8.28 hr	β+, ec
^{53m}Fe		2.54 sec	i.t.
^{53}Fe		8.51 min	β+
^{54}Fe	5.8%		
^{55}Fe		2.7 yr	ec
^{56}Fe	91.72%		
^{57}Fe	2.2%		
^{58}Fe	0.28%		
^{59}Fe		44.51 day	β-
^{60}Fe		1×10^5 yr	β-
^{61}Fe		6 min	β-
^{62}Fe		68 sec	β-
^{63}Fe		4.9 sec	β-

26-6 Iron has isotopes with atomic weights between 49 and 63.

26-5 Steel is produced in oxygen furnaces.

Rapidly cooling the steel object, usually by plunging it into water, hardens the steel. This is known as quench tempering. Sometimes, however, this steel is too hard; it is full of stresses and apt to shatter. The stresses can be removed by tempering the steel. This involves heating the steel again and holding the temperature until the stresses are relieved. This is the tempering process.

Some compounds of iron

Iron has two oxidation states, $+2$ and $+3$. The iron ions are thus Fe^{2+} and Fe^{3+}. This means the typical oxides are:

Iron(II) oxide, FeO

$$Fe^{2+} + O^{2-} \rightarrow FeO$$

Iron(III) oxide, Fe_2O_3 (also called iron sesquioxide, but best known as ordinary rust)

$$2Fe^{3+} + 3O^{2-} \rightarrow Fe_2O_3$$

Some other representative examples of iron compounds are:

Iron(II) carbonate, $FeCO_3$ (also known as the mineral *siderite*)

$$Fe^{2+} + CO_3{}^{2-} \rightarrow FeCO_3$$

Iron(III), FeF_3 (also called ferric fluoride)

$$Fe^{3+} + 3F^- \rightarrow FeF_3$$

Iron(III) phosphide, FeP (also called iron monosphosphide)

$$Fe^{3+} + P^{3-} \rightarrow FeP$$

Iron(IV) silicide, FeSi

$$Fe^{4+} + Se^{4-} \rightarrow FeSi$$

Iron and most iron alloys can corrode in the presence of air and moisture. This familiar, reddish brown nuisance is properly known as a *hydrated oxide* and has the formula, $Fe_2O_3 \cdot xH_2O$—iron(III) oxide and water. The substance is more commonly known as rust.

The rusting process is somewhat more complicated than the formula might suggest. Water and oxygen must both be present in order for rusting to take place. Remove either one, and the iron does not corrode. Also, the rusting process behaves as though it is an electrolytic process. This accounts for the way a spot of rust can gradually spread through a metal and across its surface.

Rust can be removed from iron and steel objects in a number of ways. One of the most effective is by *pickling* it—dissolving the rust with an acid. If the acid happens to be hydrochloric acid, the reaction is:

$$Fe_2O_3 + 6HCl \rightarrow 2FeCl_3 + 3H_2O$$
(iron sesquioxide + hydrochloric acid → ferric chloride + water)

The acid converts the rust to a harmless iron salt that can be washed away from the metal.

There are two principal chlorides of iron, iron(II) and iron(III) chloride. These are better known by their older nomenclature as *ferrous chloride* ($FeCl_2$) and *ferric chloride* ($FeCl_3$).

Ferrous chloride is a colorless crystalline substance that is used mainly in the textile industry to make dyes colorfast. It is produced by passing hot chlorine gas over iron:

$$Fe + Cl_2 \rightarrow FeCl_2$$
(iron + chlorine → ferrous chloride)

Ferric chloride is a dark-colored crystal that is used as a disinfectant and in the processing of industrial waste products. The crystals possess a peculiar optical property whereby they transmit red light and reflect green light. This compound is available as a byproduct of pickling iron and steel products.

Ferrous sulfide, FeS, is a dark brown or black substance that is found in nature as the mineral *pyrrhotite*. It is used mainly in the manufacture of hydrogen sulfide. *Ferrous sulfate*, $FeSO_4$, is a pale green crystalline substance that is used chiefly in the treatment of iron-deficiency anemia. It can be produced by the reaction between iron and sulfuric acid:

$$Fe + H_2SO_4 \rightarrow FeSO_4 + H_2$$
(iron + sulfuric acid → ferrous sulfate + hydrogen)

The Stock nomenclature for these two sulfur compounds are iron(II) sulfide and iron(II) sulfate.

Isotopes of iron

Figure 26-6 on p. 109 lists all of the known isotopes of iron. This list shows that most naturally occurring iron is iron-56, although there are traces of -54, -57 and -58 as well. These are all stable, nonradioactive isotopes. The remaining isotopes are man-made and radioactive.

Element 27: Cobalt

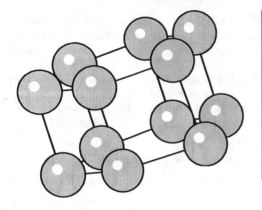

Name	Cobalt
Symbol	Co
Atomic Number	27
Atomic Weight	58.9332
Melting Point	1857°C
Boiling Point	2672°C
Specific Gravity	8.90 (20°C)
Oxidation States	+2, +3
Electron Config.	(Ar) $3d^7 4s^2$

- Name pronounced as **KO-bolt**
- Name taken from the German word *kobold*, "goblin"
- Compounds known in ancient times; isolated in 1739 by Georg Brandt
- Hard, ductile, lustrous bluish-gray metal

Cobalt is closely associated with cobalt glass and its characteristic deep blue color. A radio-active isotope of cobalt is a valuable source of radiation for medical equipment and indus-trial measuring devices. It is an important alloying agent in the steel industry, and a fourth of the world's cobalt production goes into making powerful permanent magnets.

Cobalt exists in the earth's crust with an average concentration of about 25 parts-per-million. That puts it on the same scale of abundance as lithium and nitrogen.

Historical background

The most ancient civilizations, those in Mesopotamia and Egypt, were aware of the fact that minerals containing high levels of cobalt would impart a striking, deep blue color to glass.

By the middle of the 16th century, chemists and mineralogists were referring to the min-eral that produced blue glass and pigments as *zaffer*. German miners who had to cull the stuff out of the ground called it *kobald*, referring to their mythological imp that caused the day-to-day difficulties of the mining profession. (The thinking is not unlike the "bugs" we say get into our modern high-tech equipment and computer software.) By the 18th century, the mineral was being called cobalt instead of zaffer.

Around 1730, Sweden's Georg Brandt (1694 – 1768), was preparing a case for cobalt as an element that was distinct from bismuth. During this particular era, it was fashionable to attribute the blue-coloring properties of cobalt to the element bismuth—a confusion that can be justified on the grounds that bismuth and cobalt are often found in the same location.

There is some dispute over the exact date of Brandt's announcement of his proof that cobalt is an element in its own right. The date of publication of his key paper was thought to have been 1735, but more recent historical research has shown that 1739 is a more probable date. In this case, a four-year discrepancy is of no practical significance because no one else was trying to isolate cobalt and could not therefore, make a claim to prior discovery. Incidentally, there are some striking resemblances between the historical background of cobalt and nickel. (*See* Element 28: Nickel.)

Properties of cobalt

Cobalt is a silvery-white, brittle metal that has a slight bluish color when polished. Cobalt stands between iron (Fe) and nickel (Ni) on the periodic table. These three metals are similar in many respects and are usually found together in ore deposits.

This element is best known for its remarkable magnetic properties. Like iron, cobalt is easily magnetized and readily retains its magnetism under a wide range of environmental conditions. In fact, one-fourth of the world's cobalt production is used in a "super magnet" alloy known as *alnico*, aluminum-nickel-cobalt.

Cobalt has the highest Curie point of any known metal or alloy. The Curie point is the temperature at which a metal loses its magnetic properties, usually just a bit below the melting point. In the case of cobalt, the Curie point is $1121\,°C$.

Cobalt has two common allotropes. The one that is stable at room temperature, the beta form, has a close-packed hexagonal crystalline structure. The transition to the alpha form, one having a face-centered cubic structure, takes place at about $417\,°C$.

Production of cobalt

Cobalt is refined from its ores and recovered as a byproduct of nickel, copper, and iron refining operations. The most important ores are *cobaltite* ($CoAsS$) and *erythrite* $Co_3(AsO_4)_2$.

The ores are treated in a blast furnace to produce *cobalt arsenide*, Co_2As. This arsenide is then mixed with sulfuric acid to yield *cobalt hydroxide*, $Co(OH)_2$; then the hydroxide is reacted with oxygen to produce *cobalt tetroxide*, Co_3O_4. Finally, the cobalt is reduced by hot carbon:

$$Co_3O_4 + C \rightarrow 3Co + 2CO_2$$
(cobalt tetroxide + carbon → cobalt + carbon dioxide)

Cobalt is recovered as a byproduct of refining operations for other metals that happen to come from areas that yield cobalt-rich "impurities." In many instances, this source is more economical and productive than the cobalt ores.

Some compounds of cobalt

Cobalt has two oxidation states, $+2$ and $+3$; its ionic forms are Co^{2+} and Co^{3+}. This means the oxides have these forms:

Cobalt(II) oxide, CoO

$$Co^{2+} + O^{2-} \rightarrow CoO$$

Cobalt(III) oxide, Co_2O_3

$$2Co^{3+} + 3O^{2-} \rightarrow Co_2O_3$$

Both cobalt oxides are solids. The monoxide (CoO) has a greenish-gray color, while the sesquioxide (Co_2O_3) is black. Mixed with alumina (Al_2O_3), however, the cobalt oxides form a deep blue solid which forms the basis for *cobalt blue* glass and pigments.

Examples of some cobalt halides and other salts are:

Cobalt(II) chloride, $CoCl_2$

$$Co^{2+} + 2Cl^- \rightarrow CoCl_2$$

Cobalt(II) sulfate, $CoSO_4$

$$Co^{2+} + (SO_4)^{2-} \rightarrow CoSO_4$$

Cobalt(III) fluoride, CoF_3

$$Co^{3+} + 3F^- \rightarrow CoF_3$$

Cobalt(III) sulfate, $Co_2(SO_4)_3$

$$2Co^{3+} + 3(SO_4)^{2-} \rightarrow Co_2(SO_4)_3$$

Cobalt(II) chloride is a crystal that changes color according to its degree of hydration, or combination with water molecules. The formula for hydrated cobalt(II) chloride is $CoCl_2 \cdot 6H_2O$ and it has a dark red color. The dehydrated version, $CoCl_2$, is dark blue.

Isotopes of cobalt

Figure 27-1 shows that all naturally occurring cobalt is cobalt-59. Radioactive cobalt-60, with its long half-life of about 5.3 years, is a commercially valuable source of radiation. This synthetic, radioactive form of cobalt is used in the manufacturing industry in place of X-rays for detecting internal flaws in materials and products. It is also used in the same general capacity in medicine and medical research.

Cobalt-60 is produced by irradiating natural cobalt-59.

$$^{59}Co_{27} + {}^1 n_0 \rightarrow {}^{60}Co_{27}$$

Isotope	Natural Abundance	Half-Life	Decay Mode
^{53m}Co		250 ms	β+, p
^{53}Co		260 ms	β+
^{53m}Co		1.46 min	β+
^{54}Co		190 ms	β+
^{55}Co		17.5 hr	β+, ec
^{56}Co		77.7 da	β+, ec
^{57}Co		271 da	ec
^{58m}Co		9.1 hr	i.t.
^{58}Co		70.91	β+, ec
^{59}Co	100%		
^{60m}Co		10.48 min	ec, β-
^{60}Co		5.272 yr	β-
^{61}Co		1.65 hr	β-
^{62m}Co		13.9 min	β-
^{62}Co		1.5 min	β-
^{63}Co		27.5 sec	β-
^{64}Co		300 ms	β-

27-1 Cobalt has isotopes with atomic weights between 53 and 64.

Element 28: Nickel

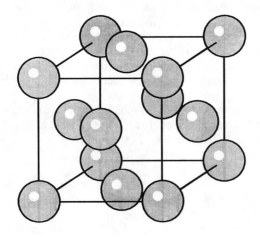

Name	Nickel
Symbol	Ni
Atomic Number	28
Atomic Weight	58.69
Melting Point	1453°C
Boiling Point	2732°C
Specific Gravity	8.908 (20°C)
Oxidation States	+2, +3
Electron Config.	(Ar) $3d^8\,4s^2$

- Name pronounced as **NIK-'l**
- Name from the German *kupfernickel*, "Old Nick's copper"
- Isolated by Baron Axel Fredrik Cronstedt in 1751
- Hard, malleable, silvery-white metal

Yes, the United States five-cent piece is made of nickel—25% of it is, anyway. Besides its use in the American coin, the metal is used as an important steel alloying agent and a component in some of the world's most powerful permanent magnets.

Nickel is found in the earth's crust in portions averaging about 70 parts per million. That is about the same proportion as some other common metals such as zinc and copper. There is a good chance that the core of the earth includes a very high proportion of molten nickel.

Historical background

The historical background of nickel is quite similar to that of cobalt (*See* Element 27: Cobalt). Their minerals were both known for their peculiar glass-coloring properties—blue for cobalt and green for nickel.

The mineral that was known to produce green colors was a reddish-brown rock that often had large blotches of green on it. By the middle of the 1700s, miners who dug this mineral from the ground began calling it *kupfernickel*, which can mean two things: the name of a troll or "false copper." The latter interpretation correctly suggests that nickel ores are often found in the same location as copper ores.

In 1751, Baron Axel Fredrik Cronstedt (1722–1765) attempted an analysis of a new mineral, *niccolite*, that was taken from the copper and cobalt mining region of Sweden. He fully expected to find a large percentage of copper, but he found none at all. Instead, he obtained a white metal that was completely unlike copper. By the end of the year, Cronstedt announced his discovery of the new element; and he called it nickel, referring to the *niccolite* that provided his first samples.

Properties of nickel

Nickel is a hard, malleable, and ductile metal. It has a silvery white appearance, and it can be polished to a lustrous finish. Corrosion under normal environmental conditions is practically nonexistent, making nickel a natural choice for a coinage material.

Nickel is a Group-VII transition metal on the periodic table of the elements. Unlike neighboring copper, nickel is only a fair conductor of electricity (copper is an excellent conductor). Like its neighbor on the other side, cobalt, nickel possesses outstanding magnetic properties. Nickel alloyed with cobalt and iron is a combination that accounts for most powerful kinds of permanent magnet.

Nickel is unusually resistant to corrosion by alkalis. For this reason, industrial-strength sodium and potassium hydroxide are shipped and stored in nickel containers. Nickel reacts with most acids to produce hydrogen gas and the Ni^{2+} ion.

Production of nickel

The primary commercial nickel ore is *pentlandite*, $NiS \cdot 2FeS$. Heating this ore in a blast furnace drives off the sulfur and replaces it with oxygen. The two oxides are then treated with an acid that is more reactive to the iron oxide than the nickel oxide. The nickel oxide thus remains behind in the solution. Heating the nickel oxide with water gas (a mixture of carbon monoxide and hydrogen) reduces the metallic nickel. The purity of the metal is on the order of 92%.

The Monde process is used for transforming refinery-grade nickel to a higher grade of 99.95% purity. The process relies on the unusual properties of a highly toxic gas, *nickel carbonyl*, $Ni(CO)_4$. The lower-grade nickel metal is warmed to about 50 °C in an atmosphere of carbon monoxide to produce nickel carbonyl:

$$Ni + 4CO \rightarrow Ni(CO)_4$$
(nickel metal + carbon monoxide → nickel carbonyl gas)

The nickel carbonyl is then heated to about 200 °C where it decomposes, reversing the previous reaction to yield carbon monoxide and pure nickel metal.

Some compounds and the isotopes of nickel

Nickel has two oxidation states, 2 and +3. The +3 state rarely turns up in actual practice, however; so the only oxide you can find on the shelf is:

Nickel(II) oxide, NiO

$$Ni^{2+} + O^{2-} \rightarrow NiO$$

Among the halides and other salts are:

Nickel chloride, $NiCl_2$

$$Ni^{2+} + 2Cl^- \rightarrow NiCl_2$$

Nickel carbonate, $NiCO_3$

$$Ni^{2+} + CO_3^{2-} \rightarrow NiCO_3$$

Nickel(II) phosphide, Ni_3P_2

$$3Ni^{2+} + 2P^{3-} \rightarrow Ni_3P_2$$

Nickel(II) silicide, Ni_2Si

$$2Ni^{2+} + Si^{4-} \rightarrow Ni_2Si$$

Nickel sulfate, Ni_2SO_4, is a green or yellow-green crystal that is industrially important as the medium for nickel plating iron and copper products.

Nickel compounds tend to have green colors.

Figure 28-1 shows the known isotopes of nickel. Naturally occurring nickel is scattered among five different stable, nonradioactive species. The remaining isotopes of nickel are both artificial and radioactive.

28-1 Nickel has isotopes with atomic weights between 53 and 67.

Isotope	Natural Abundance	Half-Life	Decay Mode
^{53}Ni		50 ms	β+, p
^{55}Ni		190 ms	β+
^{56}Ni		6.1 da	ec
^{57}Ni		36.1 hr	β+, ec
^{58}Ni	68.27%		
^{59}Ni		7.6×10^4 yr	ec
^{60}Ni	26.10%		
^{61}Ni	1.13%		
^{62}Ni	3.59%		
^{63}Ni		100 yr	β-
^{64}Ni	0.91%		
^{65}Ni		2.52 hr	β-
^{66}Ni		54.8 hr	β-
^{67}Ni		20 sec	β-

Element 29: Copper

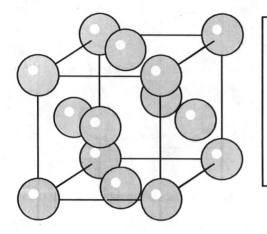

Name	Copper
Symbol	Cu
Atomic Number	29
Atomic Weight	63.546
Melting Point	1083°C
Boiling Point	2567°C
Specific Gravity	8.94 (20°C)
Oxidation States	+1, +2
Electron Config.	(Ar) $3d^{10}\,4s^1$

- Name pronounced as **KOP-er**
- Chemical symbol, Cu, taken from the Latin *cuprum*, "from the island of Cyprus"
- Prehistoric origin
- Malleable, ductile, reddish-brown metal

The United States penny used to be made of solid copper. Now, it is simply copper plated. The American slang expression for a policeman, *cop* or *copper*, probably has its origin in the fact that policeman once wore uniform buttons made of copper.

Copper and its characteristic orange-brown color, is familiar to most people in the civilized world. Most copper that is mined today is refined and drawn into wire for use in the electrical industries, although a significant percentage is also used in the manufacture of water pipes.

Copper is not one of more abundant elements in the earth's crust, but the fact that it occurs in very large and highly concentrated ore deposits makes it seem to be a common element. The most significant deposits of copper ores are in the Northern United States and Canada, the Soviet Union, Chile, and Zambia.

Historical background

The use of copper stretches back to the earliest history of mankind; a handful of copper beads found in Iraq date back to 9000 B.C. These items represent the first objects made from a metal. Around 5000 B.C., people learned to refine copper from copper ores; and by 4000 B.C., people in the North African civilizations were making copper pottery. There is ample evidence that American Indians living in the Great Lakes area were making copper tools and jewelry around 100 A.D.

Copper is relatively easy to mine and refine. This accounts for its use in early human history. It is a soft metal, however; it is unsuitable for making reliable tools and weapons.

The metalsmiths of 3000 B.C. learned to combine copper with other metals to produce alloys that were harder and more durable than the original elements. Brass, for example, is an alloy of copper and zinc, while bronze is an alloy of copper and tin. Some copper alloys of more modern origin include copper-aluminum and copper-nickel.

Cyprus was the leading supplier of copper ore for the Roman Empire, thus the origin of the modern name for this element.

Properties of copper

Copper is commonly described as a reddish-brown, malleable, and ductile metal that is one of the best conductors of heat and electricity. It resists corrosion from most acids (hot nitric acid and concentrated sulfuric acid are exceptions). Since it also resists the action of air, moisture, and even seawater, copper is an ideal material for making coins.

Copper that is exposed to natural elements for an extended period of time develops a blue-green coating, or *patina*. This is actually copper carbonate—a natural protective coating that discourages further wear and corrosion.

Copper heads the list of Group-IB elements on the periodic table. It is in good company with two other well-known metals, silver (Ag) and gold (Au).

Production of copper

Some copper is obtained from deposits of native ore deposits so rich in copper metal that it is better than 99% pure as it comes from the ground. Most copper, however, is obtained from deposits of copper compounds—deposits where the concentration of the element is between 10 and 80%.

Copper ores tend to be oxide and sulfide ores. The oxide ores appear closer to the surface of the earth where the copper can be exposed to atmospheric oxygen. Examples include *cuprite* (CuO_2), *tenorite* (CuO) and *malachite* ($CuCO_3 \cdot Cu(OH)_2$). Deeper deposits, on the other hand, tend to be sulfide compounds such as *chalcocite* (Cu_2S), *covellite* (CuS), and *bornite* (Cu_6FeS_4).

Copper is recovered from the ores either by a smelting process or by a leaching process. Smelting is generally used for the sulfide ores, while leaching is reserved for the oxide ores.

The primary objective of a smelting operation is to liberate a metal—copper in this case—from its ore by one or more high-temperature operations. Few metals, including copper, can be directly melted away from their ores. In the copper-smelting procedure, for example, an initial heating operation releases the sulfur atoms and replaces them with oxygen atoms; the sulfides are changed to oxides. Heating the oxides to a very high temperature in a blast furnace and in the presence of carbon (coke) releases the basic metal and drives off the oxygen in the form of carbon monoxide or dioxide.

A leaching operation uses a solvent of some sort to dissolve the metal-bearing compound and produce a different metal compound that can be readily converted to the pure metal. The solvent process separates the metal from most of its impurities; the resulting compound is usually converted to the pure metal by an electrolytic process.

In the case of copper, the solvent is usually sulfuric acid, and the compound that it forms is copper sulfate. The copper sulfate solution is then electrolyzed as shown in Fig. 29-1. The impurities that gather beneath the anode are often called anode slime. This is a source of rarer metals, such as selenium, that are commonly mixed with copper ores.

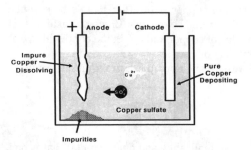

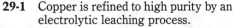

29-1 Copper is refined to high purity by an electrolytic leaching process.

Isotope	Natural Abundance	Half-Life	Decay Mode
^{58}Cu		3.21 sec	β+, ec
^{59}Cu		82 sec	β+
^{60}Cu		23.2 min	β+, ec
^{61}Cu		3.41 hr	β+
^{62}Cu		9.74 min	β+, ec
^{63}Cu	69.17%		
^{64}Cu		12.7 hr	β-, ec
^{65}Cu	30.83%		
^{66}Cu		5.1 min	β-
^{67}Cu		61.9 hr	β-
^{68m}Cu		3.8 min	β-, i.t.
^{68}Cu		31 sec	β-
^{69}Cu		3 min	β-
^{70m}Cu		46 sec	β-
^{70}Cu		5 sec	β-
^{71}Cu		20 sec	β-
^{72}Cu		6.6 sec	β-
^{73}Cu		3.9 sec	β-

29-2 Copper has isotopes with atomic weights between 58 and 73.

Some compounds of copper

Copper has two oxidation states, +1 and +2: Cu^+ and Cu^{2+}. This means there are often two different formulations for the same combination of elements. Here are a few examples:

Copper(I) fluoride, CuF

$$Cu^+ + F^- \rightarrow CuF$$

Copper(II) fluoride, CuF_2

$$Cu^{2+} + 2F^- \rightarrow CuF_2$$

Copper(I) carbonate, Cu_2CO^3

$$2Cu^+ + CO_3^{2-} \rightarrow Cu_2CO_3$$

Copper(II) carbonate, $CuCO_3$ (also known as the mineral *malachite*)

$$Cu^{2+} + CO_3^{2-} \rightarrow CuCO_3$$

Copper(II) sulfate

Copper(II) sulfate, $CuSO_4$, is the best known and most popular of the copper compounds. It is a white crystal in its pure, anhydrous (waterless) form. It is better known in its pentahydrate form, $CuSO_4 \cdot H_2O$, which is a deep blue crystal. Sometimes called *blue vitrol*, the primary commercial applications of hydrated copper sulfate are in fungicides and algicides, and in ink pigments. It is also extensively used in the refinement of copper metal.

Copper(II) sulfate is produced by heating one of the copper-sulfur compounds ores in air. For example, heating copper(II) sulfide, or covellite, in the presence of oxygen:

$$CuS + 2O_2 \rightarrow CuSO_4$$
$$\text{(copper sulfide + oxygen} \rightarrow \text{copper sulfate)}$$

It is also produced by the reaction of copper metal and sulfuric acid:

$$Cu + H_2SO_4 \rightarrow CuSO_4 + H_2$$
(copper + sulfuric acid → copper sulfate + hydrogen gas)

Copper sulfate is also the main ingredient in the minerals *chalcanthite* and *brochantite*.

The copper oxides

There are two copper oxides, Cu_2O and CuO. The Stock names for these oxides are *copper(I) oxide* and *copper(II) oxide*; the traditional names are cuprous and cuperic oxide.

As described earlier in this chapter, Copper(I) oxide is readily available as the mineral cuprite. It shows a variety of colors, from yellow to red, and can be powdery or crystalling. Cu_2O can also be produced in the laboratory by heating copper in air.

Copper(II) oxide is a black powder that occurs in nature as the minerals paramelaconite and tenorite.

Other important copper compounds

Copper(II) chloride, $CuCl_2$, is a yellowish-brown powder that is used as a dye fixer in the textile industry. It is also used to produce other chemicals, including cuprous chloride ($CuCl$).

Copper(I) chloride, $CuCl$, is a poisonous white powder that is chiefly used as an absorbing agent for carbon dioxide gas. It is produced commercially by reducing a copper(II) chloride solution with copper metal. $CuCl$ is traditionally known as cuprous chloride.

A chemical commonly used in electroplating operations is known as copper cyanide, $CuCN$. This is a white crystalline powder that is produced by the reaction between copper(I) chloride and sodium cyanide:

$$CuCl + NaCN \rightarrow CuCN + NaCl$$
(cuprous chloride + sodium cyanide → copper cyanide + sodium chloride)

Isotopes of copper

Figure 29-2 lists the isotopes of copper. Naturally occurring copper is a mixture of copper-63 and copper-65. The remaining isotopes are both artificial and radioactive.

Element 30: Zinc

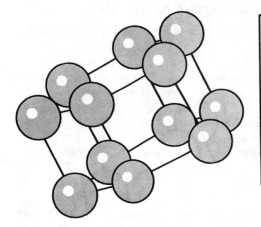

Name	Zinc
Symbol	Zn
Atomic Number	30
Atomic Weight	65.39
Melting Point	419.58°C
Boiling Point	907°C
Specific Gravity	7.14 (20°C)
Oxidation State	+2
Electron Config.	(Ar) $3d^{10}\ 4s^2$

- Name pronounced as **ZINK**
- Name of German origin, *zink*, but any literal meaning has been obscured with time
- Prehistoric origin
- Bluish-silver, ductile metal

Zinc is relatively resistant to corrosion from reactions with oxygen and moisture in the atmosphere. A thin layer of zinc applied to iron or steel products tends to extend their useful life by protecting them (at least for a reasonable period of time) from corrosion. When the zinc coating is applied by an electrolytic process, the product is said to be *galvanized*.

Zinc is easily die cast, or molded, into intricate shapes. Much of the metal is used in the manufacture of automotive engine parts and electrical equipment.

Historical background

The historical background for zinc is undistinguished. Zinc compounds, most notably the zinc oxide in calamine, have enjoyed commercial applications dating back to the time of Marco Polo's ventures in the 1400s. The zinc compounds were made into healing lotions and alloyed with copper to produce brass.

No one receives credit for identifying zinc as an element. Chemists of the 1800s simply accepted the metal as an element without any sort of fanfare.

Perhaps the only name that can be legitimately attached to the history of zinc is that of Andreas Sigismund Marggraf (1709–1782). One of the difficulties inherent in reducing zinc from its ores is that temperatures chemists were using for the refining operation tended to be so high that the zinc would vaporize and blow away. The boiling point of zinc is only 907°C—far below that of similar metals. Margraff developed a technique for distilling zinc metal from calamine, suggested the metal could be obtained from other ores, and promptly set about to discover beet sugar, instead. The discovery of beet sugar notwithstanding, Margraff's procedure for obtaining zinc from calamine and other ores was made commercially practical by 1752.

Properties of zinc

Zinc is characterized as a fairly hard, blue-white metal. In its purest state, it is shiny and ductile; but few people ever see zinc in that state. The more common commercial grades of zinc have a dull finish and are quite brittle.

Zinc heads the short list of Group-IIB metals on the periodical table of the elements. Other members of this group of cadmium (Cd) and mercury (Hg).

Production of zinc metal

Most zinc is obtained from a zinc sulfide (ZnS) mineral known as *zinc blende* or *sphalerite*. Just as in the earliest days of zinc refining, some still comes from zinc carbonate ($ZnCO_3$)— *smithsonite* or *calamine*. Some of the world's largest deposits of zinc ores are in the United States, Canada, and the Soviet Union.

Until recent years, most zinc was extracted from its ores by roasting the ground ores in a blast furnace of one kind or another. Some of the zinc is driven off as a hot vapor, which can be condensed in a molten zinc bath. Most of the zinc vapor, however, is absorbed in a spray of molten lead; as this mixture cools, the zinc is easily separated from the molten lead.

Nowadays, more than half the world's production of zinc is carried out by the electrolysis of aqueous zinc sulfate. The zinc sulfate, itself, is produced by treating finely ground zinc ores with sulfuric acid.

Some compounds of zinc

Zinc has a single oxidation state of $+2$ and a typical metallic ion, Zn^{2+}. It thus combines with -1 anions in this way:

Zinc chloride, $ZnCl_2$

$$Zn^{2+} + 2Cl^- \rightarrow ZnCl_2$$

Zinc hydroxide, $Zn(OH)_2$

$$Zn^{2+} + 2(OH)^- \rightarrow Zn(OH)_2$$

and with -2 anions as:

Zinc oxide, ZnO

$$Zn^{2+} + {}^{2-} \rightarrow AnO$$

Zinc sulfate, $ZnSO_4$

$$Zn^{2+} + (SO_4)^{2-} \rightarrow ZnSO_4$$

Examples of Zn^{2+} combining with ions having an oxidation states of -3 are:

Zinc nitride, Zn_3N_2

$$3Zn^{2+} + 2N^{3-} \rightarrow Zn_3N_2$$

Zinc phosphate, $Zn_3(PO_4)_2$

$$3Zn^{2+} + 2(PO_4)^{3-} \rightarrow Zn_3(PO_4)_2$$

Zinc oxide, ZnO, is perhaps the most popular zinc compound. It is characterized as a white, insoluable powder. It has applications as diverse as pigment bases for white paints and pharmaceutical ointments. Zinc oxide is available from nature in the form of the mineral *zincite*. Commercial amounts are more economically produced by burning zinc metal in air.

Zinc chloride is used in the production of other chemicals and often applied to building lumber to make it more fire resistant. This poisonous salt is usually produced by a reaction between zinc and hydrochloric acid:

$$2Zn + 2HCl \rightarrow 2ZnCl + H_2$$
(zinc metal + hydrochloric acid → zinc chloride + hydrogen gas)

Zinc sulfate is an important ingredient in dyes, pigments, and galvanizing processes. It can be produced easily by a reaction between zinc metal and sulfuric acid:

$$Zn + H_2SO_4 \rightarrow ZnSO_4 + H_2$$
(zinc metal + sulfuric acid → zinc sulfate + hydrogen gas)

Zinc sulfide, ZnS, occurs naturally in the minerals *sphalerite* and *wurtzite*. This fluorescent crystalline compound is commonly used as a white pigment for fluorescent paints. It is combined with barium sulfide to produce a common white paint pigment known as *lithopone*. Most zinc sulfide is derived from natural sources, but ZnS can be produced in the laboratory by reacting hydrogen sulfide (HS) with a zinc salt.

Two zinc-chromium compounds find applications as paint pigments. *Zinc dichromate* ($ZnCr_2O_7$) provides an orange-red pigment, while *zinc chromate* ($ZnCrO_4$) is a brilliant yellow.

Isotopes of zinc

Figure 30-1 lists the isotopes of zinc. Naturally occurring zinc is composed of five different, nonradioactive isotopes. The remaining isotopes are both radioactive and manmade.

Isotope	Natural Abundance	Half-Life	Decay Mode
^{57}Zn		40 ms	β+, p
^{59}Zn		184 ms	β+, p
^{60}Zn		2.4 min	β+, ec
^{61}Zn		89.1 sec	β+
^{62}Zn		9.26 hr	β+, ec
^{63}Zn		38.1 min	β+, ec
^{64}Zn	48.6%		
^{65}Zn		243.8 da	β+, ec
^{66}Zn	27.9%		
^{67}Zn	4.1%		
^{68}Zn	18.8%		
^{69m}Zn		13.8 hr	i.t.
^{69}Zn		57 min	β-
^{70}Zn	0.6%		
^{71m}Zn		3.97 hr	β-
^{71}Zn		2.4 min	
^{72}Zn			β-
^{73}Zn		24 sec	β-
^{74}Zn		96 sec	β-
^{75}Zn		10.2 sec	β-
^{76}Zn		5.7 sec	β-
^{77}Zn		1.4 sec	β-
^{78}Zn		1.5 sec	β-

30-1 Zinc has isotopes with atomic weights between 57 and 78.

Element 31: Gallium

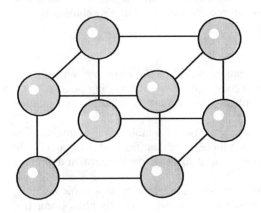

Name	Gallium
Symbol	Ga
Atomic Number	31
Atomic Weight	69.72
Melting Point	29.78°C
Boiling Point	2403°C
Specific Gravity	5.903 (25°C)
Oxidation State	+3
Electron Config.	(Ar) $3d^{10}\ 4s^2\ 4p^1$

- Name pronounced as **GAL-i-em**
- Name from the Latin, *Gallia*, "France"
- Existence predicted by Mendeleyev; located and isolated by Paul-Emile Lecoq de Boisbaudran in 1875
- Soft, blue-white metal

Gallium was once an obscure metal that was known only to chemistry professors and people interested in science trivia. But that all changed in the early 1970s when gallium arsenide (GaAs) light-emitting diodes, or LEDs, exploded onto the electronics scene. Within a few years, these economical and efficient little lamps transformed our ideas of electronic indicators and displays. Gallium has become a viable commercial commodity, used in producing LEDs and GaAs laser diodes.

Historical background

The existence of gallium was predicted theoretically by Mendeleyev in 1871. He suggested it would resemble aluminum, so he gave the undiscovered metal the name *ekaaluminum* and suggested the chemical symbol, Ea. Furthermore, Mendeleyev predicted Ea would have an atomic weight of 68 (atomic weight of Ga is 69.7), its oxide would have the formula Ea_2O_3 (gallium oxide is Ga_2O_3), the specific gravity would be 5.9 (gallium has a specific gravity of 5.9), and the element would be discovered spectroscopically (gallium was discovered with the aid of the spectroscope). There were other predictions about Mendeleyev's ekaaluminum that fit the specifications for gallium when it was finally found around 1875.

With the aid of Mendeleyev's clues, but chiefly through his own mastery of spectroscopic science, the French chemist Paul-Emile Lecoq de Boisbaudran (1838–1912) set out to find the metals that were missing between aluminum and indium. He knew he was on the right track when he located a set of new spectral lines from samples of the zinc mineral, *sphalerite*, or zinc blende.

Sphalerite is basically a zinc-sulfide mineral which, oddly enough, was sometimes called *galena inanis*, useless lead. As Boisbaudran suspected (and as we now know for certain), sphalerite often includes a wide range of metallic impurities, including gallium. A few months later he isolated the pure element by electrolyzing a mixture of gallium hydroxide and potassium hydroxide.

Sphalerite is no longer regarded as useless lead. Although *gallite* is now recognized as a legitimate gallium ore, most gallium is still recovered from Boisbaudran's sphalerite.

Properties of gallium

Gallium is a soft metal. Like pure lead, gallium can be cut with a knife at room temperature. When the metal is chilled, however, it becomes hard and brittle. Its melting point is just a bit above ordinary room temperature; unlike most other elements, gallium expands upon cooling.

Gallium belongs to the Group-IIIA elements on the periodic table of the elements. The other elements in this group are boron (B), aluminum (Al), indium (In), and thallium (Tl). In the chemical sense, gallium is most like aluminum, but it shares a few chemical and physical characteristics with indium and thallium.

Gallium is best known today for its tendency to conduct electricity as a semiconductor, but only when "doped" with one of the Group-VA compounds, especially phosphorus (P), arsenic (As), and antimony (Sb).

Production of gallium

Although gallium is just about as abundant as lead in the earth's crust, gallium and gallium ores are not the main source of this metal because the extraction procedures are not economical. Most gallium is recovered as a byproduct of other refinery operations, notably those for zinc, aluminum, and iron.

Some compounds and the isotopes of gallium

Gallium's primary oxidation state is $+3$. This means it combines with -1 anions in this way:

Gallium chloride, $GaCl_3$

$$Ga^{3+} + 3Cl^- \rightarrow GaCl_3$$

Gallium hydroxide, $Ga(OH)_3$

$$Ga^{3+} + 3(OH)^- \rightarrow Ga(OH)_3$$

With $^-2$ anions gallium forms compounds such as:

Gallium oxide, Ga_2O_3

$$2Ga^{3+} + 3O^{2-} \rightarrow Ga_2O_3$$

Gallium sulfate, $Ga_2(SO_4)_3$

$$2Ga^{3+} + 3(SO_4)^{2-} \rightarrow Ga_2(SO_4)_3$$

And with $^-3$ anions:

Gallium arsenide, $GaAs$

$$Ga^{3+} + As^{3-} \rightarrow GaAs$$

Gallium nitride, GaN

$$Ga^{3+} + N^{3-} \rightarrow GaN$$

There are a few compounds that show gallium can also exist in a +1 oxidation state—gallium suboxide, Ga_2O, for example. The existence of gallium dichloride, $GaCl_2$, would normally show that gallium can also exist with a +2 oxidation state. This is not true, however. This compound is actually made up of equal amounts of gallium(I) and gallium(III) chloride.

Figure 31-1 lists the known isotopes of gallium.

Isotope	Natural Abundance	Half-Life	Decay Mode
^{62}Ga		116 ms	β+
^{63}Ga		32 sec	β+, ec
^{64}Ga		2.63 min	β+
^{65}Ga		15.2 min	β+, ec
^{66}Ga		9.4 hr	β+, ec
^{67}Ga		78.25 hr	ec
^{68}Ga		68.1 min	β+, ec
^{69}Ga	60.1%		
^{70}Ga		21.1 min	β-, ec
^{71}Ga	39.9%		
^{72}Ga		13.95 hr	β-
^{73}Ga		4.87 hr	
^{74m}Ga		9.5 sec	i.t.
^{74}Ga		8.1 min	β-
^{75}Ga		2.10 min	β-
^{76}Ga		29.1 sec	β-
^{77}Ga		13 sec	β-
^{78}Ga		5.09 sec	β-
^{79}Ga		3.0 sec	β-
^{80}Ga		1.66 sec	β-
^{81}Ga		1.23 sec	β-
^{82}Ga		1.9 sec	β-
^{83}Ga		1.2 sec	β-

31-1 Gallium has isotopes with atomic weights between 62 and 83.

Element 32: Germanium

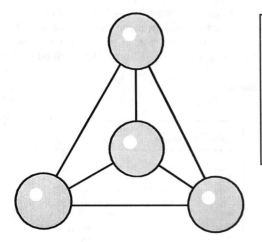

Name	Germanium
Symbol	Gė
Atomic Number	32
Atomic Weight	72.59
Melting Point	937.4°C
Boiling Point	2830°C
Specific Gravity	5.323 (25°C)
Oxidation States	+2, +4
Electron Config.	(Ar) $3d^{10}\ 4s^2\ 4p^2$

- Name pronounced as **jer-MAY-ni-em**
- Name from the Latin *Germania*, "Germany"
- Existence predicted by Mendeleyev in 1871; discovered by Clemens Winkler in 1886
- Grayish-white metal

Germanium was one of the first, and is still one of the most popular, elements used in the manufacture of electronic semiconductor devices. There is not much germanium in the earth's crust (only about one part per 10-million), and none of it is found as the metal, itself. Natural germanium is all compounded with other elements, especially oxygen.

The chemical and physical properties of this element are very close to those of ordinary silicon.

Historical background

The existence of germanium was predicted theoretically by Mendeleyev in 1871. He suggested it would resemble silicon, so he gave the undiscovered metal the name *ekasilicon* and suggested the chemical symbol, Es. Furthermore, Mendeleyev predicted Es would have an atomic weight of 72 (atomic weight of Ge is 72.59), and would have a specific gravity of 5.5 (germanium has a specific gravity of 5.32). There were other predictions about Mendeleyev's ekasilicon that fit the specifications for germanium when it was finally found.

The German chemist and inventor, Clemens Alexander Winkler (1838 – 1904), transformed the theoretical existence of ekasilicon into reality. This part of the story begins in the autumn of 1885 when a new ore, later named *argyrodite*, was found in the Himmelsfurst silver mine. When Winkler ran a careful analysis of the new mineral, he repeatedly found 75% silver, 18% sulfur, and 7% of something else that had properties similar to arsenic and antimony. That extra 7%, of course, turned out to be the new element, germanium.

Properties of germanium

Germanium is a semimetal, or metalloid. In other words, it is not a metal such as aluminum, tin or lead; but neither is it a nonmetal such as phosphorus and sulfur. Like a few other elements in its general neighborhood on the periodic table of the elements, germanium is like a metal in some respects, but like a nonmetal in others.

Pure germanium is usually described as a crystal that closely resembles silicon—the world's most important semimetal. It even combines with oxygen to produce germanium dioxide and the analogue of silicon dioxide (which is ordinary beach sand).

Germanium is a good semiconductor when combined with tiny amounts of phosphorus (P), arsenic (As), gallium (Ga), and antimony (Sb). Notice that these elements are all in the same general vicinity as germanium on the periodic table.

Production of germanium

Although germanium is included in minerals such as *germanite* and *argyrodite*, the metal is more economically recovered as a byproduct of commercial zinc refining operations.

With zinc already removed from the ores, germanium is easily separated by dissolving the zinc byproduct in strong hydrochloric acid. This produces a highly volatile gas known as *germanium tetrachloride*. (Also see a description of *germanium(IV) chloride* presented later in this chapter.) A partial reaction showing only the relevant ions looks like this:

$$Ge^{+4} + 4HCl \rightarrow 4H^+ + GeCl_4$$
(germanium + hydrochloric acid → hydrogen + germanium tetrachloride)

The next step in the procedure is to allow the tetrachloride to react with water molecules—H^+ and OH^- ions—to yield *germanium dioxide* (described later in this chapter as *germanium(IV) oxide*). The germanium dioxide is finally reduced with hydrogen gas to produce germanium metal and some water:

$$GeO_2 + 2H_2 \rightarrow Ge + 2H_2O$$
(germanium dioxide + hydrogen → germanium metal + water)

Some compounds and the isotopes of germanium

Germanium has two oxidation states, $+2$ and $+4$, which produce germanium ions Ge^{2+} and Ge^{4+}. The oxides of germanium are germanium monoxide and germanium dioxide, or, to describe them another way:

Germanium(II) oxide, GeO

$$Ge^{2+} + O^{2-} \rightarrow GeO$$

Germanium(IV) oxide, GeO_2

$$Ge^{4+} + 2O^{2-} \rightarrow GeO_2$$

Some other examples of germanium compounds are:

Germanium(II) chloride, $GeCl_2$

$$Ge^{2+} + 2Cl^- \rightarrow GeCl_2$$

Germanium(IV) chloride, $GeCl_4$

$$Ge^{4+} + 4Cl^- \rightarrow GeCl_4$$

Germanium(IV) oxide occurs in most sulfide ores, especially zinc ores. The tetrachloride, $GeCl_4$, is a volatile liquid that is formed by heating germanium metal in the presence of chlorine gas.

Figure 32-1 shows the known isotopes of germanium.

Isotope	Natural Abundance	Half-Life	Decay Mode
^{64}Ge		63 sec	β+, ec
^{65}Ge		31 sec	β+, ec
^{66}Ge		2.27 hr	β+, ec
^{67}Ge		19 min	β+, ec
^{68}Ge		288 day	ec
^{69}Ge		39.1 hr	β+, ec
^{70}Ge	20.5%		
^{71}Ge		11.2 day	ec
^{72}Ge	27.4%		
^{73}Ge	78%		
^{74}Ge	36.5%		
^{75m}Ge		48 sec	i.t.
^{75}Ge		82.8 min	β-, ec
^{76}Ge	7.8%		
^{77m}Ge		53 sec	β-
^{77}Ge		11.3 hr	β-
^{78}Ge		1.45 hr	β-
^{79m}Ge		19 sec	β-
^{79}Ge		42 sec	β-
^{80}Ge		29 sec	β-
^{81m}Ge		7.6 sec	β-
^{81}Ge		7.6 sec	β-
^{82}Ge		4.6 sec	β-
^{83}Ge		1.9 sec	β-

32-1 Germanium has isotopes with atomic weights between 64 and 83.

Element 33: Arsenic

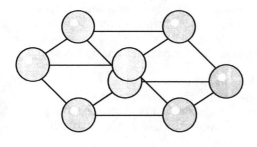

Name	Arsenic
Symbol	As
Atomic Number	33
Atomic Weight	74.9216
Melting Point	817°C (28 atm)
Sublimation Point	613°C
Specific Gravity	5.73 (25°C)
Oxidation States	+3, -3, +5
Electron Config.	(Ar) $3d^{10}\ 4s^2\ 4p^3$

- Name pronounced as **AR-s'n-ik**
- Name from the Latin, *arsenicum*, and Greek, *arsenikon*; both are names for a popular pigment, yellow orpiment
- Possibly first identified by Albertus Magnus in 1250 A.D.
- Steel gray, brittle semimetal
- Popularly known for its highly poisonous compounds

Arsenic and many arsenic compounds are fairly plentiful and useful. Tiny amounts of arsenic are added to gallium, for example, to produce electronic light-emitting diodes (LEDs) and laser diodes. Some compounds of arsenic, called arsenides, are used in the manufacture of paints, wallpapers, and ceramics.

Arsenic is also used as a weed killer and rat poison; of course, more sinister applications are described in the histories of crime. At one time, arsenic (actually arsenious oxide) was a popular poison for the homicidally inclined. Ingesting arsenic in small doses over a period of time, the victim would develop symptoms similar to those of pneumonia, then die without a trace of any known poison in his body. Intentional arsenic poisoning is rare these days, however, because coroners have found techniques for detecting its presence during an autopsy.

Historical background

The earliest history of arsenic and its compounds is obscure. The early Greeks and Romans used slave labor to mine deadly arsenious sulfides, orpiment, and sandarac. Early medieval Greek alchemists and ancient Chinese scholars apparently knew how to prepare and apply certain compounds of arsenic, but it is unlikely we will ever know the person and circumstances of the original discovery. Nevertheless, the honor of discovering the element is often given to German scholar and alchemist Albertus Magnus (1193–1280), who extracted it from a heated mixture of orpiment and soap.

Properties of arsenic

Arsenic is a semimetal, or metalloid element. It isn't quite a metal such as aluminum or tin, and it isn't quite a nonmetal such as sulfur and bromine. It belongs to a fairly small group of semimetals that share the same general area on the periodic table of the elements.

The principal allotrope of arsenic is gray arsenic. This is characterized as a brittle, silvery-gray metal. Two other allotropes, yellow and black arsenic, are unstable crystalline substances that can be produced by first heating, then cooling, gray arsenic. Gray arsenic tends to sublimate rather than go through a molten state. Heating gray arsenic to its sublimation temperature, 613 °C, causes it to generate an arsenic vapor. If you cool this vapor slowly, you will see the black form of arsenic condensing on the sample. As the sample continues to cool and passes through the 360 °C mark, the black arsenic changes back to the gray form.

Cooling gray arsenic rapidly from its sublimation temperature, however, causes yellow arsenic to condense on the sample. Unlike black arsenic, the yellow attotrope does not automatically return to the gray form upon further cooling. The yellow allotrope is stable with respect to changes in temperature but is sensitive to light. Light energy converts yellow arsenic to the stable gray form.

Production of arsenic

Arsenic is most often produced by means of a two-step process. In the first, the sulfide is heated in air to yield the oxide. Then the oxide is heated with carbon to produce carbon dioxide and elemental arsenic.

Step 1:
$$2As_2S_3 + 9O_2 \rightarrow 2As_2O_3 + 6SO_2$$
(arsenic trisulfide + oxygen → arsenic trioxide + sulfur dioxide)

Step 2:
$$As_2O_3 + 3C \rightarrow 3CO + 2As$$
(arsenic trioxide + carbon → carbon dioxide + arsenic)

Some compounds and the isotopes of arsenic

Three arsenic-bearing minerals are *realgar* (arsenic monosulfide, AsS), *orpiment* (arsenic trisulfide, As_2S_3) and *arsenopyrite* (iron arsenosulfide, FeAsS). Realgar has a reddish color, while orpiment is yellow; both are used as paint pigments. Arsenopyrite, often called *mispikel*, is one of the leading commercial sources of arsenic. Elemental arsenic can be obtained from arsenopyrite by heating; the arsenic sublimes and condenses as pure arsenic, leaving behind ferrous sulfide residue.

There are two oxides of arsensic, *arsenic trioxide* (As_3O_3) and *arsenic pentoxide* (As_2O_5). The trioxide is an extremely poisonous, colorless crystal that can be found in nature as *arsenolite* and *claudetite*. It is used mainly as an insecticide and weed killer. The pentoxide is formed by oxidizing the trioxide, and it is applied mostly in the manufacture of other compounds of arsenic.

Figure 33-1 shows the known isotopes of arsenic. All natural arsenic is arsenic-75. The radioactive isotopes are all very unstable; the longest half-life is less than three months.

Isotope	Natural Abundance	Half-Life	Decay Mode
^{67}As		43 sec	β+, ec
^{68}As		2.53 min	β+
^{69}As		15.1 min	β+, ec
^{70}As		52.6 min	β+, ec
^{71}As		62 hr	β+, ec
^{72}As		26 hr	β+
^{73}As		80.3 day	ec
^{74}As		17.8 day	β+, ec
^{75}As	100%		
^{76}As		26.3 hr	β-
^{77}As		38.8 hr	β-
^{78}As		1.15 hr	β-
^{79}As		9 min	β-
^{80}As		16 sec	β-
^{81}As		33 sec	β-
^{82m}As		14 sec	β-
^{82}As		19 sec	β-
^{83}As		13 sec	β-
^{84}As		5.5 sec	β-, n
^{85}As		2.03 sec	β-, n
^{86}As		900 ms	β-, n

33-1 Arsenic has isotopes with atomic weights between 67 and 86.

Element 34: Selenium

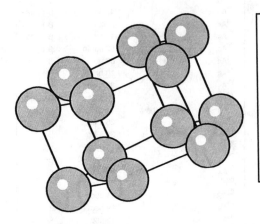

Name	Selenium
Symbol	Se
Atomic Number	34
Atomic Weight	78.96
Melting Point	50° (amorphous form)
	217°C (gray form)
Boiling Point	685°C
Specific Gravity	4.28 (amorphous form)
	4.79 (gray form)
Oxidation States	-2, +4, +6
Electron Config.	(Ar) $3d^{10}\,4s^2\,4p^4$

- Name pronounced as **si-LEE-ni-em**
- Name from the Greek, *selene*, "moon"
- Identified as an element by Jöns Jacob Berzelius in 1818
- A soft metalloid similar to sulfur

The most striking feature of selenium is the degree to which its electrical conductivity increases in response to light shining onto it. The conductivity of pure selenium can increase as much as a thousandfold when a sample is taken from darkness into bright sunlight. This property accounts for the most common applications of the element and its compounds. Selenium can be found in all kinds of light-sensitive devices, from robotic sensors to xerography machines.

Historical background

During the autumn of 1817, Jöns Jacob Berzelius (1779 – 1848) wrote to a colleague concerning the unexpected presence of tellurium in the product of a sulfuric acid factory in Sweden. His account went so far as to describe how this could technically happen—how tellurium could be showing up in that particular acid factory and no other anywhere else.

Nearly a year later, he changed his mind about the nature of the impurity. He found it to be something only similar to tellurium. It was not tellurium. The differences were subtle, but sufficient to arouse the famous chemist's appetite for discovery. A few months later he confirmed the existence of element 34. A few days before making a formal announcement of his discovery, Berzelius identified a mineral that is rich in selenium. He called it *eucairite*, which loosely translates from the Greek as "just in time."

Properties of selenium

Selenium is a soft metalloid, or semimetal. It is quite similar to sulfur in a number of respects, but overall it is more like tellurium. It is difficult to describe the physical appearance of selenium because it can exist in several allotropic forms that range from a gray metallic appearance to a red glassy appearance.

Selenium is in the VIA, or oxygen, group of elements on the periodic table. It is a metalloid, or semimetal. This means it has some characteristics of metals and some of nonmetals.

Some of the most important properties—heat conductivity and density, for example—change dramatically with the allotropic form and only small amounts of impurities.

Production of selenium

Eucairite, CuAgSe, is the only mineral that is rich in selenium; however, it is too thinly distributed to be of any commercial value. Virtually all commercial selenium is recovered from anode slimes in copper refineries and in the sludge that remains after producing sulfuric acid. Selenium is usually found in the company of copper and sulfur, and these two highly profitable operations simply cast off selenium as a byproduct. In fact, the profits from refining copper and making sulfuric acid pay the way for refining selenium. If selenium had to be recovered from its eucairite ore, it would be too costly for the applications it enjoys today.

The impure selenium from these operations is usually the red allotrope. When it is mixed with sulfuric acid, the selenium becomes bound up in molecules of selenious acid and selenic acid, H_2SeO_3 and H_2SeO_4, respectively. These acids are then easily separated from the remaining slime and sludge.

Several other recovery methods use procedures that vary according to the source of the slime of sludge.

Some compounds and the isotopes of selenium

There are relatively few inorganic compounds of selenium, and none has any significant commercial application. Most of the compounds listed here are used for producing other selenium compounds, including a wide variety of organic substances.

The chlorides are *selenium dichloride* ($SeCl_2$) and *selenium tetrachloride* ($SeCl_4$). A *selenium oxychloride* ($SeOCl_2$) is sometimes used as a solvent.

Figure 34-1 shows the known isotopes of selenium. None of the naturally occurring species is radioactive.

Isotope	Natural Abundance	Half-Life	Decay Mode	Isotope	Natural Abundance	Half-Life	Decay Mode
^{69}Se		27.4 sec	β+, ec	^{79}Se		6x10^4 yr	β-
^{70}Se		41.1 min	β+	^{80}Se	49.6%		
^{71}Se		4.7 min	β+, ec	^{81m}Se		57.3 min	β-
^{72}Se		8.4 day	ec	^{81}Se		18.5 min	β-
^{73m}Se			β+, i.t.	^{82}Se	9.4%		
^{73}Se		7.1 hr	β+, ec	^{83m}Se		70 sec	β-
^{74}Se	0.9%			^{83}Se		22.3 min	β-
^{75}Se		118.5 day	ec	^{84}Se		3.3 min	β-
^{76}Se	9%			^{85}Se		32 sec	β-
^{77m}Se		17.4 day	i.t.	^{86}Se		15 sec	β-
^{77}Se	7.6%			^{87}Se		5.6 sec	β-
^{78}Se	23.5%			^{88}Se		1.5 sec	β-, n
^{79m}Se		3.89 min	i.t.	^{89}Se		410 ms	β-, n

34-1 Selenium has isotopes with atomic weights between 69 and 89.

Element 35: Bromine

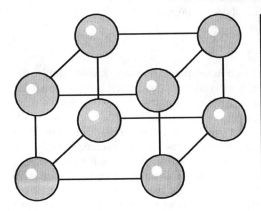

Name	Bromine
Symbol	Br
Atomic Number	35
Atomic Weight	79.904
Melting Point	-7.2°C
Boiling Point	58.78°C
Density	7.59 g/l (gas, 1 atm)
	3.12 g/l (liquid, 20°C)
Oxidation States	+1, -1, +5
Electron Config.	(Ar) $3d^{10}\ 4s^2\ 4p^5$

- Name pronounced as **BRO-meen**
- Name from the Greek *bromos*, "stench"
- Isolated in 1826 by Antoine-Jérôme Balard
- Reddish-brown liquid

Bromine is a reddish-brown, heavy (but watery) liquid that gives off thick, red-brown fumes that have a biting odor similar to chlorine. It is the only nonmetallic element that is in a liquid state at normal room temperatures.

Bromine was once produced in large commercial quantities in order to manufacture a compound that prevented the buildup of lead compounds in automobile engines burning antiknock gasolines. For environmental protection, leaded gasolines have been taken from the consumer marketplace, and the production of bromine has suffered accordingly. However, other applications in dyes, disinfectants, and photographic chemicals manage to maintain a modest market demand for bromine.

Historical background

The historical roots of bromine stretch back to the dawn of civilization and a sea mussel, the straight-spined murex, or *M. brandaris Linne*. The murex secretes a liquid that was made into an expensive purple die known as Tyrian purple. The fact that an organic compound of bromine was the key ingredient was not known until the early 1900s.

In 1825, a freshman chemistry student at Heidelberg walked up to his professor and showed him a container of a red, chlorine-smelling liquid. These days, freshmen bring small refrigerators, portable TVs, teddy bears, and poor posture from home. Young Carl Löwig brought a new chemical element he had concocted at home during his summer break. His professor, Leopold Gmelin didn't know what the smelly liquid was, but he knew it didn't belong to the world of common chemicals. Gmelin asked the student to prepare some more of the liquid so they could begin some thorough testing. Winter exams and the holidays interrupted the student's special project long enough to let another youthful chemist, Antoine-Jérôme Balard, announce his results in a paper presented in early 1826.

Balard gets credit for discovering bromine and he, as is the custom, chose the name for the new element. Löwig and Balard both went on to distinguished careers in chemistry and teaching, but neither managed to discover another element.

Bromine was discovered at a time when analytical procedures were improving at a rapid pace. These improved techniques were actually responsible for the discovery of a great many elements because they allowed chemists to distinguish the various components of a substance more accurately. If your equipment and analytical techniques are only good to an accuracy of 1%, for example, and the bromine content of a chlorine sample is only 0.02%, then you aren't going to detect the presence of the bromine. The new and improved procedures, as exemplified by the discovery of bromine, made it possible to study many new substances that could not be detected before.

Properties of bromine

Bromine is one of the halogens that make up Group-VIIA on the periodic table of the elements. The pure element is a reddish-brown liquid that volatilizes with a thick vapor at room temperature and atmospheric pressure. Bromine is poisonous and can cause severe burns on the skin.

Like the other halogen gasses, bromine is diatomic. That is, its most stable molecular form is Br_2 The bromine ion, Br^-, combines with most metals with nearly the same vigor as chlorine. There is a bromine analogue for just about every compound of fluorine and chlorine.

Production of bromine

Most bromine is obtained almost directly from ordinary seawater and brine mixtures left over from the production of potassium salts. The commercial process takes advantage of the fact that bromine ions (Br^-) in water are easily oxidized by chlorine to yield bromine gas (Br_2):

$$2Br^- + Cl_2 \rightarrow Br_2 + 2Cl^-$$

The process of producing bromine gas begins by treating seawater with chlorine gas at a temperature slightly above the boiling point of bromine. The result is a mixture of bromine and chlorine gasses that separate as soon as you allow the mixture to cool to the point where the bromine liquifies but the chlorine remains a gas.

Where additional refining is necessary, bromine gas is mixed with sulfur dioxide and forced up through a cylinder that has water running down the inside surface. The gasses react with the water to produce hydrobromic and sulfuric acids:

$$SO_2 + Br_2 + H_2O \rightarrow 2HBr + H_2SO_4$$
(sulfur dioxide + bromine + water → hydrobromic acid + sulfuric acid)

Treatment with chlorine once again oxidizes the bromine to release bromine gas. The chlorine is then removed by passing the mixture over wet iron filings.

Small amounts of bromide can be produced by reacting HBr and manganese dioxide:

$$4HBr + MnO_2 \rightarrow MNBr_2 + 2H_2O + Br_2$$
(hydrobromic acid + manganese dioxide → manganese bromide + water + bromine)

Some compounds of bromine

The principal oxidation state of bromine is -1, so it reacts with the alkali metals to produce rather ordinary compounds such as:

Sodium bromide, NaBr

$$Na^+ + Br^- \rightarrow NaBr$$

Potassium bromide, KBr

$$K^+ + Br^- \rightarrow KBr$$

Among the metals having multiple oxidation states, bromine tends to combine with the lowest values. For example:

Nickel(II) bromide, $NiBr_2$

$$Ni^{2-} + 2Br^- \rightarrow NiBr_2$$

Manganese(II) bromide, $MnBr_2$

$$Mn^{2+} + 2Br^- \rightarrow MnBr_2$$

It tends to combine with the nonmetals according to the lowest-valued, positive oxidation state:

Phosphorus(III) bromide, PBr_3

$$P^{3+} + 3Br^- \rightarrow PBr_3$$

Selenium(IV) bromide, $SeBr_4$

$$Se^{4+} + 4Br^- \rightarrow SeBr_4$$

Two of the most common compounds of bromine are hydrobromic acid (HBr) and *silver bromide* (AgBr). Hydrobromic acid is commercially produced by the action of phosphoric acid on one of the alkali bromides:

$$KBr + H_3PO_4 \rightarrow KH_2PO_4 + HBr$$

(potassium bromide + phosphoric acid → potassium orthophosphate + hydrobromic acid)

Silver bromide occurs in nature as the mineral *bromyrite*. It is produced commercially for photographic applications by combining aqueous solutions of a silver salt and a bromide, for example:

$$AgNO_3 + KBr \rightarrow AgBr + KNO_3$$

(silver nitrate + potassium bromide → silver bromide + potassium nitrate)

Isotopes of bromine

Figure 35-1 shows the isotopes of bromine. All naturally occurring bromine is a mixture of bromine-79 and bromine-81. The rest of the isotopes are both man-made and radioactive.

Isotope	Natural Abundance	Half-Life	Decay Mode
^{72}Br		1.31 min	β+
^{73}Br		3.4 min	β+
^{74m}Br		41.5 min	β+
^{74}Br		25.3 min	β+
^{75}Br		98 min	β+, ec
^{76m}Br		1.49 sec	i.t.
^{76}Br		16.1 hr	β+, ec
^{77m}Br		4.3 min	i.t.
^{77}Br		57.0 hr	β+, ec
^{78}Br		6.46 min	β+, ec
^{79m}Br		4.86 sec	i.t.
^{79}Br	50.69%		
^{80m}Br		4.42 hr	i.t.
^{80}Br		17.6 min	β+, ec
^{81}Br	49.31%		
^{82m}Br			β-, i.t.
^{82}Br		35.3 hr	β-
^{83}Br		2.39 hr	β-
^{84m}Br		6 min	β-
^{84}Br		31.8 min	β-
^{85}Br		2.87 min	β-
^{86}Br			β-
^{87}Br		56.1 sec	β-
^{88}Br		16.4 sec	β-, n
^{89}Br		4.4 sec	β-, n
^{90}Br		1.9 sec	β-, n
^{91}Br		540 ms	β-, n
^{92}Br		360 ms	β-, n

35-1 Bromine has isotopes with atomic weights between 72 and 92.

Element 36: Krypton

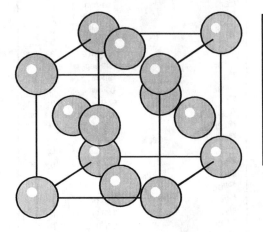

Name	Krypton
Symbol	Kr
Atomic Number	36
Atomic Weight	83.80
Melting Point	-156.6°C
Boiling Point	-152.30°C
Density	3.773 g/l (0°C, 1 atm)
Oxidation State	0
Electron Config.	$1s^2\ 2s^2\ 2p^6\ 3s^2\ 3p^6$ $3d^{10}4s^24p^6$

- Name pronounced as **KRIP-ton**
- Name from the Greek, *kryptos*, "hidden"
- Discovered by Sir William Ramsay and Morris W. Travers in 1898
- Rare noble gas

Any resemblance between the element krypton and Superman's strength-sapping nemesis, kryptonite, is purely coincidental. Maybe the people who thought of the names were thinking of the Greek word for "hidden." Nevertheless, krypton, the element, is a very real atmospheric gas as shown in Fig. 36-1.

Gas (Sea level)	Content by volume	
	(percent)	(ppm)
Nitrogen, N_2	78.09	—
Oxygen, O_2	20.95	—
Argon, Ar	0.93	—
Carbon Dioxide, CO_2	0.03	—
Neon, Ne	—	18.18
Helium, He	—	5.24
Krypton, Kr	—	1.14
Methane, CH_4	—	2
Nitrous oxide, N_2O	—	0.5
Hydrogen, H_2	—	.05
Xenon, Xe	—	.087

36-1 Krypton ranks seventh on the list of gasses in the earth's atmosphere.

The commercial applications of krypton are in lighting products. Some krypton is used as the inert filler-gas in incandescent bulbs; some is used, mixed with argon, in fluorescent lamps. The most important application is in the flashing stroboscopic lamps that outline modern airport runways during hours of darkness.

Historical background

Sir William Ramsay (1852 – 1916), was already recognized as an expert on atmospheric gasses when he and a Ph.D. candidate, Morris W. Travers, started working together on a new problem in 1898. The wide disparity between the atomic weights of helium and argon (approximately 4 and 40, respectively), suggested to Ramsay that they might be members of a new group of elements—a group made up of more gassy elements than the two that were already known. We now know he was putting together the far right-hand column of elements on the periodic table.

They first tried looking for new inert gasses by heating certain minerals. Ramsay had used this technique successfully in the past as part of his work with nitrogen and the discovery of argon. The idea did not work this time, so they turned to their liquid-air machine.

They set up the machine to produce argon, as they had done many times before. This time, however, they were determined to be especially careful about capturing all the cold residues that remained after the liquid helium and argon were drawn off. The experiment was so well-conceived and executed that the two researchers discovered the new noble gas and produced enough of it to determine its density in a single day, May 30, 1898, between lunch and bedtime. Before turning out the lights for the night, they agreed to call it krypton.

Incidentally, the method they used for isolating krypton yielded up neon as well. They didn't see the neon while looking for krypton because it was mixed with the liquified helium and argon they were setting aside. But the story continues: they discovered the neon a few weeks later (*see* Element 10: Neon).

Properties of krypton

Krypton is characterized as a dense, colorless, odorless, and tasteless gas. Its naturally occurring, nonradioactive isotopes are completely harmless to life forms.

The Group-0, noble gasses (now sometimes called Group VIIIA) were thought to be totally inert until 1967. At that time, chemists began finding ways to get these so-called inert elements to combine with others. Today krypton fluoride, KrF_2, is not exactly a common household chemical, but it is a prototype for producing similar compounds of krypton and other noble gasses that are called *clathrates*.

Production of krypton

Krypton is produced today using the same principles as those used for its discovery. The gas is captured and separated for commercial and laboratory applications by fractional distillation of liquid air. Figure 36-2 shows that the critical temperature of krypton is between that of carbon dioxide (CO_2) and oxygen (O_2). A company that produces liquid oxygen, for instance, is going to find krypton among the impurities. The active impurities, carbon dioxide and methane (CH_4), are easy to remove because they are readily absorbed by common materials such as activated charcoal and titanium. Minute amounts of xenon remain in the krypton, but not enough to degrade its commercial applications.

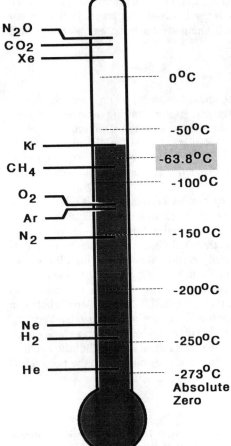

Isotope	Natural Abundance	Half-Life	Decay Mode
^{72}Kr		17 sec	β+, ec
^{73}Kr		27 sec	β+, ec
^{74}Kr		11.5 min	β+, ec
^{75}Kr		4.5 min	β+, ec
^{76}Kr		14.8 hr	ec
^{77}Kr		1.24 hr	β+, ec
^{78}Kr	0.35%		
^{79m}Kr		50 sec	i.t.
^{79}Kr		35.0 hr	β+, ec
^{80}Kr	2.25%		
^{81m}Kr		13.3 sec	i.t.
^{81}Kr		2.1×10^5 yr	ec
^{82}Kr	11.6%		
^{83m}Kr		1.86 hr	i.t.
^{83}Kr	11.5%		
^{84}Kr	57.0%		
^{85m}Kr		4.48 hr	β-
^{85}Kr		10.72 yr	β-
^{86}Kr	17.3%		
^{87}Kr		76.3 min	β-
^{88}Kr		2.84 hr	β-
^{89}Kr		3.16 min	β-
^{90}Kr		32.3 sec	β-
^{91}Kr		8.6 sec	β-
^{92}Kr		1.84 sec	β-, n
^{93}Kr		1.29 sec	β-, n
^{94}Kr		210 ms	β-, n

36-3 Krypton has isotopes with atomic weights between 72 and 94.

36-2 The critical temperature for krypton is above that of oxygen, making it a natural byproduct of commercial gas-liquification operations.

Isotopes of krypton

Figure 36-3 shows the isotopes of krypton. None of the isotopes of naturally occurring krypton is radioactive. The radioactive isotopes of krypton are produced artificially as byproducts of nuclear power plants. Radioactive krypton-85 is used as a low-cost source of radiation for industrial thickness gauges and leak-testing instruments.

Krypton-86 is the basis for the current international definition of a meter. One meter is now defined as 1,650,762.73 wavelengths of the red-orange spectral line of krypton-86.

Element 37: Rubidium

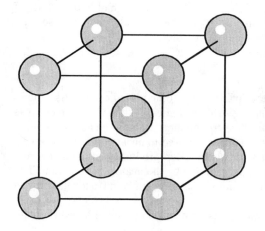

Name	Rubidium
Symbol	Rb
Atomic Number	37
Atomic Weight	85.468
Melting Point	38.89°C
Boiling Point	686°C
Specific Gravity	1.53 (20°C)
Oxidation State	+1
Electron Config.	(Kr) $5s^1$

- Name pronounced as **roo-BID-i-em**
- Name taken from the Latin, *rubidus*, "deep red"
- Discovered by Robert Bunsen and Gustav Kirchhoff in 1861
- Soft, silvery-white, highly reactive metal

Rubidium is one of the few metals that can exist in its liquid form in a natural environment—if you happen to consider 39 °C or 102 °F, a natural environment. You can melt rubidium metal in your hand if you happen to have a fever; and if you are technically inclined, you can substitute the expression, "It's hot enough to fry an egg on the sidewalk" with "It's hot enough to melt rubidium on the sidewalk!" Mercury is the metal having a boiling point low enough to exist in its liquid state at normal room temperatures in the 20 °C, or 68 °F, range.

Applications of rubidium and its compounds are currently limited to the manufacture of vacuum and cathode-ray tubes. Recent discoveries of large deposits of rubidium-bearing minerals place it in 16th place on the abundance list of elements in the earth's crust. As this metal becomes better understood, we can expect to find more applications for it.

Historical background

The story of rubidium begins with the mineral *lepidolite*, a potassium-lithium-aluminum mica. There is also an OH⁻ ion that gives the mineral alkaline properties. During the late 1700s, lepidolite was of special interest to chemists because it exhibited the qualities of potassium hydroxide (KOH)—the substance of vegetable alkali and potash that soon led to the discovery of the alkali metals.

Although lepidolite exists in a number of different formulations, rubidium is not included in any of them. Nevertheless, you might still find significant amounts of other chemicals—especially an alkali metal such as rubidium—accompanying the buckets of lepidolite you might dig from the earth. Chemists had learned this lesson by the middle part of the 1800s, and many were making a habit of looking for new elements among the impurities accompanying samples of known elements.

In 1861, chemistry's dynamic duo of the time, Robert Bunsen and Gustav Kirchhoff, were busy isolating various alkalis from samples of lepidolite. They were putting the samples into their special piece of new equipment called a spectroscope. They were finding the familiar spectral lines for potassium, iron, and lithium. Then, as they had hoped, a set of uncharted spectral lines appeared. The lines had a very distinctive, ruby-red color, so Bunsen and Kirchhoff decided to name their new element rubidium (as in *ruby*).

Properties of rubidium

Rubidium belongs to the family of alkali metals in Group IA of the periodic table. As a member of this group, it is highly reactive, it cannot exist in its elemental state in nature because it reacts with ordinary air and moisture to produce compounds. Rubidium is so reactive, in fact, that it undergoes spontaneous combustion when exposed to air at room temperature, forming a mixture of its oxides. It also reacts violently in water, producing rubidium hydroxide and liberating hydrogen gas that is immediately ignited by the heat of the reaction. The pure metal has to be stored and transported in containers of kerosene or nitrogen gas, or in a vacuum bottle.

Rubidium is a very soft, silvery-white metal. Its compounds produce a yellow-violet color when subjected to a flame test.

Because rubidium was considered a very rare element until recently, its properties are not as well documented as those of the lighter alkali metals.

Production of rubidium

Rubidium has no significant mineral of its own. Rather, it is found as an impurity in other minerals such as lepidolite and pollucite, the primary ores of lithium and cesium, respectively. Most rubidium is thus recovered from the byproducts of lithium-refining operations. These refining operations involve treating lepidolite with hydrochloric acid at a very high temperature. The lithium is removed in the form of lithium chloride (*see* Element 3: Lithium), leaving behind a carbonate sludge that can contain up to 23% rubidium. The remainder of the sludge is mostly potassium carbonate and a small percentage of cesium carbonate. Rubidium and cesium are nearly identical twins as far as their chemical properties are concerned. This means the two can be difficult to separate.

Until recent times, the two could be separated only by lengthy and tedious crystallization processes. Today, however, it is more practical to reduce the carbonates with calcium and then separate the metals by fractional distillation.

Compounds and isotopes of rubidium

The oxidation state for rubidium is $+1$, and the most stable ion is Rb^+. Since this is a highly reactive metal, it can form a fairly large number of compounds; however, not a single one has a notable commercial application. Setting aside economic interests, compounds that use the Rb^+ ion include:

Rubidium chloride, RbCl

$$Rb^+ + Cl^- \rightarrow RbCl$$

Rubidium monoxide, Rb_2O

$$2Rb^+ + O^{2-} \rightarrow Rb_2O$$

Rubidium has a tendency to form double sulfates, or alums:

Rubidium cobalt(II) sulfate, $Rb_2SO_4 \cdot CoSO_4 \cdot 6H_2O$

Rubidium copper sulfate, $Rb_2SO_4 \cdot CuSO_4 \cdot 6H_2O$

Rubidium iron(II) sulfate, $Rb_2SO_4 \cdot FeSO_4 \cdot 6H_2O$

Rubidium magnesium sulfate, $Rb_2SO_4 \cdot MgSO_4 \cdot 6H_2O$

The cobalt compound is a ruby-red crystal, the copper version is white, the iron crystal is deep green, and the magnesium compound is colorless.

A couple of other interesting double-radical compounds are:

Rubidium iron(II) selenate, $Rb_2S_4 \cdot FeSO_4 \cdot 6H_2O$

Rubidium praseodymium nitrate, $Rb_2NO_3 \cdot Pr(NO_3)_3 \cdot 4H_2O$

Figure 37-1 shows that about a quarter of the world's supply of natural rubidium is the radioactive isotope, rubidium-87.

37-1 Rubidium has isotopes with atomic weights between 75 and 98.

Isotope	Natural Abundance	Half-Life	Decay Mode
^{75}Rb		17 sec	β+
^{76}Rb		17 sec	β+
^{77}Rb		3.8 min	β+
^{78m}Rb		5.7 min	β+, ec
^{78}Rb		17.6 min	β+, ec
^{79}Rb		23 min	β+, ec
^{80}Rb		34 sec	β+
^{81m}Rb		32 min	β+, ec
^{81}Rb		4.58 hr	β+, ec
^{82m}Rb		6.47 hr	β+, ec
^{82}Rb		1.27 min	β+, ec
^{83}Rb		86.2 day	ec
^{84m}Rb		20.3 min	i.t.
^{84}Rb		32.9 day	β+, ec
^{85}Rb	72.17%		
^{86m}Rb		1.02 min	i.t.
^{86}Rb		18.63 day	β-
^{87}Rb	27.83%	4.9×10^{10} yr	β-
^{88}Rb		17.7 min	β-
^{89}Rb			
^{90m}Rb		4.28 min	β-
^{90}Rb		2.6 min	β-
^{91}Rb		58.4 sec	β-
^{92}Rb			
^{93}Rb		5.85 sec	β-
^{94}Rb		2.73 sec	β-, n
^{95}Rb		380 ms	β-, n
^{96}Rb		200 ms	β-, n
^{97}Rb		170 ms	β-, n
^{98}Rb		130 ms	β-, n

Element 38: Strontium

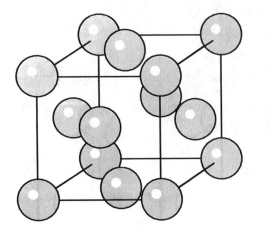

Name	Strontium
Symbol	Sr
Atomic Number	38
Atomic Weight	87.62
Melting Point	769 °C
Boiling Point	1384 °C
Specific Gravity	2.54 (20°C)
Oxidation State	+2
Electron Config.	(Kr) $5s^2$

- Name pronounced as **STRON-she-em**
- Named for the Scottish town, *Strontian*
- Existence noted by Adair Crawford in 1790; isolated by Sir Humphry Davy in 1808
- Silvery, malleable metal

Strontium has two faces, a good face and a bad one. On the positive side, the salts on strontium produce brilliant red flames that are at the heart of many kinds of pyrotechnic devices. On the negative side, the strontium-90 isotope is a deadly and long-lived fallout product of atomic-bomb explosions. Fortunately, the natural isotopes of strontium are not radioactive.

The pure metal cannot be found in nature, but an abundant supply of compounds have been naturally formed by reactions between strontium, atmospheric gasses, and water. Its compounds comprise about .025% of the earth's crust, putting it in the same general category as carbon and sulfur: it is not exactly popping out of the ground wherever you look, but there is plenty to go around.

Historical background

If it were not for the careful eye and experimental technique of one Dr. Adair Crawford (1748 – 1795), strontium may not have been discovered until more recently. It is difficult to say when someone else would have thought about looking for strontium. It was discovered purely by accident when, in 1878, Dr. Crawford began examining samples of the mineral *witherite* (barium carbonate) that had been on display in Scottish museums for a number of years. Mixing the samples with hydrochloric acid, Crawford found that the resulting crystalline substances did not all resemble barium chloride, the expected product of the reaction. He suggested that the samples were contaminated with a theretofore unknown mineral.

Dr. Crawford named his new mineral *strontianite*, indicating that it had originated near the town of Strontian. As other researchers studied strontianite and attempted to sort out its foundational elements, there was a widespread belief that the mineral was a mixture of lime and baryta (oxides of calcium and barium). This error was caused by the fact that tests on strontianite displayed some characteristics of lime and some of baryta.

By 1807, it was clear that strontium was an element in its own right. A year later the venerable Sir Humphry Davy was well into his second season of isolating all kinds of new metallic elements. Strontium was next on his list of successes; this time he inserted the electrodes into a mixture of strontium chloride and mercuric oxide. A strontium amalgam—an alloy of strontium and mercury—formed at the cathode. Heating the amalgam released the mercury as a vapor, leaving behind strontium metal.

Properties of strontium

Strontium is a soft, shiny metal. Like calcium and the other metals on the left-hand side of the periodic table, strontium is an active metal. It has a shiny, silver-gray appearance when it is first cut, but soon tarnishes with a duller, slightly yellow color. This tarnishing effect is due to strontium's reaction with atmospheric gasses, notably oxygen and nitrogen:

$$2Sr + O_2 \rightarrow 2SrO$$
(strontium metal + atmospheric oxygen → strontium oxide)
$$3Sr + N_2 \rightarrow Sr_3N_2$$
(strontium metal + atmospheric nitrogen → strontium nitride)

Both of these compounds are quite effective at preventing further corrosion of the metal. Finely ground strontium, however, burns spontaneously in air.

Strontium readily combines with water, too. In this situation, the reaction yields hydrogen gas and the hydroxide of strontium:

$$Sr + 2H_2O \rightarrow Sr(OH)_2 + H_2$$
(strontium metal + water → strontium hydroxide + hydrogen gas)

Production of strontium metal

Strontium metal is ultimately produced from one of its two most common ores, *celestite* ($SrSO_4$) and *strontianite* ($SrCO_3$). In either case, the ore is treated with hydrochloric acid to yield strontium chloride. The reactions are:

$$SrSO_4 + 2HCl \rightarrow SrCl_2 + H_2SO_4$$
(strontium sulfate + hydrochloric acid → strontium chloride + sulfuric acid)
$$SrCO_3 + 2HCl \rightarrow SrCl_2 + H_2CO_3$$
(strontium carbonate + hydrochloric acid → strontium chloride + carbonic acid)

As shown in Fig. 38-1, strontium chloride is then electrolyzed in a molten state to produce molten strontium metal and chlorine gas. The reactions are:

$$2Cl^- \rightarrow Cl_2 + 2e^- \text{ (anode reaction)}$$
$$Sr^+ + e^- \rightarrow Sr \text{ (cathode reaction)}$$
$$2Sr^+ + 2Cl^- \rightarrow 2Sr + Cl_2 \text{ (cell reaction)}$$

Molten strontium metal gathers around the cathode, while chlorine gas bubbles off at the anode.

The melting temperature of the electrolyte can be dramatically lowered by using a mixture of strontium chloride and potassium chloride (KCl). In this eutectic mixture, the potassium ion is simply a spectator—it takes no part in the reaction. As in any eutectic mixture, the melting point is lower than the melting point of any of the individual compounds.

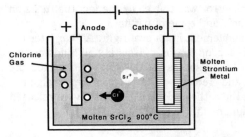

38-1 Strontium can be produced by the electrolysis of its chloride.

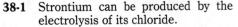

Isotope	Natural Abundance	Half-Life	Decay Mode
^{79}Sr		2.1 min	β+
^{80}Sr		106 min	β+
^{81}Sr		22.2 min	β+, ec
^{82}Sr		25.6 day	ec
^{83m}Sr		5.0 sec	i.t.
^{83}Sr		32.4 hr	β+, ec
^{84}Sr	0.56%		
^{85m}Sr		67.6 min	i.t.
^{85}Sr		64.8 day	ec
^{86}Sr	9.86%		
^{87m}Sr		2.80 hr	i.t.
^{87}Sr			
^{88}Sr	82.58%		
^{89}Sr		50.52 day	β-
^{90}Sr		29 yr	β-
^{91}Sr		9.5 hr	β-
^{92}Sr		2.71 hr	β-
^{93}Sr		7.5 min	β-
^{94}Sr		75 sec	β-
^{95}Sr		25 sec	β-
^{96}Sr		1.06 sec	β-
^{97}Sr		400 ms	β-
^{98}Sr		650 ms	β-

38-2 Strontium has isotopes with atomic weights between 79 and 98.

Strontium metal can also be produced by reducing strontium oxide (SrO) with aluminum metal:

$$3SrO + 2Al \rightarrow 3Sr + Al_2O_3$$
(strontium oxide + aluminum → strontium + aluminum oxide)

Some compounds of strontium

Like the other elements in Group IIA on the periodic table, strontium has a single oxidation state of +2 and ionic formula, Sr^{2+}. This means it combines with oxygen and other anions having an oxidation state of −2 this way:

Strontium oxide, SrO

$$Sr^{2+} + O^2 \rightarrow SrO$$

Strontium sulfate, $SrSO_4$

$$Sr^{2+} + (SO_4)^{2-} \rightarrow Sr\,SO_4$$

It combines with anions having an oxidation state of −1 to form compounds such as:

Strontium chloride, $SrCl_2$

$$Sr^{2+} + 2Cl^- \rightarrow SrCl_2$$

Strontium hydroxide, $Sr(OH)_2$

$$Sr^{2+} + 2(OH)^- \rightarrow Sr(OH)_2$$

Strontium oxide looks and feels much like powdered lime. It is used in the chemical process for producing strontium metal.

Strontium carbonate, $SrCO_3$, is derived directly from the mineral *strontianite*. It is necessary to remove impurities often found in the same area as this mineral. Niobium compounds, nearly always found in samples of strontianite, are especially difficult to remove. This carbonate is used in the manufacture of fireworks, certain kinds of glass, and other strontium compounds.

Strontium nitrate, $Sr(NO_3)_2$, is also responsible for red colors appearing in fireworks, signal flares, and other pyrotechnic devices. It is produced on a commercial scale by reacting strontium carbonate with nitric acid to yield strontium nitrate and carbonic acid:

$$SrCO_3 + 2HNO_3 \rightarrow Sr(NO_3)_2 + H_2CO_3$$
(strontium carbonate + nitric acid → strontium nitrate + carbonic acid)

Isotopes of strontium

Figure 38-2 lists all of the known isotopes of strontium. Several are not radioactive and account for all the strontium that is naturally present on the earth. The remainder of the isotopes are radioactive and man-made.

Strontium-89 and -90 are noteworthy inasmuch as they are common fallout products of atomic-bomb explosions. Strontium-90 is especially deadly because it is a strong beta emitter and has a long half-life. Furthermore, anyone exposed to strontium-90 particles will show a rapid accumulation of the isotope in bone tissue. Because it is so highly radioactive, it interfers with the production of new blood cells and eventually causes death.

Element 39: Yttrium

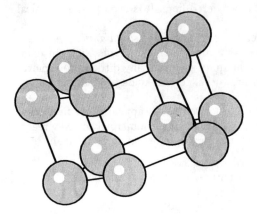

Name	Yttrium
Symbol	Y
Atomic Number	39
Atomic Weight	88.906
Melting Point	1522 °C
Boiling Point	5338 °C
Specific Gravity	4.469 (25°C)
Oxidation State	+3
Electron Config.	(Kr) $4d^1 5s^2$

- Name pronounced as **IT-ri-em**
- Named for the Swedish village, Ytterby
- Discovered by Johan Gadolin in 1789; isolated by Friedrich Wöhler in 1828
- Silvery, ductile, fairly reactive metal

Yttrium is a rare-earth metal that is no longer regarded as a rarity. Figure 39-1 shows that yttrium is one of the most abundant rare-earth elements. The supply meets the commercial demand for its oxide: more than 15 tons per year. The best-known application is as phosphor that produces the brilliant red color available with today's color television tubes.

Apparent similarities between the rare-earth elements have caused a great many headaches for chemists over the years. Such matters are being sorted out, but at least one point of possible confusion remains: do not confuse this element, yttrium, with another rare earth known as ytterbium (atomic number 70).

Historical background

In 1788, Bengt Reinhold Geijer described a new mineral, *gadolinite*, which was found near the Swedish town of Ytterby. He described it as resembling asphalt or coal and suggested that it contained tungsten.

Eleven years later, Johan Gadolin (1760 – 1852) ran a series of studies on the mineral that bears his name (gadolinite), and concluded that it contained 23% silica (silicon dioxide), 4.5% glucina (beryllium oxide), 16.5% iron oxide, 0.5% volatile matter, and 55.5% a new oxide he called yttria.

No one possessed the equipment and know-how to isolate the metal, itself, until Friedrich Wöhler turned the trick in 1828. In this case, he obtained a crude sample of yttrium metal by reducing the chloride with potassium:

$$YCl_3 + K \rightarrow 2KCl + Y$$
(yttrium chloride + potassium → potassium chloride + yttrium)

Rank (Rare Earths)	Rare-Earth Element	Abundance (ppm)
1	Cerium, Ce	46.0
2	Yttrium, Y	28.0
3	Neodymium, Nd	24.0
4	Lanthanum, La	18.0
5	Samarium, Sm	6.5
6	Gadolinium, Gd	6.4
7	Praseodymium, Pr	5.5
8	Scandium, Sc	5.0
9	Dysprosium, Dy	4.5
10	Ytterbium, Yb	2.7
11	Erbium, Er	2.5
12	Holmium, Ho	1.2
13	Europium, Eu	1.1
14	Terbium, Tb	0.9
15	Lutetium, Lu	0.8
16	Thulium, Tm	0.2
17	Promethium, Pm	0.0

39-1 Yttrium is ranked second on the abundance chart for rare earths found in the earth's crust.

Isotope	Natural Abundance	Half-Life	Decay Mode
^{80}Y		36 sec	β+
^{81}Y		72 sec	β+
^{82}Y		9.5 sec	β+
^{83m}Y		2.85 min	β+, ec
^{83}Y		7.1 min	β+, ec
^{84m}Y		4.6 sec	β+, ec
^{84}Y		40 min	β+, ec
^{85m}Y		4.9 hr	β+, ec
^{85}Y		2.6 hr	β+, ec
^{86m}Y		48 min	β+, i.t.
^{86}Y		14.74 hr	β+, ec
^{87m}Y		13 hr	β+, i.t.
^{87}Y		80.3 hr	ec
^{88}Y		106.6 day	β+, ec
^{89m}Y		15.7 sec	i.t.
^{89}Y	100%		
^{90m}Y		3.19 hr	i.t.
^{90}Y		64.0 hr	β-
^{91m}Y		49.7 min	i.t.
^{91}Y		58.5 day	β-
^{92}Y		3.54 hr	β-
^{93m}Y		820 ms	β-
^{93}Y		10.2 hr	β-
^{94}Y		18.7 min	β-
^{95}Y		10.3 min	β-
^{96m}Y		9.8 sec	β-
^{96}Y		6.2 sec	β-
^{97m}Y		1.21 sec	β-
^{97}Y		3.7 sec	β-
^{98m}Y		2.0 sec	β-
^{98}Y		650 ms	β-
^{99}Y		1.5 sec	β-

39-2 Yttrium has isotopes with atomic weights between 80 and 99.

Properties of yttrium

Yttrium is a silvery, ductile metal. Powdered samples burn easily, and thin turnings of the metal from metalworking lathes have been known to ignite spontaneously.

Yttrium is a Group-IIIB element. Among other things, this means it is a fairly active and moderately lightweight rare-earth metal. Some chemists still argue that scandium (Sc) is not a rare-earth element and that yttrium is the first on the table and the lightest of all the rare earths.

Production of yttrium

Most commercial-grade yttrium is obtained from *monazite sand*, a mixture of phosphates of calcium, thorium, cerium, and most of the other rare earths. This sand, in fact, is often 50% rare earth by weight and 3% yttrium. Most of the impurities and other unwanted metals can be removed magnetically or by flotation processes. The difficult step remains, however—separating one rare earth from the other.

Like most rare-earth metals, yttrium can be separated from the others by an ion-exchange displacement process. The result is an yttrium ion which can react with a fluoride or chloride ion to form yttrium fluoride (YF_3) and yttrium chloride (YCl_3).

Yttrium is also produced by reducing yttrium fluoride with calcium metal:

$$3Ca + 2YF_3 \rightarrow 2Y + 3CaF_2$$

(calcium metal + yttrium fluoride → yttrium metal + calcium fluoride)

The same kind of reaction is possible with lithium metal and yttrium chloride:

$$3Li + YCl_3 \rightarrow Y + 3LiCl$$

(lithium metal + yttrium chloride → yttrium metal + lithium chloride)

In either case, the yttrium halide and active metal are loaded into a tantalum crucible and fired in a helium atmosphere. As the reaction progresses, the molten yttrium, halide compound, and excess active metal separate due to differences in density. When this layered mixture is allowed to cool, the yttrium is simply cut away from the impurities. The operation can be repeated as often as necessary to achieve the desired level of purity.

Compounds and isotopes of yttrium

Yttrium has a single oxidation state, $+3$. This means it combines with oxygen to form *yttrium oxide*, Y_2O_3:

$$2Y^{3+} + 3O^{2-} \rightarrow Y_2O_3$$

A couple of yttrium salts are:

Yttrium chloride, YCl_3

$$Y^{3+} + 3Cl^- \rightarrow YCl_3$$

Yttrium sulfate, $Y_2(SO_4)_3$

$$2Y^{3+} + 3(SO_4)^{2-} \rightarrow Y_2(SO_4)_3$$

Yttrium compounds are generally white or colorless. The oxide is characterized as a heavy white powder.

The red phosphor on the face of color television tubes is actually yttrium oxide compounded with another rare-earth metal, europium. A second phosphor is made up of *yttrium orthovanadate*, YVO_4, which is also activated by the addition of europium.

Yttrium garnet is both a gemstone and a tough crystalline material used in solid-state microwave communications equipment. The gemstone garnate is yttrium oxide compounded with iron, $Y_3Fe_5O_{12}$. *Yttrium aluminum garnate*, $Y_2Al_5O_{12}$, is the one used in solid-state microwave devices.

Figure 39-2 on p. 151 lists the isotopes of yttrium. All naturally occurring yttrium is nonradioactive yttrium-89. Some of the artificial, radioactive isotopes have been suggested as convenient sources of radiation for the treatment of cancer.

Element 40: Zirconium

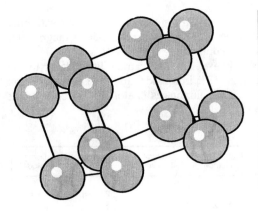

Name	Zirconium
Symbol	Zr
Atomic Number	40
Atomic Weight	91.22
Melting Point	1852°C
Boiling Point	4377°C
Specific Gravity	6.506 (20°C)
Oxidation State	+4
Electron Config.	(Kr) $4d^2\ 5s^2$

- Name pronounced as **zer-KO-ni-em**
- Named for the mineral, *zircon*
- Identified by Martin Heinrich Klaproth in 1789; isolated by Jöns Jacob Berzelius in 1824
- Gray-white, lustrous, corrosion-resistant metal

Zirconium is known in engineering and industry as a tough, corrosion-resistant metal that is suitable for high-technology applications in electronics and nuclear power. It is perhaps more commonly known, however, for the role it plays in the gemstone zircon. There are several varieties of zircon, but the one with the greatest commercial and asthetic value is clear, transparent, and faceted like diamond.

The element, zirconium, was discovered among ordinary, nongem samples of zircon, $ZrSiO_4$. The modern commercial process for producing zirconium begins with this same mineral.

The properties of zirconium are remarkably similar to those of hafnium, and chemists generally agree that there are no other pairs of chemical elements that are so much alike. On the positive side, this means just about everything known about the more abundant zirconium applies more or less equally to hafnium. On the other hand, it is virtually impossible to obtain samples of one that are not contaminated by traces of the other. Zirconium and hafnium are adjacent to one another vertically in Group IVB. For more information about hafnium, the twin element of zirconium, *see* Element 72: Hafnium.

Historical background

Zirconium minerals have been known since ancient times, but more so by their older names, *jargon, jacinth*, and *hyacinth*. Jacinth, for example, is mentioned three times in the Bible. No one suspected that these minerals might contain an undiscovered chemical element until Martin Heinrich Klaproth (1743 – 1817) took a good look at the mineral during the closing years of the 1700s.

Good science is often a matter of knowing what to look for and how to go about looking for it. Most experiments fail on one of these points. Klaproth's success at identifying zirconium as a new element followed on the heels of reports of other researchers who failed at the same effort.

Some reported that jargon contained mostly silica with mere traces of magnesia, lime, and iron. Silica is better known today as silicon dioxide, SiO_2, and magnesia as magnesium oxide, MgO. Both are among the more abundant compounds in the earth's crust.

Another researcher, hiring students to do his experiments, came a little closer to the true analysis of jargon: 25% silican, 40% alumina, 13% iron oxide, and 20% lime. Alumina is now known as aluminum oxide, Al_2O_3; like silica, alumina is one of the more abundant compounds on earth. (See Fig. 40-1.)

Compound	Weight (ppm)
Silica (silicon dioxide), SiO_2	428,600
Magnesium oxide, MgO	350,700
Iron oxide (ferrous oxide), FeO	89,700
Alumina (aluminum oxide), Al_2O_3	69,900
Lime (calcium Oxide), CaO	43,700
Sodium oxide, Na_2O	4500
Ferric oxide, Fe_2O_3	3600
Titanium dioxide, TiO_2	3300
Chromic oxide, Cr_2O_3	1800
Manganese oxide, MnO	1400

40-1 Compounds once commonly confused with zirconium are among the ten most abundant compounds in the earth's crust.

Isotope	Natural Abundance	Half-Life	Decay Mode
^{82}Zr		2.5 min	$\beta+$
^{83m}Zr		8 sec	$\beta+$
^{83}Zr		44 sec	$\beta+$
^{84}Zr		28 min	$\beta+$, ec
^{85m}Zr		10.9 sec	$\beta+$, i.t.
^{85}Zr		7.9 min	$\beta+$, ec
^{86}Zr		16.5 hr	ec
^{87m}Zr		14.0 sec	i.t.
^{87}Zr		1.73 hr	$\beta+$, ec
^{88}Zr		83.4 day	ec
^{89m}Zr		4.18 min	$\beta+$, i.t.
^{89}Zr		78.4 hr	$\beta+$, ec
^{90m}Zr		809 ms	i.t.
^{90}Zr	51.45%		
^{91}Zr	11.27%		
^{92}Zr	17.17%		
^{93}Zr		1.5×10^6 yr	$\beta-$
^{94}Zr	17.33%		
^{95}Zr		64.03 day	$\beta-$
^{96}Zr	2.78%		
^{97}Zr		16.8 hr	$\beta-$
^{98}Zr		30.7 sec	$\beta-$
^{99}Zr		2.1 sec	$\beta-$
^{100}Zr		7.1 sec	$\beta-$
^{101}Zr		2.0 sec	$\beta-$

40-2 Zirconium has isotopes with atomic weights between 82 and 101.

Knowing what to look for and knowing exactly how to go about it, Herr Klaproth ran his own analysis on the very same specimen the chemistry students used. In 1789, he announced the results of his work: 25% silica, 5% iron oxide, and 70% zirconia. The students had hit the silica analysis right, but they confused alumina and lime with Klaproth's new element, zirconia (later named *zirconium*).

The odd thing about the man—one Torbern Bergman—who hired students to do his research is that he pulled the same trick less than ten years later with beryllium, with the same result: the students fouled up the analysis and Herr Klaproth did the job properly.

Properties of zirconium

Zirconium reacts with the oxygen and nitrogen in the atmosphere to form a protective film that prevents further corrosion of the metal. This is not to say that zirconium is a metal that is prone to destruction by natural elements, though. On the contrary, zirconium, even without its protective film of oxide or nitride, is resistant to weak acids. It is, in fact, known in industry as a tough, corrosion-resistant metal that is suitable for use in high-performance pumps and valves.

Zirconium becomes superconductive when alloyed with niobium.

Laboratory and commercial production of zirconium

Laboratory quantities of pure zirconium metal are produced by vaporizing zirconium tetraiodide (ZrI_4) on a hot wire in a vacuum.

Commercial quantities of zirconium are produced by the Kroll process, which begins with either of two natural minerals that are commonly found in ordinary beach sand; *zircon* ($ZrSiO_4$) and *baddeleyite* (ZrO_2). The temperature of the ore is raised to a red-hot level, then treated with hot chlorine gas and a carbon catalyst. The result is a vapor that is rich in zirconium tetrachloride. As the temperature falls, the process of fractional distillation of the vapors separates them and yields a fairly pure version of the chloride, $ZrCl_4$. The chloride is then reduced with molten magnesium metal to produce a sponge of zirconium metal. Impurities such as magnesium chloride and excess magnesium metal are vaporized and burned away by raising the temperature to about 1000 °C.

Some compounds and isotopes of zirconium

Zirconium is listed as having a single oxidation state of $+4$, although there are a few compounds that indicate oxidation states of $+2$ and $+3$ as well. The only oxide, for example, is ZrO_2:

$$Zr^{4+} + 2O^{2-} \rightarrow ZrO_2$$

There are three chlorides, which suggests the existence of the two lower oxidation states:

$$Zr^{2+} + 2Cl^- \rightarrow ZrCl_2, \text{ zirconium dichloride}$$

$$Zr^{3+} + 3Cl^- \rightarrow ZrCl_3, \text{ zirconium trichloride}$$

$$Zr^{4+} + 4Cl^- \rightarrow ZrCl_4, \text{ zirconium tetrachloride}$$

Zirconium oxide, ZrO_2, forms as a natural barrier against further corrosion as a sample of zirconium metal reacts with atmospheric oxygen. This same oxide is found in nature as the mineral *baddeleyite*—an alternative zirconium ore.

Zirconium nitride (ZrN) occurs naturally as zirconium metal reacts with atmospheric nitrogen to produce a film that prevents further corrosion. The compound is commercially produced by heating zirconium in an atmosphere of nitrogen gas.

Zirconium tetrachloride ($ZrCl_4$) and *zirconium tetraiodide* (ZrI_4) are both produced by heating zirconium or a zirconium ore in an atmosphere of the corresponding halogen gas. Consider the reaction involved in obtaining zirconium tetrachloride from zircon, for example:

$$ZrSiO_4 + 2Cl_2 \rightarrow ZrCl_4 + SiO_2 + O_2$$
(zircon + chlorine gas → zirconium tetrachloride + silicon dioxide + oxygen)

Also consider the reaction for zirconium tetraiodide from baddelyite, or zirconium dioxide:

$$ZrO_2 + 2I_2 \rightarrow ZrI_4 + O_2$$
(baddelyite + iodine vapor → zirconium tetraiodide + oxygen)

Zirconium hydroxide, $Zr(OH)_4$, is a white amorphous powder that is usually formed by the reaction of a zirconium salt with an alkali hydroxide. By way of an example, consider a reaction between zirconium tetrachloride and sodium hydroxide:

$$ZrCl_4 + 4NaOH \rightarrow Zr(OH)_4 + 4NaCl$$
(zirconium tetrachloride + sodium hydroxide → zirconium hydroxide + sodium chloride)

Look for basic *zirconium carbonate*, $3ZrO_2 \cdot CO_2 \cdot H_2O$, in poison ivy lotions.

Figure 40-2 on p. 155 shows the isotopes of zirconium. Most of the naturally occurring zirconium is in the form of zirconium-90. All natural zirconium is stable, or nonradioactive.

There are no significant commercial or laboratory applications of radioactive zirconium.

Element 41: Niobium

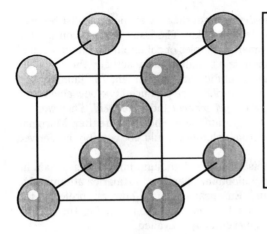

Name	Niobium
Symbol	Nb
Atomic Number	41
Atomic Weight	92.906
Melting Point	2468°C
Boiling Point	4742°C
Specific Gravity	8.57 (20°C)
Oxidation States	+3, +5
Electron Config.	(Kr) $4d^4\ 5s^1$

- Name pronounced as **ni-OH-bee-em**
- Named after *Niobe*, the mythological daughter of Tantalus
- Discovered by Charles Hatchett in 1801
- Also known as *columbium*
- Shiny white, soft, ductile metal

Not many people have heard of niobium, and some prefer to call it *columbium*. It was discoverd in a museum and mistaken for a compound of chromium. Later it was determined to be tantalum, and not an element at all. If niobium were a person, we might say he or she would suffer from a serious problem with personal identity.

Niobium exists in the earth's crust in proportions of about 20 parts-per-million. Nowadays it is commercially refined and used as an alloy with iron and nickel. It can be used in atomic reactors and it is known to be superconductive when alloyed with tin or aluminum.

Historical background

The historical account of the discovery of niobium is not a straightforward one, and there are still some details missing from the puzzle. There can be no doubt, however, that the story begins in the opening years of the 18th century when one Mr. Winthrop of Massachusetts discovered a new mineral near one of the iron mines of New England. Mr. Winthrop named his mineral *columbite*, and sent a sample to the British Museum in London. The date that the British Museum received the sample of columbite is unclear, but there is a reference to the shipment in a journal dated June 27, 1734.

In any event, Charles Hatchett (1765 – 1847), came across the sample while browsing through the museum's mineral collection. He was attracted to it because it looked much like a sample of Siberian chromate of iron he was studying at the time. He probably thought it would indeed be interesting to verify that the chromate mineral existed in America as well as Russia.

Hatchett's preliminary analyses, however, proved the American sample was not a chromate at all, but rather the oxide of an unknown element. He was unable to isolate the new metal from its oxide; but in 1801 he was awarded the privilege of naming the element. His choice was *columbium*.

Obviously the book was not closed on the discovery of the new element in 1801 because columbium is not recognized as a chemical element today. The issue became confused in 1809 when a Dr. William Hyde Wollaston compared samples of columbite and tantalite, and concluded that their basic elements, columbium and tantalum, were actually the same element. Tantalum survived this error, but columbium did not (*See* Element 73: Tantalum.)

The story is picked up again in 1846 when Heinrich Rose produced two new acids from samples of columbite and tantalite. He called them *pelopic acid* and *niobic acid*. They were so similar, however, that he found it impossible to separate them. Shortly thereafter, Marignac separated the acids and proved that the acid from columbite could not possibly be derived from tantalum.

Heinrich Rose did not realize he was rediscovering columbium, but he was certain he was looking at a new element which he named niobium. Chemists in America attempted to resurrect Hatchett's original name, columbium. European chemists, however, preferred the newer name. And since European scientific publications were commanding the greater amount of respect in those days, the new name eventually prevailed.

Properties of niobium

Although it looks much like steel, pure niobium is soft and ductile. It resists corrosion at room temperature, presumably because of a thin film of niobium oxide that forms on all surfaces of the samples. The only acid that attacks niobium at room temperature is hydrofluoric acid. The metal becomes much more active at temperatures above 200 °C. Niobium alloys quite well with iron and nickel to enhance the stability of these metals during welding operations. Alloys of niobium-tin and niobium-aluminum are superconductive.

Niobium is a Group-VB, vanadium-type element. Niobium's chemical and physical properties are nearly identical to those of tantalum—the element appearing directly below niobium on the periodic table of the elements.

Production of niobium

Niobium occurs naturally in *columbite* and *pyrochlor*. The problem is that tantalum ores are usually mixed with the niobium ores; these two elements are so similar that they can be difficult to separate. The processes for refining these nearly identical elements usually begin by dissolving them out of the other impurities with hydrofluoric acid. This produces fluorides of the two elements which are, quite fortunately, easy to separate by fractional crystallization. At this point in the refining operation, we have a niobium fluoride in one vat and a tantalum fluoride in another. Niobium metal is then produced by the electrolysis of molten niobium potassium fluoride, K_2NbF_7.

Some compounds of niobium

There are few natural compounds of niobium, but they have no significant commercial value. Niobium is far more useful in its elemental form and when alloyed with other metals. Some compounds are worth noting, however.

Heating niobium in atmospheres of oxygen and halogen gasses produces pentavalent (oxidation-state 5) compounds:

$$2Nb + 5O_2 \rightarrow 2Nb_2O_5$$
(niobium + oxygen → niobium pentoxide)

$$Nb + 5Cl \rightarrow NbCl_5$$
(niobium + chlorine gas → niobium pentachloride)

$$Nb + 5F \rightarrow NbF_5$$
(niobium + fluorine gas → niobium pentafluoride)

Chemical engineers and applications-minded chemists might be content with pentavalent compounds of niobium, but the theory guys do not have to be content with the situation. Consider oxygen compounds for example. The laboratory and theory chemists want to find ways to create niobium oxides made up of one, two, or three oxygen atoms instead of the Nb_2O_5 formulation of the garden variety oxide. Such people rarely care whether or not their work has any direct practical application. They are more interested in taking on the challenge and, perhaps, making a contribution to human knowledge. So efforts to produce lower-valence oxides of niobium paid off for the theory guys—paid off with new compounds but confusing names and formulae.

Niobium monoxide, for example, would have the formula, NbO, and the niobium would have an oxidation state of $+2$. It turned out that the molecule was somewhat bigger, and the formula was found to be Nb_2O_2. The original name was no longer technically correct, so it was changed to niobium dioxide.

But then there should be a niobium dioxide, NbO_2, where the niobium has an oxidation state of 4. In order to avoid confusion with oxidation-state 2 oxides, the name and formula were changed to niobium tetroxide, Nb_2O_4.

Another way around such points of confusion is to show the oxidation state in the name of the compound—to use the Stock convention for naming them. Niobium dioxide, for example, can take the form of niobium(II) dioxide or niobium(IV) dioxide. The Roman numerals in parentheses indicate the oxidation state of the niobium.

Isotopes of niobium

Figure 41-1 on the next page shows all the known isotopes of niobium. Niobium-93 accounts for all the elements that occur in nature. The other isotopes are quite rare, being radioactive and artificially produced.

Isotope	Natural Abundance	Half-Life	Decay Mode
^{86}Nb		1.45 min	β+
^{87m}Nb		3.7 min	β+, ec
^{87}Nb		2.6 min	β+, ec
^{88m}Nb		7.8 min	β+, ec
^{88}Nb		14.3 min	β+, ec
^{89m}Nb		122 min	β+, ec
^{89}Nb		66 min	β+, ec
^{90m}Nb		18.8 sec	i.t.
^{90}Nb		14.6 hr	β+, ec
^{91m}Nb		62 day	ec, i.t.
^{91}Nb		700 yr	
^{92m}Nb		10.13 day	ec
^{92}Nb		3×10^7 yr	ec
^{93m}Nb		13.6 yr	i.t.
^{93}Nb	100%		
^{94m}Nb		6.26 min	β-, i.t.
^{94}Nb		2.4×10^4 yr	β-
^{95m}Nb		3.61 day	β-, i.t.
^{95}Nb		34.98 day	β-
^{96}Nb		23.4 hr	β-
^{97m}Nb		54 serc	i.t.
^{97}Nb		73.6 min	β-
^{98m}Nb		51 min	β-
^{98}Nb		2.8 sec	β-
^{99m}Nb		2.6 min	β-, i.t
^{99}Nb		15 sec	β-
^{100m}Nb		1.5 sec	β-
^{100}Nb		3.1 sec	β-.
^{101}Nb		7.1 sec	β-
^{102m}Nb		1.3 sec	β-
^{102}Nb		4.3 sec	β-
^{103}Nb		1.5 sec	β-

41-1 Niobium has isotopes with atomic weights between 86 and 103.

Element 42: Molybdenum

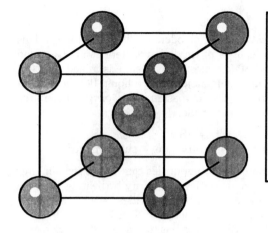

Name	Molybdenum
Symbol	Mo
Atomic Number	42
Atomic Weight	95.94
Melting Point	2617°C
Boiling Point	4612°C
Specific Gravity	10.22 (20°C)
Oxidation State	+6
Electron Config.	(Kr) $4d^5\ 5s^1$

- Name pronounced as **meh-LIB-deh-nem**
- Name taken from the Greek, *molybdos*, "lead"
- Identified as a new element by Carl Welhelm Scheele in 1778
- Silvery white, hard metal

During World War II, the German army constructed a giant piece of artillery that was moved about as desired on a railroad car. The Allies called the gun Big Bertha, and soon discovered that the special formulation for the gun steel included molybdenum—a metal that previously had no practical application. Now we know "moly steel" as another important technological advance brought about by modern warfare.

Historical background

In the winter of 1777, Carl Welhelm Scheele (1742–1786) was writing to the most famous mineralogists and chemists of his time, seeking samples of a mineral known at the time as *molybdaena* (now known as *molybdenite*). Although molybdenum has little in common with lead, certain compounds of the two were often confused before Scheele started his experiments.

In 1778, Scheele announced to the Royal Academy that the Molybdaena he borrowed from his contemporaries was not a special kind of lead ore, as was commonly believed, but the sulfide of an unknown metal. His claim rested mainly on his successful production of molybdic acid, $H_2MoO_2 \cdot H_2O$.

As was the custom of that time, Scheele named his new element after the mineral that lead to its discovery. He could not isolate the element. That task was left to a friend, Peter Jacob Hjelm, who managed to produce samples of the pure metal in 1781.

Properties of molybdenum

Molybdenum can be described as a hard, silver-white metal, but it is more often produced, stored, and used as a gray, powdery substance. Chemically it resembles a cross between chromium (Cr) and tungsten (W)—elements appearing directly above and below molybdenum on the periodic table of the elements.

Production of molybdenum

The primary ore for molybdenum is *molybdenite*, or molybdenum disulfide (MoS_2). This mineral is commonly associated with vein deposits of tin and tungsten. It is also found around cerain kinds of granite. In the United States, most molybdenite is mined near Climax, Colorado. The mineral is first ground and then subjected to a liquid-flotation procedure that separates common impurities. If the "pulp" is roasted in air, oxygen enters the reaction to yield molybdenum trioxide and sulfur monoxide:

$$2MoS_2 + 5O_2 \rightarrow 2MoO_3 + 4SO$$
(molybdenum disulfide + oxygen → molybdenum trioxide + sulfur monoxide)

Molybdenum trioxide is quite volatile compared to impurities that might remain after this roasting operation, so it is easily raised to a higher level of purity by heating until the MoO_3 vaporizes. The vapors are easily lead away from the impurities; when cooled, the vapors condense to produce crystalline MoO_3 having purities of 99% or better.

The trioxide is finally reduced with carbon or hydrogen gas to produce the pure metal. Using carbon as the reducing agent, the reaction is:

$$2MoO_3 + 3C \rightarrow 2Mo + 3CO_2$$
(molybdenum trioxide + carbon + heat → molybdenum metal + carbon dioxide)

Using hydrogen gas as the reducing agent, the reaction is:

$$MoO_3 + 3H_2 \rightarrow Mo + 3H_2O$$
(molybdenum trioxide + hydrogen gas + heat → molybdenum metal + water vapor)

Some compounds and the isotopes of molybdenum

The principal oxidation state of molybdenum is +6, although some of the ionic compounds suggest lower oxidation states. The principal ion, Mo^{6+} appears in compounds such as:

Molybdenum hexafluoride, MoF_6

$$Mo^{6+} + 6F^- \rightarrow MoF_6$$

Molybdenum phosphide, MoP_2

$$Mo^{6+} + 2P^{3-} \rightarrow MoP_2$$

The most common compound having the Mo^{6+} ion, however, is the molybdenum trioxide, MoO_3, described earlier in this section.

The following examples illustrate the presence of molybdenum ions having lower oxidation states:

Molybdenum(II) chloride, $MoCl_2$

$$Mo^{2+} + 2Cl^- \rightarrow MoCl_2$$

Molybdenum(III) chloride, $MoCl_3$

$$Mo^{3+} + 3Cl^- \rightarrow MoCl_3$$

Molybdenum(IV) chloride, $MoCl_4$

$$Mo^{4+} + 4Cl^- \rightarrow MoCl_4$$

Molybdenum readily forms several acids, the simplest of which is *molybdic acid*, H_2MoO_4.

Figure 42-1 lists the isotopes of molybdenum. You can see that natural molybdenum is a mixture of seven different isotopes. The remaining isotopes are radioactive and artificially produced.

Isotope	Natural Abundance	Half-Life	Decay Mode
^{88}Mo		8.0 min	β+, ec
^{89m}Mo		190 ms	i.t.
^{89}Mo		2.2 min	β+, ec
^{90}Mo		5.67 hr	β+, ec
^{91m}Mo		65 sec	β+, ec
^{91}Mo		15.5 min	β+, ec
^{92}Mo	14.84%		
^{93m}Mo		6.9 hr	i.t.
^{93}Mo		3.5×10^3 yr	β-
^{94}Mo	9.25%		
^{95}Mo	15.92%		
^{96}Mo	16.68%		
^{97}Mo	9.55%		
^{98}Mo	24.13%		
^{99}Mo		65.94 hr	β-
^{100}Mo	9.63%		
^{101}Mo		14.6 min	β-
^{102}Mo		11.2 min	β-
^{103}Mo		68 sec	β-
^{104}Mo		60 sec	β-
^{105m}Mo		30 sec	β-.
^{105}Mo		50 sec	β-
^{106}Mo		8.4 sec	β-

42-1 Molybdenum has isotopes with atomic weights between 88 and 106.

Element 43: Technetium

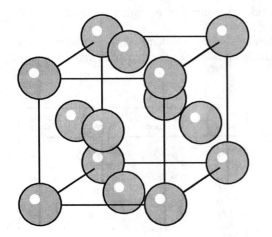

Name	Technetium
Symbol	Tc
Atomic Number	43
Atomic Weight	98 Note
Melting Point	2172°C
Boiling Point	4877°C
Specific Gravity	11.50 (20°C)
Oxidation States	+4, +6, +7
Electron Config.	(Kr) $4d^5\,5s^2$

Note: Most stable isotope.

- Name pronounced as **tek-NEE-shi-em**
- Name taken from the Greek, *technetos*, "artificial"
- Discovered by E.G. Segrè and C. Perrier in 1937
- First synthetically produced element

Technetium is a corrosion-resistant metal. There is nothing unusual about that; many of the transition elements are corrosion-resistant metals. Technetium is unusual in a couple of other aspects, however. First, technetium is quite unusual because it is one of the very few artificially produced elements that has a practical industrial application. Second, technetium is unusual inasmuch as portions as small as 55 part-per-million can transform iron into a corrosion-resistant alloy.

Historical background

By 1934, it was evident that neutron bombardment would help fill gaps in the periodic table for elements 43, 61, 85, and 87. Knowing that something is supposed to exist, and having at least a few notions about its nature, goes a long way toward finding it. A lot of people went looking for element 43, known in Mendeleyevian terminology as ekamanganese.

Between 1934 and 1937, there were dozens of claims of discovery; and among the claims were suggested names such as davyum, illmenium, lucium, and nipponium. None of these claims could be clearly substantiated according to the international standards of the time.

In December, 1936, Italian chemists Emilio Gino Segrè (1905 –) and C. Perrier studied a sample of molybdenum that had been bombarded with deuterons in a cyclotron. The sample was highly radioactive, moreso than one would suspect if it were an isotope of niobium, zirconium, or molybdenum. However, the sample did appear to contain traces of manganese and rhenium—elements found directly above and below element 43 on the periodic table. Could this be element 43? The evidence was becoming more compelling. The biggest difficulty facing Segrè and Perrier was that they had to work with a microscopic, unweighably small sample. The researchers estimated the sample weighed only about 10^{-1}gm. But that was enough.

In 1936, the claims of Segrè and Perrier were accepted by the scientific community, and technetium became a new element. It was also the first synthetically produced element, and there was some controversy about whether or not synthetic elements belonged on the official periodic table of elements. The arguments were not settled until 1947 when the fallout from secret World War II atomic research suddenly brought to light a dozen new, artificially produced, heavy elements. Today all elements, synthetic or otherwise, are regarded together as building blocks of matter.

Properties of technetium

Technetium is a silvery-gray metal that would look much like platinum if it were ever produced in that form. It is normally produced, stored, and used in a powdered form.

Chemically, it resembles a cross between manganese and rhenium. Technetium is located directly below manganese (Mn) and directly above rhenium (Re) on the periodic table of the elements. This is not an uncommon phenomenon throughout the middle part of the periodic table, where an element will resemble its fellow group members.

Production of technetium

Technetium was not only the first artificially produced element, but also the first to have a viable industrial application. The element was originally produced by bombarding molybdenum-96 with deuterons to yield technetium-97:

$$^{96}Mo(d,n)^{97}Tc$$

Technetium is now produced in kilogram quantities as Tc-99. This process requires bombarding molybdenum-98 with neutrons:

$$^{98}Mo(n, \gamma)^{99}Mo \rightarrow {}^{99}Tc + \beta -$$

Some compounds and the isotopes of technetium

Very few compounds of technetium have been studied. The oxidation states are $+4$, $+6$, and $+7$.

The main oxide, produced by heating technetium in an oxygen-rich atmosphere, is Tc_2O_7. This compound suggests the existence of the Tc^{7+} ion:

$$2Tc^{7+} + 7O^{2-} \rightarrow Tc_2O_7$$

The simpler, Stock-convention name for this oxide is *technetium(VII) oxide*, although you might call it ditechnetium septoxide whenever you want to impress someone with the extent of your knowledge.

A lesser oxide, TcO_2 (*technetium dioxide*, or *technetium(IV) oxide*), uses a Tc^{4+} ion:

$$Tc^{4+} + 2O^{2-} \rightarrow TcO_2$$

Here is an example of a Tc^{6+} compound:

Technetium(VI) chloride, $TcCl_6$

$$Tc^{6+} + 6Cl^- \rightarrow TcCl_6$$

Other compounds that have been prepared for experimental purposes include *potassium technetate(VII)*, $KTcO_4$ and *technetium(IV) sulfide*, TcS_2.

Figure 43-1 shows all of the known isotopes of technetium. All are artificial and radioactive.

Isotope	Natural Abundance	Half-Life	Decay Mode
^{90}Tc		49.2 sec	β+
^{91m}Tc		8.3 sec	β+, ec
^{91}Tc		3.3 min	β+, ec
^{92}Tc		4.4 min	β+, ec
^{93m}Tc		43 min	ec, i.t.
^{93}Tc		2.83 hr	β+, ec
^{94m}Tc		52 min	β+, ec
^{94}Tc		4.88 hr	β+, ec
^{95m}Tc		61 day	ec, i.t.
^{95}Tc		20.0 hr	ec
^{96m}Tc		52 min	β+, i.t.
^{96}Tc		4.3 day	ec
^{97m}Tc		90 day	i.t.
^{97}Tc		2.6×10^6 yr	ec
^{98}Tc		4.2×10^6 yr	β-
^{99m}Tc		6.01 hr	i.t.
^{99}Tc		2.13×10^5 yr	β-
^{100}Tc		15.8 sec	β-
^{101}Tc		14.2 min	β-
^{102m}Tc		4.4 min	β-, i.t.
^{102}Tc		5.3 sec	β-
^{103}Tc		54 sec	β-
^{104}Tc		18.3 min	β-
^{105}Tc		7.6 min	β-
^{106}Tc		36 sec	β-
^{107}Tc		21.2 sec	β-
^{108}Tc		5.0 sec	β-

43-1 Technetium has isotopes with atomic weights between 90 and 108.

Element 44: Ruthenium

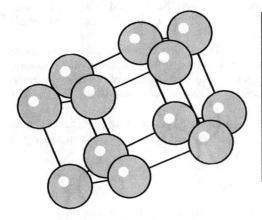

Name	Ruthenium
Symbol	Ru
Atomic Number	44
Atomic Weight	101.07
Melting Point	2310°C
Boiling Point	3900°C
Specific Gravity	12.45 (20°C)
Oxidation State	+3
Electron Config	(Kr) $4d^7\ 5s^1$

- Name pronounced as **roo-THE-ni-em**
- Name taken from the Latin *Ruthenia*, "Russia"
- Existence predicted by G. Wilhelm Osann in 1828; isolated by Karl Karlovich Klaus in 1844
- Rare, silver-gray, extremely brittle metal

Ruthenium is found among a family of elements including iridium and osmium, that are commonly found in platinum ores. The quantities of ruthenium in these ores rarely exceeds 2%, and is usually much lower. Ruthenium is thus a common byproduct of the refiner process for platinum. Although pure platinum is readily refined from its ores (*see* Element 78: Platinum), sorting ruthenium from the residue is a relatively difficult task.

The only commercial application for the metal is as an alloying agent for hardening platinum and palladium to be used in fine jewelry.

Historical background

Element 44 was first isolated by Jedrzej Sniadecki (1768 – 1838) in 1807. He authored several papers and a book about his new element and his procedures for isolating it. Because he was relatively unknown in the scientific community, his claims were not immediately accepted by the Paris commission. The members of that commission, in fact, were unable to find the new element among ores of platinum as Sniadecki described.

Rather than suggesting the panel of big shots in Paris were not doing their job right, this undistinguished Polish professor quietly withdrew his claims. In big-time science, withdrawing a claim is tantamount to saying nothing had ever happened.

Sniadecki had named his new element *vestium*, in recognition of the recent discovery of the planet Vesta (which was later determined to be nothing more than a big asteroid).

More than two decades later, evidence for element 44 was found among the residues that result from scorching platinum ores with aqua regia. This time, the work was being done by some of the real scientific heavyweights of the era—names such as Berzelius Wollaston, and Tennant. Two newcomers were involved, G.W. Osann and Karl Klaus; unlike Professor Sniadecki, these two were linked up with the good-ol'-boy network.

When Gottfried Wilhelm Osann claimed he found three new elements in his platinum samples; pluranium, ruthenium, and polinium; the scientific community eagerly anticipated the meager evidence required for placing them onto the periodic chart. The year was 1828. Nothing more happened that year. A few more years passed. No one said Osann was wrong, but no one was proving him right, either. Unlike Sniadecki, Osann did not withdraw his claims.

Finally in 1844, Karl Karlovich Klaus (1796 – 1864), also known as Carl Ernst Claus, produced convincing evidence that two of Osann's three metals, pluranium and polinium, were not new metals at all. Osann's ruthenium was a very poor grade of the oxide; so poor, in fact, that it could not qualify as a new discovery. Having thus shown where Osann went wrong, Klaus was able to straighten out the mess.

Osann gets the credit for finding the element, and Klaus for isolating it. It can be shown today that Sniadecki had done the complete job much earlier, but you cannot win a race you quit.

Properties of ruthenium

Ruthenium is a rare metal, occupying no more than 0.01 parts-per-million of the matter in the earth's crust. Whenever enough is put together in one place, it has a gray-white appearance and a hard, brittle character.

At room temperature, ruthenium is impervious to virtually all acids, including aqua regia. It is vulnerable to alkalis, however, and it oxidizes explosively in the presence of potassium chlorate.

The high melting temperature and brittleness make it difficult to refine and cast into useful shapes, and these features seriously limit commercial applications.

Ruthenium is a Group-VIII metal. There is some chemical similarity to iron (Fe), which is located directly above ruthenium on the periodic table of the elements. It is more like osmium (Os), though, which is located directly below it on the table.

Production of ruthenium

Virtually all the world's supply of ruthenium is recovered from the byproducts of platinum-refining operations. Osmium is first removed from the residue by dissolving it in a solution of nitric acid. Further steps produce an ammoniated ruthenium oxychloride which, in effect, get the ruthenium ions away from the rest of the residues. The final steps are to reduce the ruthenium, usually by a reaction with hydrogen gas.

Some compounds and the isotopes of ruthenium

The principal oxidation state of ruthenium is $+3$, and the Ru^{3+} metal ion forms compounds such as:

Ruthenium trichloride, $RuCl_3$

$$Ru^{3+} + 3Cl^- \rightarrow RuCl_3$$

Ruthenium hydroxide, $Ru(OH)_3$

$$Ru^{3+} + 3(OH)^- \rightarrow Ru(OH)_3$$

The oxides of ruthenium illustrat the presence of other oxidation states for this metal:

Ruthenium(IV) oxide, RuO_2

$$Ru^{4+} + 2O^{2-} \rightarrow RuO_2$$

Ruthenium(VIII) oxide, RuO_4

$$Ru^{8+} + 4O^{2-} \rightarrow RuO_4$$

The ruthenium salts are usually very colorful. A few are colorless black or gray, but most have bright colors such as reddish brown, dark green, dark blue, and yellow.

Figure 44-1 shows the isotopes of ruthenium. Many are found in nature as stable, or nonradioactive, isotopes. The artificial and radioactive isotopes of ruthenium have relatively short half-lives.

44-1 Ruthenium has isotopes with atomic weights between 92 and 110.

Isotope	Natural Abundance	Half-Life	Decay Mode
^{92}Ru		3.7 min	β+, ec
^{93m}Ru		10.8 sec	β+, ec
^{93}Ru		1 min	β+, ec
^{94}Ru		52 min	ec
^{95}Ru		1.64 hr	β+, ec
^{96}Ru	5.52%		
^{97}Ru		2.89 day	ec
^{98}Ru	1.88%		
^{99}Ru	12.7%		
^{100}Ru	12.6%		
^{101}Ru	17.0%		
^{102}Ru	31.6%		
^{103}Ru		39.24 day	β-
^{104}Ru	18.7%		
^{105}Ru		4.44 hr	β-
^{106}Ru		372.6 day	β-
^{107}Ru		3.8 min	β-
^{108}Ru		4.6 min	β-
^{109}Ru		35 sec	β-
^{110}Ru		15 sec	β-

Element 45: Rhodium

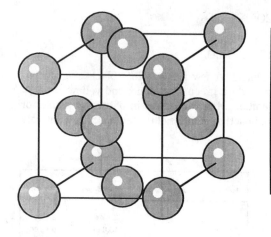

Name	Rhodium
Symbol	Rh
Atomic Number	45
Atomic Weight	102.906
Melting Point	1966°C
Boiling Point	3727°C
Specific Gravity	12.41 (20°C)
Oxidation State	+3
Electron Config.	(Kr) $4d^8\ 5s^1$

- Name pronounced as **RO-di-em**
- Name taken from the Greek, *rhodon*, "rose"
- Discovered by William Hyde Wollaston in 1803
- Silvery white, hard metal

Rhodium is one of those relatively rare metals that has few, if any applications in its own right, but acts as an important alloying agent with other metals. World production of rhodium is on the order of 10 tons per year. Some are used in the manufacture of special high-temperature crucibles for laboratory applications; most, however, are used as a hardener for platinum and palladium.

Rhodium is one of the so-called platinum elements. This means it is most often found in nature in the company of platinum. It also shares some of the notable properties of platinum, including its high level of resistance to corrosion, its hardness and its ductility.

This is the rarest of the platinum metals, found in the earth's crust in concentrations averaging about 1 part in 200-million.

Historical background

Having just announced his discovery of palladium (element 46) in 1803, William Hyde Wollaston set out to find another element in his South American platinum ores. He first dissolved the platinum ore in aqua regia, a mixture of nitric and hydrochloric acids. After neutralizing the excess acid with sodium hydroxide, he treated it with ammonium chloride to remove the platinum as ammonium chloroplatinate. Then he treated the sample with mercuric cyanide to precipitate the palladium as palladious cyanide. This is how he discovered palladium a few months earlier.

After filtering, washing, and drying the part that remained, Wollaston ended up with a dark red powder now known as *sodium rhodium chloride*. The new metal was easily reduced from the salt by reducing it with hydrogen. Wollaston named the element for the distinctive red-to-rosy color of its salts.

Properties of rhodium

This element is usually described as a shiny white metal that is quite hard, yet ductile. It is a *platinum metal*, and thus resists corrosion by moisture, oxygen, and most acids at room temperature.

Rhodium is one of the Group-VIII elements that are sometimes called the transition metals. Like many of the transition metals, rhodium has chemical properties similar to the metals directly above and below it on the periodic table. In this case you can see that rhodium would be similar to cobalt (Co) in some respects and to iridium (Ir) in others.

Production of rhodium

Rhodium and a few other metals always accompany lodes of platinum. Wherever there is platinum in the earth, there is rhodium as well. Most rhodium is extracted from a sludge that remains after platinum is removed from the ore. A high percentage of rhodium is also found in certain nickel deposits in Canada. The extraction processes are quite similar in principle.

Rhodium is so hard and corrosion-resistant that it can be refined by simply dissolving away other metals and impurities. This is the same approach that William H. Wollaston used when he discovered the element nearly two centuries ago.

Assuming the platinum has already been removed, any osmium and ruthenium can be removed by forming their volatile oxides. Iridium and palladium can be removed by adding ammonium and chlorine compounds. The rhodium compounds that remain can be reduced with titanium trichloride.

Some compounds and the isotopes of rhodium

The principal oxidation state of rhodium is $+3$, although the family of rhodium compounds indicates an oxidation state of $+4$ as well:

Rhodium(III) chloride, $RhCl_3$

$$Rh^{3+} + 3Cl^- \rightarrow RhCl_3$$

Rhodium(III) oxide, Rh_2O_3

$$2Rh^{3+} + 3O^{2-} \rightarrow Rh_2O_3$$

Rhodium(IV) oxide, RhO_2

$$Rh^{4+} + 2O^{2-} \rightarrow RhO_2$$

Sodium rhodium chloride, Na_3RhCl_6, played an important role in the discovery of rhodium. It normally exists in a hydrated form where each molecule of the compound is surrounded by 12 molecules of water: $Na_3RhCl_6 \cdot 12H_2O$. The hydrate is produced today by heating one of the rhodium oxides with sodium chloride and chlorine.

Rhodium has an affinity for potassium and sulfate ions, forming a couple of relatively complex inorganic molecules: hydrated *potassium rhodium alum*, $K_2SO_4 \cdot Rh_2(SO_4)_3 \cdot 24H_2O$, and *potassium rhodium sulfate*, $K_3Rh(SO_4)_3$. Both of these rosy-colored crystals are produced by burning rhodium oxide and controlled amounts of potassium bisulfate ($KHSO_4$).

Figure 45-1 shows the isotopes of rhodium that have been investigated thus far. Note that all naturally occurring rhodium is rhodium-103; the remaining isotopes are both radioactive and synthetically produced.

Isotope	Natural Abundance	Half-Life	Decay Mode
^{94m}Rh		71 sec	β+
^{94}Rh		25.8 sec	β+
^{95m}Rh		1.96 min	β+, i.t.
^{95}Rh		5 min	β+
^{96m}Rh		1.51 min	β+, i.t.
^{96}Rh		9.9 min	β+, ec
^{97m}Rh		46 min	β+, ec
^{97}Rh		31 min	β+
^{98m}Rh		3.5 min	β+
^{98}Rh		8.6 min	β+
^{99m}Rh		4.7 hr	β+, ec
^{99}Rh		16.1 day	β+, ec
^{100m}Rh		4.7 min	β+, i.t.
^{100}Rh		20.8 hr	β+, ec
^{101m}Rh		4.34 day	ec, i.t.
^{101}Rh		3.3 yr	ec
^{102m}Rh		206 day	β-, ec
^{102}Rh		2.9 yr	ec
^{103m}Rh		56.12 min	i.t.
^{103}Rh	100%		
^{104m}Rh		4.36 min	β-
^{104}Rh		41.8 sec	β-
^{105m}Rh		45 sec	β-
^{105}Rh		35.4 hr	β-
^{106m}Rh		2.18 hr	β-
^{106}Rh		29.8 sec	β-
^{107}Rh		21.7 min	β-
^{108m}Rh		17 sec	β-
^{108}Rh		6 min	β-
^{109}Rh		81 sec	β-
^{110m}Rh		3.1 sec	β-
^{110}Rh		29 sec	β-
^{111}Rh		11 sec	β-
^{112}Rh		800 ms	β-

45-1 Rhodium has isotopes with atomic weights between 94 and 112.

Element 46: Palladium

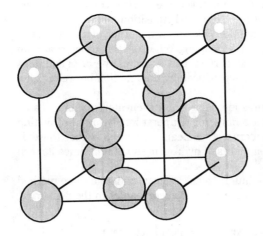

Name	Palladium
Symbol	Pd
Atomic Number	46
Atomic Weight	106.42
Melting Point	1554°C
Boiling Point	3140°C
Specific Gravity	12.02 (20°C)
Oxidation State	+2, +4
Electron Config.	(Kr) $4d^{10}$

- Name pronounced as **peh-LAY-di-em**
- Named after the asteroid, *Pallas*
- Discovered by William Hyde Wollaston in 1803
- Silvery-white, soft, malleable and ductile metal

Palladium is not a very familiar element, but it has some applications to familiar objects. This soft, corrosion-resistant metal is frequently used as a substitute for silver in dental items and jewelry; it stands on its own as the delicate mainsprings in analog wristwatches.

This is a rare metal. On the average, the earth's crust contains palladium in proportions of only 1 part per 100 million. Fortunately, the metal is not difficult to find; it turns up naturally in the byproducts of refining operations for more common metals such as copper, silver, and gold.

Historical background

During the closing years of the 1700s and the opening of the 1800s, researchers were having a heyday sorting new elements from platinum ores. One element to come out of this environment was element 46, which was sorted from platinum ore samples by William Hyde Wollaston (1766 – 1828).

These ore samples were taken from a region in Brazil that was noted for gold mines that were contaminated with "white gold." Later, the same region yielded up a peculiar, silver-white platinum. It is now suspected that both were alloys of palladium and gold.

In 1803, Wollaston separated gold and a new element from samples of South American platinum. He started by dissolving the crude platinum in aqua regia (a mixture of nitric and hydrochloric acids), then slowly adding mercuric cyanide to produce a yellow precipitate that was later identified as palladious cyanide. Metallic palladium was then reduced from this compound by igniting it.

Less than a year later, Wollaston would use the same general procedure to isolate yet another new element, rhodium.

Properties and production of palladium

Palladium is described as a silver-white metal that is both ductile and malleable. Because of the latter features, it is often found as a substitute for silver in electrical components, jewelry, and dental materials. Palladium is one of the Group-VII transition metals.

Palladium is more prone to attack from common acids than the other platinum metals (rhodium iridum, ruthenium, and osmium, for example). Whereas the other platinum metals hardly respond at all to hydrochloric acid at room temperature, one of palladium's most useful compounds, palladium(II) chloride, is produced by the reaction between palladium metal and hydrochloric acid.

All metals soften somewhat at temperatures just a bit below their melting point. Palladium, however, softens over an unusually wide range of temperatures below the melting point. As far as practical applications are concerned this means palladium is easy to weld.

Palladium has an ability to absorb large amounts of hydrogen—up to 900 times its own volume.

Palladium is found in conjuction with platinum, nickel, copper, and gold. The method for extracting the palladium depends mainly on the metal it accompanies to the refinery.

Some compounds and the isotopes of palladium

Palladium exhibits oxidation states of $+2$ and $+4$. The oxides of this element are thus:

Palladium(II) oxide, PdO

$$Pd^{2+} + O^{2-} \rightarrow PdO$$

Palladium(IV) oxide, PdO_2

$$Pd^{4+} + 2O^{2-} \rightarrow PdO_2$$

The chlorides are:

Palladium(II) chloride, $PdCl_2$

$$Pd^{2+} + 2Cl^- \rightarrow PdCl_2$$

Palladium(IV) chloride, $PdCl_4$

$$Pd^{4+} + 4Cl^- \rightarrow PdCl_4$$

Palladium(II) chloride, variously called palladous chloride or palladium dichloride, can selectively absorb large quantities of carbon monoxide gas (CO). For this reason, $PdCl_2$ is used in instruments that detect the presence of this deadly gas.

Figure 46-1 shows all of the known isotopes of palladium. None of the naturally occurring species is radioactive; all of the synthetic isotopes are radioactive.

Isotope	Natural Abundance	Half-Life	Decay Mode
^{96}Pd		2 min	ec
^{97}Pd		3.1 min	β+, ec
^{98}Pd		18 min	β+, ec
^{99}Pd		21.4 min	β+, ec
^{100}Pd		3.6 day	ec
^{101}Pd		8.4 hr	β+, ec
^{102}Pd	1.02%		
^{103}Pd		16.97 day	ec
^{104}Pd	11.14%		
^{105}Pd	22.33%		
^{106}Pd	27.33%		
^{107m}Pd		20.9 sec	i.t.
^{107}Pd		6.5x10^6 yr	β-
^{108}Pd	26.46%		
^{109m}Pd		4.68 min	i.t.
^{109}Pd			β-
^{110}Pd	11.72%		
^{111m}Pd		5.5 hr	β-, i.t.
^{111}Pd		22 min	β-
^{112}Pd		21 hr	β-
^{113m}Pd		89 sec	β-
^{113}Pd		98 sec	β-
^{114}Pd		2.48 min	β-
^{115}Pd		47 sec	β-
^{116}Pd		12.7 sec	β-

46-1 Palladium has isotopes with atomic weights between 96 and 116.

Element 47: Silver

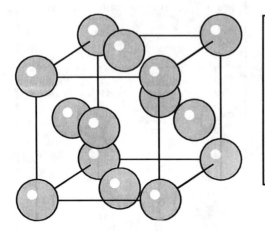

Name	Silver
Symbol	Ag
Atomic Number	47
Atomic Weight	107.868
Melting Point	961.93°C
Boiling Point	2212°C
Specific Gravity	10.50 (20°C)
Oxidation State	+1
Electron Config.	(Kr) $4d^{10} 5s^2$

- Name pronounced as **SIL-ver**
- Name taken from the Anglo-Saxon, *siolful*, "silver"
- Chemical symbol, Ag, taken from the Latin name, *argentium*
- The element is of ancient origin
- Silvery-ductile, and malleable metal

Silver is considered a precious metal—a member of a special group that also includes gold, iridium, palladium, and platinum. There are other metals that are far more scarce, but no one really cares about them.

Silver is present in the earth's crust in portions on the order of 0.05 parts-per-million. This means, on the average, you have to dig up 20 million shovels of dirt in order to find one shovelful of silver. By contrast, tin is present in 6 parts-per-million, lead in 13, copper in 50, and iron in 50,000 parts-per-million.

Silver is of ancient origin, with products and refining methods described in the Bible and early Egyptian writings. There was a period in early history when silver was regarded more highly than gold, probably because gold was easier to locate and refine at the time. We now know that silver is ten times more abundant in the earth's crust than gold.

Properties of silver

Silver is a Group-IB metal that appears directly below copper (Cu) and above gold (Au) on the periodic table of the elements. Pure silver is the best conductor of heat and electricity.

Of course it is a *silvery* metal. Freshly exposed silver is bright and mirrorlike, but its appearance gradually dulls as a thin oxide coating forms on the surfaces. It is ductile and malleable, too. Among other things, this means silver is easily hammered or molded into shapes and can be drawn into very fine wire.

Jewelry and ornaments made from pure silver would be too expensive for the ordinary pocketbook, and pure silver utensils would be too soft and fragile for practical use. The same ideas apply to industrial applications of the metal. Therefore, silver is usually alloyed with at least one other metal. The alloying metals not only dilute the silver in order to make it more economical, but enhance its physical properties as well. The purity of silver is expressed in terms of its *fineness*.

The fineness of a silver alloy is a numerical value that is equal to 10 times the percentage of silver in the mix. Sterling silver, for example, is about 93% silver and 7% other metals, mostly copper. The fineness of this alloy is 930. Fine silver jewelry usually has a fineness of 800. Of course, the fineness rating of pure silver is 1000.

Production of silver

Although silver can be found in high concentrations in silver ores such as argentite (Ag_2S), most is recovered as a byproduct of refining operations of less costly metals such as copper, lead, and zinc. In the United States, Canada, and Mexico, most silver is now recovered from copper-nickel ores. Today a great deal of United States silver is recovered from the sludge, or "anode mud," that is produced during the electrolytic purification of copper (*see* Element 29: Copper).

Silver can be recovered and purified from the byproducts of other refining operations by chemical and electrolytic procedures.

Some compounds of silver

The principal oxidation state of silver is $+1$, so you can expect to see the Ag^+ ion forming compounds such as:

Silver sulfide, AgS

$$Ag^+ + S^- \rightarrow AgS$$

Silver oxide, Ag_2O

$$2Ag^+ + O^{2-} \rightarrow Ag_2O$$

Silver phosphate, Ag_3PO_4

$$3Ag^+ + (PO_4)^{3-} \rightarrow Ag_3PO_4$$

Silver nitrate, $AgNO_3$, is a commercially valuable compound. It is one of the essential ingredients in photographic emulsions and it is a key compound in the production of other silver compounds. This colorless and highly toxic chemical is produced by the reaction between silver metal and nitric acid:

$$Ag + HNO_3 \rightarrow AgNO_3 + H_2$$
(silver + nitric acid → silver nitrate + hydrogen gas)

Silver bromide, AgBr, occurs in nature as the mineral *bromyrite*. It is produced commercially for photographic applications by combining aqueous solutions of a silver salt and a bromide, for example:

$$AgNO_3 + KBr \rightarrow AgBr + KNO_3$$
(silver nitrate + potassium bromide → silver bromide + potassium nitrate)

Silver chloride, AgCl, can be found in nature as the mineral *cerargyrite*. Like silver bromide, silver chloride is used extensively in the manufacture of photographic emulsions. In order to meet the commercial demand, most silver chloride is produced synthetically by combining aqueous solutions of a silver salt and a chloride. For instance:

$$AgNO_3 + KCl \rightarrow AgCl + KNO_3$$
(silver nitrate + potassium chloride → silver chloride + potassium nitrate)

Silver nitrate and hydrochloric acid also produce silver chloride:

$$AgNO_3 + HCl \rightarrow AgCl + HNO_3$$
(silver nitrate + hydrochloric acid → silver chloride + nitric acid)

Silver iodide, AgI, is used in photographic emulsions as, indeed, are all the silver halides, AgI, however, is better known as the rain-making chemical. Yellowish crystals of silver iodide can be sprinkled into moisture-bearing clouds to encourage precipitation. Unlike many other silver compounds, silver iodide is quite harmless to animal and vegetable life, particularly when diluted and dispersed by the rainfall it causes. The chemical is produced in commercial quantities by reacting silver nitrate and potassium iodide in a solution of concentrated nitric acid.

Silver cyanide, AgCN, is a white poisonous substance that is used in the manufacture of more complex, silver compounds, including *potassium argentocyanide*, $KAg(CN)_2$, a vital chemical in commercial silver plating operations.

Fulminated mercury, or mercury fulminate $(Hg(CNO)_2)$, is a well-known explosive. *Silver fulminate* (AgCNO) is less well-known, but more violently explosive.

Isotopes of silver

Figure 47-1 lists the isotopes of silver that have been positively identified. Notice that the silver that occurs in nature is divided between two isotopic species, Ag-107 and Ag-109. The remaining isotopes of silver are both radioactive and artificially produced.

Isotope	Natural Abundance	Half-Life	Decay Mode	Isotope	Natural Abundance	Half-Life	Decay Mode
^{96}Ag		5.1 sec	β+, ec	^{109m}Ag		39.8 sec	i.t.
^{97}Ag		19 sec	β+, ec	^{109}Ag	46.16%		
^{98}Ag		46.7 sec	β+, ec	^{110m}Ag		249.8 day	β-, i.t.
^{99m}Ag		11 sec	i.t.	^{110}Ag		24.6 sec	β-
^{99}Ag		2.07 min	β+, ec	^{111m}Ag		65 sec	β-, i.t.
^{100m}Ag		2.3 min	β+, ec	^{111}Ag		7.47 day	β-
^{100}Ag		2 min	β+, ec	^{112}Ag		3.14 hr	β-
^{101m}Ag		3.1 sec	i.t.	^{113m}Ag		68 sec	β-, i.t.
^{101}Ag		11.1 min	β+, ec	^{113}Ag		5.3 hr	β-
^{102m}Ag		7.8 min	β+, ec	^{114}Ag		4.5 sec	β-
^{102}Ag		13 min	β+, ec	^{115m}Ag		18.7 sec	β-
^{103m}Ag		5.7 sec	i.t.	^{115}Ag		20 min	β-
^{103}Ag		66 min	β+, ec	^{116m}Ag		10 sec	β-, i.t.
^{104m}Ag		33 min	β+, ec	^{116}Ag		2.68 min	β-
^{104}Ag		69 min	β+, ec	^{117m}Ag		5.3 sec	β-
^{105m}Ag		7.2 min	ec, i.t.	^{117}Ag		73 sec	β-
^{105}Ag		41.3 day	ec	^{118m}Ag		2.8 sec	β-, i.t.
^{106}Ag		8.5 day	ec	^{118}Ag		4 sec	β-
^{106}Ag		24 min	β+, ec	^{119}Ag		2.1 sec	β-
^{107m}Ag		44.2 sec	i.t.	^{120m}Ag		320 ms	β-, i.t.
^{107}Ag	51.84%			^{120}Ag		1.2 sec	β-
^{108m}Ag		130 yr	ec, i.t.	^{121}Ag		800 sec	β-
^{108}Ag		2.42 min	β-, ec	^{122}Ag		1.5 sec	β-

47-1 Silver has isotopes with atomic weights between 96 and 122.

Element 48: Cadmium

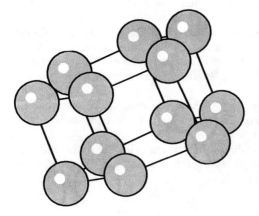

Name	Cadmium
Symbol	Cd
Atomic Number	48
Atomic Weight	112.41
Melting Point	320.9°C
Boiling Point	765°C
Specific Gravity	8.65 (20°C)
Oxidation State	+2
Electron Config.	(Kr) $4d^{10}\,5s^2$

- Name pronounced as **KAD-me-em**
- Name from the Greek *kadmeia*, ancient name for calamine (zinc oxide)
- Discovered by Friedrich Strohmeyer in 1817, and independently, in the same year, by K.S.L. Hermann and J.C.H. Roloff
- Soft, malleable, blue-white metal

Cadmium is rather scarce for a metal that has everyday industrial applications. People do not have to go out looking for cadmium ore, however, because the element turns up in every truckload of common zinc ore. A company that refines ordinary zinc can recover significant amounts of cadmium as a byproduct.

Cadmium metal is used mostly for electroplating steel and in the manufacture of bearings. The cadmium compounds are found in paint pigments in a wide variety of intense colors.

Historical background

The discovery of cadmium in 1871 is closely associated with attempts to produce pharmaceutical-grade zinc oxide. As an inspector of apothecaries, Friedrich Strohmeyer (1776–1835) wrote, " . . . instead of the proper oxide of zinc, [I found] carbonate of zinc, which had been almost entirely procured from the chemical manufactory at Salzgitter. This carbonate of zinc had a dazzling white color; but when heated to redness, it assumed a yellow color, inclining to orange, though no sensible portions of iron or lead could be detected in it.'' Pure oxides and carbonates of zinc should not change color when heated.

Strohmeyer's curiosity led him to a deeper analysis of samples that exhibited this peculiar behavior. After performing a series of treatments with acids, all known metals, including zinc, were removed. He mixed the powdery residue with lampblack and compacted it in a retort. After heating the mixture, he found a small ingot of a soft, lustrous, bluish-white metal.

Properties and production of cadmium

Cadmium is a bluish-white, malleable and ductile metal. Like zinc, it "cries" when rapidly bent. It can be polished to a lustrous finish, but gradually dulls as a thin layer of oxide forms.

Cadmium is in the middle of the IIB zinc group on the periodic table. Zinc and cadmium share a few chemical and physical properties. Mercury, located just below cadmium on the periodic table, has the lowest melting point of all the metals. Cadmium's melting point is not that low, but it can be made to boil at about 321 °C. Boiling cadmium gives off a poisonous and weird, yellow-colored vapor.

Although cadmium can be found in a few, widely scattered minerals, it is not economically feasible to extract the metal from those minerals. Cadmium, however, is nearly always found as an impurity in natural zinc ores.

Where zinc is refined in a blast furnace, cadmium can be found in dust that is regularly scraped from the flues and stacks. In electrolytic zinc-refining operations, the anode slime contains a high percentage of cadmium metal.

Some compounds of cadmium

Cadmium is bivalent—it has a single oxidation state of $+2$. This oxidation state is responsible for producing cadmium compounds of these general forms:

Cadmium iodide, CdI_2

$$Cd^{2+} + 2I^- \rightarrow CdI_2$$

Cadmium oxide, CdO

$$Cd^{2+} + O^{2-} \rightarrow CdO$$

Most cadmium compounds are produced from cadmium metal which is, in turn, derived from its natural sulfide ore, greenockite.

White soluable crystals of *cadmium chloride*, $CdCl_2$, are formed by a reaction between cadmium metal and hydrochloric acid:

$$Cd + 2HCl \rightarrow CdCl_2 + H_2$$
(cadmium + hydrochloric acid → cadmium chloride + hydrogen gas)

Cadmium chloride is most stable in a hydrated form where there are $2^1/_2$ molecules of water per molecule of the chloride. For example: $2CdCl_2 \cdot 5H_2O/$

Hydrated *cadmium sulfate*, $3CdSO_4 \cdot 8H_2O$, is a white soluble crystal that is commonly used in an electrical cell—the Weston cell—that serves as a precise voltage standard for calibrating laboratory and medical electronic instruments. It is produced by the reaction between cadmium metal and dilute sulfuric acid:

$$Cd + H_2SO_4 \rightarrow CdSO_4 + H_2$$
(cadmium + sulfuric acid → cadmium sulfate + hydrogen gas)

Cadmium hydroxide, $Cd(OH)_2$, is formed by a reaction between aqueous solutions of cadmium sulfate and sodium hydroxide:

$$CdSO_4 + NaOH \rightarrow Cd(OH)_2 + 2NaSO_4$$
(cadmium sulfate + sodium hydroxide → cadmium hydroxide + sodium sulfate)

One of the applications for cadmium hydroxide is in the manufacture of *cadmium oxide*, CdO.

Isotopes of cadmium

Figure 48-1 shows the known isotopes of cadmium. You can see that none of the natural isotopes is radioactive, while all of the synthetic species are.

48-1 Cadmium has isotopes with atomic weights between 99 and 124.

Isotope	Natural Abundance	Half-Life	Decay Mode
^{99}Cd		16 sec	β+, ec
^{100}Cd		1.1 min	β+, ec
^{101}Cd		1.2 min	β+, ec
^{102}Cd		5.5 min	β+, ec
^{103}Cd		7.7 min	β+, ec
^{104}Cd		58 min	ec
^{105}Cd		55.3 min	β+, ec
^{106}Cd	1.25%		
^{107}Cd		6.5 hr	β+, ec
^{108}Cd	0.89%		
^{109}Cd		462.3 day	ec
^{110}Cd	12.49%		
^{111m}Cd		48.7 min	i.t.
^{111}Cd	12.8%		
^{112}Cd	24.13%		
^{113m}Cd		13.7 yr	
^{113}Cd	12.22%		β-
^{114}Cd	28.73%		
^{115m}Cd		44.6 day	β-
^{115}Cd		53.5 hr	β-
^{116}Cd	7.49%		
^{117m}Cd		3.4 hr	β-
^{117}Cd		2.49 hr	β-
^{118}Cd		50.3 min	β-
^{119m}Cd		2.20 min	β-
^{119}Cd		2.69	β-
^{120}Cd		50.8 sec	β-
^{121m}Cd		8 sec	β-
^{121}Cd		13.5 sec	β-
^{122}Cd		5.8 sec	β-
^{124}Cd		900 ms	β-

Element 49: Indium

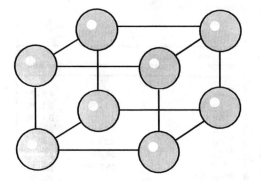

Name	Indium
Symbol	In
Atomic Number	49
Atomic Weight	114.82
Melting Point	156.61°C
Boiling Point	2080°C
Specific Gravity	7.31 (20°C)
Oxidation State	+3
Electron Config.	(Kr) $4d^{10}\ 5s^2\ 5p^1$

- Name pronounced as **IN-di-em**
- Name taken from the Latin, *indicum*, the color indigo
- Discovered by Ferdinand Reich and Theodor Richter in 1863
- Very soft, silvery-white metal

Indium is a rare metal; its abundance in the earth's crust is identical to that of silver—about 0.05 parts-per-million. Fortunately, indium is almost always found in the company of plentiful and ordinary zinc ores. Therefore, zinc refineries are the world's major source of indium.

Indium is used mostly for electroplating steel bearings and as an alloy that lowers the melting point of other metals. Relatively small amounts are used in dental items and electronic semiconductors.

Historical background

In 1863, Ferdinand Reich (1799 – 1882) was searching for traces of the newly discovered element, thallium, in zinc ores from the nearby Himmelsfürst mine. Some chemical treatments convinced Reich he had accidentally produced the yellowish sulfide of a new element. The situation required a spectroscopic examination of the samples in order to confirm the presence of a new element. Spectroscopic work was routine in those days, and the bands of colors, fingerprints as it were, provided conclusive qualitative analysis. Reich was on the verge of success, but he suffered from a particularly annoying handicap: he was totally colorblind.

Reich had to entrust the spectrographic analysis to an assistant named Hieronymous Theodor Richter. Using a simple spectrographic setup, Richter was the first to see the bright indigo lines of the new element. Codiscoverers, Reich and Richter thus named it *indium*.

Properties and production of indium

Indium is characterized as a soft and malleable, silvery-white metal. It looks a lot like aluminum, but feels more like tin. Like tin, pure indium emits a squealing sound when it is bent.

This metal is so soft that you can wipe it onto other objects in much the same way as you can wipe graphite or pencil lead. Pure indium can be highly polished, and it will retain the shine because it is corrosion resistant.

The low melting point contributes to its commercial value as an alloying agent for soldering material. Indium is a member of the carbon group of elements, Group IIIA, on the periodic table.

Over a thousand kilograms of indium are recovered each year from the flue dust of zinc refineries. Concentrations from this source are typically on the order of 1 part per 1000. An acid leaching process allows the indium to be recovered, usually as indium sulfate, $In_2(SO_4)_3$, from other flue metals such as aluminum, arsenic, antimony, cadmium, and zinc.

The indium that is recovered from the flue dusts can be purified by means of an electrolysis procedure. The electrolyte in this case is aqueous *indium sulfate*, $In_2(SO_4)_3 \cdot 9H_2O$.

Some compounds and the isotopes of indium

Indium is trivalent—it has a stable oxidation state of $+3$. The In^{3+} ion forms compounds that look like this:

Indium trichloride, $InCl_3$

$$In^{3+} + 3Cl^- \rightarrow InCl_3$$

Indium sesquioxide, In_2O_3

$$2In^{3+} + 3O^{2-} \rightarrow In_2O_3$$

Lower oxidation states are unusual but evident in compounds such as InCl and $InCl_2$—indium(I) chloride and indium(II) chloride, respectively. Triindium tetroxide, In_3O_4, uses indium in more than one oxidation state.

Figure 49-1 shows all the known isotopes of indium. Naturally occurring indium consists mostly of radioactive indium-115, although it is usually diluted with a small percentage of nonradioactive indium-113.

Isotope	Natural Abundance	Half-Life	Decay Mode	Isotope	Natural Abundance	Half-Life	Decay Mode
^{102}In		24 sec	ec	^{117}In		43.1 min	β-
^{103}In		1.1 min	β+, ec	^{118m2}In		8.5 sec	β-, i.t.
^{104}In		1.82 min	β+, ec	^{118m1}In		4.4 min	β-
^{105m}In		43 sec	i.t.	^{118}In		5 sec	β-
^{105}In		4.9 min	β+, ec	^{119m}In		18 min	β-, i.t.
^{106m}In		6.2 min	β+, ec	^{119}In		2.4 min	β-
^{106}In		5.3 min	β+, ec	^{120m}In		3 sec	β-
^{107m}In		51 sec	i.t.	^{120}In		44 sec	β-
^{107}In		32.5 min	β+, ec	^{121m}In		3.9 min	β-, i.t.
^{108m}In		40 min	β+, ec	^{121}In		23 sec	β-
^{108}In		57 min	β+, ec	^{122m}In		1.5 sec	β-
^{109m}In		1.3 min	i.t.	^{122}In		10.1 sec	β-
^{109}In		4.2 hr	β+, ec	^{123m}In		48 sec	β-
^{110m}In		4.9 hr	ec	^{123}In		6 sec	β-
^{110}In		69 min	β+, ec	^{124m}In		2.4 sec	β-
^{111m}In		7.7 min	i.t.	^{124}In		3.2 sec	β-
^{111}In		2.8 day	ec	^{125m}In		12.2 sec	β-
^{112m}In		20.9 min	i.t.	^{125}In		2.33 sec	β-
^{112}In		14.4 min	β+, ec	^{126m}In		1.45 sec	β-
^{113m}In		1.66 hr	i.t.	^{126}In		1.53 sec	β-
^{113}In	4.3%			^{127m}In		3.76 sec	β-
^{114m}In		49.5 day	ec, i.t.	^{127}In		1.12 sec	β-
^{114}In		71.9 day	β-, ec	^{128m}In		832 ms	β-
^{115m}In		4.49 hr	β-, i.t.	^{128}In		900 ms	β-
^{115}In	95.7%	4.4×10^{14} yr	β-	^{129m}In		1.25 sec	β-, n
^{116m2}In		2.16 sec	β-	^{129}In		590 ms	β-
^{116m1}In		54.1 min	β-	^{130}In		510 ms	β-
^{116}In		14.1 sec	β-	^{131}In		280 ms	β-
^{117m}In		1.9 hr	β-, i.t.	^{132}In		220 ms	β-

49-1 Indium has isotopes with atomic weights between 102 and 132.

Element 50: Tin

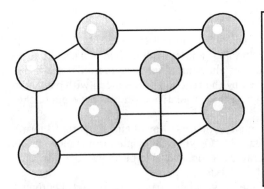

Name	Tin
Symbol	Sn
Atomic Number	50
Atomic Weight	118.69
Melting Point	231.97°C
Boiling Point	2270°C
Specific Gravity	5.75 (gray, 20°C)
	7.31 (white, 20°C)
Oxidation States	+2, +4
Electron Config.	(Kr) $4d^{10}\, 5s^2\, 5p^2$

- Name pronounced as **TIN**
- Named after the Etruscan god, Tinia
- Chemical symbol, Sn, taken from the Latin name for the element, *stannum*
- Identified and applied in ancient times
- Silvery-white, soft, malleable and ductile metal

Tin is perhaps best known for its use in the manufacture of tin cans. A very thin coating of tin on steel food containers prevents corrosion that would otherwise spoil the contents. Tin is an ideal metal for this application because it is nontoxic, noncorrosive, and can be easily applied to the surface of other metals. Tin cans are no longer as widely used as they once were, however; they are being replaced in many instances by containers made from less expensive materials such as plastic and paper.

This is not to say that tin is no longer a useful metal. Tin is (and always has been) a popular alloying agent used in the manufacture of solders for electronic components to the special alloys used in the finest bell metals.

Historical background

Tin is of ancient origin. Mining, refining, and metalworking operations are described in the oldest written records of the Mediterranean world. The book of Numbers in the Old Testament, for examples, cites tin as one of the seven known metals of the time (the others are gold, silver, copper, iron, lead, and brass). It was not universally understood at the time that brass is not an elemental metal, but rather an alloy of zinc and copper. In many parts of the ancient world, bronze—an alloy of copper and tin—was considered an elemental metal.

The ancients knew that bronze was a harder metal and was easier to cast into shapes than pure copper. Most metalsmiths knew how to find tin, then refine it and alloy it with copper to produce bronze. In fact, an entire age of human history is formally known as the Bronze Age because of the popularity of bronze tools, weapons, and household utensils.

Unalloyed tin is generally too soft for fashioning tools and utensils, although tin bowls, cups, and other dining utensils were quite popular in 17th-century Europe and somewhat later in America.

Since the end of the Bronze Age, the most common application of tin has been as a plating medium for iron. A thin layer of tin prevents the oxidation that would otherwise corrode away iron objects. Even today, in this age of paper, plastic, and aluminum food containers, tin-plated steel cans are still found on the grocery shelves.

Properties of tin

Tin is a IVA metal. Pure tin is ductile and malleable, and therefore adaptable to a wide range of forming processes such as rolling, spinning, and extruding. Tin is basically a silvery-white metal that looks much like freshly cut aluminum, but feels more like lead. Polished tin has a slight bluish color that is caused by the reaction of the metal with oxygen in the atmosphere. This oxide, tin(IV) oxide, forms a thin protective layer that prevents further oxidation of the sample.

Tin has two, well-defined allotropes known as *gray tin* (α form) and *white tin* (β form). The gray form is stable at temperatures below 13.2 °C, while the white form is more stable above that temperature. Normal room temperature is considered to be about 20 °C, so it follows that the most common form is the white, or β, form.

Both of these allotropes have highly defined crystalline structures. In fact, bending a bar of tin produces a characteristic squealing sound, or "cry," as the crystals are separated.

Production of tin

Tin is found naturally in deposits of *cassiterite* as stannic oxide, SnO_2. There are some minor sources in California and Alaska, but the bulk of the World's tin mining takes place in Bolivia, Indonesia, Zaire, Thailand, Nigeria, and China.

Tin is obtained directly from cassiterite by roasting it with coke (carbon):

$$SnO_2 + C \rightarrow Sn + CO_2$$
(stannic oxide + carbon $\rightarrow$ tin + carbon dioxide gas)

The tin can be further refined by a special electrolytic process, illustrated in Fig. 50-1, whereby the impure tin is the anode of the cell. As the electrolytic operation progresses, pure tin collects on the cathode.

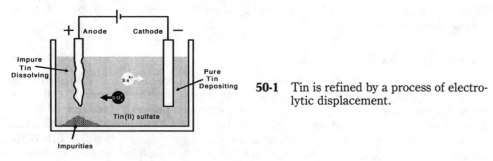

50-1 Tin is refined by a process of electrolytic displacement.

Some compounds of tin

Tin has two oxidation states, +2 and +4, and two common ions, Sn^{2+} and Sn^{4+}. Some compounds of Sn^{2+} are:

Tin(II) oxide, SnO (also known as stannous monoxide under the older system of nomenclature)

$$Sn^{2+} + O^{2-} \rightarrow SnO$$

Tin(II) chloride, $SnCl_2$ (also known as stannous chloride)

$$Sn^{2+} + 2Cl^- \rightarrow SnCl_2$$

Tin(II) sulfate, $SnSO_4$ (also known as stannous sulfate)

$$Sn^{2+} + SO_4^{2-} \rightarrow SnSO_4$$

Stannous(II) fluoride, SnF_2 (also known as fluoristan), is an active ingredient in some fluoride toothpastes.

The corresponding compounds of the Sn^{4+} ion are:

Tin(IV) oxide, SnO_2 (also called stannic oxide)

$$Sn^{4+} + 2O^{2-} \rightarrow SnO_2$$

Tin(IV) chloride, $SnCl_4$ (also called stannic chloride)

$$Sn^{4+} + 4Cl^- \rightarrow SnCl_4$$

Tin(IV) sulfate, $Sn(SO_4)_2$ (also called stannic sulfate)

$$Sn^{4+} + 2SO_4^{2-} \rightarrow Sn(SO_4)_2$$

Notice that tin(II) compounds are traditionally called *stannous*, while tin(IV) compounds are called *stannic*.

Isotopes of tin

Figure 50-2 lists the isotopes of tin. Notice that there is an unusually large number of stable (nonradioactive) isotopes of tin. Most tin in the earth's crust is tin-118 and tin-120. Tin-126 is the most stable of the radioactive isotopes, having a half-life of 100,000 years.

Isotope	Natural Abundance	Half-Life	Decay Mode	Isotope	Natural Abundance	Half-Life	Decay Mode
^{106}Sn		2.1 min	β+, ec	^{121m}Sn		55 yr	β-, i.t.
^{107}Sn		2.9 min	β+, ec	^{121}Sn		27 hr	β-
^{108}Sn		10.3 min	β+, ec	^{122}Sn	4.6%		
^{109}Sn		18 min	β+, ec	^{123m}Sn		40.1 min	β-, i.t.
^{110}Sn		4 hr	ec	^{123}Sn		129.2 day	β-
^{111}Sn		35.3 min	β+, ec	^{124}Sn	5.66%		
^{112}Sn	1.0%			^{125m}Sn		9.52 min	β-
^{113m}Sn		21.4 min	ec, i.t.	^{125}Sn			β-
^{113}Sn		115 day	ec	^{126}Sn		10^5 yr	β-
^{114}Sn	0.7%			^{127m}Sn		4.15 min	β-
^{115}Sn	0.4%			^{127}Sn		2.1 hr	β-
^{116}Sn	14.7%			^{128}Sn		59.1 min	β-
^{117m}Sn		13.6 day	i.t.	^{129m}Sn		6.9 min	β-
^{117}Sn	7.7%			^{129}Sn		2.5 min	β-
^{118}Sn	24.3%			^{130m}Sn		1.7 min	β-
^{119m}Sn		293 day	i.t.	^{130}Sn		3.7 min	β-
^{119}Sn	8.6%			^{131m}Sn		39 sec	β-
^{120}Sn	32.4%			^{131}Sn		61 sec	β-
				^{132}Sn		40 sec	β-

50-2 Tin has isotopes with atomic weights between 106 and 132.

Element 51: Antimony

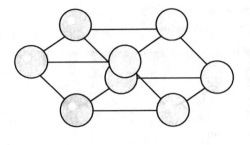

Name	Antimony
Symbol	Sb
Atomic Number	51
Atomic Weight	121.75
Melting Point	630.74°C
Boiling Point	1750°C
Specific Gravity	6.684 (25°C)
Oxidation States	+3, -3, +5
Electron Config.	(Kr) $4d^{10} 5s^2 5p^3$

- Name pronounced as **AN-teh-MOH-ni**
- Name from the Greek *anti + monos*, "not alone"; suggests that the metal is not found alone in nature
- The chemical symbol, Sb, is taken from the name of the mineral *stibnite*, the most common natural source of antimony
- Compounds of antimony are of ancient origin; the element had been identified by the early part of the 17th century
- Hard, silvery-white, brittle semimetal

Antimony is one of the few elements that was studied, mined, and applied during the opening centuries of recorded history. It is unusual that an element with such a long history is so little known today. Historically speaking, antimony is on about the same level as some of the more familiar elements such as zinc, tin, lead, silver, and phosphorus. Nevertheless, few people can name a single application or a common item that uses antimony.

Today, antimony is alloyed with other metals to increase their hardness. It is also used in the manufacture of a few special types of electronic semiconductor devices. A few kinds of over-the-counter cold and flu remedies include small amounts of antimony compounds.

Antimony does not make it to any of the top-ten abundance charts, but it is not exactly a rare element, either. The estimated average proportion of antimony in the earth's crust is about 0.2 parts-per-million. This puts it into the same category of abundance as germanium, arsenic, cadmium, and bismuth.

Historical background

The discovery of antimony and its compounds is lost in ancient history. One practical application of its chief mineral, *stibnite*, goes as far back as the Egyptian nineteenth dynasty and Biblical times where it was known as *stick-stone*, or *stibick-stone*. At that time, it was used as a popular black eye paint for women of wealth and power.

Antimony has long been associated with arsenic, sulfides, and lead. Sulferous minerals of antimony and arsenic are commonly found together, and elemental arsenic looks and feels very much like lead. It is understandable, then, that ancient and medieval chemists (or alchemists) could confuse these various substances. According to Pedanius Dioscorides, a first-century Greek physician and pharmacologist, "One roasts this ore [stibnite] by placing it on charcoal and heating to incandescence; if one continues the roasting, it changes into lead." Even Pliny, the renowned first-century Roman scholar, provides a warning about baking your stibnite too long: "But the main thing of all is to observe such a degree of nicety in heating it, as not to let it become lead." It's little wonder that the alchemists liked to experiment with antimony—if it can be turned into lead, maybe it could be transmuted into gold!

Nicolas Lémery (1645 – 1715), a French chemist and author of the classic *Cours de Chymie*, is regarded as the pioneer in the truly scientific study of antimony and its compounds.

Properties of antimony

Antimony is a silvery-white crystalline substance that has a metallic luster. It is brittle, yet soft—that is, it fractures readily into small pieces, yet scratches easily, too. This element is in the oxygen group, Group VIA, on the periodic chart.

Physically, antimony behaves more like a nonmetal such as sulfur. It is a poor conductor of heat and electricity, and it flakes and crumbles easily. Chemically, antimony resembles a metal. It alloys readily with most metals, it is found in nature in the company of other metals such as lead and silver, and it behaves ionically like a metal.

There are two allotropic forms of antimony: the normal metallic form and an amorphous gray form. Older texts refer to explosive and yellow forms as well, but these have been shown to be compounds rather than two additional allotropes of the element.

Production of antimony

The chief source of antimony is its mineral, stibnite (Sb_2S_3). The metal is recovered from this sulfide by means of a two-step process. In the first, ground-up stibnite is roasted in air to drive off the sulfur atoms and replace them with oxygen:

$$2Sb_2S_3 + 9O_2 \rightarrow 2Sb_2O_3 + 6SO_2$$
(antimony trisulfide + oxygen → antimony trioxide + sulfur dioxide)

Then the oxide is heated with carbon to produce carbon dioxide and elemental antimony:

$$2b_2O_3 + 3C \rightarrow 3CO + 2Sb$$
(antimony trioxide + carbon → carbon dioxide + antimony)

Antimony can also be produced by direct reduction of the sulfide with iron:

$$Sb_2S_3 + 3Fe \rightarrow 3FeS + 2Sb$$
(antimony trisulfide + iron → iron sulfide + antimony)

Some compounds and the isotopes of antimony

The primary oxidation states of antimony are $+3$, $+5$, and -3. The $+3$ state is demonstrated by the following compounds of chlorine and sulfur:

Antimony trichloride, $SbCl_3$ (also known as *butter of antimony*)

$$Sb^{3+} + 3Cl^- \rightarrow SbCl_3$$

Antimony trisulfide, Sb_2S_3 (also known as the mineral *stibnite*)

$$2Sb^{3+} + 3S^{2-} \rightarrow Sb_2S_3$$

The +5 state by these compounds of chlorine and sulfur are:

Antimony pentachloride, $SbCl_5$

$$Sb^{5+} + 5Cl^- \rightarrow SbCl_5$$

Antimony pentasulfide, Sb_2S_5

$$2Sb^{5+} + 5S^{2-} \rightarrow Sb_2S_5$$

The -3 oxidation state occurs in some of the antimonides of heavy metals such as *indium antimonide*, InSb. Another notable compound of antimony is *antimony hydride*, or *stibine*, SbH_3.

Figure 51-1 lists the known isotopes of antimony. Naturally occurring antimony is fairly evenly split between the isotopes antimony-121 and antimony-123. The remaining isotopes are both synthetic and radioactive.

Isotope	Natural Abundance	Half-Life	Decay Mode		Isotope	Natural Abundance	Half-Life	Decay Mode
^{109}Sb		18.3 sec	β+, ec		^{124m1}Sb		96 sec	β-
^{110}Sb		23.5 sec	β+, ec		^{124}Sb		60.2 day	β-, i.t.
^{111}Sb		75 sec	β+, ec		^{125}Sb		2.76 yr	β-
^{112}Sb		51 sec	β+, ec		^{126m2}Sb		11 sec	i.t.
^{113}Sb		6.7 min	β+, ec		^{126m1}Sb		19 min	β-, i.t.
^{114}Sb		3.5 min	β+, ec		^{126}Sb		12.4 day	β-
^{115}Sb		32.1 min	β+, ec		^{127}Sb		3.84 day	β-
^{116m}Sb		60 min	β+, ec		^{128m}Sb		10 min	β-, i.t.
^{116}Sb		16 min	β+, ec		^{128}Sb		9.1 hr	β-
^{117}Sb		2.8 hr	β+, ec		^{129m}Sb		17.7 min	β-
^{118m}Sb		5 hr	ec		^{129}Sb		4.4 hr	β-
^{118}Sb		3.6 min	β+, ec		^{130m}Sb		6.3 min	β-
^{119}Sb		36.1 hr	ec		^{130}Sb		38.4 min	β-
^{120m}Sb		5.76 day	ec		^{131}Sb		23 min	β-
^{120}Sb		15.9 min	β+, e		^{132m}Sb		3.1 min	β-
^{121}Sb	57.3%				^{132}Sb		4.12 min	β-
^{122m}Sb		4.21 min	i.t.		^{133}Sb		2.5 min	β-
^{122}Sb		2.71 day			^{134m}Sb		850 ms	β-
^{123}Sb	42.7%		β-		^{134}Sb		10.4 sec	β-
^{124m2}Sb			i.t.		^{135}Sb		1.71 sec	β-

51-1 Antimony has isotopes with atomic weights between 109 and 135.

Element 52: Tellurium

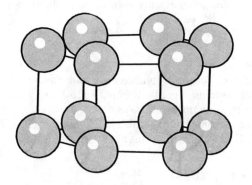

Name	Tellurium
Symbol	Te
Atomic Number	52
Atomic Weight	127.60
Melting Point	449.5°C
Boiling Point	4877°C
Specific Gravity	11.50 (20°C)
Oxidation States	-2, +4, +6
Electron Config.	(Kr) $4d^{10}\ 5s^2\ 5p^4$

- Name pronounced as **te-LOOR-i-em**
- Name taken from the Latin, *tellus*, "earth"
- Discovered by Franz Joseph Müller von Reichenstein in 1782
- Silvery-white, brittle semimetal

Tellurium is a relatively rare element that is found in the earth's crust in about the same proportions as platinum—about 0.02 parts-per-million.

Alloyed with copper and stainless steel, tellurium increases the machinability of those metals. Some are used in the rubber industry and it is also a basic ingredient in the manufacture of blasting caps.

Historical background

In the latter part of the 1770s, Franz Joseph Müller von Reichenstein was appointed chief inspector of all mines, smelters, and saltworks in the tiny province of Transylvania. Possessing something more than a bureaucrat's passing interest in the subject of his work, Müller began experimenting with the ores from his mines. An ore of gold, known at the time as *aurum album*, caught his attention when he extracted a different metal from it. He and other chemists working on similar samples assumed it to be antimony. By 1783, Müller was beginning to think the metal was not antimony at all, but a new metal.

His work was all but forgotten until the famous chemist, M. H. Klaproth mentioned Müller's metal in a paper read before the Berlin Academy of Sciences in 1798. Klaproth, in fact, was so certain that Müller had discovered a new element that he took the liberty of suggesting a name: tellurium. The discovery was actually made by Müller in 1782, but the new element remained largely unknown and unnamed until Klaproth delivered his paper some 16 years later. Klaproth later gave Franz Joseph Müller von Reichenstein full credit for the discovery.

Properties of tellurium

Tellurium is usually described as a silvery-white, brittle crystal. Tellurium belongs to the carbon group of elements, Group VIA, on the periodic table.

Tellurium is a semimetal, sharing properties with metals and nonmetals. (Semimetals are also called *metalloids*.) In its purest state, for example, tellurium has a metallic luster; but like a nonmetal, it is easily pulverized to a powder.

Tellurium is not affected by nitric acid, but it combines readily with nitric acid to produce tellurous acid. It burns easily in air to produce the oxide.

Production of tellurium

Elemental tellurium is occasionally found in nature, but more reliable sources include the minerals *sylvanite*, *calaverite*, and *krennerite* (all containing gold telluride, $AuTe_2$), and the anode slime recovered from electrolytic copper refining operations.

The procedure for recovering tellurium from its principal minerals is to digest the tellurium with nitric acid to produce *tellourous acid*, H_2TeO_3. Treating this acid with sulfur dioxide yields elemental tellurium:

$$H_2TeO_3 + 2SO_2 \rightarrow Te + 2H_2SO_4$$
(tellourous acid + sulfur dioxide → tellurium + sulfuric acid)

Some compounds of tellurium

The metallic oxidation states for tellurium account for its behavior as Te^{4+} and Te^{6+} ions:

Tellurium tetrachloride, $TeCl_4$

$$Te^{4+} + 4Cl^- \rightarrow TeCl_4$$

Tellurium trioxide, TeO_3

$$Te^{6+} + 3O^{2-} \rightarrow TeO_3$$

There is also a Te^{2+} ion as indicated by the existence of the following examples:

Tellurium dichloride, $TeCl_2$

$$Te^{2+} + 2Cl^- \rightarrow TeCl_2$$

Tellurium monoxide, TeO

$$Te^{2+} + O^{2-} \rightarrow TeO$$

The $^-2$ oxidation state becomes evident when tellurium plays the role of an anion, combining with hydrogen and a few metals according to the following examples:

Hydrogen telluride, H_2Te

$$2H^+ + Te^{2-} \rightarrow H_2Te$$

Aluminum telluride, Al_2Te_3

$$2Al^{3+} + 3Te^{2-} \rightarrow Al_2Te_3$$

Sodium telluride, Na_2Te

$$2Na^+ + Te^{2-} \rightarrow Na_2Te$$

Isotopes of tellurium

Figure 52-1 shows the isotopes of tellurium. Nearly 34% of the naturally occurring tellurium is radioactive tellurium-130. Tellurium-123 is also a natural, radioactive form. The remaining natural isotopes are not radioactive.

Isotope	Natural Abundance	Half-Life	Decay Mode
^{108}Te		2.1 sec	β+, ec
^{109}Te		4.2 sec	β+, ec
^{110}Te		18.5 sec	β+, ec
^{111}Te		19.3 sec	β+, ec
^{112}Te		2.0 min	β+, ec
^{113}Te		1.7 sec	β+, ec
^{114}Te		15 min	β+, ec
^{115m}Te		6.7 min	β+, ec
^{115}Te		5.8 min	β+, ec
^{116}Te		2.5 hr	ec
^{117}Te		62 min	β+, ec
^{118}Te		6 day	ec
^{119m}Te		4.7 day	ec
^{119}Te		16 hr	β+, e
^{120}Te	0.096%		
^{121m}Te			ec, i.t.
^{121}Te		16.8 day	ec
^{122}Te	2.6%		
^{123m}Te		119.7 day	i.t.

Isotope	Natural Abundance	Half-Life	Decay Mode
^{123}Te	0.903%	1.3×10^{13} yr	ec
^{124}Te	4.186%		
^{125m}Te		58 day	i.t.
^{125}Te	7.14%		
^{126}Te	18.95%		
^{127m}Te		109 day	β-, i.t.
^{127}Te		9.5 hr	β-
^{128}Te	31.69%		
^{129m}Te		33.4 day	β-, i.t.
^{129}Te		69.5 day	β-
^{130}Te	33.8%	2.4×10^{21} yr	
^{131m}Te		32.4 hr	β-, i.t.
^{131}Te		25 min	β-
^{132}Te		78.2 hr	β-
^{133m}Te		55.4 min	β-, i.t.
^{133}Te		12.5 min	β-
^{134}Te		42 min	β-
^{135}Te		19.2 sec	β-
^{136}Te		18 sec	β-
^{137}Te		4 sec	β-, n

52-1 Tellurium has isotopes with atomic weights between 108 and 137.

Element 53: Iodine

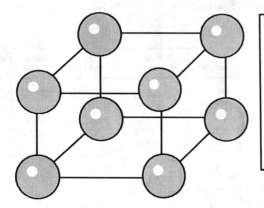

Name	Iodine
Symbol	I
Atomic Number	53
Atomic Weight	126.904
Melting Point	113.5°C
Boiling Point	184.35°C
Specific Gravity	4.93 (20°C)
Oxidation States	+1, -1, +5, +7
Electron Config.	(Kr) $4d^{10}\, 5s^2\, 5p^5$

- Name pronounced as **EYE-eh-dine** or **EYE-eh-din**
- Name taken from the Greek, *ioeides*, "violet colored"
- Discovered by Bernard Courtois in 1811
- Shiny, black, nonmetallic solid

It is difficult for most people to think of iodine in its pure state—as a black solid. People rather perceive it as a deep purple liquid that you put onto cuts and scrapes on the skin. That substance, however, is a tincture of iodine—a dilute mixture of alcohol and iodine.

As described later, most iodine is obtained indirectly from seawater through the seaweeds that absorb and concentrate it. The human thyroid gland secretes an iodine-bearing hormone called thyroxin. The body obtains this iodine from foods such as seafood and iodized salt.

Historical background

Iodine was discovered by accident one day in 1811 along the western coast of France. Barnard Courtois (1777–1838), was working at his business of recovering sodium and potassium compounds from seaweed commonly washed ashore at high tides. The general procedure was to burn the seaweed, then leach out the sodium chloride, potassium chloride, and potassium sulfate. The remaining mother liquor contained some undesirable sulfides in addition to small amounts of valuable carbonates and cyanides. The next step in the process was to treat the mother liquor with sulfuric acid in order to remove the unwanted compounds.

For some unknown reason, Courtois, who was a skilled chemist and pharmacologist, added a great excess of sulfuric acid. The bubbling mess belched clouds of a chlorine-smelling, violet-colored gas. When the gas condensed on metallic surfaces in the room, it formed a black, lustrous solid that had the feel of a metal.

Courtois immediately launched a series of experiments aimed at determining the chemical nature of the new element. For a time, his chemical company was the only one supplying iodine for chemical research and a rapidly growing pharmaceutical market.

One of Courtois' contemporaries wrote, "The mother liquor from seaweed ash contains quite a large quantity of a very peculiar and curious substance; it is easily extracted; one merely pours sulfuric acid on the mother liquor and heats the mixture . . . the substance which is precipitated in the form of a black, shining powder immediately after the addition of sulfuric acid, rises, when heated, in vapor of a superb violet color."

Properties of iodine

Iodine appears near the end of the Group-VIIA elements, or halogens: fluorine (F), chlorine (Cl), bromine (Br), iodine (I), and astatine (At). Iodine is the heaviest of the group to occur in nature (the heaviest halide, astatine, is a synthetic element).

Iodine tends to form a diatomic molecule that can be represented as I_2. The black solid sublimes at room temperature, producing a violet gas that is intensely irritating to the eyes, nose, and throat.

Production of iodine

Iodine is produced from three different kinds of resources: seaweed, salt brines, and Chilean saltpeter. Iodine is present in ordinary seawater, but in proportions too low to be of commercial value. Seaweed, such as the giant kelp found along California's Pacific coast, extracts and concentrates iodine from seawater. In a manner of speaking, then, seawater is a primary source of iodine; we simply let nature handle the first step in the production process.

Iodine can be derived from the powdery ashes of cremated seaweed. The ashes are first leached with water, slowly and gently. Then most of the unwanted salts, mainly sodium compounds, are allowed to crystalize out of solution by evaporation. Manganese dioxide (MnO_2) is finally added to oxidize the iodine ions (I^-) to produce elemental iodine (I_2). For example:

$$4I^- + MnO_2 \rightarrow MnI_2 + I_2 + 2O^{2-}$$

Technically speaking, Chilean saltpeter is potassium nitrate (KNO_3) and there is no way that iodine can be derived from it. Saltpeter, however, is mined directly from the earth and includes a number of impurities. One common impurity, especially in saltpeter shipments from Chile, includes significant amounts of sodium and calcium iodate, $NaIO_3$ and $Ca(IO_3)_2$. The iodine is thus extracted from the impurities, rather than the saltpeter, itself.

First, the saltpeter is dissolved in water so that evaporation can remove most of the unwanted salts by crystallization. The remaining liquid, or *mother liquor*, is poured off and treated with a reducing agent such as sodium hydrogen sulfite. The result is solid molecular iodine that is easily separated from the solution and distilled to remove all remaining water. An example of the reaction is:

$$2NaIO_3 + 5NaHSO_3 \rightarrow 3NaHSO_4 + 2Na_2SO_4 + H_2O + I_2$$
(sodium iodate + sodium hydrogen sulfite → sodium hydrogen sulfate
+ sodium sulfate + water + iodine)

It is commercially feasible to produce iodine from salt brines that can be found in abundance around salt mines and many oil wells. One way to release the iodine is by oxidizing the iodine ions with chlorine, exactly as described earlier for producing iodine from water that has been leached through baked seaweed. Another approach begins by filtering the brine through a copper wire mesh to form copper iodide Cu_2I_2. This compound is easily removed from the mesh; then it is dried and ground to a powder. The powdered copper iodide is heated with potassium carbonate (K_2CO_3) to yield potassium iodide:

$$Cu_2I_2 + K_2CO_3 \rightarrow 2KI + Cu_2O + CO^2$$

The potassium iodide is, in turn, treated with sodium dichromate to oxidize iodine ions to free iodine:

$$6KI + Na_2Cr_2O_7 + 7H_2SO_4 \rightarrow 3I_2 + Cr_2(SO_4)_3 + Na_2SO_4 + 3K_2SO_4 + 7H_2O$$
(potassium iodide + sodium dichromate + sulfuric acid → iodine
+ chromium sulfate + sodium sulfate + potassium sulfate + water)

Some compounds of iodine

Iodine, like all of the lighter halogens, combines readily with most metals to form iodide salts. The I⁻ ion, for example, combines with sodium and potassium to form two of the most common compounds of iodine:

Sodium iodide, NaI

$$Na^+ + I^- \rightarrow NaI$$

Potassium iodide, KI

$$K^+ + I^- \rightarrow KI$$

Iodine combines readily with oxygen to form the iodate ion, IO_3^-, thus accounting for iodine's +5 oxidation state:

$$I^{5+} + 3O^{2-} \rightarrow IO_3^-$$

The most common iodates are those that occur naturally and serve as one of the world sources of iodine:

Sodium iodate, $NaIO_3$

$$Na^+ + IO_3^- \rightarrow NaIO_3$$

Calcium iodate, $Ca(IO_3)_2$

$$Ca^{2+} + 2IO_3^- \rightarrow Ca(IO_3)_2$$

Then there is the moderately strong acid, *iodic acid*, HIO_3.

Iodine's +7 oxidate state shows up in the periodates such as *potassium metaperiodate*, KIO_4:

$$K^+ + I^{7+} + 4O^{2-} \rightarrow KIO_4$$

The simplest and one of the most commercially important compounds of iodine is *hydrogen iodide*, HI. When it is dissolved in water, it becomes one of the strongest aqueous acids, *hydriodic acid*. Hydriodic acid is a starting point in the production of virtually all iodine compounds that are not readily obtained from nature.

Isotopes of iodine

Figure 53-1 shows the isotopes of iodine. You can see that all naturally occurring iodine is iodine-127. Radioactive iodine-131 is used in medical diagnosis to monitor and trace the flow of thyroxin from the thyroid gland.

Isotope	Natural Abundance	Half-Life	Decay Mode
^{110}I		650 ms	β+, ec
^{111}I		7.5 sec	β+, ec
^{112}I		3.4 sec	β+, ec
^{113}I		5.9 sec	β+, ec
^{114}I		2.1 sec	β+, ec
^{115}I		28 sec	β+, ec
^{116}I		2.9 sec	β+, ec
^{117}I		2.3 min	β+, ec
^{118m}I		8.5 min	β+, ec
^{118}I		14.3 min	β+, ec
^{119}I		19.2 min	β+, ec
^{120m}I		53 min	β+, ec
^{120}I		1.35 hr	β+, ec
^{121}I		2.12 hr	β+, ec
^{122}I		3.6 min	β+, ec
^{123}I		13.1 hr	ec
^{124}I		4.17 day	β+, e
^{125}I		59.9 day	ec
^{126}I		13 day	β+, ec
^{127}I	100%		
^{128}I		25 min	β-, ec
^{129}I		1.6×10^7 yr	β-, ec
^{130m}I		9 min	β-
^{130}I		12.36 hr	β-
^{131}I		8.04 day	β-
^{132}I		83 min	β-
^{133m}I		9 sec	i.t.
^{133}I		20.8 hr	β-
^{134m}I		3.5 min	β-, i.t.
^{134}I		52.5 min	β-
^{135}I		6.59 hr	β-
^{136m}I		45 sec	β-
^{136}I		83.6 sec	β-
^{137}I		24.5 sec	β-
^{138}I		6.4 sec	β-
^{139}I		2.3 sec	β-
^{140}I		860 ms	β-, n

53-1 Iodine has isotopes with atomic weights between 110 and 140.

Element 54: Xenon

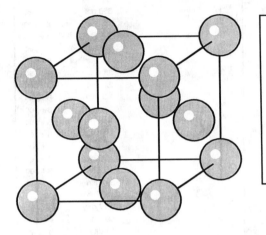

Name	Xenon
Symbol	Xe
Atomic Number	54
Atomic Weight	131.30
Melting Point	-111.9°C
Boiling Point	-107.1°C
Density	5.88 g/l
	(gas, 1 atm, 0°C)
Specific Gravity	3.52 (liquid, -109°C)
Oxidation State	0
Electron Config.	$(Kr)\ 4d^{10}\ 5s^2\ 5p^6$

- Name pronounced as **ZEE-non**
- Name taken from the greek, *xenos*, "strange"
- Discovered by Sir William Ramsay and M.W. Travers in 1898
- Heavy, colorless, and odorless noble gas

Xenon is the rarest of the gassy elements in the earth's atmosphere (see Fig. 54-1). For every 1000-million atoms of air, only 87 are xenon atmos. Even so, it is commonly recovered from liquified air in commercially useful amounts.

Xenon is by far the most popular choice for the gas used in strobe lamps; electrical excitation of xenon causes it to produce a burst of brilliant white light. This heavy gas also finds applications in modern nuclear power reactors.

Historical background

Most people never get around to discovering a new element. Few have discovered three of them, and even fewer have discovered three new elements in as many consecutive months; but Sir William Ramsay (1852 – 1916), and Morris William Travers (1872 – 1961), pulled off the hat trick in May, June, and July of 1898. The elements they added to the periodic table were krypton (May 30), neon (sometime in June), and xenon (July 12, 1898).

Their astounding achievement was based on their mastery of the new technology of refrigeration. With access to the finest refrigeration pumps and valves of the day, Ramsay and Travers could liquify large quantities of air and adjust the pressures and temperatures in order to fraction the liquid into its essential components.

Xenon was the last to be discovered in this series, mainly because of its relative scarcity in the atmosphere. They had to produce about 10,000 pounds of liquid krypton and neon in order to obtain one pound of xenon. The separation was made possible by two facts: xenon is so much more dense and has a much higher critical temperature than the other two gasses. Nevertheless, Ramsay thought it appropriate to call element 54, *xenon*, the "strange one." (After all, it took the researchers nearly a whole month to find it.)

Gas (Sea level)	Content by volume	
	(percent)	(ppm)
Nitrogen, N_2	78.09	—
Oxygen, O_2	20.95	—
Argon, Ar	0.93	—
Carbon Dioxide, CO_2	0.03	—
Neon, Ne	—	18.18
Helium, He	—	5.24
Krypton, Kr	—	1.14
Methane, CH_4	—	2
Nitrous oxide, N_2O	—	0.5
Hydrogen, H_2	—	.05
Xenon, Xe	—	.087

54-1 Xenon is the least abundant of the gasses in the earth's atmosphere.

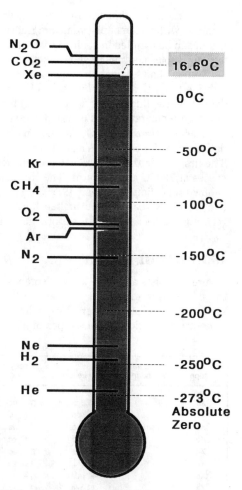

54-2 The critical temperature of xenon is well above that of oxygen, so it easily boils away from quantities of commercially prepared liquid oxygen.

Properties and production of xenon

Xenon is one of the Group-0, noble gasses. It is a heavy gas—about 4.5 times heavier than air—and is colorless, odorless, and tasteless.

Xenon is recovered on a commercial scale by the fractional distillation of liquid air. Figure 54-2 shows that xenon, with a critical temperature of 16.6 °C, is among the gasses that boil off between carbon dioxide and oxygen.

Some compounds of xenon

Before 1962, it would have been a mistake to suggest that there could be any compounds of xenon. The noble gasses were known to be absolutely inert—they could not combine with any other element. In 1962, however, Neil Bartlett coaxed a sample of xenon to combine with an ion of platinum and fluorine to produce the first noble-gas compound. Now xenon can be handled in such a way that it exhibits four different oxidation states, although periodic tables commonly show a single oxidation state of 0.

Xenon shows oxidation states of $+2$, $+4$, and $+6$, respectively when it combines with fluoride to form *xenon difluoride* (XeF_2), *xenon tetrafluoride* (XeF_4), and *xenon hexafluoride* (XeF_6). These fluorides of xenon are all formed by reacting the gasses in a nickel container at a high temperature and elevated pressures.

Xenon tetraoxide (XeO_4) is a fascinating gas. For one thing, it shows xenon with an oxidation state of $+8$; but it is also characterized as a highly unstable and extremely explosive. The first step in the process is to prepare xenon hexafluoride by reacting xenon and fluorine gasses at 700 °C and 200 atm. The XeF_6 from this reaction is a white solid that melts to a yellow-green liquid at just 49.5 °C. The second step is to produce sodium perxenate (Na_4XeO_6) by reacting the molten hexafluoride with sodium hydroxide (NaOH). Finally, reacting the perxenate with sulfuric acid yields the XeO_4 gas.

Isotopes of xenon

Figure 54-3 lists all of the known isotopes of xenon. Most naturally occurring xenon (what there is of it) is xenon-129 -131, and -132. Xenon-133 is the only radioactive version being seriously considered as a practical source of radiation. Xenon-133 and -135 are byproducts of neutron radiation in some types of nuclear reactors.

Isotope	Natural Abundance	Half-Life	Decay Mode
^{114}Xe		10.3 sec	β+, ec
^{115}Xe		18 sec	β+, ec
^{116}Xe		57 sec	β+, ec
^{117}Xe		61 sec	β+, ec
^{118}Xe		4 min	β+, ec
^{119}Xe		5.8 min	β+, ec
^{120}Xe		40 min	β+, ec
^{121}Xe		39 min	β+, ec
^{122}Xe		20 hr	ec
^{123}Xe		2 hr	β+, ec
^{124}Xe	0.10%		
^{125m}Xe		57 sec	i.t.
^{125}Xe		17.1 hr	ec
^{126}Xe	0.09%		
^{127m}Xe		69 sec	i.t.
^{127}Xe		36.3 day	ec
^{128}Xe	1.91%		
^{129m}Xe		8.88 day	i.t.

Isotope	Natural Abundance	Half-Life	Decay Mode
^{129}Xe	26.4%		i.t.
^{130}Xe	4.1%		i.t.
^{131m}Xe		11.9 day	i.t.
^{131}Xe	21.2%		
^{132}Xe	26.9%		
^{133m}Xe		2.19 day	i.t.
^{133}Xe		5.25 day	β-
^{134}Xe	10.4%		
^{135m}Xe		15.3 min	i.t.
^{135}Xe		9.1 hr	β-
^{136}Xe	8.9%		
^{137}Xe		3.84 min	β-
^{138}Xe		14.1 min	β-
^{139}Xe		40.4 sec	β-
^{140}Xe		13.6 day	β-
^{141}Xe		1.72 sec	β-
^{142}Xe		1.2 sec	β-

54-3 Xenon has isotopes with atomic weights between 114 and 142.

Element 55: Cesium

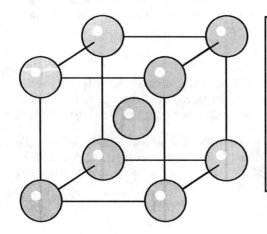

Name	Cesium
Symbol	Cs
Atomic Number	55
Atomic Weight	132.905
Melting Point	28.40°C
Boiling Point	669.3°C
Specific Gravity	1.873 (20°C)
Oxidation State	+1
Electron Config.	(Xe) $6s^1$

- Name pronounced as **SEE-zi-em**
- Name taken from the Latin *coesius*, "sky blue"; named for the characteristic blue lines of its spectrum
- Discovered by Robert Bunsen and Gustav Kirchoff in 1860
- Very soft, ductile, light gray metal

Cesium is an element of extremes. It is the most electropositive of all the elements, for example; and its hydroxide is the strongest base known. It is one of the few metals that is in a molten state at normal temperatures; and in its solid form, cesium is the softest of all metals. It reacts explosively with water and readily absorbs atmospheric oxygen.

Because cesium reacts so readily with most kinds of gasses, it is used as a *getter*—an absorber of unwanted gasses—in electronic vacuum tubes and cathode-ray tubes. It is also used in the production of photoelectric devices and atomic clocks.

It is hoped that cesium will one day supply the vast doses of massive, high-energy ions required for plasma-drive engines for interstellar vehicles.

Historical background

In November, 1859, Robert Wilhem Bunsen (1811 – 1899), was expressing to his contemporaries his great enthusiasm for the new technology of spectroscopic chemical analysis. His coworker, Gustav Robert Kirchhoff (1824 – 1887), shared his enthusiasm. The two established the technology, publishing a classic work in 1860, *Chemical Analysis through Observation of the Spectrum*.

During the course of their studies, Bunsen and Kirchhoff came up with the idea of using the spectroscope to look at the lines identifying the principal elements in Durkheim mineral water. (Maybe that is what happened to be in the water cooler down the hall.) Anyway, they found spectral lines for sodium, potassium, lithium, calcium, and strontium. Then they started chemically removing the metals and observing the absence of their lines from the spectrum. As the lines began disappearing, however, two bright blue lines unexpectedly appeared.

If Bunsen and Kirchhoff understood their new technology properly, the discovery of new spectral lines was tantamount to discovering a new element. That was indeed the case, and Bunsen suggested the name, *cesium*, "sky blue."

Properties of cesium

Cesium is one of the Group-IA alkali metals. This group includes more familiar active metals such as lithium (Li), sodium (Na), and potassium (K). These have been called alkali metals because they react explosively with water to produce a caustic metal hydroxide, or alkali, compound.

Few people have ever seen a blob of pure cesium metal. Those who have seen the solid form say it is a silvery white, soft, and ductile metal. It is easily melted at 28.4 °C, or about 83 °F, so it often exists as a liquid that looks much like mercury. In fact, mercury is the only metal that has a melting point lower than cesium.

Production of cesium

The main source of cesium is the mineral *pollucite*, $CsAlSi_2O_6$, although carbonates of cesium are usually mixed with the potassium ore, *lepidolite*. The main problem with refining cesium metal is that rubidium is always mixed with the ores, and this element has many critical properties that are nearly identical to cesium. As a result, rubidium and cesium can be difficult to separate from one another.

A mixture of rubidium and cesium is obtained from one of the ores—sometimes lepidolite, but usually pollucite. This mixture was originally obtained by a lengthy and tedious crystallization process; nowadays it is accomplished more economically by reducing the metals with elemental sodium. In this process, the ores are finely ground and heated to about 650 °C with sodium metal. The result is an alloy of sodium, cesium, and rubidium. The three metals are then separated by fractional distillation, much the same way the atmospheric gasses are separated from liquid air.

Some compounds and the isotopes of cesium

The most abundant natural compound of cesium is the mineral, pollucite. This compound is used only as a source of cesium metal. Cesium chloride (CsCl) and cesium nitrate ($CsNO_3$) are the most popular compounds and the starting point for the production of other chemicals.

The most stable cesium ion has a $+1$ charge, so it reacts with anions of -1 and -2 in the following ways:

Cesium chloride, CsCl

$$Cs^+ + Cl^- \rightarrow CsCl$$

Cesium nitrate, $CsNO_3$

$$2Cs^+ + NO_3^- \rightarrow CsNO_3$$

Cesium chloride can be produced by reacting cesium metal with chlorine gas at a high temperature. Cesium nitrate can be produced by the reaction between nitric acid and the cesium carbonate that is available in the byproducts of a lithium refinery.

A close cousin of cesium nitrate is *cesium azide*, CsN_3. This compound serves as a convenient commercial source of cesium metal. While the metal, itself, is difficult and dangerous to handle, cesium azide can be safely and easily shipped and stored. When someone needs a bit of cesium metal, he only has to heat the azide until it decomposes into cesium metal and nitrogen gas.

Cesium hydroxide is the most powerful base yet discovered. It is easily manufactured by dropping cesium metal into water. The resulting violent reaction produces cesium hydroxide and hydrogen gas:

$$2Cs + H_2O \rightarrow 2CsOH + H_2$$

(cesium + water → cesium hydroxide + hydrogen gas)

Figure 55-1 lists the isotopes of cesium. Notice that all naturally occurring cesium is cesium-133.

Isotope	Natural Abundance	Half-Life	Decay Mode	Isotope	Natural Abundance	Half-Life	Decay Mode
^{114}Cs		570 ms	β+, ec	^{130}Cs		29.2 min	β+, ec
^{115}Cs		1.4 sec	β+, ec	^{131}Cs		9.69 day	ec
^{116m}Cs		700 ms	β+, ec	^{132}Cs		6.47 day	β+, ec
^{116}Cs		3.8 sec	β+, ec	^{133}Cs	100%		
^{117}Cs		6.7 sec	β+, ec	^{134m}Cs		2.91 hr	i.t.
^{118}Cs		15 sec	β+, ec	^{134}Cs		2.1 yr	β-
^{119}Cs		38 sec	β+, ec	^{135m}Cs		53 min	i.t.
^{120}Cs		64 sec	β+, ec	^{135}Cs		3x10^6 yr	β-
^{121m}Cs		212 sec	β+, i.t.	^{136m}Cs		19 sec	β-, i.t.
^{121}Cs		136 sec	β+, ec	^{136}Cs		13.1 day	β-
^{122m}Cs		4.4 min	β+, ec	^{137}Cs		30.2 yr	β-
^{122}Cs		21 sec		^{138m}Cs		2.9 min	β-, i.t.
^{123m}Cs		1.7 sec	β+, ec	^{138}Cs			β-
^{123}Cs		5.9 min	β+, ec	^{139}Cs			β-
^{124}Cs		30.8 sec	β+, i.t.	^{140}Cs		63.7 sec	β-
^{125}Cs		45 min	β+, ec	^{141}Cs		24.9 sec	β-
^{126}Cs		64 min	ec	^{142}Cs		1.8 sec	β-
^{127}Cs		6.2 hr	β+, ec	^{143}Cs		1.78 sec	β-
^{128}Cs		3.62 min	β+, ec	^{144}Cs		1.01 sec	β-
^{129}Cs		32.3 hr	ec	^{145}Cs		580 ms	β-

55-1 Cesium has isotopes with atomic weights between 114 and 145.

Element 56: Barium

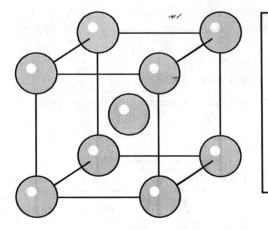

Name	Barium
Symbol	Ba
Atomic Number	56
Atomic Weight	137.33
Melting Point	725°C
Boiling Point	1640°C
Specific Gravity	3.51 (20°C)
Oxidation State	+2
Electron Config.	(Xe) $6s^2$

- Name pronounced as **BAR-i-em**
- Name from the Greek *barys*, "heavy"
- Isolated by Sir Humphry Davy in 1808
- Soft, slightly malleable, silvery-white metal

The historical background for barium is just about as varied and colorful as its modern-day applications—from the eerie, glowing Bologna stone of sixteenth-century alchemists to the modern day technology of ultrasonics. Barium ranks sixth in abundance among the elements in the earth's crust; however, its applications, though well established and wide ranging, consume relatively small amounts of this natural source.

Historical background

The recorded history of barium begins with the discovery of Bologna stones near Bologna, Italy, in the very early 1500s. These smooth, rounded pebbles glowed in the presence of light from the sun, moon, or a lamp. They would glow in the dark for nearly six years after heating them intensely in the presence of carbon black, or charcoal.

Researchers, including some alchemists and witches, were attracted to the strange stones that could be forced to glow in the dark. We now know they were working with the mineral, *barite*, or barium sulfate, $BaSO_4$.

Chemists in the late 1700s were able to prepare compounds of barium and, in the process, discovered natural *witherite*, or barium carbonate, $BaCO_3$.

The metal, itself, could not be isolated until the invention of Volta's electric pile and the technique of electrolysis. In 1808, Sir Humphry Davy (1778 – 1829) managed to electrolyze metallic barium from a mixture of molten barium compounds commonly known as *baryta*.

Properties of barium

Barium belongs to the set of Group-IIA metals known as the *alkaline-earth metals*. This means they have a number of significant properties in common. They are all very metallic in nature, for example. They are silvery white, fairly hard, and are good conductors of electricity. They all have much higher melting temperatures than their alkali-metal counterparts in Group IA.

They are traditionally called alkaline earths because, to the eyes of early chemists, they appeared to share the properties of both alkalis and earths. They missed the metallic properties because none of this group occurs in an elemental form in nature.

Barium metal burns easily in air to produce barium oxide:

$$2Ba + O_2 \rightarrow 2BaO$$
$$(barium + oxygen \rightarrow barium\ oxide)$$

it reacts with water to yield barium hydroxide and hydrogen:

$$Ba + 2H_2O \rightarrow Ba(OH)_2 + H_2$$
$$(barium + water \rightarrow barium\ hydroxide + hydrogen)$$

Production of barium

Small amounts of barium metal are prepared by the electrolysis of molten, or fused, barium chloride. The reactions are:

$$2Cl^- \rightarrow Cl_2 + 2e^-\ (anode\ reaction)$$
$$bA^+ > + e^- \rightarrow Ba\ (cathode\ reaction)$$
$$2Ba^+ + 2Cl^- \rightarrow 2Ba + Cl_2\ (cell\ reaction)$$

The melting point of barium chloride is 963 °C, and the melting point of barium metal is 725 °C. Therefore, maintaining a temperature of 963 °C allows the electrolysis to take place and causes liquid barium metal to collect at the cathode. (See Fig. 56-1.)

56-1 Barium can be produced by the electrolysis of its chloride.

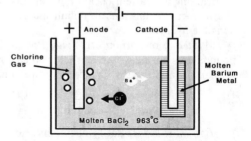

Most commercial-grade barium, however, is produced by reducing barium oxide with aluminum under carefully controlled conditions of temperature and low pressure. The reaction is:

$$3BaO + 2Al \rightarrow 3Ba + Al_2O_3$$
$$(Barium\ oxide + aluminum \rightarrow barium + aluminum\ oxide)$$

Some compounds of barium

Barium's most stable oxidation state is +2, so the most common ionic form is Ba^{2+}. Ionic bonds with anions having a −1 charge form compounds such as:

Barium chloride, $BaCl_2$

$$Ba^{2+} + 2Cl^- \rightarrow BaCl1_2$$

Barium hydroxide, $Ba(OH)_2$

$$Ba^{2+} + 2OH^- \rightarrow Ba(OH)_2$$

There are two oxides of barium, one using the stable Ba^{2+} ion and the other a less stable Ba^{4+} ion:

Barium oxide, BaO

$$Ba^{2+} + O^2 \rightarrow BaO$$

Barium peroxide, BaO_2

$$Ba^{4+} + 2O^2 \rightarrow BaO_2$$

Barium arsenide is an example of one of the few stable compounds where Ba^{2+} combines with an anion having a charge greater than 2 – :

$$3Ba^{2+} + 2As^{3-} \rightarrow Ba_3As_2$$

Barite, or barium sulfate ($BaSO_4$, is the primary natural source of barium compounds and, ultimately the metal, itself. It has some interesting applications of its own, however. Ground barite is used as a filler for rubber, plastics, and resins. Purified barite is used as a paint pigment. A white pigment commonly known as *lithophone* is a mixture of barium sulfate and zinc oxide. *Blanc fixe*, a very high-quality white pigment and base for other oil-based colors, is a mixture of barium sulfate and sodium sulfate.

Barium sulfate is unusually insoluble in water. So, in spite of the fact that it is technically considered a deadly poison (as all barium compounds are), it can be swallowed and passed through the body before any of it can be absorbed. Why would anyone want to swallow this toxin that cannot harm you? Well, it also happens to be unusually opaque to X-rays. So drinking a "barium cocktail" soon fills your digestive system with barium sulfate and allows X-ray technicians to obtain images of the soft internal tissues that are otherwise invisible to X-rays.

Witherite, or *barium carbonate*, $BaCO_3$, is a secondary source of barite and its compounds. It is normally found in veins of lead ore, or *galena*. Higher grades of barium carbonate can be produced by a reaction between barium chloride and sodium carbonate:

$$BaCl_2 + Na_2CO_3 \rightarrow BaCO_3 + 2NaCl$$
(barium chloride + sodium carbonate → barium carbonate + sodium chloride)

Barium chloride, $BaCl_2$, has applications in the chemical industry and as a water softener. It is prepared by heating barite in the presence of coal and calcium chloride ($CaCl_2$), by adding a chloride to barium sulfide, and by treating witherite with hydrochloric acid (HCl).

Barium oxide, BaO, can appear as a white powder or grayish lumps, depending on the purity. It strongly absorbs moisture and is thus used as an industrial drying agent. It also absorbs carbon dioxide quite readily. Other names for this compound of barium are *baryta* and *calcined baryta*.

When *barium peroxide*, BaO_2, is mixed with ordinary water, it forms hydrogen peroxide (H_2O_2)—a bleaching agent. Barium peroxide is available as a "dry" bleaching agent that releases its bleaching qualities when mixed with cold water. This grayish-white powder can be formed by exposing barium oxide (BaO) to dry oxygen at about 100 °C.

Barium nitrate, $Ba(NO_3)_2$, burns with a brilliant green color and is thus used in pyrotechnic products such as signal flares and fireworks. It is easily produced by treating barium carbonate with nitric acid. The byproduct in this case is carbonic acid:

$$BaCO_3 + 2HNO_3 \rightarrow Ba(NO_3)_2 + H_2CO_3$$
(barium carbonate + nitric acid → barium nitrate + carbonic acid)

Barium titanate, $BaTiO_3$, has a high dielectric property that makes it a popular electrolytic material for capacitors in electronic applications.

Isotopes of barium

Figure 56-2 lists the isotopes of barium. Seven species of stable barium isotopes occur in nature. The radioactive isotopes are all produced in the laboratory.

Isotope	Natural Abundance	Half-Life	Decay Mode
^{120}Ba		32 sec	β+, ec
^{121}Ba		30 sec	β+, ec
^{122}Ba		2 min	β+, ec
^{123}Ba		2.7 min	β+, ec
^{124}Ba		11.4 min	β+, ec
^{125}Ba		3.5 min	β+, ec
^{126}Ba		99 min	β+, ec
^{127}Ba		12 min	β+, ec
^{128}Ba		2.43 day	ec
^{129m}Ba		2.1 hr	β+, ec
^{129}Ba		2.5 hr	β+, ec
^{130}Ba	0.106%		
^{131m}Ba		14.6 min	i.t.
^{131}Ba		11.8 day	ec
^{132}Ba	0.101%		
^{133m}Ba		38.9 hr	i.t.
^{133}Ba		10.53 yr	ec
^{134}Ba	2.417%		
^{135m}Ba		28.7 hr	i.t.
^{135}Ba	6.592%		
^{136m}Ba		306 ms	i.t.
^{136}Ba	7.854%		
^{137m}Ba		2.55 min	i.t.
^{137}Ba	11.23%		
^{138}Ba	71.7%		
^{139}Ba		1.41 hr	β-
^{140}Ba		12.76 day	β-
^{141}Ba		18.3 min	β-
^{142}Ba		10.7 min	β-
^{143}Ba		15 sec	β-
^{144}Ba		11.5 sec	β-
^{145}Ba		4 sec	β-
^{146}Ba		2.2 sec	β-
^{147}Ba		700 ms	β-
^{148}Ba		470 ms	β-, n

56-2 Barium has isotopes with atomic weights between 120 and 148.

Element 57: Lanthanum

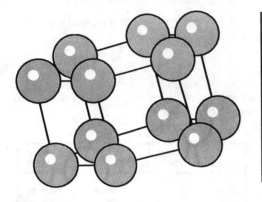

Name	Lanthanum
Symbol	La
Atomic Number	57
Atomic Weight	138.91
Melting Point	918°C
Boiling Point	3464°C
Specific Gravity	6.145 (25°C)
Oxidation State	+3
Electron Config.	(Xe) $5d^1 6s^2$

- Name pronounced as **LAN-the-nem**
- Name taken from the Greek, *lanthanein*, "to be hidden"
- Identified as a rare earth by Carl Gustaf Mosander in 1893
- Silvery-white, soft, malleable, and ductile metal
- Heads the list of important lanthanide elements

Lanthanum is the fourth most common rare-earth element in the earth's crust (see Fig. 57-1). At 18 parts per million, the abundance of lanthanum is on the same order as some of the better-known metals such as nickel, lead, and zinc. It is most influential as the first of an important series of elements called the *lanthanide* series.

Lanthanum is one of the rare-earth metals included in the electrodes for high-intensity, carbon-arc lights—the kind typically used in commercial motion picture projectors and searchlights. It also plays an important role in the production of high-grade europium metal.

Historical background

Today we know that all sixteen of the naturally occurring rare earths are found mixed together in their oxide forms, but that was not known in the last decades of the 1800s. At that time, there were just two rare-earth oxides, yttria and ceria. Carl Gustav Mosander and others saw the possibility that their samples of yttria and ceria were not absolutely pure, so they set out to look for the impurities.

In 1839, for example, Mosander obtained some cerium nitrate and treated it with dilute nitric acid. The reaction yielded a new oxide which Mosander called lanthana. So the cerium was indeed contaminated with a new element—one we now call lanthanum.

Mosander not only discovered a new element, but upset all of the physical properties of the element known as cerium. Until that time, all chemical research on cerium was conducted with samples that included lanthanum. Once the lanthanum was removed, the figures had to change. In a manner of speaking, Mosander discarded one element from the periodic table and added two new ones. He could have had cerium erased from the periodic table of his time, substituting a name of his own invention; but he chose not to do so.

Rank (Rare Earths)	Rare-Earth Element	Abundance (ppm)
1	Cerium, Ce	46.0
2	Yttrium, Y	28.0
3	Neodymium, Nd	24.0
4	Lanthanum, La	18.0
5	Samarium, Sm	6.5
6	Gadolinium, Gd	6.4
7	Praseodymium, Pr	5.5
8	Scandium, Sc	5.0
9	Dysprosium, Dy	4.5
10	Ytterbium, Yb	2.7
11	Erbium, Er	2.5
12	Holmium, Ho	1.2
13	Europium, Eu	1.1
14	Terbium, Tb	0.9
15	Lutetium, Lu	0.8
16	Thulium, Tm	0.2
17	Promethium, Pm	0.0

57-1 Lanthanum is ranked fourth on the abundance chart for rare earths found in the earth's crust.

Isotope	Natural Abundance	Half-Life	Decay Mode
^{125}La		76 sec	$\beta+$, ec
^{126}La		1 min	$\beta+$, ec
^{127}La		3.8 min	$\beta+$, ec
^{128}La		4.6 min	$\beta+$, ec
^{129}La		11.6 min	$\beta+$, ec
^{130}La		8.7 min	$\beta+$, ec
^{131}La		59 min	$\beta+$, ec
^{132m}La		24 min	$\beta+$, i.t.
^{132}La		4.8 hr	$\beta+$, ec
^{133}La		3.91 hr	$\beta+$, ec
^{134}La		6.5 min	$\beta+$, ec
^{135}La		19.5 hr	ec
^{136}La		9.87 min	$\beta+$, ec
^{137}La		6×10^4 yr	ec
^{138}La	0.09%	1.06×10^{11} yr	β-, ec
^{139}La	99.91%		
^{140}La		40.28 hr	β-
^{141}La		3.93 hr	β-
^{142}La		92 min	β-
^{143}La		14.1 min	β-
^{144}La		40 sec	β-
^{145}La		25 sec	β-
^{146}La		10 sec	β-
^{147}La		4.1 sec	β-
^{148}La		2.6 sec	β-
^{149}La		1.2 sec	β-

57-2 Lanthanum has isotopes with atomic weights between 125 and 149.

Mosander's notion of finding a new rare-earth element as an impurity in an older one was applied throughout the discovery of the remaining natural rare-earth elements. Like Mosander, all the discoverers chose to retain the name of the parent earth.

Properties of lanthanum

Lanthanum is silvery white, malleable, and ductile. It is soft enough to be cut with a knife. It is a reactive rare earth, second only to europium in that respect. It reacts in dry air, burning at about 440 °C, and it reacts vigorously in hot water.

Lanthanum is in a unique position on the periodic table, at the beginning of the lanthanide series. Beginning with lanthanum, itself (element 57), the series resumes on a separate line below the main body of the table. This line begins with cerium (element 58) and ends with lutetium (element 71). Lutetium is not only the last of the lanthanide series, but the last of the rare-earth metals as well. The periodic sequence then returns to the main body of the table with hafnium (element 72).

Commercial production of lanthanum

Most commercial-grade lanthanum is obtained from *monazite sand*, which is a mixture of phosphates of calcium, thorium, cerium, and most of the other rare earths. This sand, in fact, is often 50% rare earth by weight, and about 25% lanthanum. Most of the unwanted metals are removed magnetically or by flotation processes. The remaining problem is one of separating the rare earths from one another.

Like most rare-earth metals, lanthanum can be separated from other rare earths by means of ion-exchange displacement. The result is a lanthanum ion which can react with a fluoride or chloride ion to form lanthanum fluoride (LaF_3) and lanthanum chloride ($LaCl_3$).

Lanthanum is also produced by reducing lanthanum fluoride with calcium metal:

$$3Ca + 2LaF_3 \rightarrow 2La + 3CaF_2$$
(calcium metal + lanthanum fluoride → lanthanum metal + calcium fluoride)

The same kind of reaction is possible with lithium metal and lanthanum chloride:

$$3Li + LaCl_3 \rightarrow La + 3LiCl$$
(lithium metal + lanthanum chloride → lanthanum metal + lithium chloride)

In either case, the lanthanum halide and active metal are loaded into a tantalum crucible and fired in a helium atmosphere. As the reaction progresses, the molten lanthanum halide compound and excess active metal separate due to differences in density. When this layered mixture is allowed to cool, the lanthanum is simply cut away from the impurities. The operation can be repeated as often as necessary to achieve the desired level of purity.

Some compounds and the isotopes of lanthanum

Like most rare-earth metals, lanthanum's most stable oxidation state is +3; and like most rare earths, the lanthanum metal ion, La^{3+}, readily combines with chlorine and oxygen to form two of its most common compounds:

Lanthanum chloride, $LaCl_3$

$$La^{3+} + 3Cl^- \rightarrow LaCl_3$$

Lanthanum oxide, La_2O_3 (also known as *lanthana*)

$$2La^{3+} + 3O^{2-} \rightarrow La_2O_3$$

Higher oxidation states are indicated by the existence of lanthanum pentacholride and lanthanum carbide, LaC_2: $La^{8+} + 2C^{4-} \rightarrow LaC_2$

Most lanthanum compounds are colorless or white.

Figure 57-2 on p. 209 lists all of the known isotopes of lanthanum. More than 99.9% of naturally occurring lanthanum is stable, or nonradioactive, lanthanum-139; a small fraction of native lanthanum is radioactive lanthanum-138. The remainder of the isotopes are both synthetic and radioactive.

Element 58: Cerium

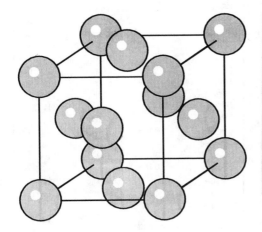

Name	Cerium
Symbol	Ce
Atomic Number	58
Atomic Weight	140.12
Melting Point	798°C
Boiling Point	3443°C
Specific Gravity	6.672 (25°C)
Oxidation States	+3, +4
Electron Config.	(Xe) $4f^2\ 6s^2$

- Name pronounced as **SER-i-em**
- Named for the asteroid, Ceres, discovered just two years before the element
- The oxide form was discovered in 1803 by Jons Jacob Berzelius and Wilhelm Hisinger, and found independently by Martin Klaproth in the same year
- Malleable, ductile, iron-gray metal

Cerium is the most abundant of the rare-earth metals. As indicated in Fig. 58-1, it is found in 46 parts per million among the other elements in the earth's crust. Even so, its existence was unknown until 1804, and it was not isolated in its pure metallic form until 1875. There were no practical applications until the middle part of this century.

Cerium metal is too unstable under ordinary environmental conditions to be of any practical importance. Its oxides are stable, however, and find commercial applications in the optics and glass-making industries. Other salts, notably the halides, are used in the photography and the textile industry. Cerium, as well as several other rare-earth elements, are used in high-intensity carbon lamps and as alloying agents in special metals.

Historical background

Jöns Jacob Berzelius (1779 – 1848) was certainly the father of many elements that were discovered and isolated through the first half of the nineteenth century. He was also a prolific and skilled writer. The following is taken from one of his accounts of the discovery of cerium:

> In the iron mine at Bastnäs, now abandoned, "Berzelius wrote," . . . one finds a mineral of exceedingly high specific gravity, called 'heavy stone of Bastnas'; that is why [Karl Wilhelm] Scheele searched there, but in vain, for tungsten. This mineral remained in oblivion until 1803, when it was simultaneously examined by Klaproth, by Hisinger and by myself. We found in it a new substance; Klaproth called it terre ochrioite. Hisinger and I called it cerous oxide . . .

Rank (Rare Earths)	Rare-Earth Element	Abundance (ppm)
1	Cerium, Ce	46.0
2	Yttrium, Y	28.0
3	Neodymium, Nd	24.0
4	Lanthanum, La	18.0
5	Samarium, Sm	6.5
6	Gadolinium, Gd	6.4
7	Praseodymium, Pr	5.5
8	Scandium, Sc	5.0
9	Dysprosium, Dy	4.5
10	Ytterbium, Yb	2.7
11	Erbium, Er	2.5
12	Holmium, Ho	1.2
13	Europium, Eu	1.1
14	Terbium, Tb	0.9
15	Lutetium, Lu	0.8
16	Thulium, Tm	0.2
17	Promethium, Pm	0.0

58-1 Cerium is ranked first on the abundance chart for rare earths found in the earth's crust.

Isotope	Natural Abundance	Half-Life	Decay Mode
^{129}Ce		3.5 min	β+, ec
^{130}Ce		25 min	β+, ec
^{131m}Ce		5 min	β+, ec
^{131}Ce		9.5 min	β+, ec
^{132}Ce		3.5 hr	ec
^{133m}Ce		97 min	β+, ec
^{133}Ce		5.4 hr	β+, ec
^{134}Ce		76 hr	ec
^{135m}Ce		20 sec	i.t.
^{135}Ce		17.8 hr	
^{136}Ce	0.19%		
^{137m}Ce		34.4 hr	ec, i.t.
^{137}Ce		9 hr	β+
^{138}Ce	0.25%		
^{139m}Ce		56 sec	i.t.
^{139}Ce			β-
^{140}Ce	88.48%		
^{141}Ce		32.5 day	β-
^{142}Ce	11.08%		
^{143}Ce		33 hr	β-
^{144}Ce		284.4 day	β-
^{145}Ce		2.9 min	β-
^{146}Ce		13.6 min	β-
^{147}Ce		56 sec	β-
^{148}Ce		48 sec	β-
^{149}Ce		5.2 sec	β-
^{150}Ce		4.4 sec	β-
^{151}Ce		1.0 sec	β-

58-2 Cerium has isotopes with atomic weights between 129 and 151.

Ironically, Berzelius and Hisinger were searching the new mineral for traces of yttria, but found the oxide of the new element instead. Klaproth was evidently looking for the new element mixed with the yttria that was commonly found around the Bastnas mine.

Properties of cerium

Cerium is a shiny gray, malleable, soft, and ductile metal. It readily oxidizes in moist air and decomposes rapidly in hot water. The heat of friction caused by scratching a sample of the pure metal can ignite it.

Cerium is classified as a lanthanide—a member of the series of elements from lanthanum (element 57) through lutetium (element 71). Cerium is also prominent among the rare-earth elements, which include the lanthanide series as well as scandium (element 21) and yttrium (element 39).

There are four allotropes of cerium, α (alpha) through δ (delta). Most of them exist at relatively low temperatures:

- α form, below – 172 °C
- β form, between – 172 °C and – 16 °C

- γ form, between $-16\,°C$ and $726\,°C$
- δ form, above $726\,°C$

The γ (gamma) form is the one that exists under normal environmental conditions.

Production of cerium

Most commercial-grade cerium is obtained from *monazite sand*, which is a mixture of phosphates of calcium, thorium, cerium, and most of the other rare earths. This sand, in fact, is often 50% rare earth by weight. Most of the unwanted metals can be removed magnetically or by flotation processes. The task that remains is to separate cerium from the other rare earths.

Like most rare-earth metals, cerium can be separated from the others by an ion-exchange displacement process. The result is a cerium ion which can react with a fluoride or chloride ion to form cerium fluoride (CeF_3) or cerium chloride ($CeCl_3$).

Cerium is also produced by reducing cerium fluoride with calcium metal:

$$3Ca + 2CeF_3 \rightarrow 2Ce + 3CaF_2$$
(calcium metal + cerium fluoride → cerium metal + calcium fluoride)

The same kind of reaction is possible with lithium metal and cerium chloride:

$$3Li + CeCl_3 \rightarrow Ce + 3LiCl$$
(lithium metal + cerium chloride → cerium metal + lithium chloride)

In either case, the cerium halide and active metal are loaded into a tantalum crucible and fired in a helium atmosphere. As the reaction progresses, the molten cerium, halide compound, and excess active metal separate due to differences in density. When this layered mixture is allowed to cool, the cerium is simply cut away from the impurities. The operation can be repeated as often as necessary to achieve the desired level of purity.

Cerium metal can be produced from molten cerium salts by electrolysis. Here the molten metal collects at the cathode while anion gasses, such as chlorine or fluorine, gather around the anode.

Some compounds and isotopes of cerium

Cerium has two oxidation states, $+3$ and $+4$. Compounds of the $+3$ oxidation state are called cerous, or cerium (III) compounds; those having an oxidation state of $+4$ are called ceric, or cerium (IV) compounds. The fluoride, for example can be cerous fluoride (CeF_3) or ceric fluoride (CeF_4). Although many elements have two or more oxidation states, cerium is unusual inasmuch as the oxidation state apparently changes with temperature and pressure.

The oxides of cerium are:

Cerium (III) oxide, Ce_2O_3

$$2Ce^{3+} + 3O^{2-} \rightarrow Ce_2O_3$$

Cerium (IV) oxide, CeO_2

$$Ce^{4+} + 2O^{2-} \rightarrow CeO_2$$

Examples of other cerium salts are:

Cerium (III) chloride, $CeCl_3$

$$Ce^{3+} + 3Cl^- \rightarrow CeCl_3$$

Cerium (IV) chloride, $CeCl_4$

$$Ce^{4+} + 4Cl^- \rightarrow CeCl_4$$

Cerium (III) sulfate, $Ce_2(SO_4)_3$

$$2Ce^{3+} + 3(SO_4)^{2-} \rightarrow Ce_2(SO_4)_3$$

Cerium (IV) sulfate, $Ce(SO_4)_2$

$$Ce^{4+} + 2(SO_4)^{2+} \rightarrow Ce(SO_4)_2$$

There is also a Ce^{8+} ion as shown by:

Cerium carbide, CeC_2

$$Ce^{8+} + 2C^{4-} \rightarrow CeC_2$$

Cerium silicide, $CeSi_2$

$$Ce^{8+} + 2Si^{4-} \rightarrow CeSi_2$$

Cerium (III) compounds tend to be white or colorless, while cerium (IV) compounds have yellow-to-reddish colors.

Isotopes of cerium

Figure 58-2 on p. 212 shows the known isotopes of cerium. Most of the cerium found in nature is cerium-140.

Element 59: Praseodymium

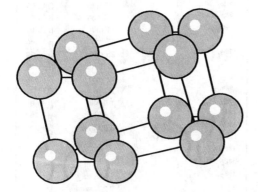

Name	Praseodymium
Symbol	Pr
Atomic Number	59
Atomic Weight	140.908
Melting Point	931°C
Boiling Point	3520°C
Specific Gravity	6.773 (25°C)
Oxidation State	+3
Electron Config.	(Xe) $4f^3 6s^2$

- Name pronounced as **pra-si-eh-DIM-i-em**
- Name taken from the Greek, *prasios + didymos*, "green twin"
- Isolated and identified by Carl Auer von Welsbach in 1885
- Silvery white, moderately soft, malleable, and ductile metal

The most critical application of praseodymium is as high-strength alloying agent in the magnesium used in parts of modern aircraft engines. Misch metal, an important alloying agent in steel and a flint for creating sparks, contains about 5% praseodymium metal.

The yellow didymium glass used in welder's goggles contains a mixture of praseodymium and neodymium. Certain praseodymium compounds are used as yellow pigments.

Figure 59-1 shows that praseodymium ranks seventh in abundance among the rare-earth elements found in the earth's crust.

Historical background

1882 was an important year in the history of rare-earth elements. A number of influential chemists were suggesting that an earth called didymium was actually a mixture of elements, and not a fundamental substance in its own right. A professor at the University of Prague, Professor Bohuslave Brauner, ran a sample of didymium through his spectroscopic lab and discovered two new groups of absorption bands—one in the blue region and another in the yellow. This was clear evidence that there were at least two unknown elements in didymium. They had to be separated, however, before they could be registered as bona fide chemical elements; few people possessed the necessary skill for the job.

One who had the necessary skill was Baron Auer von Welsbach (1858–1929). This Austrian had grown up with a passion for collecting and studying rare earths, and it paid off during the evening of June 18, 1885, when he announced to the Vienna Academy of Sciences that he had split didymium into two new earths by repeated fractionation of ammonium didymium nitrate. He proposed the names praseodymia (green didymia) and neodymia (new didymia), which were later modified to conform to standardized nomenclature requiring such metals to have an *-ium* suffix.

Rank (Rare Earths)	Rare-Earth Element	Abundance (ppm)
1	Cerium, Ce	46.0
2	Yttrium, Y	28.0
3	Neodymium, Nd	24.0
4	Lanthanum, La	18.0
5	Samarium, Sm	6.5
6	Gadolinium, Gd	6.4
7	Praseodymium, Pr	5.5
8	Scandium, Sc	5.0
9	Dysprosium, Dy	4.5
10	Ytterbium, Yb	2.7
11	Erbium, Er	2.5
12	Holmium, Ho	1.2
13	Europium, Eu	1.1
14	Terbium, Tb	0.9
15	Lutetium, Lu	0.8
16	Thulium, Tm	0.2
17	Promethium, Pm	0.0

59-1 Praseodymium is ranked seventh on the abundance chart for rare earths found in the earth's crust.

Isotope	Natural Abundance	Half-Life	Decay Mode
^{132}Pr		1.6 min	$\beta+$, ec
^{133}Pr		6.7 min	$\beta+$, ec
^{134m}Pr		11 min	$\beta+$, ec
^{134}Pr		17 min	$\beta+$, ec
^{135}Pr		25 min	$\beta+$, ec
^{136}Pr		13.1 min	$\beta+$, ec
^{137}Pr		77 min	$\beta+$, ec
^{138m}Pr		2.1 hr	$\beta+$, ec
^{138}Pr		1.5 min	$\beta+$, ec
^{139}Pr		4.41 hr	$\beta+$, ec
^{140}Pr		3.39 min	$\beta+$, ec
^{141}Pr	100%		
^{142m}Pr		14.6 min	i.t.
^{142}Pr		19.13 hr	$\beta-$
^{143}Pr		13.58 day	$\beta-$
^{144m}Pr		7.2 min	i.t.
^{144}Pr			$\beta-$
^{145}Pr		5.98 hr	$\beta-$
^{146}Pr		24.1 min	$\beta-$
^{147}Pr		13.4 min	$\beta-$
^{148m}Pr		2.0 min	$\beta-$
^{148}Pr		2.28 min	$\beta-$
^{149}Pr		2.3 min	$\beta-$
^{150}Pr		6.2 sec	$\beta-$
^{151}Pr		4 sec	$\beta-$
^{152}Pr		3.2 sec	$\beta-$

59-2 Praseodymium has isotopes with atomic weights between 132 and 152.

Properties of praseodymium

Praseodymium is a silvery white, fairly soft, malleable, and ductile metal. It is moderately reactive in air, developing a green oxide coating that eventually falls away to expose fresh metal for further oxidation. The metal is quite reactive in water as well, generating some heat and hydrogen gas.

Praseodymium, aside from being a rare-earth metal, is also a member of the lanthanide series of elements—a series that begins with lanthanum (element 57) and ends with lutetium (element 71).

Production of praseodymium

Most commercial-grade praseodymium is obtained from *monazite sand*—a mixture of phosphates of calcium, thorium, cerium, and most of the other rare earths. This sand is often 50% rare earth by weight. Once the unwanted metals are removed by means of magnetic or flotation processes, the only remaining problem is separating the rare earths from one another.

Like most rare-earth metals, praseodymium can be separated from the others by an ion-exchange displacement process. The result is a praseodymium ion that reacts with an anion to form a binary compound such as praseodymium fluoride (PrF_3), praseodymium chloride ($PrCl_3$), or praseodymium oxide (Pr_2O_3). Where a higher grade of purity is required, praseodymium oxide is distilled to separate remaining traces of rare earth metals and compounds. Reducing rare-earth compounds with calcium or lithium is normally an efficient process for obtaining high-grade metals, but not in the case of praseodymium.

Some compounds and isotopes of praseodymium

The principal oxidation state of praseodymium is $+3$. This means that the most stable compounds are built around the Pr^{3+} metal ion. Some examples are:

Praseodymium chloride, $PrCl_3$

$$Pr^{3+} + 3Cl^- \rightarrow PrCl_3$$

Praseodymium (III) oxide, Pr_2O^3 (also called praseodymium sesquioxide)

$$2Pr^{3+} + 3O^{2-} \rightarrow Pr_2O_3$$

A Pr^{4+} ion shows up in a second oxide, praseodymium dioxide:

Praseodymium (IV) oxide, PrO_2

$$Pr^{4+} + 2O^{2-} \rightarrow PrO_2$$

Figure 59-2 shows the isotopes of praseodymium. All naturally occurring praseodymium is Pr-141. The remainder are radioactive and synthetic (at least as far as the earth environment is concerned).

Element 60: Neodymium

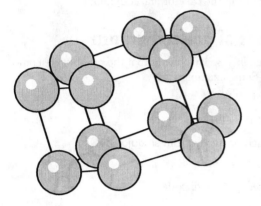

Name	Neodymium
Symbol	Nd
Atomic Number	60
Atomic Weight	144.24
Melting Point	1021°C
Boiling Point	3074°C
Specific Gravity	7.007 (20°C)
Oxidation State	+3
Electron Config.	(Xe) $4f^4 6s^2$

- Name pronounced as **nee-eh-DIM-i-em**
- Name from the Greek *neos* + *didymos*, "new" + "twin"
- Discovered by Carl Auer von Welsbach in 1885
- Silvery-white, rare-earth metal that oxidizes easily in air

Neodymium is used in the fabrication of artificial ruby for laser applications. The element also finds applications in the electronics and ceramics industries; and it has been used to eliminate the greenish tint in glass that happens to have a high iron content. The neodymium content of Misch metal, an important steel-alloying agent, is about 18%.

Figure 60-1 shows that neodymium is relatively abundant in the earth's crust. Its average distribution is 24 parts-per-million, making it the third most abundant rare-earth element. It is far more abundant than some of the most familiar metals such as gold, silver, tin, lead, and platinum.

Historical background

The technical skills of one Baron Auer von Welsbach (1858 – 1929) paid off in June, 1885, when he announced to the Vienna Academy of Sciences that he had split a relatively common earth called didymium into two new earths. He called the two new elements praseodymia (green didymia) and neodymia (new didymia), which are now known as praseodymium and neodymium, respectively. Based on recent spectrographic evidence and the advice of his mentor, Robert Bunsen of Bunsen burner fame, the baron separated the elements by a painstaking process of repeated fractionation of ammonium didymium nitrate.

Properties of neodymium

Neodymium is reactive with both air and moisture. In dry air, it tarnishes to form the light-blue oxide, Nd_3O_3, that flakes away and exposes more metal that is susceptible to further oxidation. It reacts in water to form neodymium hydroxide, $Nd(OH)_3$, and hydrogen gas—a reaction that becomes more vigorous at higher temperatures. Because this metal is so reactive to normal environmental conditions, it is shipped and stored in containers of mineral oil and other nonreactive liquids.

Rank (Rare Earths)	Rare-Earth Element	Abundance (ppm)
1	Cerium, Ce	46.0
2	Yttrium, Y	28.0
3	Neodymium, Nd	24.0
4	Lanthanum, La	18.0
5	Samarium, Sm	6.5
6	Gadolinium, Gd	6.4
7	Praseodymium, Pr	5.5
8	Scandium, Sc	5.0
9	Dysprosium, Dy	4.5
10	Ytterbium, Yb	2.7
11	Erbium, Er	2.5
12	Holmium, Ho	1.2
13	Europium, Eu	1.1
14	Terbium, Tb	0.9
15	Lutetium, Lu	0.8
16	Thulium, Tm	0.2
17	Promethium, Pm	0.0

60-1 Neodymium is ranked third on the abundance chart for rare earths found in the earth's crust.

Isotope	Natural Abundance	Half-Life	Decay Mode
^{133}Nd		1.2 min	β+, ec
^{134}Nd		8.5 min	β+, ec
^{135}Nd		12 min	β+, ec
^{136}Nd		50.7 min	β+, ec
^{137m}Nd		1.6 sec	it.
^{137}Nd		38 min	β+, ec
^{138}Nd		5.1 hr	ec
^{139m}Nd		5.5 hr	β+, i.t.
^{139}Nd		30 min	β+, ec
^{140}Nd		3.37 day	ec
^{141m}Nd		61 sec	β+, i.t.
^{141}Nd		2.5 hr	β+, ec
^{142}Nd	27.13%		
^{143}Nd	12.18%		
^{144}Nd	23.80%	2.1x10^{15} yr	
^{145}Nd	8.30%		
^{146}Nd	17.19%		
^{147}Nd		11 day	β-
^{148}Nd	5.76%		
^{149}Nd		1.73 hr	β-
^{150}Nd	5.64%		
^{151}Nd		12.4 min	β-
^{152}Nd		11.4 min	β-
^{154}Nd		40 sec	β-

60-2 Neodymium has isotopes with atomic weights between 133 and 154.

Neodymium, aside from being a rare-earth metal, is also a member of the lanthanide series of elements—a series that begins with lanthanum (element 57) and ends with lutetium (element 71).

Production of neodymium

Most commercial-grade neodymium is obtained from monazite sand, which is a mixture of phosphates of calcium, thorium, cerium, and most of the other earths. This sand, in fact, is often 50% rare earth by weight. Most of the unwanted metals can be removed magnetically or by flotation processes. What remains, then, is to separate one rare earth from the other.

Like most rare-earth metals, neodymium can be separated from the others by an ion-exchange displacement process. The result is a neodymium ion that reacts with a fluoride or chloride ion to form neodymium fluoride (NdF_3) or neodymium chloride ($NdCl_3$).

Neodymium is also produced by reducing its fluoride with calcium metal:

$$3Ca + 2NdF_3 \rightarrow 2Nd + 3CaF_2$$
(calcium metal + neodymium fluoride → neodymium metal + calcium fluoride)

The same kind of reaction is possible with lithium metal and neodymium chloride:

$$3Li + NdCl_3 \rightarrow Nd + 3LiCl$$
(lithium metal + neodymium chloride → neodymium metal + lithium chloride)

In either case, the neodymium halide and active metal are loaded into a tantalum crucible and fired in a helium atmosphere. As the reaction progresses, the molten halide and excess active metal separate due to differences in density. When this layered mixture is allowed to cool, the neodymium is simply cut away from the impurities. The operation can be repeated as often as necessary to achieve the desired level of purity.

Some compounds and the isotopes of neodymium

Neodymium usually takes on an oxidation state of $+3$. The examples cited below illustrate the role of the Nd^{3+} ion:

Neodymium chloride, $NdCl_3$

$$Nd^{3+} + 3Cl^- \rightarrow NdCl_3$$

Neodymium oxide, Nd_2O_3 (also called neodymia)

$$2Nd^{3+} + 3O^{2-} \rightarrow Nd_2O_3$$

Neodymium nitride, NdN

$$Nd^{3+} + N^{3-} \rightarrow NdN$$

An Nd^{8+} ion appears in neodymium carbide, NdC_2

$$Nd^{8+} + 2C^{4-} \rightarrow NdC_2$$

Neodymium compounds tend to be colorful. Most are rose colored or black. The oxide is light blue, however, and the sulfide (Nd_2S_2) is olive green.

Figure 60-2 on p. 219 lists the known isotopes of neodymium. Nearly a fourth of naturally occurring neodymium is made up of radioactive Nd-144. Its incredibly long half-life of 1,000,000,000,000,000 years, however, has preserved its existence since the creation of the earth.

Element 61: Promethium

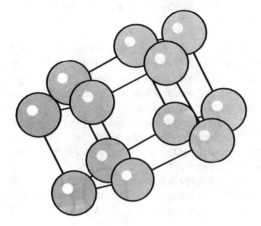

Name	Promethium
Symbol	Pm
Atomic Number	61
Atomic Weight	145 Note 1
Melting Point	1042°C
Boiling Point	3000°C Note 2
Specific Gravity	7.22 (25°C)
Oxidation State	+3
Electron Config.	(Xe) $4f^5 6s^2$

Note 1: Most stable isotope.
Note 2: Estimated value.

- Name pronounced as **pro-MEE-thi-em**
- Named for the Greek god, Prometheus
- Formerly called *illinium* and *florentium*
- Existence predicted in 1912
- Existence confirmed by J.A. Marinsky, L.E. Glendenin, and C.D. Coryell in 1947
- Rare-earth metal of synthetic origin on the earth

The spectral lines of promethium have been observed in the light from some stars, but it is a well established fact that this element does not occur naturally on the earth. So as provincial as it might seem, earthling chemists regard promethium as a synthetic element.

The pure metal is produced in such small amounts that chemists have had little opportunity to study anything beyond its most fundamental properties. A few compounds have been used as sources of radioactivity for thickness-measuring gages, and there are suggestions that promethium might find applications in long-life storage batteries and portable sources of atomic energy. It might be used as a source of X-rays for medical applications in areas of the world where electrical power is not generally available.

Historical background

When Henry G.J. Moseley (1887 – 1915) developed the present-day scheme for assigning integer values—atomic number—to the elements in 1912, it became apparent that a rare-earth metal was missing between neodymium and samarium. Rare earths have always been difficult to separate from one another, thereby making it extremely difficult to isolate any one of them with a level of purity sufficient to prove its existence as a true element. It figures that the last to be discovered would also be the most difficult; it took more than a decade to obtain the first evidence of element 61 and more than three decades to confirm its existence.

The first evidence appeared on two occasions between 1924 and 1926. A group of researchers at the Royal University of Florence, Italy, delivered a sealed package to the

Accademia de Lincei that supposedly contained a sample of element 61, which they called *florentium*. Some clerk must have blown his job, so the news did not reach the scientific world until it was time to dispute the claims of a couple of American chemists who announced their discovery of element 61 in 1926. The Americans suggested the name *illinium*; like their Italian counterparts, however, the Americans failed to provide sufficient evidence for the discovery of element 61.

More time passed, and more claims of discovery were rejected. Hope awakened in 1941 when another group of Americans, working at Ohio State University, claimed they had synthesized element 61 in a cyclotron. They suggested *cyclonium* as the name. Their claim was probably valid, and the experiment has since been successfully repeated with more powerful cyclotrons. Nevertheless, the evidence did not meet the standards of the time.

The issue was finally settled in 1947 at the Clinton Laboratories at Oak Ridge, Tennessee. J.A. Marinsky, L.E. Glendenin, and C.D. Coryell found traces of all the known rare earths in the residue from their atomic reactor. Using the latest ion-exchange techniques for separating rare earths, they isolated element 61 in a most convincing fashion.

The element is appropriately named after the Greek god and Titan, Prometheus. According to the mythology, Prometheus is the one who gave mankind the gift of fire. The element, promethium, was certainly born of the first fires of the Atomic Age.

Properties of promethium

Promethium is the least abundant of all rare-earth elements in the earth's crust. There is absolutely none. It is remarkable that anything at all is known about its properties.

Promethium belongs to the lanthanide series (between elements 57 and 71) and indicates that it is classified as a rare-earth metal. This sort of classification is largely responsible for the facts that are known about the element.

Promethium has at least two allotropic forms.

Production of promethium

The methods for producing promethium follow the procedures used in efforts to confirm its very existence. Much of it is derived from the "ashes" of nuclear reactors. Today's more powerful accelerators make it feasible to produce the element by neutron bombardment. In this case, bombardment of neodymium-146 with neutrons yields neodymium-147, and natural decay of the latter leads to promethium-147:

$$^{146}Nd(n,\gamma)^{147}Nd \rightarrow \, ^{147}Pm + \beta^-$$

Some compounds and isotopes of promethium

The principal oxidation state for promethium is $+3$. Researchers have prepared more than thirty different compounds of promethium, but none has any significant commercial value. The variety and formulae for promethium compounds follow the general pattern for other metals in the lanthanide series.

Promethium trichloride, $PrCl_3$

$$Pr^{3+} + 3Cl^- \rightarrow PrCl_3$$

Promethium sesquioxide, Pr_2O_3

$$2Pr^{3+} + 3O^{2-} \rightarrow Pr_2O3$$

Promethium nitride, PrN

$$Pr^{3+} + N^{3-} \rightarrow PrN$$

Due to their high levels of radioactivity, promethium salts glow in the dark with an eerie pale blue or yellow-green glow.

The salts of promethium tend to have a pink or rosy color.

As shown in Fig. 61-1, there are 27 isotopes of promethium. All are radioactive, with the longest half-life being just a bit less than 18 years.

61-1 Promethium has isotopes with atomic weights between 134 and 155.

Isotope	Natural Abundance	Half-Life	Decay Mode
^{134}Pm		24 sec	β+, ec
^{135}Pm		48 sec	β+, ec
^{136}Pm		1.8 min	β+, ec
^{137}Pm		2.4 min	β+, ec
^{138}Pm		3.2 min	β+, ec
^{139}Pm		4.1 min	β+, ec
^{140m}Pm		5.9 min	β+, ec
^{140}Pm		9.2 sec	β+, ec
^{141}Pm		20.9 min	β+, ec
^{142}Pm		40.5 sec	β+, ec
^{143}Pm		265 day	ec
^{144}Pm		363 day	ec
^{145}Pm		17.7 yr	ec
^{146}Pm		5.53 yr	β-, ec
^{147}Pm		2.62 yr	β-
^{148m}Pm		41. 3 day	β-, i.t.
^{148}Pm		5.37 day	β-
^{149}Pm		53.1 hr	β-
^{150}Pm		2.69 hr	β-
^{151}Pm		28.4 hr	β-
^{152m2}Pm		15 min	β-, i.t.
^{152m1}Pm		7.52 min	β-
^{152}Pm		4.1 min	β-
^{153}Pm		5.4 min	β-
^{154m}Pm		2.7 min	β-
^{154}Pm		1.7 min	β-
^{155}Pm		48 sec	β-

Element 62: Samarium

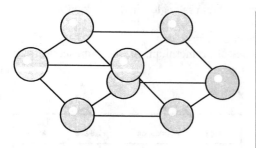

Name	Samarium
Symbol	Sm
Atomic Number	62
Atomic Weight	150.36
Melting Point	1074°C
Boiling Point	1794°C
Specific Gravity	7.52 (25°C)
Oxidation States	+2, +3
Electron Config.	(Xe) $4f^6 6s^2$

- Name pronounced as **seh-MER-i-em**
- Named for the mineral *samarskite*
- Isolated and identified as an element by Locoq de Boisbaudran in 1879
- Silvery rare-earth metal

Samarium is a fairly abundant rare-earth metal that is just beginning to find significant commercial applications in high-technology industries. It is currently being used in the electronics and ceramics industries. It is easily magnetized and, as far as anyone knows at this time, no other material is more difficult to demagnetize. This property suggests important applications in solid-state and superconductor technologies.

Historical background

As early as 1853, Jean Charles Galissard de Marignac (1817 – 1894) believed that a popular earth, dydimia, was not a pure substance, but rather a mixture of yet undiscovered elements. His suspicion was further supported by the fact that the absorption spectra of dydimia varied according to where it was found.

Marignac later received credit for discovering and isolating two other rare-earth elements, ytterbium and gadolinium, but he could not figure out how to split the unknown element or elements he believed were hiding away in samples of dydimia. It was one Paul-Émile Locoq de Boisbaudran (1838 – 1912) who came up with the proper technique in 1879.

The difficult and time-consuming process of chemical fractionation was being perfected to a point where it was responsible for the discovery of most of the rare-earth elements. The problem then, as now, is that the rare earths are never found in isolation. Dydimia, for example, is now known to include most of the rare-earth elements and especially high concentrations of samarium, gadolinium, neodymium, and praseodymium. Boisbaudran found that ammonium hydroxide caused a new precipitate to form before the one commonly known as dydimia formed.

Boisbaudran was acutely aware of Marignac's attempts to establish the existence of this element by spectroscopic techniques. Marignac was finding high-quality spectra for the new element in samples of the mineral *samarskite*. In deference to Marignac's contribution, Boisbaudran named the new element after the mineral Marignac was studying at the time.

Properties of samarium

Samarium has a silver luster that is not significantly tarnished under normal room conditions. It can be ignited in air at 150 °C, however.

As shown in Fig. 62-1, samarium is a rare earth that ranks fifth in abundance. It is also a member of the lanthanide series of elements: lanthanum (La) through lutetium (Lu).

There are three allotropic forms known at the present time. The α form exists up to 734 °C and the β to 922 °C.

Rank (Rare Earths)	Rare-Earth Element	Abundance (ppm)
1	Cerium, Ce	46.0
2	Yttrium, Y	28.0
3	Neodymium, Nd	24.0
4	Lanthanum, La	18.0
5	Samarium, Sm	6.5
6	Gadolinium, Gd	6.4
7	Praseodymium, Pr	5.5
8	Scandium, Sc	5.0
9	Dysprosium, Dy	4.5
10	Ytterbium, Yb	2.7
11	Erbium, Er	2.5
12	Holmium, Ho	1.2
13	Europium, Eu	1.1
14	Terbium, Tb	0.9
15	Lutetium, Lu	0.8
16	Thulium, Tm	0.2
17	Promethium, Pm	0.0

62-1 Samarium is ranked fifth on the abundance chart for rare earths found in the earth's crust.

Isotope	Natural Abundance	Half-Life	Decay Mode
^{138}Sm		3.0 min	$\beta+$, ec
^{139m}Sm		9.5 sec	$\beta+$, i.t.
^{139}Sm		2.6 min	$\beta+$, ec
^{140}Sm		14.8 min	$\beta+$, ec
^{141m}Sm		22.6 min	$\beta+$, ec
^{141}Sm		10.2 min	$\beta+$, ec
^{142}Sm		72.5 min	$\beta+$, ec
^{143m}Sm		66 sec	i.t.
^{143}Sm		8.83 min	$\beta+$, ec
^{144}Sm	3.1%		
^{145}Sm		340 day	ec
^{146}Sm		1.03×10^8 yr	α
^{147}Sm	15.0%	1.08×10^{11} yr	α
^{148}Sm	11.3%	7×10^{15} yr	α
^{149}Sm	13.8%	10^{16} yr	α
^{150}Sm	7.4%		
^{151}Sm		90 yr	$\beta-$
^{152}Sm	26.7%		
^{153}Sm		46.7 hr	$\beta-$
^{154}Sm	22.7%		
^{155}Sm		22.2 min	$\beta-$
^{156}Sm		9.4 hr	$\beta-$
^{157}Sm		8.1 min	$\beta-$
^{158}Sm		5.5 min	$\beta-$

62-2 Samarium has isotopes with atomic weights between 138 and 158.

Production of samarium

Most commercial-grade samarium is obtained from *monazite sand*, which is a mixture of phosphates of calcium, thorium, cerium, and most of the other rare earths. This sand, in fact, is often 50% rare earth by weight, and 2.8% samarium. Most of the unwanted metals can be removed from finely ground monazite by magnetic or flotation processes. The task that remains is to separate the samarium from the other rare earths.

Like most rare-earth metals, samarium can be separated from the others by an ion-exchange displacement process. The result is a samarium ion that reacts with a fluoride or chloride ion to form samarium fluoride (SmF_3) or samarium chloride ($SmCl_3$).

Samarium is also produced by reducing samarium fluoride with calcium metal:

$$3Ca + 2SmF_3 \rightarrow 2Sm + 3CaF_2$$
(calcium metal + samarium fluoride $\rightarrow$ samarium metal + calcium fluoride)

The same kind of reaction is possible with lithium metal and samarium chloride:

$$3Li + SmCl_3 \rightarrow Sm + 3LiCl$$
(lithium metal + samarium chloride $\rightarrow$ samarium metal + lithium chloride)

In either case, the samarium halide and active metal are loaded into a tantalum crucible and fired in a helium atmosphere. As the reaction progresses, the molten halide and excess active metal separate due to differences in density. When this layered mixture is allowed to cool, the samarium is simply cut away from the impurities. The operation can be repeated as often as necessary to achieve the desired level of purity.

Samarium can be produced in the laboratory by reducing samarium oxide with barium:

$$Sm_2O_3 + 3Ba \rightarrow 2Sm + 3BaO$$
(samarium oxide + barium $\rightarrow$ samarium + barium oxide)

Some compounds and the isotopes of samarium

Samarium is an unusual rare-earth metal inasmuch as it has two oxidation states, $+2$ as well as the usual $+3$. As a result, there are sometimes two different compounds available from the same set of elements. Samarium can combine with chlorine, for instance, to yield one of two different compounds:

Samarium (II) chloride, $SmCl_2$ (also called samarium dichloride)

$$Sm^{2+} + 2Cl^- \rightarrow SmCl_2$$

Samarium (III) chloride, $SmCl_3$ (also called samarium trichloride)

$$Sm^{3+} + 3Cl^- \rightarrow SmCl_3$$

Most other compounds use the Sm^{3-} ion. For instance:

Samarium sesquioxide, Sm_2O_3

$$2Sm^{3+} + 3O^{2-} \rightarrow Sm_2O_3$$

Samarium hydroxide, $Sm(OH)_3$

$$Sm^{3+} + 3(OH)^- \rightarrow Sm(OH)_3$$

Like most other elements in the lanthanide series, a carbide compound is made possible by the existence of an otherwise unusual $+8$ oxidation state:

Samarium carbide, SmC_2

$$Sm^{8+} + 2C^{4-} \rightarrow SmC_2$$

Samarium (II) compounds tend to have reddish brown color, while samarium (III) compounds tend toward yellow colors.

Figure 62-2 on p. 225 lists all the known isotopes of samarium. Few elements have so many different stable isotopes that occur naturally on earth.

Element 63: Europium

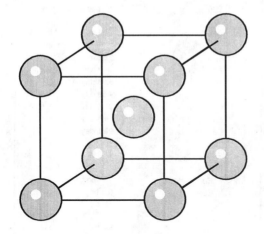

Name	Europium
Symbol	Eu
Atomic Number	63
Atomic Weight	151.96
Melting Point	822°C
Boiling Point	1527°C
Specific Gravity	5.243 (25°C)
Oxidation States	+2, +3
Electron Config.	(Xe) $4f^7\,6s^2$

- Name pronounced as **yoo-RO-pi-em**
- Named for the continent of Europe
- Discovered and isolated by Eugène-Antole Demarcay in 1896 and 1901, respectively
- Soft, silvery-white metal

As shown in Fig. 63-1, europium ranks thirteenth in abundance among the rare earths. It is even lower on the list of abundances for all the elements, but it turns out there is 20 times as much europium in the earth than silver and gold combined.

There are few practical applications of europium metal, but the oxide more than makes up the difference. The oxide, for example, is often used as an activator and red phosphor in color cathode-ray tubes for televisions and computer screens.

Historical background

In 1896, Eugène-Antole Demarcay (1852 – 1904) was taking a close look at a recently dis-covered element called samarium (Sm). Demarcay suspected that the samples used for the discovery were not absolutely pure and, in fact, contained an element that had not yet been identified. Demarcay set out to separate and identify the intruder.

The separation procedure was a long and tedious one, but the payoff was the discovery of a new chemical element. Demarcay announced his discovery of element 63, which he decided to call europium.

Five years later, Demarcay perfected his separation technique for europium and isolated some suitably pure samples.

Properties and production of europium

Europium looks and feels much like ordinary lead; it is slightly less heavy, but about as soft and shiny. Chemically, it is the most reactive of the rare-earth metals. It reacts much like

Rank (Rare Earths)	Rare-Earth Element	Abundance (ppm)
1	Cerium, Ce	46.0
2	Yttrium, Y	28.0
3	Neodymium, Nd	24.0
4	Lanthanum, La	18.0
5	Samarium, Sm	6.5
6	Gadolinium, Gd	6.4
7	Praseodymium, Pr	5.5
8	Scandium, Sc	5.0
9	Dysprosium, Dy	4.5
10	Ytterbium, Yb	2.7
11	Erbium, Er	2.5
12	Holmium, Ho	1.2
13	Europium, Eu	1.1
14	Terbium, Tb	0.9
15	Lutetium, Lu	0.8
16	Thulium, Tm	0.2
17	Promethium, Pm	0.0

63-1 Europium is ranked thirteenth on the abundance chart for rare earths found in the earth's crust.

Isotope	Natural Abundance	Half-Life	Decay Mode
^{141m}Eu		3.3 sec	β+, i.t.
^{141}Eu		40 sec	β+, ec
^{142m}Eu		1.22 min	β+, ec
^{142}Eu			ec
^{143}Eu		2.62 min	β+, ec
^{144}Eu		10.2 sec	β+, ec
^{145}Eu		5.93 day	β+, ec
^{146}Eu		4.58 day	β+, ec
^{147}Eu		24.3 day	β+, ec
^{148}Eu		54.5 day	ec
^{149}Eu		93.1 day	ec
^{150m}Eu		36 yr	ec
^{150}Eu		12.6 hr	β+, ec
^{151}Eu	51.8%		
^{152m2}Eu		96 min	i.t.
^{152m1}Eu		9.3 hr	β-, ec
^{152}Eu		13.4 yr	β-, ec
^{153}Eu	52.2%		
^{154m}Eu		46.1 min	i.t.
^{154}Eu		8.5 yr	β-, ec
^{155}Eu		4.73 yr	β-
^{156}Eu		15.2 day	β-
^{157}Eu		15.15 hr	β-
^{158}Eu			β-
^{159}Eu		18 min	β-
^{160}Eu		53 sec	β-

63-2 Europium has isotopes with atomic weights between 141 and 160.

calcium in water, for instance, bubbling off a gentle but continuous stream of hydrogen gas:

$$2Eu + 3H_2O \rightarrow Eu_2O_3 + 3H_2$$

(europium + water → europium oxide + hydrogen gas)

Europium is one of the lanthanide series of elements. This is a series of rare-earth elements that begins with lanthinum (La, element 57) and ends with lutetium (Lu, element 71).

Most europium is obtained from *monazite sand*, which is a mixture of phosphates of calcium, thorium, cerium, and most of the other rare earths. Most of the unwanted metals can be removed magnetically or by flotation processes. The most difficult part of the process, however, is separating the rare earths from one another.

Limited amounts of europium are available from the residue of conventional nuclear reactors.

Like most rare-earth metals, europium can be separated from the others by an ion-exchange displacement process. The result is an europium ion that reacts with oxygen ions to form europium oxide, Eu_2O^3. This oxide then becomes the primary vehicle for the production of europium metal.

Europium is reduced from europium oxide by mixing it with powdered lanthanum metal in a tantalum crucible. This apparatus is then fired in a vacuum oven to produce europium metal and lanthanum oxide:

$$Eu_2O_3 + 2La \rightarrow 2Eu + La_2O_3$$
(europium oxide + lanthanum metal → europium metal + lanthanum oxide)

Some compounds and isotopes of europium

Europium's most stable oxidation state is $+3$. This accounts for the general form of its formulations:

Europium (III) chloride, $EuCl_3$

$$Eu^{3+} + 3Cl^- \rightarrow EuCl_3$$

Europium (III) sulfate, $Eu_2(SO_4)_3$

$$2Eu^{3+} + 3(SO_4)^{2-} \rightarrow Eu_2(SO_4)_3$$

Figure 63-2 lists the isotopes of europium. You can see that naturally occurring europium is fairly evenly divided between europium-151 and -153. These two isotopes are not radioactive. The remaining species, however, are both synthetic and radioactive.

Element 64: Gadolinium

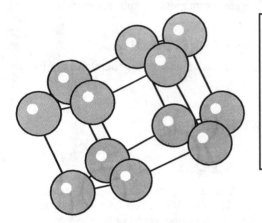

Name	Gadolinium
Symbol	Gd
Atomic Number	64
Atomic Weight	157.25
Melting Point	1313°C
Boiling Point	3273°C
Specific Gravity	7.90 (25°C)
Oxidation State	+3
Electron Config.	(Xe) $4f^7 5d^1 6s^2$

- Name pronounced as **GAD-eh-LIN-i-em**
- Named after *gadolinite*, a mineral named for the Finnish Chemist, Johan Gadolin
- Discovery shared by J. de Marignac (1880) and Lecoq de Boisbaudran (1886)
- Soft, ductile, silvery-white metal

Gadolinium is not a well-known metal, although its compounds are common enough to place it sixth on the abundance chart for rare earths contained in the earth's crust (see Fig. 64-1). Current applications are limited to steel alloying agents and the manufacture of electronic components. It is ferromagnetic below 17 °C and naturally superconductive near absolute zero.

Historical background

Jean Charles Galissard de Marignac (1817 – 1894) publicized his belief that a popular earth known as *dydimia* was a mixture of elements rather than an element in its own right. His spectroscopic studies in 1853 supported his theory. The new spectral lines were badly scrambled in dydimia, but became clearer in similar minerals such as *samarskite* and *gadolinite*. The laboratory methods he chose were to prove inadequate, however, for substantiating the existence of new elements.

Working from clues offered by Marignac, Paul-Émile Locoq de Boisbaudran (1838 – 1912) isolated element 62 from samples of dydimia in 1879; in 1886 he isolated element 64 from the same source. Boisbaudran was aware of Marignac's efforts to uncover the same elements, so he offered to name the new elements samarium and gadolinium, after the minerals Marignac had been studying, samarskite and gadolinite.

Properties of gadolinium

Gadolinium is described as a soft, ductile, silvery-white metal. It is relatively stable in air, but tarnishes in moist air to produce a white oxide that eventually flakes off to expose more metal. Gadolinium is in the middle of the lanthanide series of elements (atomic numbers 57 through 71).

Rank (Rare Earths)	Rare-Earth Element	Abundance (ppm)
1	Cerium, Ce	46.0
2	Yttrium, Y	28.0
3	Neodymium, Nd	24.0
4	Lanthanum, La	18.0
5	Samarium, Sm	6.5
6	Gadolinium, Gd	6.4
7	Praseodymium, Pr	5.5
8	Scandium, Sc	5.0
9	Dysprosium, Dy	4.5
10	Ytterbium, Yb	2.7
11	Erbium, Er	2.5
12	Holmium, Ho	1.2
13	Europium, Eu	1.1
14	Terbium, Tb	0.9
15	Lutetium, Lu	0.8
16	Thulium, Tm	0.2
17	Promethium, Pm	0.0

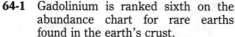

64-1 Gadolinium is ranked sixth on the abundance chart for rare earths found in the earth's crust.

Isotope	Natural Abundance	Half-Life	Decay Mode
^{143m}Gd		1.83 min	β+, ec
^{143}Gd		39 sec	β+, ec
^{144}Gd		4.5 min	β+, ec
^{145m}Gd		85 sec	β+, i.t.
^{145}Gd		23 min	β+, ec
^{146}Gd		48.3 day	β+, ec
^{147}Gd		38.1 hr	ec
^{148}Gd		75 yr	α
^{149}Gd		9.3 day	ec
^{150}Gd		1.8×10^6 yr	α
^{151}Gd		120 day	ec
^{152}Gd	0.20%		
^{153}Gd		241.6 day	ec
^{154}Gd	2.18%		
^{155}Gd	14.80%		
^{156}Gd	20.47%		
^{157}Gd	15.65%		
^{158}Gd	24.84%		
^{159}Gd		18.6 hr	β-
^{160}Gd	20.86%		
^{161}Gd		3.7 min	β-
^{162}Gd		8.4 min	β-
^{163}Gd		68 sec	β-

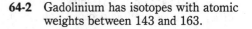

64-2 Gadolinium has isotopes with atomic weights between 143 and 163.

There are two different crystalline, allotropic forms. The α form is the one that exists at room temperature. The β form takes shape at temperatures above 1235 °C.

Gadolinium has the capacity for absorbing larger concentrations of thermal neutrons than any other naturally occurring element. This makes it an ideal material for control rods in nuclear power generators.

Production of gadolinium

Most commercial-grade gadolinium is obtained from *monazite sand*, which is a mixture of phosphates of calcium, thorium, cerium, and most of the other rare earths. This sand, in fact, is often 50% rare earth by weight. Most of the unwanted metals can be removed magnetically or by flotation processes. The most difficult step, however, is separating the rare earths from one another.

Like most rare-earth metals, gadolinium can be separated from the others by an ion-exchange displacement process. The result is a gadolinium ion which can react with a fluoride or chloride ion to form gadolinium fluoride (GdF_3) and gadolinium chloride ($GdCl_3$).

Gadolinium is also produced by reducing gadolinium fluoride with calcium metal:

$$3Ca + 2GdF_3 \rightarrow 2Gd + 3CaF_2$$
(calcium metal + gadolinium fluoride → gadolinium metal + calcium fluoride)

The same kind of reaction is possible with lithium metal and gadolinium chloride:

$$3Li + GdCl_3 \rightarrow Gd + 3LiCl$$
(lithium metal + gadolinium chloride → gadolinium metal + lithium chloride)

In either case, the gadolinium halide and active metal are loaded into a tantalum crucible and fired in a helium atmosphere. As the reaction progresses, the molten gadolinium, halide compound, and excess active metal separate due to differences in density. When this layered mixture is allowed to cool, the gadolinium is simply cut away from the impurities. The operation can be repeated as often as necessary to achieve the desired level of purity.

Gadolinium can be produced in the laboratory by heating anhydrous gadolinium chloride with calcium:

$$2GdCl_3 + 3Ca \rightarrow 2Gd + 3CaCl_3$$
(gadolinium chloride + calcium metal → gadolinium metal + calcium chloride)

Some compounds and isotopes of gadolinium

Gadolinium has an oxidation state of $+3$. This means the metal ion is Gd^{3+}. All gadolinium compounds of any significance are built around this ion. Consider the following examples:

Gadolinium chloride, $GdCl_3$

$$Gd^{3+} + 3Cl^- \rightarrow GdCl_3$$

Gadolinium oxide, Gd_2O_3 (also called *gadolinia*)

$$2Gd^{3+} + 3O^{2-} \rightarrow Gd_2O_3$$

Compounds of gadolinium tend to be white or colorless.

Figure 64-2 on p. 231 shows the isotopes of gadolinium. Few elements have so many different stable (nonradioactive) isotopes that occur in nature.

Element 65: Terbium

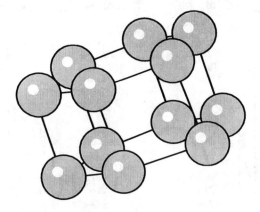

Name	Terbium
Symbol	Tb
Atomic Number	65
Atomic Weight	158.925
Melting Point	1356°C
Boiling Point	3230°C
Specific Gravity	8.23 (25°C)
Oxidation State	+3
Electron Config.	(Xe) $4f^9 6s^2$

- Name pronounced as **TUR-bi-em**
- Named after Ytterby, a village in Sweden
- Discovered by Gustaf Mosadner in 1843
- Soft, ductile, silvery-gray, rare-earth metal

Terbium is definitely not a household word. It is a safe bet that most students in high school and first-year college chemistry classes would not recall hearing anything about it. Figure 65-1 shows that terbium ranks fourteenth in abundance among the seventeen rare earths in the earth's crust. You can expect to find one teaspoon of the element for every 63 tons of earth.

Terbium is used in modest amounts in special lasers and solid-state devices.

Historical background

Having previously shown that supposedly pure samples of ceria, or ceric oxide, were actually contaminated with a new element, lanthanum, Gustaf Mosadner set out to find any new elements that might be hiding away in another popular earth called yttria. He used a separation procedure, fractioning the compounds with ammonium hydroxide.

Starting with available samples of yttria, Mosander first removed three other earths already known to accompany yttria: ceria, lanthana, and didymia—the oxides of cerium, lanthanum, and didymium, respectively. He found that the portion that remained contained the oxides of at least three new elements. For the colorless oxide, Mosander retained the name of the original source, yttria. He named the yellow oxide *erbia* and the rose-colored oxide *terbia*. So with a single set of experiments in 1843, Mosander added two new elements to the periodic table, erbium and terbium.

Properties of terbium

Terbium is a soft, silvery metal. It feels something like lead, but looks a bit more like aluminum. It is a lot heavier than either of those familiar elements, though. Terbium is a member of the lanthanide series, from lanthanum (element 57) through lutetium (element 71).

Rank (Rare Earths)	Rare-Earth Element	Abundance (ppm)
1	Cerium, Ce	46.0
2	Yttrium, Y	28.0
3	Neodymium, Nd	24.0
4	Lanthanum, La	18.0
5	Samarium, Sm	6.5
6	Gadolinium, Gd	6.4
7	Praseodymium, Pr	5.5
8	Scandium, Sc	5.0
9	Dysprosium, Dy	4.5
10	Ytterbium, Yb	2.7
11	Erbium, Er	2.5
12	Holmium, Ho	1.2
13	Europium, Eu	1.1
14	Terbium, Tb	0.9
15	Lutetium, Lu	0.8
16	Thulium, Tm	0.2
17	Promethium, Pm	0.0

65-1 Terbium is ranked fourteenth on the abundance chart for rare earths found in the earth's crust.

Isotope	Natural Abundance	Half-Life	Decay Mode
^{145}Tb		30 sec	$\beta+$, ec
^{146}Tb		23 sec	$\beta+$, ec
^{147m}Tb		1.8 min	$\beta+$, ec
^{147}Tb		1.6 hr	$\beta+$, ec
^{148m}Tb		2.2 min	$\beta+$, ec
^{148}Tb		1 hr	$\beta+$, ec
^{149m}Tb		4.2 min	$\beta+$, ec
^{149}Tb		4.15 hr	$\alpha+$, $\beta+$
^{150m}Tb		6.0 min	$\beta+$, ec
^{150}Tb		3.3 hr	$\beta+$, ec
^{151m}Tb		50 sec	i.t.
^{151}Tb		17.6 hr	$\beta+$, ec
^{152m}Tb		4.1 min	i.t., ec
^{152}Tb		17.6 hr	$\beta+$, ec
^{153}Tb		2.34 day	ec
$^{154m2}Tb$		23 hr	ec, i.t.
$^{154m1}Tb$		9 hr	$\beta+$, i.t.
^{154}Tb		22 hr	$\beta+$, ec
^{155}Tb		5.3 day	ec
$^{156m2}Tb$		24 hr	i.t.
$^{156m1}Tb$		5.0 hr	i.t.
^{156}Tb		5.3 day	ec
^{157}Tb		150 yr	ec
^{158m}Tb		10.5 sec	i.t.
^{158}Tb		150 yr	$\beta-$, i.t.
^{159}Tb	100%		
^{160}Tb		72.4 day	$\beta-$
^{161}Tb		6.91 day	$\beta-$
^{162}Tb		7.6 min	$\beta-$
^{163}Tb		19.5 min	$\beta-$
^{164}Tb		3.0 min	$\beta-$
^{165}Tb		2.1 min	$\beta-$

65-2 Terbium has isotopes with atomic weights between 145 and 165.

The element has two, temperature-dependent crystal forms, or allotropes. The α form is the one that exists at room temperature—up to 1298 °C, in fact. The β form prevails above that temperature.

Production of terbium

Most commercial-grade terbium is obtained from *monazite sand*, which is a mixture of phosphates of calcium, thorium, cerium, and most of the other rare earths. This sand, in fact, is often 50% rare earth by weight and typically 0.03% terbium. Other sources of some commercial value are *xenotime* and *euxenite*, both being oxide mixtures that often contain up to 1% terbium. Unwanted metals can be removed from these ores by magnetic or flotation processes. The final task is to sort the rare-earth metals from one another.

Like most rare-earth metals, terbium can be separated from the others by an ion-exchange displacement process. The result is a terbium ion that reacts with a fluoride or chloride ion to form terbium fluoride (TbF_3) or terbium chloride ($TbCl_3$).

Terbium is also produced by reducing terbium fluoride with calcium metal:

$$3Ca + 2TbF_3 \rightarrow 2Tb + 3CaF_2$$
(calcium metal + terbium fluoride → terbium metal + calcium fluoride)

The same kind of reaction is possible with lithium metal and terbium chloride:

$$3Li + TbCl_3 \rightarrow Tb + 3LiCl$$
(lithium metal + terbium chloride → terbium metal + lithium chloride)

In either case, the terbium halide and active metal are loaded into a tantalum crucible and fired in a helium atmosphere. As the reaction progresses, the molten terbium, halide compound, and excess active metal separate due to differences in density. When this layered mixture is allowed to cool, the terbium is simply cut away from the impurities. The operation can be repeated as often as necessary to achieve the desired level of purity.

Some compounds and isotopes of terbium

Although it has been demonstrated that terbium has more than one oxidation state, the +3 state is the most stable. Using the Tb^{3+} ion, we get compounds such as:

Terbium fluoride, $TbFl_3$

$$Tb^{3+} + 3Fl^- \rightarrow TbFl_3$$

Terbium oxide, Tb_2O_3 (also called *terbia*)

$$2Tb^{3+} + 3O^{2-} \rightarrow Tb_2O_3$$

A second oxide, *terbium peroxide*, has the approximate formula, Tb_4O_7. This is one of those rare instances where the oxidation state of the metal cannot be expressed as an integer value: $4Te^{3.5+} + 7O^{2-} \rightarrow Tb_4O_7$.

Figure 65-2 lists the known isotopes of terbium. Notice that terbium-159 accounts for all of the elements as it exist in nature.

Element 66: Dysprosium

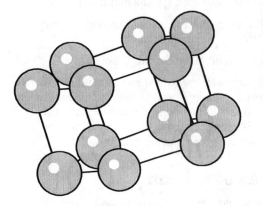

Name	Dysprosium
Symbol	Dy
Atomic Number	66
Atomic Weight	162.50
Melting Point	1412°C
Boiling Point	2567°C
Specific Gravity	8.540 (25°C)
Oxidation State	+3
Electron Config.	(Xe) $4f^{10} 6s^2$

- Name pronounced as **dis-PRO-si-em** or **dis-PRO-shi-em**
- Name taken from the Greek work *dysprositos*, "hard to get at"
- Discovered by Lecoq de Boisbaudran in 1886, then isolated by Georges Urbain in 1906
- Soft, lustrous, silvery metal

There are modest amounts of natural dysprosium in the world. Figure 66-1 shows that it ranks ninth in abundance among the 17 rare earths. It is not exactly scarce when compared with other metals. For example, there is more than twice as much dysprosium in the earth's crust as there is uranium.

Nevertheless, applications of disprosium and its oxide, *disprosia*, are limited to the experimental and the esoteric.

Historical background

Paul-Émile Lecoq de Boisbaudran (1838 – 1912) became interested in the properties of a newly discovered element, erbium (Er, element 68). Other researchers had recently been successful with the task of sorting new elements from mixtures previously thought to be pure elements.

Taking a close look at the oxide of erbium, *erbia*, Boisbaudran found he could carefully extract small amounts of an unlisted oxide. He called the new oxide *dysprosia* and in 1886, he boldly announced it was the oxide of a new element that would be called dysprosium.

Subsequent research clearly indicated that Boisbaudran's discovery did indeed fit the specifications for element 66 on the periodic table.

The pure metal and oxide were not isolated until the 1950s.

Properties and production of dysprosium

Dysprosium is a fairly dense, soft, and silvery metal. It oxidizes fairly rapidly in air, continuously flaking off the white disprosium oxide.

Rank (Rare Earths)	Rare-Earth Element	Abundance (ppm)
1	Cerium, Ce	46.0
2	Yttrium, Y	28.0
3	Neodymium, Nd	24.0
4	Lanthanum, La	18.0
5	Samarium, Sm	6.5
6	Gadolinium, Gd	6.4
7	Praseodymium, Pr	5.5
8	Scandium, Sc	5.0
9	Dysprosium, Dy	4.5
10	Ytterbium, Yb	2.7
11	Erbium, Er	2.5
12	Holmium, Ho	1.2
13	Europium, Eu	1.1
14	Terbium, Tb	0.9
15	Lutetium, Lu	0.8
16	Thulium, Tm	0.2
17	Promethium, Pm	0.0

66-1 Dysprosium is ranked ninth on the abundance chart for rare earths found in the earth's crust.

Isotope	Natural Abundance	Half-Life	Decay Mode
^{147m}Dy		58 sec	i.t., $\beta+$, ec
^{147}Dy		80 sec	$\beta+$, ec
^{148}Dy		3.1 min	$\beta+$, ec
^{149}Dy		4.2 min	$\beta+$, ec
^{150}Dy		7.17 min	α, $\beta+$, ec
^{151}Dy		17 min	α, $\beta+$, ec
^{152}Dy		2.3 hr	α, ec
^{153}Dy		6.3 hr	α, $\beta+$, ec
^{154}Dy		3×10^6 yr	α
^{155}Dy		10 hr	$\beta+$, ec
^{156}Dy	0.06%		
^{157}Dy		8.1 hr	ec
^{158}Dy	0.10%		
^{159}Dy		144 day	ec
^{160}Dy	2.34%		
^{161}Dy	18.9%		
^{162}Dy	25.5%		
^{163}Dy	24.9%		
^{164}Dy	28.2%		
^{165m}Dy		1.26 min	i.t., $\beta-$
^{165}Dy		2.33 hr	$\beta-$
^{166}Dy		81.6 hr	$\beta-$
^{167}Dy		6.2 min	$\beta-$
^{168}Dy		8.5 min	$\beta-$

66-2 Dysprosium has isotopes with atomic weights between 147 and 168.

Dysprosium is a member of the lanthanide series of metals, beginning with lanthanum (La, element 57) and running through consecutive atomic numbers to lutetium (Lu, element 71).

Most dysprosium is obtained from *monazite sand*, which is a mixture of phosphates of calcium, thorium, cerium, and most of the other rare earths. This sand is often 50% rare earth by weight. Most of the unwanted metals can be removed magnetically or by flotation processes. The next step, separating dysprosium from the other rare-earth metals, is more difficult.

Like most rare-earth metals, dysprosium can be separated by an ion-exchange displacement process. The result is a dysprosium ion which can react with a fluoride or chloride ion to form dysprosium fluoride (DyF_3) and dysprosium chloride ($DyCl_3$).

Dysprosium is also produced by reducing dysprosium fluoride with calcium metal:

$$3Ca + 2DyF_3 \rightarrow 2Dy + 3CaF_2$$
(calcium metal + dysprosium fluoride → dysprosium metal + calcium fluoride)

The same kind of reaction is possible with lithium metal and dysprosium chloride:

$$3Li + DyCl_3 \rightarrow Dy + 3LiCl$$
(lithium metal + dysprosium chloride → dysprosium metal + lithium chloride)

In either case, the dysprosium halide and active metal are loaded into a tantalum crucible and fired in a helium atmosphere. As the reaction progresses, the molten dysprosium, halide compound, and excess active metal separate due to differences in density. When this layered mixture is allowed to cool, the dysprosium is simply cut away from the impurities. The operation can be repeated as often as necessary to achieve the desired level of purity.

Some compounds and the isotopes of dysprosium

The dysprosium has an oxidation state of $+3$. The Dy^{3+} metallic ion thus combines with anions to form a small group of compounds. The halides all take the same general form: DyX_3, where X is an F^- (fluoride ion), Cl^- (chloride ion), Br^- (bromide ion), or I^- (iodide ion). The halides tend toward yellow colors.

Dysprosium oxide, also called *dysprosia*, is put together this way:

$$2Dy^{3+} + 3O^{2-} \rightarrow Dy_2O_3$$

Dysprosium carbonate, $Dy_2(CO_3)_3$, and *dysprosium sulfate*, $Dy_2(SO_4)_3$, are ionically assembled in much the same fashion.

Figure 66-2 on p. 237 shows the isotopes of dysprosium. More than 99% of natural dysprosium is divided among consecutive isotopes Dy-160 through Dy-164. The rest is made up of Dy-156 and -158. Dysprosium is not naturally radioactive.

All of the synthetic species are radioactive, however. Dysprosium-154 is worthy of special attention because its half-life of 3 million years is so far out of line with the half-lives of other radioactive isotopes of dysprosium.

Element 67: Holmium

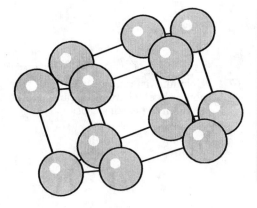

Name	Holmium
Symbol	Ho
Atomic Number	67
Atomic Weight	164.930
Melting Point	1474°C
Boiling Point	2700°C
Specific Gravity	8.795 (25°C)
Oxidation State	+3
Electron Config.	(Xe) $4f^{11} 6s^2$

- Name pronounced as **HOLE-mi-em**
- Name taken from *Holmia*, the Latinized version of the name of the Swedish city, Stockholm
- Discovered by Per Theodor Cleve in 1879
- Fairly soft, malleable, lustrous, silvery metal

For a short time prior to its acceptance as an element, holmium was known in some circles as *Element X*. Most of its basic secrets have been uncovered; it is about as well understood as the other minor rare earths. Figure 67-1 shows that it occurs in the earth's crust in a proportion of 1.2 parts per million.

Holmium has very few practical applications; however, it has some unusual magnetic properties that offer some hope for applications in the future.

Historical background

The discovery of new rare-earth elements through the middle part of the 1800s prompted chemists to employ the same general procedures and philosophies when searching out more new elements in the series. For example, Carl Gustaf Mosander had shown that "pure" samples of ceria were actually contaminated with the oxide of a new element, lanthanum. Using the same line of reasoning, Mosander showed that yttria could be fractioned into two new elements, erbium and terbium. It is not surprising, then, that scientists such as Per Theodore Cleve (1840 – 1905) would take a second and more careful look at "pure" samples of rare-earth oxides.

Cleve's approach paid off in 1879 when he carefully fractionated samples of erbia, or erbium oxide. Following Marignac's procedure announced a year earlier, Cleve quickly separated ytterbia and scandia from the sample. Then the truly original work began—resolving the remaining erbia even further. In this instance, he knew the rose-colored oxide was a purified erbium; the brownish and greenish precipitates he named *holmia* and *thulia*, respectively.

Rank (Rare Earths)	Rare-Earth Element	Abundance (ppm)
1	Cerium, Ce	46.0
2	Yttrium, Y	28.0
3	Neodymium, Nd	24.0
4	Lanthanum, La	18.0
5	Samarium, Sm	6.5
6	Gadolinium, Gd	6.4
7	Praseodymium, Pr	5.5
8	Scandium, Sc	5.0
9	Dysprosium, Dy	4.5
10	Ytterbium, Yb	2.7
11	Erbium, Er	2.5
12	Holmium, Ho	1.2
13	Europium, Eu	1.1
14	Terbium, Tb	0.9
15	Lutetium, Lu	0.8
16	Thulium, Tm	0.2
17	Promethium, Pm	0.0

67-1 Holmium is ranked twelfth on the abundance chart for rare earths found in the earth's crust.

J.L. Soret and M. Delafontaine had performed spectroscopic analyses on erbia a year earlier and reported seeing absorption bands for an *element X*. They failed to pull together sufficient evidence for a new element until Cleve announced his discovery of holmium, via holmia, or holmium oxide.

Laboratory-grade holmia was not produced until 1911, and the pure metal was not isolated until even more recently.

Properties of holmium

Holmium has a bright, silvery luster. It is fairly soft—much like lead—and it can be pounded or rolled into very thin sheets. It is fairly stable in normal room environments, but it tends to corrode with a dull, yellowish oxide film when subjected to conditions of high temperature and humidity.

Holmium is a lanthanide as well as a rare earth.

Production of holmium

Most commercial-grade holmium is obtained from *monazite sand*, which is a mixture of phosphates of calcium, thorium, cerium, and most of the other rare earths. This sand is often 50% rare earth by weight, with approximately 0.05% being holmium. Most of the unwanted metals can be removed from ground monazide magnetically or by a flotation process. The remaining operations deal with separating holmium from the other rare-earth metals.

Like most rare-earth metals, holmium can be separated by an ion-exchange displacement process. The result is a holmium ion, which can react with oxygen ions to form holmium oxide (Ho_2O_3). This oxide is then used for producing other holmium compounds.

Holmium fluoride and chloride, for example, can be produced by the reaction of holmium oxide with the appropriate acid:

$$HO_2O_3 + 6HF \rightarrow 2HoF_3 + 3H_2O$$
(holmium oxide + hydrofluoric acid → holmium fluoride + water)

Holmium metal can be recovered from the fluoride or chloride by reduction with an active metal such as calcium. Using holmium fluoride and calcium, the reaction is:

$$3Ca + 2HoF_3 \rightarrow 2Ho + 3CaF_2$$
(calcium metal + holmium fluoride → holmium metal + calcium fluoride)

Some compounds and isotopes of holmium

Holmium has an oxidation state of $+3$, and thus typifies the lanthanide series of rare-earth metals. The halide compounds are *holmium fluoride* (HoF_3), *holmium chloride* ($HoCl_3$), *holmium bromide* ($HoBr_3$), and *holmium iodide* (HoI_3). These are all put together this way:

$$Ho^{3+} + X^- \rightarrow HoX_3$$

where X is the halide ion.

The only *holmium oxide* is Ho_2O_3 (also called holmium sesquioxide and *holmia*):

$$2Ho^{3+} + 3O^{2-} \rightarrow Ho_2O_3$$

This is the only compound of importance; and even then, its importance is fairly well limited to the production of other holmium compounds that are, themselves, intended solely for research purposes.

The halide compounds of holmium are all yellow; the oxide is light brown.

Figure 67-2 lists all of the known isotopes of Holmium. The isotope, holmium-165, accounts for all of the element as found in nature.

Isotope	Natural Abundance	Half-Life	Decay Mode	Isotope	Natural Abundance	Half-Life	Decay Mode
^{148}Ho		9 sec	β+, ec	^{159m}Ho		8.3 sec	i.t.
^{149}Ho		21 sec	β+, ec	^{159}Ho		33 min	ec
^{150m}Ho		26 sec	β+, ec	^{160m}Ho		4.9 hr	i.t., ec
^{150}Ho		88 sec	β+, ec	^{160}Ho		25.6 min	β+, ec
^{151m}Ho		48 sec	β+, ec	^{161m}Ho		6.7 sec	i.t.
^{151}Ho		5.1 sec	β+, ec	^{161}Ho		2.5 hr	ec
^{152m}Ho		51 sec	β+, ec	^{162m}Ho		68 min	i.t., ec
^{152}Ho		2.4 min	β+, ec	^{162}Ho		15 min	ec, β+
^{153m}Ho		2.0 min	β+, ec	^{163m}Ho		1.1 sec	i.t.
^{153}Ho		9.3 min	β+, ec	^{163}Ho		33 yr	ec
^{154m}Ho		3.2 min	β+, ec	^{164m}Ho		37.5 min	i.t., ec
^{154}Ho		12 min	β+, ec	^{164}Ho		29 min	ec, β-
^{155}Ho		48 min	β+, ec	^{165}Ho	100%		
^{156m}Ho		56 min	β+, ec	^{166m}Ho		1000 yr	β-
^{156}Ho		2 min	β+, ec	^{166}Ho		1.1 day	β-
^{157}Ho		12.6 min	β+, ec	^{167}Ho		3.1 hr	β-
$^{158m2}Ho$		21 min	β+, ec	^{168}Ho		3 min	β-
$^{158m1}Ho$		27 min	i.t., ec	^{169}Ho		4.7 min	β-
^{158}Ho		11.3 min	β+, ec	^{170m}Ho		43 sec	β-
				^{170}Ho		2.8 min	β-

67-2 Holmium has isotopes with atomic weights between 148 and 170.

Element 68: Erbium

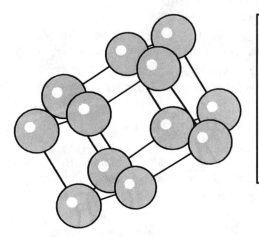

Name	Erbium
Symbol	Er
Atomic Number	68
Atomic Weight	167.26
Melting Point	1529°C
Boiling Point	2868°C
Specific Gravity	9.066 (25°C)
Oxidation State	+3
Electron Config.	(Xe) $4f^{12} 6s^2$

- Name pronounced as **UR-bi-em**
- Named for the Swedish town, Ytterby
- Discovered by C.G. Mosander in 1843
- Soft, malleable, silvery metal

Figure 68-1 shows that erbium ranks eleventh out of seventeen on the abundance chart of rare earths in the earth's crust. Having an average concentration of 2.5 parts-per-million, you might expect to find 2.5 pounds of erbium in every million pounds (500 tons) of dirt, mud, and clay. These are average estimates, however; erbium, like all of the other rare earths, are found in much higher concentrations in a few scattered localities. So if you dig in the wrong place, you will not find any erbium in 500 tons of earth. Dig in the right place, though, and you might find nearly a ton of it.

Erbium finds a few applications in the nuclear industry and as an alloying agent for other exotic metals—it increases the malleability of vanadium, for example.

Erbium might have been legitimately named *akatastasium* (from the Greek *akatastasia*, ''confusion'') because of its confusion with other rare earths during the formative years of rare-earth chemistry. The rare earths are usually found in their oxide forms in nature. Early researchers believed that the oxides of some of the rare earths were elements in their own right. One of these oxides is yttria (oxide of yttrium). In 1842, yttria was found to include *erbia* and *terbia* (oxides of erbium and terbium, respectively) as well as yttria. This is where the confusion began.

Erbia and terbia are so incredibly similar that even highly respected and skilled chemists confused the two. Throughout the literature of the time, one can find data for these two oxides being switched around. This confusion was resolved in 1877, when the scientific establishment had its ''final'' say in the matter—and they got it wrong. What we now call erbium was originally terbium and *vice versa*.

Rank (Rare Earths)	Rare-Earth Element	Abundance (ppm)
1	Cerium, Ce	46.0
2	Yttrium, Y	28.0
3	Neodymium, Nd	24.0
4	Lanthanum, La	18.0
5	Samarium, Sm	6.5
6	Gadolinium, Gd	6.4
7	Praseodymium, Pr	5.5
8	Scandium, Sc	5.0
9	Dysprosium, Dy	4.5
10	Ytterbium, Yb	2.7
11	Erbium, Er	2.5
12	Holmium, Ho	1.2
13	Europium, Eu	1.1
14	Terbium, Tb	0.9
15	Lutetium, Lu	0.8
16	Thulium, Tm	0.2
17	Promethium, Pm	0.0

68-1 Erbium is ranked eleventh on the abundance chart for rare earths found in the earth's crust.

Isotope	Natural Abundance	Half-Life	Decay Mode
^{150}Er		20 sec	$\beta+$, ec
^{151}Er		23 sec	$\beta+$, ec
^{152}Er		10.3 sec	α, $\beta+$, ec
^{153}Er		37.1 sec	α, $\beta+$, ec
^{154}Er		3.7 min	α, $\beta+$, ec
^{155}Er		5.3 min	$\beta+$, ec
^{156}Er		20 min	$\beta+$, ec
^{157}Er		24 min	$\beta+$, ec
^{158}Er		2.3 hr	$\beta+$, ec
^{159}Er		36 min	$\beta+$, ec
^{160}Er		28.6hr	ec
^{161}Er		3.24 hr	ec
^{162}Er	0.14%		
^{163}Er		75.1 min	ec
^{164}Er	1.61%		
^{165}Er		10.36 hr	ec
^{166}Er	33.6%		
^{167m}Er		2.28 sec	i.t.
^{167}Er	22.95%		
^{168}Er	26.8%		
^{169}Er		9.4 day	β-
^{170}Er	14.9%		β-
^{171}Er		7.5 hr	β-
^{172}Er		2 day	β-
^{173}Er		1.4 min	β-

68-2 Erbium has isotopes with atomic weights between 150 and 173.

Historical background

Carl Gustaf Mosander (1797 – 1858) had already proven that a new element, lanthanum, could be separated from samples of ceria, or ceric oxide. Using the same procedure, he hoped to repeat his success with another earth called yttria.

He already knew that his samples of yttria would contain three other earth oxides: ceria, lanthana, and didymia. He quickly separated them from the source sample. The portion that remained contained not one, but three, new oxides.

The first to separate from the fractions had a yellowish color; Mosander called it *erbia*. The next in line had a rosy color, and Mosander named it *terbia*. The final fraction was a colorless oxide that he named after the source material, *yttria*.

The discovery of erbium is closely associated with yttrium and terbium, and with Gustaf Mosander's work in 1843. About 30 years later, Jean-Charles Galissard de Marignac would show that Mosander's erbia included another element now known as ytterbium (atomic number 70).

Erbium metal was not isolated from its compounds until nearly a century after its discovery. In 1934, Klemm and Bommer devised a technique that used vaporized potassium to reduce erbium metal from its chloride which, in turn, was produced from erbium oxide:

$$Er_2O_3 + 6HCl \rightarrow 2ErCl_3 + 2H_2O$$
(erbium oxide + hydrochloric acid → erbium chloride + water)

$$ErCl_3 + 3K \rightarrow Er + 3KCl$$
(erbium chloride + potassium → erbium + potassium chloride)

Properties of erbium

Pure erbium is soft and malleable. It has a silvery metallic luster that tarnishes only slightly in air. It is a member of the lanthanide group of elements that fit onto the periodic chart between lantanum (element 57) and hafnium (element 72).

Erbium has unusual magnetic properties, including the fact that it is antiferromagnetic across a fairly wide range of low temperatures. It becomes superconductive at very low temperatures.

Production of erbium

Most erbium is obtained from minerals *xenotime* and *euxerite*. Erbium, as well as most of the other rare-earth metals, are technically regarded as impurities in these minerals. There are sufficient amounts of these so-called "impurities," however, to make it commercially feasible to recover the metals from them.

Like most rare-earth metals, erbium can be separated from the other rare earths by means of an ion-exchange displacement process. The result is an erbium ion, which can react with a fluoride or chloride ion to form erbium fluoride (ErF_3) and erbium chloride ($ErCl_3$).

Erbium is also produced by reducing erbium fluoride with calcium metal:

$$3Ca + 2ErF_3 \rightarrow 2Er + 3CaF_2$$
(calcium metal + erbium fluoride → erbium metal + calcium fluoride)

The same kind of reaction is possible with lithium metal and erbium chloride:

$$3Li + ErCl_3 \rightarrow Er + 3LiCl$$
(lithium metal + erbium chloride → erbium metal + lithium chloride)

Some compounds and isotopes of erbium

Erbium has a single oxidation state of +3, so its metal ion is characterized as Er^{3+}. The halide compounds are put together this way:

$$Er^{3+} + 3X^- \rightarrow ErX_3$$

where X is the halide ion. This accounts for the formulae for *erbium fluoride* (ErF_3), *erbium chloride* ($ErCl_3$), *erbium bromide* ($ErBr_3$), and *erbium iodide* (ErI_3).

The sole *erbium oxide* is Er_2O_3 (also called erbium sesquioxide and *erbia*):

$$2Er^{3+} + 3O^{2-} \rightarrow Er_2O_3$$

Figure 68-2 on p. 243 lists all of the known isotopes of erbium. Six of these occur naturally.

Element 69: Thulium

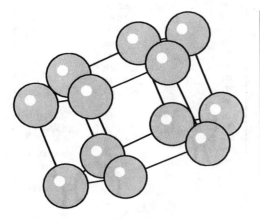

Name	Thulium
Symbol	Tm
Atomic Number	69
Atomic Weight	168.934
Melting Point	1545°C
Boiling Point	1950°C
Specific Gravity	9.321 (25°C)
Oxidation State	+3
Electron Config.	(Xe) $4f^{13} 6s^2$

- Name pronounced as **THOO-li-em**
- Named for the *Thule*, the ancient name for Scandinavia
- Discovered by Per Theodor Cleve in 1879
- Soft, malleable, ductile, silvery metal

Thulium is the least abundant of the naturally occurring rare earths. As shown in Fig. 69-1, it is found in average portions of 0.2 parts per million of the earth's crust. This means you have to dig through 5000 tons of earth to find just two pounds of thulium. The only rare earth that is any rarer is promethium—and that one does not exist on earth at all.

There are presently no commercial applications of this element.

Historical background

Through the middle part of the 1800s, Carl Gustaf Mosander had shown that ceria (cerium oxide) could be split into ceria and lanthana (lanthanum oxide), and that yttria (yttrium oxide) could be split into yttria, erbia (erbium oxide), and terbia (terbium oxide). He thus is credited with taking two known elements, cerium and turbium, and adding three more to the periodic table: lanthanum, erbium, and terbium.

So why fix something that isn't broken? That was the line of thinking that Per Theodore Cleve (1840 – 1905) adopted in 1879 when he took up a closer study of erbia. Using procedures suggested a year earlier, Cleve quickly sorted out the ytterbia and scandia already known to permeate such samples. Then the truly exciting part could begin—resolving the remaining erbia even further.

Things worked out exactly as they had for Mosander. Cleve ended up with three oxides: a rose-colored oxide he knew was purified erbium, a brownish oxide he called *holmia* and a green one he named *thulia*. The existence of the oxide of thulium was sufficient to establish thulium as a true element.

Properties of thulium

Thulium is near the end of the lanthanum series of elements. Elements in this part of the periodic chart are all metals. All are heavy, and most are lustrous and silvery gray in color. Thulium is especially soft for a lanthanide. It can be easily cut with a knife.

Rank (Rare Earths)	Rare-Earth Element	Abundance (ppm)
1	Cerium, Ce	46.0
2	Yttrium, Y	28.0
3	Neodymium, Nd	24.0
4	Lanthanum, La	18.0
5	Samarium, Sm	6.5
6	Gadolinium, Gd	6.4
7	Praseodymium, Pr	5.5
8	Scandium, Sc	5.0
9	Dysprosium, Dy	4.5
10	Ytterbium, Yb	2.7
11	Erbium, Er	2.5
12	Holmium, Ho	1.2
13	Europium, Eu	1.1
14	Terbium, Tb	0.9
15	Lutetium, Lu	0.8
16	Thulium, Tm	0.2
17	Promethium, Pm	0.0

69-1 Thulium is ranked sixteenth on the abundance chart for rare earths found in the earth's crust.

Isotope	Natural Abundance	Half-Life	Decay Mode
^{152}Tm		5.2 sec	$\beta+$, ec
^{153}Tm		1.6 sec	α, $\beta+$, ec
^{154m}Tm		3.4 sec	α, $\beta+$, ec
^{154}Tm		8.3 sec	α, $\beta+$, ec
^{155}Tm		25 sec	α, $\beta+$, ec
^{156m}Tm		19 sec	α
^{156}Tm		80 sec	α, $\beta+$, ec
^{157}Tm		3.6 min	α, $\beta+$, ec
^{158}Tm		4.0 min	$\beta+$, ec
^{159}Tm		9.0 min	$\beta+$, ec
^{160}Tm		9.2 min	$\beta+$, ec
^{161}Tm		38 min	$\beta+$, ec
^{162m}Tm		24 sec	$\beta+$, ec, i.t.
^{162}Tm		21.7 min	$\beta+$, ec
^{163}Tm		1.8 hr	$\beta+$, ec
^{164m}Tm		5.1 min	$\beta+$, ec, i.t.
^{164}Tm		2.0 min	$\beta+$, ec
^{165}Tm		30 hr	ec
^{166}Tm		7.7 hr	$\beta+$, ec
^{167}Tm		9.3 day	ec
^{168}Tm		93.1 day	ec
^{169}Tm	100%		
^{170}Tm		128.6 day	$\beta-$ ec
^{171}Tm		1.92 yr	$\beta-$
^{172}Tm		2.65 day	$\beta-$
^{173}Tm		8.24 hr	$\beta-$
^{174}Tm		5.4 min	$\beta-$
^{175}Tm		15.2 min	$\beta-$
^{176}Tm		1.9 min	$\beta-$

69-2 Thulium has isotopes with atomic weights between 152 and 176.

The melting temperature of thulium is so high that it poses special problems in operations that require forcing a metal to its molten state. For one thing, any container for molten thulium is affected by the high temperature and inevitably adds some impurities to the thulium. The vapor pressure is also so high that large amounts tend to evaporate away from the sample at atmospheric gas pressures.

Production of thulium

Most thulium is obtained from *monazite sand*—a mixture of phosphates of calcium, thorium, cerium, and most of the other rare earths. This sand is often 50% rare earth by weight, but only 0.007% thulium. Like most rare-earth metals, thulium can be separated from the others by an ion-exchange displacement process. The result is a thulium ion, which can react with an anion to form a binary compound such as thulium fluoride (TmF_3), thulium chloride ($TmCl_3$), or thulium oxide (Tm_2O_3).

Where a higher grade of purity is required, thulium oxide is distilled to further separate traces of rare-earth metals and compounds.

Reducing rare-earth compounds with calcium or lithium is normally an efficient process for obtaining high-grade metals. The procedure is not very efficient for the Group IV elements, however, including thulium.

Some compounds and isotopes of thulium

Like the other rare-earth metals in the lanthanide series, thulium has a single oxidation state of $+3$, so its metal ion is characterized as Tm^{3+}. The halide compounds are put together this way:

$$Tm^{3+} + 3X^- \rightarrow TmX_3$$

where X is the halide ion. This accounts for the formulae for *thulium fluoride* (TmF_3), *thulium chloride* ($TmCl_3$), *thulium bromide* ($TmBr_3$), and *thulium iodide* (TmI_3).

The only oxide is *thulium oxide*, Tm_2O_3. This is also called thulium sesquioxide and *thulia*. Its formulation is justified this way:

$$2Tm^{3+} + 3O^{2-} \rightarrow Tm_2O_3$$

Compounds of thulium tend to have greenish colors.

Figure 69-2 lists all of the known isotopes of thulium. All naturally occurring thulium (what there is of it) is stable, nonradioactive thulium-169. The other isotopes are radioactive.

Element 70: Ytterbium

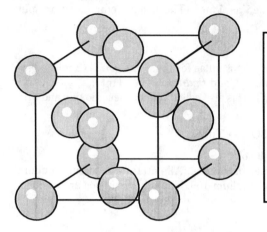

Name	Ytterbium
Symbol	Yb
Atomic Number	70
Atomic Weight	173.04
Melting Point	819°C
Boiling Point	1196°C
Specific Gravity	6.9654 (25°C)
Oxidation States	+2, +3
Electron Config.	$(Xe)\ 4f^{14}\ 6s^2$

- Name pronounced as **i-TUR-bi-em**
- Named for the Swedish village of Ytterby
- Discovered by Jean-Charles-Galinard de Marignac in 1878
- Silvery, lustrous, malleable, and ductile metal

Ytterbium was the first rare earth to be discovered. Like most of the 16 rare-earth metals discovered subsequently, ytterbium is more plentiful in the earth's crust than once thought. Figure 70-1 shows that ytterbium ranks tenth on the abundance chart for rare-earth metals in the earth's crust.

Confusion abounds in the stories about ytterbium and its fellow rare earths. For one thing, they are not earths at all—what chemists once called earths are now known to be oxides of metals. Adding to the confusion is the fact that a given rare earth is nearly always found in the company of at least three or four others; and until recently, the rare earths were separated by tedious, time consuming and expensive processes.

Finally, there is a confusion of names for ytterbium. It is also known by two other names, *aldebaranium* and *cassiopeium*; the proper name is easily confused with the name of another rare-earth element, yttrium (atomic number 39).

Historical background

Chemists were working with a form of ytterbium long before anyone knew of its existence, as was also the case with many other natural elements. In this case, chemists in the late 1800s were working with an earth they called *erbia*. They had no idea that they were attempting to unravel a substance composed of an entire family of rare-earth oxides.

In 1878, Jean Charles Galissard de Marignac (1817 – 1894), announced that he had separated a new ingredient from erbia. He called the new stuff *ytterbia* and suggested it was a compound of a new element he called ytterbium. (Thus began the common confusion between the names for elements 39 and 70—yttrium and ytterbium, respectively.)

Rank (Rare Earths)	Rare-Earth Element	Abundance (ppm)
1	Cerium, Ce	46.0
2	Yttrium, Y	28.0
3	Neodymium, Nd	24.0
4	Lanthanum, La	18.0
5	Samarium, Sm	6.5
6	Gadolinium, Gd	6.4
7	Praseodymium, Pr	5.5
8	Scandium, Sc	5.0
9	Dysprosium, Dy	4.5
10	Ytterbium, Yb	2.7
11	Erbium, Er	2.5
12	Holmium, Ho	1.2
13	Europium, Eu	1.1
14	Terbium, Tb	0.9
15	Lutetium, Lu	0.8
16	Thulium, Tm	0.2
17	Promethium, Pm	0.0

70-1 Ytterbium is ranked tenth on the abundance chart for rare earths found in the earth's crust.

Isotope	Natural Abundance	Half-Life	Decay Mode
^{154}Yb		0.4 sec	α, $\beta+$, ec
^{155}Yb		1.7 sec	α, $\beta+$, ec
^{156}Yb		24 sec	α, $\beta+$, ec
^{157}Yb		39 sec	α, $\beta+$, ec
^{158}Yb		1.5 min	$\beta+$, ec
^{159}Yb		12 sec	$\beta+$, ec
^{160}Yb		4.8 min	$\beta+$, ec
^{161}Yb		4.2 min	$\beta+$, ec
^{162}Yb		18.9 min	$\beta+$, ec
^{163}Yb		11 min	$\beta+$
^{164}Yb		1.26 hr	ec
^{165}Yb		9.9 min	$\beta+$, ec
^{166}Yb		2.36 day	ec
^{167}Yb		17.5 min	$\beta+$, ec
^{168}Yb	0.13%		
^{169m}Yb		46 sec	i.t.
^{169}Yb		32 day	ec
^{170}Yb	3.05%		
^{171}Yb	14.3%		
^{172}Yb	21.9%		
^{173}Yb	16.12%		
^{174}Yb	31.8%		
^{175}Yb		4.19 day	$\beta-$
^{176m}Yb		11.4 sec	i.t.
^{176}Yb	12.7%		
^{177m}Yb		6.41 sec	i.t.
^{177}Yb		1.9 hr	$\beta-$
^{178}Yb		1.23 hr	$\beta-$
^{179}Yb		8 min	$\beta-$

70-2 Ytterbium has isotopes with atomic weights between 154 and 179.

Whenever a new element is discovered, chemists rush to determine its physical and chemical properties. Ytterbium, as well as a few of the other newly discovered rare-earth elements, did not behave in a consistent fashion in the laboratories around the world. Less imaginative scientists believed the trouble was due to inadequate instruments or faulty procedures. A few hit the jackpot, however, when they concluded they were getting mixed results about the properties of ytterbium for an entirely different kind of reason: Ytterbium is not an element at all, but a mixture of two or more elements. As the proportions of the other, unknown elements varied, so did the apparent properties of the samples.

By 1907, Marignac's ytterbium was split into two entirely different elements. One is still called ytterbium. The "child element" is now known as lutetium (see Element 71: Lutetium).

Properties of ytterbium

Ytterbium is a very soft, silvery-white metal. It is shiny when first cut, but gradually takes on a somewhat duller appearance as the oxide forms due to chemical reaction with air. This is a rare-earth metal that is part of the lanthanide series of transition elements.

The metal has at least two allotropic forms. The common, room-temperature form has a face-centered cubic crystal. This transforms to a body-centered form as the metal is heated above 978 °C.

Production of ytterbium

Most commercial-grade ytterbium is obtained from *monazite sand*, which is a mixture of phosphates of calcium, thorium, cerium, and most of the other rare earths. This sand is usually 50% rare earth by weight, and 0.03% is ytterbium. Most of the unwanted metals and other impurities can be removed from the pulverized ore by magnetic or flotation processes. The next step is to separate the rare earths from one another.

Like most rare-earth metals, ytterbium can be separated from the others by an ion-exchange displacement process. The result is an ytterbium ion, which can react with a fluoride or chloride ion to form ytterbium fluoride (YbF_3) and ytterbium chloride ($YbCl_3$).

Ytterbium is also produced by reducing ytterbium fluoride with calcium metal:

$$3Ca + 2YbF_3 \rightarrow 2Yb + 3CaF_2$$

(calcium metal + ytterbium fluoride → ytterbium metal + calcium fluoride)

The same kind of reaction is possible with lithium metal and ytterbium chloride:

$$3Li + YbCl_3 \rightarrow Yb + 3LiCl$$

(lithium metal + ytterbium chloride → ytterbium metal + lithium chloride)

In either case, the ytterbium halide and active metal are loaded into a tantalum crucible and fired in a helium atmosphere. As the reaction progresses, the molten ytterbium, halide compound, and excess active metal separate due to differences in density. When this layered mixture is allowed to cool, the ytterbium is simply cut away from the impurities. The operation can be repeated as often as necessary to achieve the desired level of purity.

Some compounds and the isotopes of ytterbium

Like the other rare-earth metals in the lanthanide series, ytterbium has a single oxidation state of +3, so its metal ion is characterized as Yb^{3+}. There are few compounds that indicate the presence of a +2 oxidation state, of Yb^{2+}.

The halogen compounds can be represented by the element's chlorides:

Ytterbium (II) chloride, $YbCl_2$ (also called ytterbium dichloride)

$$Yb^{2+} + 2Cl^- \rightarrow YbCl_2$$

Ytterbium (III) chloride, $YbCl_3$ (also called ytterbium trichloride)

$$Yb^{3+} + 3Cl^- \rightarrow YbCl_3$$

The oxide, *ytterbium (III) oxide*, is Yb_2O_3. This is sometimes called ytterbium sesquioxide and *ytterbia*. It is the principal oxide of ytterbium and the compound produced in the largest quantities for commercial use.

Compounds of ytterbium (III) tend to be white or colorless, while those of ytterbium (II) are pale green.

Figure 70-2 on p. 249 lists the known isotopes of ytterbium.

Element 71: Lutetium

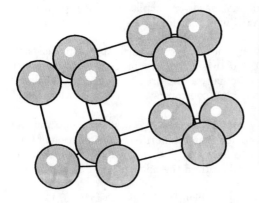

Name	Lutetium
Symbol	Lu
Atomic Number	71
Atomic Weight	174.97
Melting Point	1663°C
Boiling Point	3402°C
Specific Gravity	9.84(25°C)
Oxidation State	+3
Electron Config.	(Xe) $4f^{14} 5d^1 6s^2$

- Name pronounced as **loo-TEE-shi-em**
- Name taken from the ancient name for Paris, France, *Lutecia*
- Discovered independently by Carl Auer von Welsbach and Georges Urbain in 1907 – 08
- Silvery-white, hard, dense, rare-earth metal

Lutetium is an element that has had a lot of different names: neoytterbium, lutecium, cassiopium, and lutetium. Of those four names, the last two are still in use today. One might suspect that an element with so many different names must certainly be important. But it isn't. In fact lutetium is one of the few natural elements that has no practical application.

Figure 71-1 shows that lutetium ranks near the bottom of the list of rare earths found in the earth's crust.

71-1 Lutetium is ranked fifteenth on the abundance chart for rare earths found in the earth's crust.

Rank (Rare Earths)	Rare-Earth Element	Abundance (ppm)
1	Cerium, Ce	46.0
2	Yttrium, Y	28.0
3	Neodymium, Nd	24.0
4	Lanthanum, La	18.0
5	Samarium, Sm	6.5
6	Gadolinium, Gd	6.4
7	Praseodymium, Pr	5.5
8	Scandium, Sc	5.0
9	Dysprosium, Dy	4.5
10	Ytterbium, Yb	2.7
11	Erbium, Er	2.5
12	Holmium, Ho	1.2
13	Europium, Eu	1.1
14	Terbium, Tb	0.9
15	Lutetium, Lu	0.8
16	Thulium, Tm	0.2
17	Promethium, Pm	0.0

Historical background

The discovery of lutetium was made possible by significant advances in the technology for separating very small amounts of compounds that have very similar chemical properties. Most of the rare-earth elements were discovered with the aid of these ion-separation techniques.

During the latter part of 1907 and the first months of 1908, Carl Auer von Welsbach (1858 – 1929) and Georges Urbain (1872 – 1938) both used the new procedures to show that a recently announced element, ytterbium, was actually a mixture of at least two elements. Their work was conducted independently, so some controversy arose about who should have the privilege of naming the new elements.

Welsbach chose the names *aldebaranium* and *cassiopium*. The first is taken from the name of a bright star, Aldebaran; the second comes from the northern constellation of Cassiopia. Urbain chose the names *neoytterbium* and *lutecium*. The first of these names means "new ytterbium." The second of his names is taken from the ancient name for his hometown of Paris.

Although a few German references still refer to element 71 as cassiopium, Georges Urbain eventually won this name-the-element contest—but not without some slight changes. Most chemists had grown fond of the name ytterbium, so the prefix was dropped from Urbain's neoytterbium. And the spelling for element 71 was eventually changed from *lutecium* to *lutetium*, although the pronunciation remained unchanged.

Properties and production of lutetium

Lutetium is a rare-earth, Group-IIB transition metal. It is the final rare-earth metal on the periodic chart and it marks the end of the lantanide series of elements.

Lutetium is also the hardest and heaviest of the rare earths. It has a silvery-white color and is farily stable under normal atmospheric conditions.

This metal is usually obtained from *monazite sand*, along with most of the other rare earths, where lutetium content is on the order of 0.003%. Like most rare-earth metals, lutetium can be separated from the others by an ion-exchange displacement process. The result is a lutetium ion, which can react with a fluoride or chloride ion to form lutetium fluoride (LuF_3) and lutetium chloride ($LuCl_3$).

Lutetium is also produced by reducing lutetium fluoride with calcium metal:

$$3Ca + 2LuF_3 \rightarrow 2Lu + 3CaF_2$$
(calcium metal + lutetium fluoride → lutetium metal + calcium fluoride)

The same kind of reaction is possible with lithium metal and lutetium chloride:

$$3Li + LuCl_3 \rightarrow Lu + 3LiCl$$
(lithium metal + lutetium chloride → lutetium metal + lithium chloride)

In either case, the lutetium halide and active metal are loaded into a tantalum crucible and fired in a helium atmosphere. As the reaction progresses, the molten lutetium, halide compound, and excess active metal separate due to differences in density. When this layered mixture is allowed to cool, the lutetium is simply cut away from the impurities. The operation can be repeated as often as necessary to achieve the desired level of purity.

Some compounds and the isotopes of lutetium

Lutetium has an oxidation state of + 3, and thus typifies the lanthanide series of rare-earth metals. The halide compounds are *lutetium fluoride* (LuF_3), *lutetium chloride* ($LuCl_3$), *lute-*

tium bromide (LuBr$_3$) and *lutetium iodide* (LuI$_3$). These are all put together this way:

$$Lu^{3+} + X^- \rightarrow LuX_3$$

where X is the halide ion.

The only lutetium oxide is Lu$_2$O$_3$ (also called lutetium sesquioxide).

$$2Lu^{3+} + 3O^{2-} \rightarrow Lu_2O_3$$

Lutetium compounds are white or colorless. There are no significant practical applications of the compounds.

Figure 71-2 lists the isotopes of lutetium. Most lutetium found in nature is lutetium-175; there is also a small amount of natural lutetium-176. The other species of the element are both man-made and radioactive.

Isotope	Natural Abundance	Half-Life	Decay Mode	Isotope	Natural Abundance	Half-Life	Decay Mode
^{154}Lu		1.0 sec	α, β+, ec	^{170m}Lu		700 ms	i.t.
^{155}Lu		70 ms	α, β+, ec	^{170}Lu		2 day	ec
^{156m}Lu		210 ms	α, β+, ec	^{171m}Lu		1.3 min	i.t.
^{156}Lu		500 ms	α, β+, ec	^{171}Lu		8.24 day	ec
^{157}Lu		5.5 sec	α, β+, ec	^{172m}Lu		3.7 min	i.t.
^{158}Lu		10 sec	α, β+, ec	^{172}Lu		6.7 day	ec
^{159}Lu		12 sec	β+, ec	^{173}Lu		1.37 yr	ec
^{160}Lu		35 sec	β+, ec	^{174m}Lu		142 day	ec, i.t.
^{161}Lu		1.2 min	β+, ec	^{174}Lu		3.31 yr	ec
^{162}Lu		1.4 min	β+, ec	^{175}Lu	97.40%		
^{163}Lu		4.1 min	β+, ec	^{176m}Lu		3.6 hr	β-
^{164}Lu		3.17 min	β+, ec	^{176}Lu	2.60%		
^{165}Lu		11.8 min	β+, ec	^{177m}Lu		160 day	β-, i.t.
^{166m2}Lu		100 ms	β+, ec	^{177}Lu		6.71 day	β-
^{166m1}Lu		1.4 min	β+, ec, i.t.	^{178m}Lu		23 min	β-
^{166}Lu		2.8 min	β+, ec	^{178}Lu		28.5 min	β-
^{167}Lu		51.5 min	β+, ec	^{179}Lu		4.6 hr	β-
^{168m}Lu		6.7 min	β+, ec	^{180}Lu		5.7 min	β-
^{168}Lu		5.5 min	β+, ec	^{181}Lu		3.5 min	β-
^{169m}Lu		2.7 min	i.t.	^{182}Lu		2.0 min	β-
^{169}Lu		1.42 day	ec				

71-2 Lutetium has isotopes with atomic weights between 154 and 182.

Element 72: Hafnium

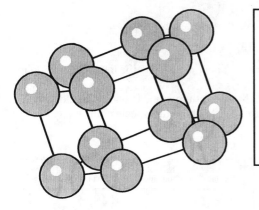

Name	Hafnium
Symbol	Hf
Atomic Number	72
Atomic Weight	178.49
Melting Point	2227°C
Boiling Point	4602°C
Specific Gravity	13.29 (25°C)
Oxidation State	+4
Electron Config.	(Xe) $4f^{14} 5d^2 6s^2$

- Name pronounced as **HAF-ni-em**
- Name taken from the Latin for city of Copenhagen, *Hafnia*
- Discovered by Dirk Coster and George Charles de Hevesy in 1923
- Silvery, ductile metal

Hafnium is a relatively abundant element—at least more abundant than some of the better known elements such as silver and gold. It might seem curious, then, that hafnium was not discovered until recent times. The reason is that hafnium so closely resembles the better-known zirconium (*see* Element 40: Zirconium). Zirconium was discovered in 1789, isolated in 1824, and purified for commercial applications in 1914. Through all these years, only a few scientists dared to suggest that a second element might be lurking in the background of even the purest known samples of zirconium.

Except for its role as a key material in the manufacture of control rods for nuclear reactors, hafnium has no real commercial value. Its primary claim to fame is a negative one—it is regarded as an impurity that has to be tolerated in commercial-grade zirconium and zirconium compounds.

Historical background

The existence of hafnium was suspected in the latter part of the 1800s. A researcher studying zirconium sulfate during that era remarked, "Zirconium is not simple; there is another element concealed in it, and when I have leisure I shall endeavor to isolate it." Unfortunately, there is usually a wide gulf between one who first perceives a truth and one who reaps the fruit of it. This particular perceiver of truth, one F.A. Genth, apparently never found the necessary leisure because he died some thirty years before anyone found a way to separate the hidden element from zirconium.

Mendeleyev, father of the modern periodic table of the elements, also predicted the existence of element 72, hafnium, but added that it would be found among titanium ores.

Neils Bohr, originator of the quantum theory of atoms, suggested the arrangement of outer electrons in atoms of element 72 to Dirk Coster (1889 – 1950) and George Charles de Hevesy (1889 – 1966). These researchers used X-ray instruments to study the patterns of outer electrons in zirconium ores. And there they were! The faint, but telltale, lines that proved Bohr's prediction.

Coster and de Hevesy announced their conclusive results in January, 1923. Acknowledging the vital role that Neils Bohr played in their discovery, the gentlemen named the new element after the ancient name for Bohr's hometown of Copenhagen.

When Coster and de Hevesy announced their discovery, the periodic table of that day had to undergo some serious revision. First, hafnium had to be added to its rightful place as element 72. Second, existing data about zirconium had to be revised as researches redefined the element's properties independent of the influence of hafnium contaminants.

Properties of hafnium

Hafnium looks and feels much like stainless steel, but it is much heavier. It is a transition Group-IVB metal; like most metals in this part of the periodic table, it is protected from corrosion by a tough oxide film that begins to form the moment the bare metal is exposed to the atmosphere.

The chemical and physical properties of hafnium and zirconium are so much alike that the two are nearly impossible to separate entirely. The highest grade zirconium metal, for example, is allowed to include as up to 1% hafnium. Likewise, hafnium containing less then 2% zirconium is considered a high-grade sample.

Hafnium is an excellent absorber of thermal neutrons. This, combined with its high resistance to corrosion, makes it an ideal material for control rods in nuclear reactors.

Production of hafnium

Small quantities of hafnium metal can be obtained by condensing it from *hafnium tetraiodide*, HfI_4, vapor on a hot tungsten wire. Commercial quantities, however, are produced by the *Kroll Process*—the same process used for refining zirconium from its ores (*see* Element 40: Zirconium). This process is appropriate for refining hafnium because zirconium and hafnium are always found together in nature.

In this process, zirconium ores such as *baddeleyite* are exposed to hot chlorine gas in the presence of a carbon catalyst. The result is a mixture of zirconium and hafnium tetrachlorides. The tetrachlorides are then reduced with molten magnesium or sodium to yield the metals. The metals separate as the temperature drops, partly because of their differences in melting points (fractionation) and partly because zirconium is only half as dense as hafnium—so the zirconium floats to the surface and the hafnium sinks to the bottom.

Common compounds and isotopes of hafnium

The principal oxidation state of hafnium is +4. Its most stable metallic ion is Hf^{4+}, so it yields compounds such as:

Hafnium chloride (-tetrachloride), $HfCl_4$

$$Hf^{4+} + 4Cl^- \rightarrow HfCl_4$$

Hafnium fluoride (-tetrafluoride), HfF_4

$$Hf^{4+} + 4F^- \rightarrow HfF_4$$

Hafnium oxide (-dioxide), HfO_2

$$Hf^{4+} + 2O^{2-} \rightarrow HfO_2$$

Hafnium carbide, HfC, has the highest melting point of all binary (2-element) compounds—a temperature in the neighborhood of 3890 °C. And *hafnium nitride*, HfN, is up there, too, with a melting point at 3305 °C.

Figure 72-1 lists the 32 known isotopes of hafnium. Naturally occurring hafnium is distributed among the six nonradioactive species.

Isotope	Natural Abundance	Half-Life	Decay Mode
^{158}Hf		2.9 sec	α, β+, ec
^{159}Hf		5.6 sec	α, β+, ec
^{160}Hf		12 sec	α, β+, ec
^{161}Hf		17 sec	α, β+, ec
^{162}Hf		37.6 sec	α, β+, ec
^{163}Hf		40 sec	β+, ec
^{166}Hf		6.8 min	β+, ec
^{167}Hf		2.05 min	β+, ec
^{168}Hf		25.9 min	β+, ec
^{169}Hf		3.25 min	β+, ec
^{170}Hf		16 hr	ec
^{171}Hf		12 hr	β+, ec
^{172}Hf		1.87 yr	ec
^{173}Hf		23.6 hr	ec
^{174}Hf	0.16%		
^{175}Hf		70 day	ec
^{176}Hf	5.2%		
^{177m2}Hf		51.4 min	i.t.
^{177m1}Hf		1.1 sec	x-ray
^{177}Hf	18.6%		
^{178m2}Hf		31 yr	i.t.
^{178m1}Hf		4.0 sec	i.t.
^{178}Hf	27.1%		
^{179m2}Hf		25.1 day	i.t.
^{179m1}Hf		18.7 sec	i.t.
^{179}Hf	13.74%		
^{180m}Hf		5.5 hr	i.t.
^{180}Hf	35.2%		
^{181}Hf		42.4 day	β-
^{182}Hf		9×10^6 yr	β-
^{183}Hf		64 min	β-
^{184}Hf		4.1 hr	β-

72-1 Hafnium has isotopes with atomic weights between 158 and 184.

Element 73: Tantalum

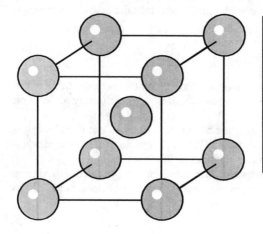

Name	Tantalum
Symbol	Ta
Atomic Number	73
Atomic Weight	180.948
Melting Point	2996°C
Boiling Point	5425°C
Specific Gravity	19.3 (20°C)
Oxidation State	+5
Electron Config.	(Xe) $4f^{14} 5d^3 6s^2$

- Name pronounced as **TAN-te-lem**
- Named for the mythological character, Tantalus, the father of Niobe
- Discovered by Anders Gustaf Ekenberg in 1802
- Gray, heavy, hard metal

Tantalum is a ductile metal that resembles the more expensive platinum in many respects. In fact, tantalum is often used as an economical substitute in applications normally requiring platinum metal. Tantalum is not simply a poor cousin of platinum—it has some unique applications of its own. Tantalum oxide, for example, is the primary ingredient in certain kinds of electronic capacitors. The metal and its alloys resist corrosion and wear, so it is often used for making surgical and dental tools. A composite of tantalum carbide (TaC) and graphite is one of the hardest materials ever produced.

Tantalum comprises only 0.0002% of the earth's crust, and most of it is concentrated in ores from South America, Africa, and Spain. The United States has very little native tantalum ore, but is the world's leading consumer.

Historical background

As the 1700s changed to the 1800s, Anders Gustaf Ekenberg (1767–1813) was having a good time studying the minerals of Ytterby, Sweden. A few years before, the mines around Ytterby provided the raw material for a new element that was later called yttrium (*see* Element 39: Yttrium). Ekenberg was a professional scientist and teacher, and he had a strong hunch that those same mines had more than one new element to offer the world.

Working from a clue offered by a colleague working in Finland, Ekenberg found that two different minerals from Ytterby contained the same unknown element. He confirmed his results and announced his findings in 1802.

The discovery did not receive universal acceptance. Many chemists believed Ekenberg was simply looking at an allotrope of niobium—a metal that is nearly an identical twin of tantalum. The matter was not settled in Ekenberg's favor during his lifetime. The first positive evidence to support Ekenberg's discovery did not come until 1844; then the final and most convincing evidence came in 1866. In both of those instances, the problem was one of demonstrating that a couple of rather esoteric acids, niobic and tantalic acids, were indeed derived from two different elements.

Properties of tantalum

Tantalum is one of the Group-VB, or vanadium group, elements on the periodic table of the elements. Notice that tantalum's twin element, niobium (Nb), is located directly above it on the table.

Tantalum is usually described as a shiny gray metal that is very hard, but ductile. It has a very high melting point that is exceeded by tungsten (W) and rhenium (Re) which, incidentally, fall directly to the right of tantalum on the periodic table.

This metal also resists attack from most chemicals at room temperature. It oxidizes very, very slowly to form the oxide. It reacts more vigorously with hydrofluoric acid (HF) to form *tantalum pentafluoride*.

Production of tantalum

Tantalum exists in a couple of ores, including *columbite* and *euxenite*. Unfortunately, niobium is found in the same ores; since tantalum and niobium are chemically very similar, it is difficult to separate the two. Tantalum and niobium are separated from the ores by a solvent-extraction procedure that yields 98% pure niobium oxide in one phase and 99.5% pure tantalum oxide in another. A similar process yields easily separable fluorides instead of the oxides.

Tantalum oxide, Ta_2O_5, is a valuable commercial compound in its own right. As a source of tantalum metal, tantalum oxide is reduced with an active metal or carbon. At high temperatures, tantalum oxide combines with carbon to produce powdery tantalum metal and carbon dioxide gas. The powdered tantalum is then pressed into bars and *sintered*—made into solid bars of metal—by electrically heating them in a vacuum furnace. The bars are finally rolled into sheets or drawn into wire.

Some compounds and the isotopes of tantalum

Tantalum's most stable oxidation state, $+5$, is represented by its most common compound, tantalum oxide. This oxide, also known as *tantalum pentoxide*, is put together this way:

$$2Ta^{5+} + 5O^{2-} \rightarrow Ta_2O_5$$

A $+4$ oxidation state shows up in one of the hardest man-made substances, *tantalum carbide*, TaC. This yellow-brown crystal is used as the cutting edges of high-speed machine tools. It is produced on a commercial scale by heating tantalum pentoxide and carbon.

Figure 73-1 lists the known isotopes of tantalum. All but a minute fraction of the tantalum found in the earth's crust is tantalum-181. There is a trace of tantalum-180. Neither is radioactive. The remaining isotopes are both man-made and radioactive.

Isotope	Natural Abundance	Half-Life	Decay Mode
^{159}Ta		600 ms	α, β+, ec
^{160}Ta			α, β+, ec
^{161}Ta			α, β+, ec
^{164}Ta		13.6 sec	α, β+, ec
^{166}Ta		32 sec	β+, ec
^{167}Ta		3 min	β+, ec
^{168}Ta		2.4 min	β+, ec
^{169}Ta		5 min	β+, i.t.
^{170}Ta		6.76 min	β+, ec
^{171}Ta		23.4 min	β+, ec
^{172}Ta		36.8 min	β+, ec
^{173}Ta		3.65 hr	β+, ec
^{174}Ta		1.18 hr	β+, ec
^{175}Ta		10.5 hr	ec
^{176}Ta		8.08 hr	ec
^{177}Ta		2.36 day	ec
^{178m}Ta		2.54 hr	ec
^{178}Ta		9.3 min	β+, ec
^{179}Ta		1.82 yr	ec
^{180m}Ta		8.15 hr	β+, ec
^{180}Ta	0.012%		
^{181}Ta	99.998%		
^{182m}Ta		15.9 min	i.t.
^{182}Ta		114.5 day	β-
^{183}Ta		5.1 day	β-
^{184}Ta		8.7 hr	β-
^{185}Ta		49 min	β-
^{186}Ta		10.5 min	β-

73-1 Tantalum has isotopes with atomic weights between 159 and 186.

Element 74: Tungsten

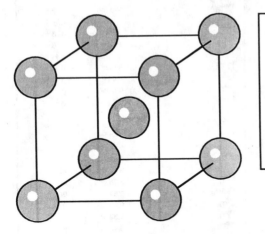

Name	Tungsten
Symbol	W
Atomic Number	74
Atomic Weight	183.85
Melting Point	3410°C
Boiling Point	5660°C
Specific Gravity	19.3 (20°C)
Oxidation State	+6
Electron Config.	(Xe) $4f^{14} 5d^4 6s^2$

- Name pronounced as **TUNG-sten**
- Name taken from the Swedish, *tung sten*, "heavy stone"
- Chemical symbol, *W*, is taken from the alternative name, wolfram
- First isolated by brothers Juan José and Fausto Elhuyar in 1783
- Tough, steel-gray to white metal
- Highest melting point of all metals

Tungsten is known as the metal used for making filaments in common incandescent light bulbs. This application takes advantage of the fact that tungsten has the highest melting temperature of any metal. Its temperature can be raised to the point where it glows with a brilliant white light. Most other metals vaporize before they can produce that much light.

A lot of tungsten is also used in the manufacture of tungsten carbide. This is an extremely hard material that is used for making industrial cutting tools and abrasives.

The remainder of the world's production of tungsten metal is used as an alloy in steel. Tungsten steel is noted for its toughness and stability at high temperatures. Nozzles for rocket engines, for example, are made from tungsten steel.

Historical background

Tungsten was originally called *wolfram*. This was back in the late 1700s when it was discovered. In fact, a few conservative German journals prefer to call element 74 by its original name. Wolfram is an appropriate name because the mineral, *wolframite*, played an important role in the discovery of this element.

In 1761, one J.G. Lehmann was studying wolframite in his mineral lab. In one of his experiments, he ground the ore and melted it with sodium nitrate. Dissolving the mixture in water, he found it turned the water green, then red. Having added some hydrochloric acid, he noticed that a spongy white precipitate formed which, upon standing for a week or so, became yellow.

Those were the kinds of clues the chemists used in those days. Unfortunately, Lehmann had the right idea but missed the conclusion. He reported his colorful results as indicating the presence of iron mixed with a bit of zinc. Today we know that wolframite is a mixture of iron and manganese compounded with *tungsten tetroxide*, $(Fe,Mn)WO_4$.

It is both interesting and informative to attempt to construct accounts of old experiments in the light of modern knowledge. Fusing the wolframite with sodium nitrate, for example, produced a sodium manganate (green color) which changed to sodium permangante (red color). The brilliant show of colors masked the interesting part of the reaction where tungsten and tungsten oxides were being reduced from the ore. Adding the acid produced *tungstic acid*, H_2WO_4. Hydrated tungstic acid is a white substance. Drying it produces anhydrous tungstic acid, which we know today as a yellow powder.

Wolframite and other tungsten-bearing ores were later confused with tin and arsenic. In 1783, brothers Juan José and Fausto Elhuyar ended the confusion by isolating pure tungsten metal from samples of wolframite. Their basic technique, now more than two centuries old, remains the primary method for producing the metal on a commercial scale.

Properties of tungsten

Very pure tungsten is relatively soft; at least it can be cut with an ordinary hacksaw. However, small amounts of impurities render the metal hard and brittle. It is sometimes described as being steely gray or tending toward a white color. The appearance, like its ductility, depends a lot on the purity of the samples.

Tungsten is a chromium metal in Group VIB on the periodic table of the elements. It is quite similar to the two elements appearing above it on the table, molybdenum (Mo) and chromium (Cr). While tungsten has the highest melting temperature of all the elements, it is straddled on the right and left by elements having the second- and third-highest melting points, rhenium (Re) and tantalum (Ta).

Production of tungsten

The chief mineral sources of tungsten are *scheelite* and *wolframite*, which are, respectively, *calcium tungstate* $(CaWO_4)$ and *iron-manganese tungstate* $(FeWO_4$ and $MnWO_4)$.

After grinding and cleaning, the ores are treated with alkalis to yield *tungsten trioxide* (WO_3). The trioxide is finally reduced with carbon or hydrogen gas to produce the pure metal. Using carbon as the reducing agent, the reaction is:

$$2WO_3 + 3C \rightarrow 2WO + 3CO_2$$
(tungsten trioxide + carbon + heat → tungsten metal + carbon dioxide)

Or using hydrogen gas as the reducing agent:

$$WO_3 + 3H_2 \rightarrow W + 3H_2O$$
(tungsten trioxide + hydrogen gas + heat → tungsten metal + water vapor)

Some compounds and the isotopes of tungsten

Tungsten's principal oxidation state is $+6$, although there are a few stable compounds having lower oxidation states. Generally, tungsten compounds look like this:

Tungsten hexachloride, WCl_6

$$W^{6+} + 6Cl^- \rightarrow WCl_6$$

Tungsten trioxide, WO_3

$$W^{6+} + 3O^{2-} \rightarrow WO_3$$

There is also a tendency to form *tungsten oxychlorides*, $WOCl_4$ and WO_2Cl_2:

$$W^{6+} + O^{2-} + 4Cl^- \rightarrow WOCl_4$$

$$W^{6+} + 2O^{2-} + 2Cl^- \rightarrow WO_2Cl_2$$

One of the lower oxidation states, namely $+4$, occurs in the hard, commercially valuable abrasive, *tungsten carbide*, WC:

$$W^{4+} + C^{4-} \rightarrow WC$$

Figure 74-1 shows the isotopes of tungsten. None of the naturally occurring species is radioactive.

Isotope	Natural Abundance	Half-Life	Decay Mode
^{160}W		80 ms	α, β+, ec
^{161}W		410 ms	α, β+, ec
^{162}W		1.39 sec	α, β+, ec
^{163}W		2.8 sec	α, β+, ec
^{164}W		6 sec	α, β+, ec
^{165}W		5 sec	α, β+, ec
^{166}W		16 sec	α, β+, ec
^{172}W		6.7 min	α, β+, ec
^{173}W		16.1 min	ec
^{174}W		1 min	ec
^{175}W		1 min	ec
^{176}W		3 min	β+, ec
^{177}W		2.2 hr	ec
^{178}W		21.5 day	ec
^{179m}W		6.4 min	i.t.
^{179}W		37.5 min	ec
^{180}W	0.13%		
^{181}W		4.8 hr	ec
^{182}W	26.3%		
^{183m}W		5.15 sec	i.t.
^{183}W	14.3%		
^{184}W	30.67%		
^{185m}W		1.65 min	i.t.
^{185}W		74.8 day	β-
^{186}W	28.6%		.t.
^{187}W		23.9 hr	β-
^{188}W		69.4 day	β-
^{189}W		11.5 min	β-
^{190}W		30 min	β-

74-1 Tungsten has isotopes with atomic weights between 160 and 190.

Element 75: Rhenium

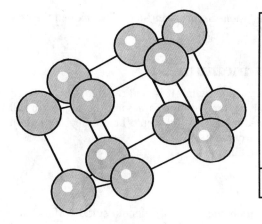

Name	Rhenium
Symbol	Re
Atomic Number	75
Atomic Weight	186.207
Melting Point	3180°C
Boiling Point	5627°C Note
Specific Gravity	21.04 (20°C)
Oxidation States	+4, +6, +7
Electron Config.	(Xe) $4f^{14}\,5d^5\,6s^2$

Note: Estimated value.

- Name pronounced as **REE-ni-em**
- Name taken from the Latin, *Rhenus*, the Rhine River
- Discovered by Ida and Walter Noddack, and Otto Carl Berg in 1925
- Dense, silvery-white metal

Rhenium is noted for being one of the most dense of the elements; it is almost as heavy as lead. Rhenium is also noted for being one of the rarest of the naturally occurring elements. You have to dig up 1000 million pounds of the earth's crust in order to get one pound of rhenium out of it. Little wonder, then, that there are so few practical applications for the pure metal.

This is not to say that rhenium is little more than a space-filler on the periodic table. The total United States annual production of rhenium is almost a half ton, and the total world reserves is on the order of 400 tons. Rhenium's commercial value is as a trace alloying agent for hardening metal components that are subjected to continuous frictional forces.

Historical background

It is not likely that an element as scarce as rhenium would be discovered accidentally. Someone would have to go looking for it; and that is exactly how element 75 was discovered in 1925.

A standard periodic chart shows four elements in Group VIIB, the manganese group. Prior to 1925, however, the only element in the group was the lead-off element, manganese (Mn). You didn't have to be a genius to suspect that there would be some elements around to fill the gaps—especially for atomic numbers 43 and 75. Using Mendeleyev's terminology, element 43 was being called *eka-manganese* and element 75 *dvi-manganese*.

Walter Noddack, Ida Tacke-Noddack and Otto Berg deduced most of the physical properties and sketched out some of the possible chemical reactions for the proposed elements. Much of this theoretical work was based on the observation that elements having odd-numbered atomic numbers are less common than those having even atomic numbers.

In May, 1925, the group managed to carry out a 100,000-fold concentration of element 75 from samples of gadolinium ore. Even so, they were a long way from a pure sample. Nevertheless, there was enough to run a spectroscopic study and see the spectral lines of a new element.

The Noddacks and Herr Berg announced their discovery in June. They named the new element for their homeland waterway, the Rhine River.

Properties and production of rhenium

Rhenium is an extremely hard, dense, silvery-white metal. It is acid resistant and does not dissolve at all in hydrochloric acid. Its melting temperature is among the highest of all known elements. If rhenium were not so heavy and rare, it would be an ideal structural metal for instruments used in hazardous environments.

Rhenium is in Group VIIB of the transition metals.

Production of rhenium

Rhenium occurs naturally as an impurity in molybdenite (molybdenum sulfide, MoS_2) and to a lesser extent in copper sulfide ores. It is far more practical, however, to recover traces of rhenium oxide, Re_2O_7, from the flue dusts of molybdenum and platinum refineries, and from the anode slime that results from the electrolytic purification of copper. Then rhenium metal can be reduced from the oxide by igniting the oxide in an atmosphere of hydrogen.

Some compounds and the isotopes of rhenium

Like manganese and technetium, which are located immediately above rhenium in Group VIIB on the periodic table, rhenium supports some of the highest oxidation states found among the elements. Oxidation states +3 and +5 are demonstrated by the rhenium chlorides:

Rhenium (III) chloride: $ReCl_3$

$$Re^{3+} + 3Cl^- \rightarrow ReCl_3$$

Rhenium (V) chloride: $ReCl_5$

$$Re^{5+} + 5Cl^- \rightarrow ReCl_5$$

The +4 and +6 oxidation states can be found among the fluorides:

Rhenium (IV) fluoride: ReF_4

$$Re^{4+} + 4F^- \rightarrow ReF_4$$

Rhenium (VI) fluoride: ReF_6

$$Re^{6+} + 6F^- \rightarrow ReF_6$$

Rhenium's highest oxidation state is determined by one of its oxides:

Rhenium heptoxide: Re_2O_7

$$2Re^{7+} + 7O^{2-} \rightarrow Re_2O_7$$

Rhenium salts tend to have green, red, and yellow colors.

Figure 75-1 shows the known isotopes of rhenium. Samples found in nature are a mixture of rhenium-185 and -187. The remaining isotopes are both artificial and radioactive.

Isotope	Natural Abundance	Half-Life	Decay Mode
^{162}Re		100 ms	α, β+, ec
^{163}Re		260 ms	α, β+, ec
^{164}Re		900 ms	α, β+, ec
^{165}Re		2.4 sec	α, β+, ec
^{166}Re		2.2 sec	α, β+, ec
^{167}Re		2.0 sec	α, β+, ec
^{168}Re		2.9 sec	α, β+, ec
^{170}Re		8 sec	β+, ec
^{172m}Re		15 sec	β+, ec
^{172}Re		2.3 min	β+, ec
^{174}Re		2.3 min	β+, ec
^{175}Re		4.6 min	β+, ec
^{176}Re		5.3 min	β+, ec
^{177}Re		14 min	β+, ec
^{178}Re		13.2 min	β+, ec
^{179}Re		19.7 min	β+, ec
^{180}Re		2.54 min	β+, ec
^{181}Re		20 hr	ec
^{182m}Re		12.7 hr	ec
^{182}Re		64 hr	ec
^{183}Re		70 day	ec
^{184m}Re		165 day	ec, i.t.
^{184}Re		38 day	ec
^{185}Re	37.4%		
^{186}Re			ec
^{187}Re	62.6%		
^{188}Re		17 hr	β-
^{189}Re		24 hr	β-
^{190m}Re		3 hr	i.t., β-
^{190}Re		3 min	β-
^{191}Re		9.8 min	β-
^{192}Re		16 sec	β-

75-1 Rhenium has isotopes with atomic weights between 162 and 192.

Element 76: Osmium

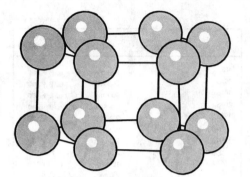

Name	Osmium
Symbol	Os
Atomic Number	76
Atomic Weight	190.2
Melting Point	3054°C
Boiling Point	5027°C
Specific Gravity	22.61 (20°C)
Oxidation States	+3, +4
Electron Config.	(Xe) $4f^{14} 5d^6 6s^2$

- Name pronounced as **OZ-mi-em**
- Name taken from the Greek, *osme*, "odor"
- Discovered by Smithson Tennant in 1803
- Blue-white, lustrous, hard metal

The oxides of osmium emit highly toxic gasses; since these oxides form readily when the metal is exposed to air, there are few commercial applications of the element itself. Osmium can be used safely as an alloying agent, however. Mixed with other metals, traces of osmium can be found where frictional wear must be minimized, as in electrical switch contacts and ballpoint pen tips.

Historical background

Osmium and its companion metal, iridium, were discovered at the same time by Smithson Tennant (1761 – 1815) in 1803. Tennant and other researchers had developed a curiosity about a black, metallic substance that appeared whenever they treated crude (unrefined) platinum with aqua regia, a mixture of nitric and hydrochloric acids. Most people thought it was graphite, and Tennant might have agreed. After all, he had just shown that diamond was actually a form of carbon, or graphite. So why not take a look at platinum?

When Tennant looked closer at the black residue and tried to alloy it with lead, he concluded he was actually dealing with a new metal instead of an allotropic form of carbon. Later that winter, Tennant performed closer analyses and found the black powder was composed of two new metals. He named one of them *iridium* because of its colorful array of compounds (*see* Element 77: Iridium); he named the other *osmium* because of its nasty smell.

It is not his discovery of osmium and iridium that marks the pinnacle of Smithson Tennant's career, however. He is better known for proving that diamond is a form of carbon.

Properties of osmium

Osmium is a tough, lustrous metal that takes on a slight blush color as a thin film of the oxide forms on the exposed surfaces. Powdered osmium emits the telltale odor of the deadly poison, osmium tetroxide.

Osmium is one of the Group-VIII elements. Its chemistry and history are closely associated with platinum (Pt) and even more so with iridium (Ir). Notice that all three of these elements—osmium, iridium, and platinum—are Group-VIII elements that are lined up in the same series on the periodic table.

Production of osmium

Osmium is generally found in the company of natural platinum. It is also found in fairly large amounts in the nickel ores of Sudbury, Ontario. Therefore, osmium is recovered as a byproduct of the mining and refining of platinum and nickel. If osmium were not found in such close association with these highly profitable enterprises, it is doubtful there would be any market for osmium. It would be far too expensive to mine and refine for its own sake.

Several methods can recover osmium metal from the residues of nickel and platinum refining operations. Boiling the osmium-bearing matter in aqua regia produces the tetroxide, which, in turn, reacts with sodium hydroxide to yield a more benign compound, sodium osmate (Na_2OsO_4). The osmium can be reduced to the metal by a reaction with an active metal such as zinc.

Some compounds and isotopes of osmium

The most stable oxidation states for osmium are $+3$ and $+4$, which accounts for the tendency to produce a variety of oxides and halides:

Osmium sesquioxide, Os_2O_3

$$2Os^{3+} + 3O^{2-} \rightarrow Os_2O_3$$

Osmium dioxide, OsO_2

$$Os^{4+} + 2O^{2-} \rightarrow OsO_2$$

Osmium (III) chloride, or osmium trichloride, $OsCl_3$

$$Os^{3+} + 3Cl^- \rightarrow OsCl_3$$

Osmium (IV) fluroide, or osmium tetrafluoride, OsF_4

$$Os^{4+} + 4F^- \rightarrow OsF_4$$

Few elements exhibit an oxidation state as high as $+8$; osmium does. In fact, this state accounts for the existence of the deadly *osmium tetroxide*:

$$Os^{8+} + 4O^{2-} \rightarrow OsO_4$$

Figure 76-1 lists the known isotopes of osmium. Seven of them occur naturally; one of them, osmium-186, is radioactive.

Isotope	Natural Abundance	Half-Life	Decay Mode
^{166}Os		180 ms	α, β+, ec
^{167}Os		700 ms	α, β+, ec
^{168}Os		2.2 sec	α, β+, ec
^{169}Os		3.3 sec	α, β+, ec
^{170}Os		7.1 sec	α, β+, ec
^{171}Os		7.9 sec	α, β+, ec
^{172}Os		19 sec	α, β+, ec
^{173}Os		16 sec	α, β+, ec
^{174}Os		44 sec	α, β+, ec
^{175}Os		1.4 min	β+, ec
^{176}Os		3.6 min	β+, ec
^{177}Os		2.8 min	β+, ec
^{178}Os		5 min	β+, ec
^{179}Os		7 min	β+, ec
^{180}Os		21.7 min	β+, ec
^{181m}Os		2.7 min	β+, ec
^{181}Os		1.75 hr	ec
^{182}Os		21.5 hr	ec
^{183m}Os		9.9 hr	ec, i.t.
^{183}Os		13 hr	ec
^{184}Os	0.02%		
^{185}Os		93.6 day	ec
^{186}Os	1.58%	2×10^{15}yr	α
^{187}Os	1.6%		
^{188}Os	13.3%		
^{189m}Os		5.8 hr	i.t.
^{189}Os	16.1%		
^{190m}Os		9.9 min	i.t.
^{190}Os	26.4%		
^{191m}Os		13.1 hr	i.t.
^{191}Os		15.4 day	β-
^{192m}Os		6.1 sec	i.t.
^{192}Os	41.0%		
^{193}Os			
^{194}Os		6 yr	β-
^{195}Os		6.5 min	β-
^{196}Os		34.9 min	β-

76-1 Osmium has isotopes with atomic weights between 166 and 196.

Element 77: Iridium

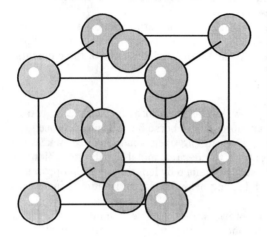

Name	Iridium
Symbol	Ir
Atomic Number	77
Atomic Weight	192.2
Melting Point	2410°C
Boiling Point	4130°C
Specific Gravity	22.65 (20°C)
Oxidation States	+3, +4
Electron Config.	(Xe) $4f^{14} 5d^7 6s^2$

- Name pronounced as **i-RID-i-em**
- Name taken from the Latin, *iris*, "rainbow"
- Discovered by Smithson Tennant in 1803
- White, brittle metal

Iridium has a reputation for being the most corrosion-resistant of all known metals. It even withstands attack with hot aqua regia and can be used routinely at temperatures up to 2000 °C. This remarkable metal is, unfortunately, very difficult to machine into useful shapes. Its most common application is as an alloying agent for hardening platinum.

Historical background

Iridium and its companion element, osmium, were discovered at the same time in 1803 by the English chemist, Smithson Tennant (1761 – 1815). Using aqua regia (a nasty mixture of nitric and hydrochloric acids) to dissolve the known minerals in samples of platinum ore, researchers found a black, shiny residue that looked much like a hard graphite or carborundum (silicon carbide).

Tennant was not satisfied with a casual identification of the black substance, and initiated a series of careful analyses. His work paid off when he positively identified two new elements. One he named *iridium* because of its colorful compounds and the other he called *osmium* because of its terrible odor (*see* Element 76: Osmium).

Properties of iridium

Iridium is one of the heaviest of the Group-VIII metals. Being in Group VIII puts it in the company of blue-chip commercial metals such as manganese, iron, cobalt, nickel, lead, and platinum.

When iridium is cast from its molten state, it cools to a crystalline form that makes it rather ductile. In this state, it can be drawn into wire or pressed into sheets. Whereas most other metals, notably steel, become less brittle after annealing (heating and slowly cooling), iridium becomes brittle and completely unworkable.

Iridium is known as a platinum metal because it is found in natural deposits of platinum. Iridium's twin element, osmium (Os, element 76), is found there, too; so osmium, iridium, and platinum are found together, both in nature and on the periodic table of the elements.

Production of iridium

The commercial demand for iridium is very low, so the procedures for separating it from osmium, platinum, and other metals appear more as cumbersome laboratory procedures than efficient industrial refining operations. The refining operations for most metals use chemical or electrochemical reactions to extract the desired metal and leave behind the impurities. Pure iridium metal, however, is usually obtained by lengthly recycling processes whereby the various impurities are removed, leaving behind a slag of iridium of increasing quality.

Most other metals found in the company of iridium are soluble in molten lead, so dissolving the impurities in molten lead can be one of the refining steps. Also, most of the metals that are chemically similar to iridium, including platinum, are soluble in aqua regia; so iridium can be further refined by dissolving away some of the impurities with that acid. Finally, most other elements vaporize at temperatures far below the melting point of iridium; so running the temperature to about 2000 °C can clear out most other impurities.

Some compounds and isotopes of iridium

The most stable oxidation states of iridium are +3 and +4. One would expect to find some simple salts such as:

Iridium (III) chloride, $IrCl_3$

$$Ir^3 + 3Cl^- \rightarrow IrCl_3$$

Iridium (IV) chloride, $IrCl_4$

$$Ir^{4+} + 4Cl^- \rightarrow IrCl_4$$

Iridium, however, tends to form more complex stable compounds such as:

Sodium iridium (III) chloride, Na_3IrCl_6

$$3Na^+ + Ir^{3+} + 6Cl^- \rightarrow Na_3IrCl_6$$

Sodium iridium (IV) chloride, Na_2IrCl_6

$$2Na^+ + Ir^{4+} + 6Cl^- \rightarrow Na_2IrCl_6$$

Ammonium iridium (IV) chloride, $(NH_4)_2IrCl_6$

$$2(NH_4)^+ + Ir^{4+} + 6Cl^- \rightarrow (NH_4)_2IrCl_6$$

Iridium (III) compounds tend to be black, white iridium (IV) compounds have greenish colors.

Figure 77-1 shows the known isotopes of iridium. All naturally occurring iridium is composed of iridium-191 and iridium-193. The remaining isotopes are synthetic and radioactive.

Isotope	Natural Abundance	Half-Life	Decay Mode
^{170}Ir		1.05 sec	α
^{171}Ir		1.6 sec	α
^{172}Ir		2.1 sec	α
^{173}Ir		3.0 sec	α
^{174}Ir		4 sec	α
^{175}Ir		4.5 sec	α
^{176}Ir		8 sec	α
^{177}Ir		21 sec	α
^{178}Ir		12 sec	β+, ec
^{179}Ir		4 min	ec
^{180}Ir		1.5 min	ec
^{181}Ir		4.9 min	β+, ec
^{182}Ir		15 min	β+, ec
^{183}Ir		56 min	β+, ec
^{184}Ir		3.0 hr	β+, ec
^{185}Ir		14 hr	β+, ec
^{186m}Ir		1.7 hr	ec
^{186}Ir		15.7 hr	β+, ec
^{187}Ir		10.5 hr	ec
^{188}Ir		41.4 hr	β+, ec
^{189}Ir		13.2 day	ec
^{190m2}Ir		3.2 hr	β+, ec, i.t.
^{190m1}Ir		1.2 hr	i.t.
^{190}Ir		11.8 day	ec
^{191m}Ir		4.93 sec	i.t.
^{191}Ir	37.3%		
^{192m2}Ir		241 yr	i.t.
^{192m1}Ir		1.44 min	i.t.
^{192}Ir		73.83 day	β-
^{193m}Ir		10.6 day	β-
^{193}Ir	62.7%		
^{194m}Ir		171 day	β-
^{194}Ir		19.2 hr	β-
^{195m}Ir		3.9 hr	β-
^{195}Ir		2.8 hr	β-
^{195m}Ir		1.4 hr	β-
^{196}Ir		52 sec	β-
^{197m}Ir		8.9 min	β-, i.t.
^{197}Ir		5.85 min	β-
^{198}Ir		8 sec	β-

77-1 Iridium has isotopes with atomic weights between 170 and 198.

Element 78: Platinum

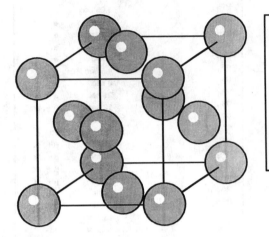

Name	Platinum
Symbol	Pt
Atomic Number	78
Atomic Weight	195.08
Melting Point	1772°C
Boiling Point	3827°C
Specific Gravity	195.09 (20°C)
Oxidation States	+2, +4
Electron Config.	(Xe) $4f^{14}\,5d^9\,6s^1$

- Name pronounced as **Plat-n-em**
- Name taken from the Spanish, *platina*, "silver"
- Discovered independently by Antonio de Ulloa in 1735, and by Charles Wood around 1741
- Very heavy, soft, silvery-white metal

Platinum is commonly classified as a precious metal, belonging to a distinctive group of metals that also includes gold (Au), silver (Ag), iridium (Ir), and palladium (Pd). There are metals on the periodic table of elements that are far more rare than any of these; but scarcity is not the sole measuring stick of value. Tradition and commercial demand combine with availability to define a precious metal.

Platinum is also the focal point for another important group of metals known as the *platinum metals*. This group includes palladium, iridium, osmium (Os), rhodium (Ro), and ruthemnium (Ru). These are known as platinum metals partly because they share a number of important physical and chemical properties, but mostly because they are found wherever natural deposits of platinum are found.

Platinum is an important metal in the manufacture of laboratory instruments, medical and dental items, and electrical contacts. It is also used in making jewelry.

Historical background

The first samples of platinum ore to reach Europe were taken from gravel pits in the Chocó district of Columbia, South America, during the 1730s and 1740s. By the end of that century, however, it was found that platinum had been used by the early South American Indians. In 1822, vast deposits of platinum were discovered in the Ural Mountains of Russia.

It is more proper to say that platinum was *rediscovered* in the eighteenth century.

Properties of platinum

Platinum is described as a silvery-white, dense metal that is quite malleable and ductile when pure. Its coefficient of expansion is very close to that of glass, so it is often used as the electrode material in sealed glass electron and X-ray tubes.

This metal is immune to oxidation in air, thus accounting for the fact that it is usually found in nature in its elemental form. Platinum is also immune to most acids, including hydrochloric acid. However, it dissolves readily in aqua regia, a mixture of nitric and hydrochloric acids, to form *chloroplatinic acid*, H_2PtCl_6.

Platinum is a Group-VIII transition metal.

Production of platinum

Most platinum is recovered from deposits of the native, or elemental, metal. In these deposits, the platinum is most often mixed with other metals such as gold, copper, nickel, iridium, osmium, palladium, ruthenium, and rhodium. *Platiniridium* is a rare, naturally occurring alloy of platinum and iridium.

Platinum is also found in the minerals *sperrylite* and *cooperite*, which are *platinum arsenate* ($PtAs_2$) and *platinum (II) sulfide* (PtS).

To a great extent, the process for refining platinum is a matter of subtraction—removing impurities until nothing but platinum remains. Consider, for example, that platinum is much more dense than most of its impurities. Therefore, the very lightweight impurities can be removed by floating them away in a simple water bath. Some of the impurities of medium density can be separated by shaking the mixture so that the lighter materials rise to the top.

Platinum is nonmagnetic, while two of its most important impurities are magnetic: nickel and iron. The magnetic materials can be removed by running the ground-up ore under a powerful electromagnet.

Next, we can take advantage of platinum's melting point, which is much higher than most other substances. So baking the mix at a high temperature burns off or melts away a lot of impurities.

Most metals and other impurities are readily attacked by hydrochloric and sulfuric acids. Platinum is not. A lot of other metals can be removed by stirring the mixture in one of those acids and recovering the platinum that is left in the container.

Eventually the process leads to a point at which we are dealing with platinum and a few of the so-called platinum metals. More complex chemical reactions involving ammonium and cyanide ions can sort platinum from its other family members.

Some compounds and isotopes of platinum

Although platinum is more often alloyed with other metals, it forms an important series of compounds with oxidation states of $+2$ and $+4$.

Platinum combines readily with the halogens to form platinum halides such as:

Platinum (II) chloride, $PtCl_2$

$$Pt^{2+} + 2Cl^- \rightarrow PtCl_2$$

Platinum (IV) chloride, $PtCl_4$

$$Pt^{4+} + 4Cl^- \rightarrow PtCl_4$$

The platinum halides tend to take on green, red, and yellow colors.

Platinum forms an interesting variety of oxides, including those that define its higher oxidation states:

Platinum (II) oxide, PtO

$$Pt^{2+} + O^{2-} \rightarrow PtO$$

Platinum (IV) oxide, PtO_2

$$Pt^{4+} + 2O^{2-} \rightarrow PtO_2$$

Platinum (II,IV) oxide, Pt_3O_4

$$2Pt^{2+} + Pt^{4+} + 4O^{2-} \rightarrow PtO_4$$

Platinum (III) oxide, Pt_2O_3

$$2Pt^{3+} + 3O^{2-} \rightarrow Pt_2O_3$$

Platinum (VI) oxide, PtO_3

$$Pt^{6+} + 3O^{2-} \rightarrow PtO_3$$

Figure 78-1 lists all of the known isotopes of platinum. Natural platinum is a mixture of six, nonradioactive isotopes.

Isotope	Natural Abundance	Half-Life	Decay Mode	Isotope	Natural Abundance	Half-Life	Decay Mode
^{172}Pt		100 ms	α, β+, ec	^{188}Pt		10.2 day	ec
^{173}Pt		340 ms	α, β+, ec	^{189}Pt		10.9 hr	β+, ec
^{174}Pt		900 ms	α, β+, ec	^{190}Pt	0.01%		
^{175}Pt		2.52 sec	α, β+, ec	^{191}Pt		2.96 day	ec
^{176}Pt		6.3 sec	α, β+, ec	^{192}Pt	0.79%		
^{177}Pt		11 sec	α, β+, ec	^{193m}Pt		4.33 day	i.t.
^{178}Pt		21 sec	α, ec	^{193}Pt		50 yr	ec
^{179}Pt		43 sec	α, β+, ec	^{194}Pt	32.9%		
^{180}Pt		3 sec	α, β+, ec	^{195m}Pt		4 day	i.t.
^{181}Pt		51 sec	α, β+, ec	^{195}Pt	33.8%		
^{182}Pt		2.7 min	β+, ec	^{196}Pt	25.3%		
^{183m}Pt		43 sec	β+, ec, i.t.	^{197m}Pt		95.4 min	β-, i.t.
^{183}Pt		7 min	β+, ec	^{197}Pt		18.3 hr	β-
^{184}Pt		17.3 min	β+, ec	^{198}Pt	7.2%		
^{185m}Pt		33 min	β+, ec	^{199m}Pt		13.5 sec	β-, i.t.
^{185}Pt		71 min	β+, ec	^{199}Pt		30.8 min	β-
^{186}Pt		2 hr	β+, ec	^{200}Pt		12.5 hr	β-
^{187}Pt		2.35 hr	β+, ec	^{201}Pt		2.5 min	β-

78-1 Platinum has isotopes with atomic weights between 172 and 201.

Element 79: Gold

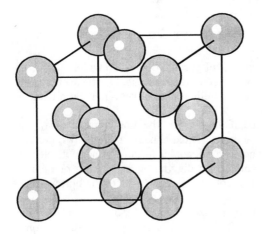

Name	Gold
Symbol	Au
Atomic Number	79
Atomic Weight	196.967
Melting Point	1064.4°C
Boiling Point	2808°C
Specific Gravity	19.3 (20°C)
Oxidation States	+1, +3
Electron Config.	(Xe) $4f^{14}\,5d^{10}\,6s^1$

- Name pronounced as **GOLD**
- Name is Anglo-Saxon in origin
- Chemical symbol, Au, taken from the Latin name, *aurum*, "shining dawn"
- Prehistoric origin
- Soft, malleable, yellow metal

Gold is a relatively rare element in the earth's crust. On the average, a million tons of earth contain just ten pounds of pure gold. Fortunately, gold is not evenly distributed through the earth's crust; rather, it is found in a few fairly rich deposits. It is estimated that there is enough gold in the world to make a cube of the metal that measures 60 feet on a side.

World history abounds with stories about the search for gold, from Egyptian inscriptions describing the deposits at Ur in 2600 B.C. to newspaper stories about gold coins and bullion salvaged from the floor of the ocean off the coast of Florida in 1989 A.D.

Gold and goldsmithing have ancient origins. Thin sheets, utensils, and threads of gold have been found among the artifacts from the earliest Egyptian dynasties. Gold and the art of working gold are mentioned numerous times in the Old Testament of the Bible.

Properties of gold

Gold has a very distinctive yellow color. It is incredibly malleable and ductile—a single ounce of pure gold can be beaten out to a sheet that is about 300 feet square. It is about as heavy as ordinary lead and, like lead, pure gold is easily cut with a knife.

Few elements react readily with gold under normal environmental conditions. This accounts for why most gold is mined as flakes and nuggets of the yellow metal itself. It does react somewhat with chlorine gas and aqua regia (a mixture of hydrochloric and nitric acids).

Gold is a very good conductor of electricity; because it does not normally corrode, it is often used as a plating material for electrical connectors. Gold is also a good reflector of heat-carrying infrared radiation, so a thin film of gold is applied to the glass in skyscrapers in order to reduce the amount of internal heating from sunlight.

The purity of gold is measured in units of *karat*. Pure gold is rated at 24 karat. An alloy that is 50% gold is 12 karat. The amount of gold in common jewelry is reckoned at 18 karat, meaning that the percentage of gold is 18/24 times 100, or 75%.

Production of gold

Although the world's oceans contain billions of tons of pure gold, it is too widely dispersed and found in concentrations far too low to be of any commercial value. On the average, you can expect to find only two-tenths of an ounce per million tons of seawater. So all gold is recovered from deposits in the earth's crust.

Placer mining is the oldest gold-mining technique and still the most popular today. The technique takes advantage of two important facts: first, gold is heavier than any other substance generally found in the same vicinity; and, second, gold is usually found in its elemental form (not as a compound). So when a sample of a digging—gravel, sand, or rock—is washed in a stream of water, nuggets or flakes of gold metal tend to fall to the bottom of the container, while impurities of lesser density are washed away.

The gold rushes of California and Alaska popularized the simple, one-man placer mining method called *panning*. In this case, a handful of gravel or sandy soil (usually from a shallow stream bed) was placed in a shallow pan—one that looks much like an ordinary pie pan having circular grooves formed on the bottom. By swirling water in this pan, the lighter materials were washed out of the pan, leaving the heavier materials, hopefully including a few tiny nuggets or flecks of yellowish gold, in the bottom.

Gold mining companies developed large-scale versions of the panning method and eventually introduced the *hydraulic method* that proved useful for recovering gold from deposits lacking the concentrations of gold required for individual panning operations. The hydraulic method uses a high pressure water hose to blast gravel and rock away from its natural deposit and wash it through flumes where the gold filters toward the bottom. Many tons of gravel could be worked each day in this fashion.

The *dredging method* replaced the hydraulic method during the early years of this century. In this instance, large mining machinery actually digs a water-filled pond that moves across the landscape. This equipment digs fresh rock at the leading edge of the moving pond, processes the rock with running water to recover the gold, then deposits the treated gravel at the trailing edge of the pond.

Lode mining is the alternative to the various placer mining techniques. In this case, the gold is mined directly from highly concentrated deposits of elemental gold or common gold minerals. The mining methods use pits and shafts that are similar to those used for mining other minerals and ores. This method does not use running water to separate gold from other materials.

Some compounds and the isotopes of gold

Gold is most often used in its pure, metallic state or in an alloyed state with another metal. There are few compounds of gold, and even fewer of any practical importance.

Gold's principal oxidation states are $+1$ and $+3$. It does not react with oxygen to form the stable oxides that typify most metals. The most common compounds are *auric chloride*, $AuCl_3$, and *chlorauric acid*, $HAuCl_4$. Both are built around the Au^{3+} metal ion.

Auric chloride is produced by a direct action between gold and hot chlorine gas:

$$Au + 2Cl_2 \rightarrow AuCl_4$$
(gold + chlorine gas → auric chloride)

Chlorauric acid is formed by a reaction between gold and the only acid known to affect it—the aqua regia of the medieval alchemists. The reaction is:

$$Au + 4HCl + HNO_2 \rightarrow HAuCl_4 + NO + 2H_2O$$
(gold + hydrochloric acid + nitric acid → chlorauric acid + nitric oxide gas + water)

Figure 79-1 shows that all gold found in nature is gold-197. All other isotopes are radio-active and artificially produced.

Isotope	Natural Abundance	Half-Life	Decay Mode	Isotope	Natural Abundance	Half-Life	Decay Mode
^{176}Au		1.3 sec	α, β+, ec	^{193m}Au		3.9 sec	i.t.
^{177}Au		1.3 sec	α	^{193}Au		17.6 hr	ec
^{178}Au		2.6 sec	α	^{194}Au		39.5 hr	β+, ec
^{179}Au		7.5 sec	α	^{195m}Au		30.5 sec	i.t.
^{180}Au		8.1 sec	ec	^{195}Au		186 day	ec
^{181}Au		11.4 sec	ec	$^{196m2}Au$		9.7 hr	i.t.
^{182}Au		21 sec	β+, ec	$^{196m1}Au$		8.1 sec	i.t.
^{183}Au		42 sec	ec	^{196}Au		6.18 day	ec
^{185m}Au		6.8 min	β+, ec, i.t.	^{197m}Au		7.8 sec	i.t.
^{185}Au		4.3 min	β+, ec	^{197}Au	100%		
^{186m}Au		2 min	β+, ec	^{198m}Au		2.3 day	β-
^{186}Au		10.7 min	β+, ec	^{198}Au		2.7 day	β-
^{187}Au		8.2 min	β+, ec	^{199}Au		3.14 day	β-
^{188}Au		8.8 min	β+, ec	^{200m}Au		18.7 hr	β-
^{189m}Au		4.6 min	β+, ec	^{200}Au		48.4 min	β-
^{189}Au		28.7 min	β+, ec	^{201}Au		26 min	β-
^{190}Au		43 min	β+, ec	^{202}Au		28 sec	β-
^{191m}Au		900 ms	i.t.	^{203}Au		53 sec	β-
^{191}Au		3.2 hr	ec	^{204}Au		40 sec	β-
^{192}Au		5.0 hr	β+, ec				

79-1 Gold has isotopes with atomic weights between 176 and 204.

Element 80: Mercury

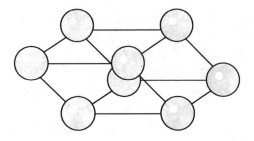

Name	Mercury
Symbol	Hg
Atomic Number	80
Atomic Weight	200.59
Melting Point	-38.87°C
Boiling Point	356.58°C
Specific Gravity	13.546 (20°C)
Oxidation States	+1, +2
Electron Config.	(Xe) $4f^{14}\,5d^{10}\,6s^2$

- Name pronounced as **MER-kyoo-ri**
- Named for the Roman god, Mercury
- Chemical symbol, Hg, taken from the Latin, *hydrargyrus*, "liquid silver"
- Also called *quicksilver*
- Known in ancient times
- Only common metal that is liquid at ordinary temperatures

Mercury is best known for being the only metallic element that is in its liquid state at normal room temperature—and at well below room temperature, for that matter. This property, combined with the facts that mercury expands and contracts evenly with changes in temperature and does not "wet" glass, makes it an ideal material for liquid thermometers and barometers. It also finds important applications in electrical switches and mercury-vapor lighting products.

Historical background

The uses of mercury have ancient origins. Evidence shows that the Chinese were using it before 2000 B.C. Ancient Egyptian tombs sometimes contain vials of mercury. The alchemists were well aware of the useful properties of mercury.

You can appreciate the enduring nature of mercury's commercial products by considering that one of the world's best-known mercury mines (the Almadén mine in Spain) has been in continuous operation since 400 B.C.

Since the historical background of mercury extends more than four millennia into the past, it is impossible to assign proper credit for its discovery.

Properties of mercury

Mercury is a heavy, silver-white metal that is in its liquid state at ordinary room temperature. When it is cooled to its freezing point, mercury looks and feels much like common lead.

Mercury is a poor conductor of heat, but a rather good conductor of electricity. It alloys easily with a number of different metals to form a family of commercially useful alloys known as *amalgams*.

Mercury is the lowest and heaviest of the Group-IIB metals on the periodic table of the elements.

Production of mercury

Virtually all mercury is derived from *cinnabar*, or mercury sulfide (HgS). Some sources of red cinnabar are so rich in mercury content that droplets of elemental mercury can be found in random samples. The mercury is easily obtained from the ore by heating it with a reducing agent. Three commonly used reducing agents are oxygen, iron, and quicklime (calcium oxide, CaO). The reactions are quite simple:

$$HgS + O_2 \rightarrow Hg + SO_2$$
(mercury sulfide + oxygen → mercury + sulfur dioxide)

$$HgS + Fe \rightarrow Hg + FeS$$
(mercury sulfide + iron → mercury + iron sulfide)

$$4HgS + 4CaO \rightarrow 4Hg + 3CaS + CaSO_4$$
(mercury sulfide + calcium oxide → mercury + calcium sulfide + calcium sulfate)

In all instances the mercury vapor is led away into vertical columns of water where the mercury liquifies and most impurities float on the surface where they can be scraped away.

Some compounds and the isotopes of mercury

The stable compounds of mercury are built around oxidation states $+1$ and $+2$. Nearly every two-element compound of mercury exists in both the mercury (I) and mercury (II) forms—forms that can also be called mercurous and mercuric.

Mercury combines with anions of a -1 oxidation state in this manner:

Mercury (I) fluoride, Hg_2F_2

$$2Hg^+ + 2F^- \rightarrow Hg_2F_2$$

Mercury (II) fluoride, HgF_2

$$Hg^{2+} + 2F^- \rightarrow HgF_2$$

It combines with -2 anions to produce compounds of these general forms:

Mercury (I) carbonate, Hg_2CO_3

$$2Hg^+ + CO_3^{2-} \rightarrow Hg_2CO_3$$

Mercury (II) carbonate, $HgCO_3$

$$Hg^{2+} + CO_3^{2-} \rightarrow HgCO_3$$

Mercury combines with ions having the -3 oxidation state in this way:

Mercury nitride, Hg_3N_2

$$3Hg^{2+} + 2N^{3-} \rightarrow Hg_3N_2$$

Mercury (II) sulfide, HgS, is better known as the minerals *cinnabar* and *metacinnabar*. Cinnabar, also called *vermillion*, has a distinct reddish color that is exploited in the manufacture of paint pigments. This red form of mercury (II) sulfide is the chief source of mercury. Metacinnabar, or black mercury sulfide, is also found in nature, but to a lesser extent than cinnabar. It is produced in the laboratory by bubbling hydrogen sulfide through an aqueous solution of mercury (II) chloride.

Mercury (I) chloride, HgCl or Hg_2Cl_2, is a heavy white powder that is found in nature under the name *calomel*. It can be produced in the laboratory by the reaction between a mercury (I) salt and hydrochloric acid. For example:

$$Hg_2SO_4 + 2HCl \rightarrow Hg_2Cl_2 + H_2SO_4$$
(mercury (I) sulfate + hydrochloric acid → mercury (I) chloride + sulfuric acid)

Mercury (I) chloride is used as a fungicide, insecticide, and in the manufacture of a type of electrical reference electrode called a *calomel electrode*.

Mercury (II) chloride, $HgCl_2$, is used as a fungicide and in the production of other compounds of mercury. It is a heavy, highly poisonous white crystal that is sometimes called *corrosive sublimate*. The simplest procedure for producing mercury (II) chloride is to allow it to sublimate from a reaction between heated mercury (II) sulfate and sodium chloride:

$$HgSO_4 + NaCl \rightarrow HgCl + NaSO_4$$
(mercury (II) sulfate + sodium chloride → mercury (II) chloride + sodium sulfate)

Mercury has two oxides: *mercury (I) oxide* and *mercury (II) oxide*, having the formulas Hg_2O and HgO, respectively. There are two forms of HgO: one is yellow and formed by a reaction between a mercury (I) salt such as *mercury (I) chloride* and sodium hydroxide; the other is red and formed by burning *mercury (II) nitrate* in oxygen. Mercury (II) oxide is formed by the reaction between a mercury (II) salt such as mercury (II) nitrate and sodium hydroxide.

Mercury cyanide, $Hg(CN)_2$, is a strong poison that is formed by a reaction between mercury (I) oxide and hydrocyanic acid. Mercury fulminate, $Hg(CNO)_2$, is one of the most unstable explosives known. No further information about producing the compound is presented here for reasons that ought to be obvious to readers blessed with good sense and the potential for living a long life.

Figure 80-1 lists the known isotopes of mercury. The seven naturally occurring isotopes of mercury are stable, or nonradioactive. The remainder are produced artificially and undergo radioactive decay.

Isotope	Natural Abundance	Half-Life	Decay Mode	Isotope	Natural Abundance	Half-Life	Decay Mode
^{178}Hg		260 ms	α, ec	^{193m}Hg		11.8 hr	β+, ec, i.t.
^{179}Hg		1.09 sec	α, ec	^{193}Hg		3.8 hr	ec
^{180}Hg		2.9 sec	α, β+, ec	^{194}Hg		520 yr	ec
^{181}Hg		3.6 sec	α, β+, ec	^{195m}Hg		40 hr	ec, i.t.
^{182}Hg		11 sec	α, β+, ec	^{195}Hg		9.5 hr	ec
^{183}Hg		8.8 sec	α, β+, ec	^{196}Hg	0.15%		
^{184}Hg		30.9 sec	α, β+, ec	^{197m}Hg		23.8 hr	i.t.
^{185m}Hg		21 sec	α, ec, i.t.	^{197}Hg		64.1 hr	ec
^{185}Hg		50 sec	β+, ec	^{198}Hg	10.1%		
^{186}Hg		1.4 min	β+, ec	^{199m}Hg		42.6 min	i.t.
^{187m}Hg		1.7 min	β+, ec	^{199}Hg	17%		
^{187}Hg		2.4 min	β+, ec	^{200}Hg	23.1%		
^{188}Hg		3.2 min	β+, ec	^{201}Hg	13.2%		
^{189m}Hg		8.6 min	ec	^{202}Hg	29.65%		
^{189}Hg		7.6 min	ec	^{203}Hg		46.6 day	β-
^{190}Hg		20 min	ec	^{204}Hg	6.8%		
^{191m}Hg		51 min	β+, ec	^{205}Hg		5.2 min	β-
^{191}Hg		49 min	β+, ec	^{206}Hg		8.5 min	β-
^{192}Hg		4.9 hr	ec				

80-1 Mercury has isotopes with atomic weights between 178 and 206.

Element 81: Thallium

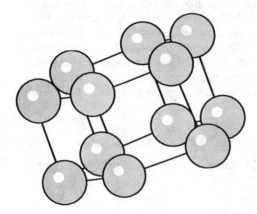

Name	Thallium
Symbol	Tl
Atomic Number	81
Atomic Weight	204.38
Melting Point	303.5°C
Boiling Point	1457°C
Specific Gravity	11.85 (20°C)
Oxidation States	+1, +3
Electron Config.	(Xe) $4f^{14} 5d^{10} 6s^2 6p^1$

- Name pronounced as **THAL-i-em**
- Name taken from the Greek, *thallos*, "green twig"
- Discovered by Sir William Crookes in 1861
- Soft, gray metal

Thallium is a metal that is very much like lead in terms of its feel and superficial appearance. Unlike lead, however, thallium reacts fairly rapidly with oxygen and moisture in the air. Lead can endure centuries of exposure to nature, but a sample of thallium crumbles into pieces of black corrosion within a few years. Because of this sensitivity to natural conditions, thallium metal has no commercial applications.

Historical background

Thallium was discovered accidentally by Sir William Crookes (1832–1919) in 1861. It was a purely serendipitous discovery—no one suspected its existence, so no one was looking for it. As far as Sir William was concerned, this contribution to the table of elements was simply a matter of doing the right thing with the right equipment at the right time.

One of Sir William's acquaintances, August Wilhelm von Hofmann, was one of the founders of Deutsche Chemische Gesellschaft which, among other things, was involved in the commercial production of sulfuric acid. One of the byproducts of this commercial process was a slag that included selenium compounds that Sir William wanted to convert into selenocyanides. So Hofmann supplied Sir William with all of the residue he could use, and Crookes promptly completed his work, removing all the selenium from the material. Rather than discarding the used residue, he decided to keep it because it might contain tellurium—something that might be useful for future experiments.

One day Sir William decided to take a look at a sample of this residue with a spectroscope. He did not see any blue selenium lines. That was not surprising because he had already removed most of the selenium. But there were not any yellow tellurium lines, either. He had expected to find tellurium in the samples. Instead he saw a brilliant green line that no one had ever described before; thus the name *thallium*, meaning *green branch*.

Properties of thallium

Thallium is a soft, gray metal that is just as malleable as lead and sometimes even softer. When thallium metal is cut, it looks a bit more like tin, but it soon takes on a dark-colored oxide and hydroxide coating. The sample first appears gray, then brown and finally black. This coating is not protective as it is for other metals such as copper and aluminum. Instead, the black oxide and hydroxide eventually flake off, exposing fresh metal which is soon corroded away. The process continues until the sample is completely destroyed. It is little wonder that thallium metal has no commercial applications.

Thallium is attacked by most acids to some extent, but especially by nitric acid, forming *thallium nitrate*:

$$2Tl + 2HNO_3 \rightarrow 2TlNO_3 + H_2$$
(thallium metal + nitric acid → thallium nitrate + hydrogen gas)

Thallium is the heaviest of the Group IIIA elements, or the so-called boron group.

Production of thallium

Although thallium can be found in ores such as *crooksite*, *hutchinsonite*, and *lorandite*, these minerals are rather rare and sparsely distributed around the world. Most thallium is recovered from the byproducts of lead and zinc refining operations. It is also recovered from sulfuric acid manufacturing processes that begin with certain pyrites.

The exact refining procedure depends on the source of the metal. The general idea, however, is to dissolve the mixture in hydrochloric acid to produce a precipitate of thallious chloride, or thallium (I) chloride, TlCl. This heavy compound is easily separated from the other substances by filtering and drying it.

Some compounds of thallium

Thallium's most stable oxidation states are $+1$ and $+3$. This suggests compounds of these general forms:

Thallium (I) fluoride, TlF

$$Tl^+ + F^- \rightarrow TlF$$

Thallium (III) chloride, TlCl₃

$$Tl^{3+} + 3Cl^- \rightarrow TlCl_3$$

Thallium (I) hydroxide, TlOH

$$Tl^+ + OH^- \rightarrow TlOH$$

Thallium (III) hydroxide, Tl(OH)₃

$$Tl^{3+} + 30H^- \rightarrow Tl(OH)_3$$

Thallium (I) sulfate, Tl_2SO_4, was once used as a pesticide. Mixture of *thallium (I) iodide* and *thallium (I) bromide*, TlI and TlBr, are presently used in the manufacture of glass for special infrared lenses. Other thallium (I) compounds of modest commercial value are *thallium (I) oxide* and *thallium (I) sulfide*, Tl_2O and Tl_2S, respectively.

Isotopes of thallium

Figure 81-1 shows the known isotopes of thallium. Thallium-207 belongs to the actinium radioactive decay series (Fig. 81-2), while thallium-208 is part of the thorium series (Fig. 81-3) and isotope 206 is part of the uranium series (Fig. 81-4). Figure 81-5 shows that thallium-209 is a member of the neptunium radioactive decay series.

Isotope	Natural Abundance	Half-Life	Decay Mode
^{184}Tl		11 sec	α, β+, ec
^{185m}Tl		1.8 sec	α+, i.t.
^{186m}Tl		4 sec	i.t.
^{186}Tl		28 sec	β+, ec
^{187m}Tl		16 sec	i.t.
^{187}Tl		45 sec	β+, ec
^{188m}Tl		71 sec	β+, ec
^{188}Tl		70 sec	β+, ec
^{189m}Tl		1.4 min	β+, ec
^{189}Tl		2.3 min	β+, ec
^{190m}Tl		3.7 min	β+, ec
^{190}Tl		2.6 min	β+, ec
^{191m}Tl		5.2 min	β+, ec
^{192m}Tl		10.8 min	β+, ec
^{192}Tl		9.4 min	β+, ec
^{193m}Tl		2.1 min	i.t.
^{193}Tl		22 min	β+, ec
^{194m}Tl		32.8 min	β+, ec
^{194}Tl		33 min	β+, ec
^{195m}Tl		3.6 sec	i.t.
^{195}Tl		1.13 hr	β+, ec

Isotope	Natural Abundance	Half-Life	Decay Mode
^{196m}Tl		1.4 hr	β+, ec
^{196}Tl		1.8 hr	β+, ec
^{197m}Tl		540 ms	β+, ec, i.t.
^{197}Tl		2.83 hr	β+, ec
^{198m}Tl		1.87 hr	β+, ec, i.t.
^{198}Tl		5.3 hr	β+, ec
^{199}Tl		7.4 hr	ec
^{200}Tl		1.1 day	ec
^{201}Tl		3 day	ec
^{202}Tl		12.23 day	ec
^{203}Tl	29.52%		
^{204}Tl		3.78 yr	β-, ec
^{205}Tl	70.48%		
^{206m}Tl		3.76 min	i.t.
^{206}Tl		4.2 min	β-
^{207m}Tl		1.33 sec	i.t.
^{207}Tl		4.77 min	β-
^{208}Tl		3.05 min	β-
^{209}Tl		2.2 min	β-
^{210}Tl		1.3 min	β-

81-1 Thallium has isotopes with atomic weights between 184 and 210.

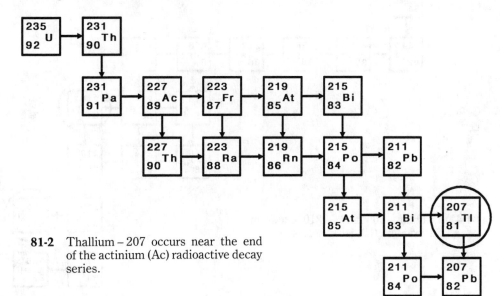

81-2 Thallium – 207 occurs near the end of the actinium (Ac) radioactive decay series.

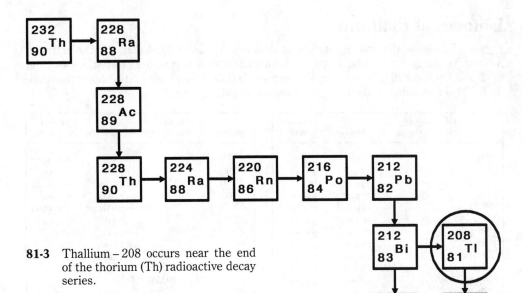

81-3 Thallium – 208 occurs near the end of the thorium (Th) radioactive decay series.

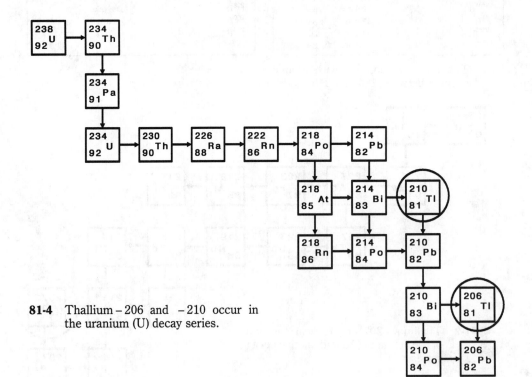

81-4 Thallium – 206 and – 210 occur in the uranium (U) decay series.

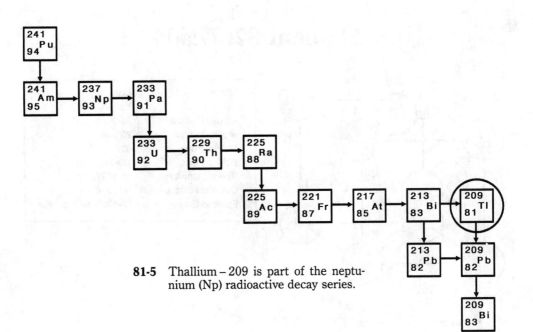

81-5 Thallium – 209 is part of the neptunium (Np) radioactive decay series.

Element 82: Lead

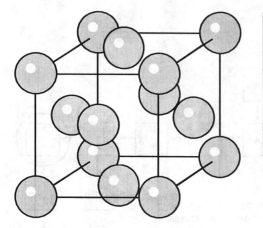

Name	Lead
Symbol	Pb
Atomic Number	82
Atomic Weight	207.19
Melting Point	327.502°C
Boiling Point	1740°C
Specific Gravity	11.35 (20°C)
Oxidation States	+2, +4
Electron Config.	(Xe) $4f^{14}\,5d^{10}\,6s^2\,6p^2$

- Name pronounced as **LED**
- Name taken from the Anglo-Saxon, *lead*
- Chemical symbol, Pb, taken from the Latin name for the element, *plumbum*
- Known in earliest civilizations
- Very soft, highly malleable and ductile, blue-white shiny metal

Lead is one of the most familiar of the metallic elements. Strangely enough, it is not among the most common elements found on the earth. In fact, lead is found in proportions of only about 13 parts-per-million. Compare that with lesser known elements such as scandium (75 ppm) and yttrium(120 ppm).

The commercial scarcity of a metal does not have as much to do with its abundance in the earth's crust as with how easily it can be mined and refined. There might be comparatively little lead in the earth, but it is easy to obtain and refine. So it is generally regarded as a common commodity.

Most lead is used in lead-acid storage batteries—the kind commonly used in automobiles. Lead is too soft for structural applications, but it is frequently used in metal products made from alloys of lead.

No one can claim to have discovered lead or to have been the first to isolate it. The history of lead has nothing to do with its discovery, simply because its discovery is hidden away in prehistory. The Bible mentions applications of lead in several passages, including one in one of the oldest books, the Book of Job.

The alchemists—those who lived in a strange world between science and fantasy— believed every element eventually changes, or transmutes, into lead. (And if a little gold happened to turn up in the mixture somewhere along the way, so much the better.)

Properties of lead

Lead is such a common element that it is often used as a standard for describing lesser-known metallic elements. This can make it difficult to describe the metal as anything but a very soft metal that has a shiny blue-white appearance when it is first cut. The luster dulls after a while due to the formation of a thin film of protective oxidation.

Lead is the last of the Group IVA elements on the periodic table. Headed up with carbon (C), this group includes some of the best-known elements: silicon (Si), germanium (Ge), and tin (Sn) as well as carbon and lead.

Production of lead

Some lead is found in its native state. This means the metal, itself, can be obtained directly from deposits in the earth. Most, however, are mined in the form of *galena*, or lead sulfide (PbS). About one-third of the lead produced in the United States is reclaimed, or recycled, from lead products and lead alloys.

In order to recover lead from natural galena, the ore is ground and roasted in hot air to produce a mixture of lead sulfide, sulfate, and oxide. The air supply is then cut off and the temperature raised again. The lead is reduced to a raw molten metal, while the sulfur and oxygen are drawn off as sulfur dioxide gas.

Some compounds of lead

Lead has an extensive variety of oxides, many being the basis for commercially important products. *Lead suboxide*, Pb_2O, is one of the few lead (l) compounds. A thin film of this black oxide forms naturally on the freshly cut surface of metallic lead; it retards further oxidation. *Lead (II) oxide*, PbO, is better known as lead monoxide or *litharge*—an insoluable yellow solid frequently used in making glass, vulcanizing rubber, and coloring paints.

Lead (III) oxide (Pb_2O_3), is a reddish-yellow solid, and *lead (IV) oxide* (PbO_2), or lead dioxide, is brown. Lead (IV) oxide is also an important ingredient in the operation of lead-acid storage batteries. Finally, there is *trilead tetraoxide*, Pb_3O^4, which is the primary ingredient in the familiar, reddish-brown rust-inhibiting paint that is applied to outdoor steel structures.

Lead (II) chloride, $PbCl_2$, occurs in nature as the mineral *cotunnite*. It is often used in the production of other compounds. *Lead (IV) chloride*, $PbCl_4$, is always produced and stored at freezing temperatures because it becomes highly unstable and explosive as it warms toward normal room temperature. This nasty yellow liquid is also known as *lead tetrachloride*.

Lead arsenate, $Pb_3(AsO_4)_2$, is a commercial insecticide that is usually produced by a reaction between a lead salt, such as lead chloride, and sodium arsenide.

Lead carbonate, $PbCO_3$, occurs in nature as the mineral *cerussite*, but it is also produced in the laboratory by a reaction between lead chloride and sodium carbonate. It is a poisonous, white crystalline substance formerly used in the manufacture of white paints. *Lead sulfate*, $PbSO_4$, is similar to a carbonate in many respects. It, too, can be found in the mineral *anglesite*; and it is used in a paint pigment commonly known as sublimed white lead.

Lead chromate, $PbCrO_4$, is a yellow crystal that occurs in nature as *crocoite* and can be commercially produced by a reaction between lead chloride and sodium dichromate. It is the basis for the popular chrome yellow paint.

Lead nitrate, $Pb(NO_3)_2$, is used in the manufacture of fireworks and other chemicals. It is produced on a commercial scale by the reaction between a lead oxide and nitric acid.

Lead silicate, $PbSiO_3$, is used in glassmaking as well as in the rubber and paint manufacturing industries.

Isotopes of lead

Figure 82-1 summarizes the known isotopes of lead. Many of them are included in one of the radioactive decay series. For example, lead-207 and -211 are both part of the actinium decay series (see Fig. 82-2), lead-212 is in the thorium series (Fig. 82-3), and lead-206, -210 and 214 are members of the uranium series (Fig. 82-4). As shown in Fig. 82-5, lead-209 and -213 are in the neptunium series. The actinium and uranium series both end with stable (nonradioactive) isotopes of lead.

Isotope	Natural Abundance	Half-Life	Decay Mode	Isotope	Natural Abundance	Half-Life	Decay Mode
^{184}Pb		600 ms	α	^{200}Pb		21.5 hr	ec
^{185}Pb		4.1 sec	α	^{201m}Pb		1.02 min	i.t.
^{186}Pb		8 sec	β+, α, ec	^{201}Pb		1.8 min	e.c.
^{187m}Pb		18.3 sec	α, ec	^{202m}Pb		1.8 min	β+, i.t.
^{187}Pb		15.2 sec	β+, ec	^{202}Pb		5.3×10^4 yr	ec
^{188}Pb		24 sec	α, ec	^{203m}Pb		6.3 sec	i.t.
^{189}Pb		51 sec	α, ec	^{203}Pb		2.17 day	.c
^{190}Pb			α, ec	^{204m}Pb		1.12 hr	i.t.
^{191m}Pb		2.2 min	β+, ec	^{204}Pb	1.4%		
^{191}Pb		1.3 min	β+, ec	^{205}Pb		1.51×10^7 yr	ec
^{192}Pb		3.5 min	β+, ec	^{206}Pb	24.1%		
^{193}Pb		5.8 min	β+, ec	^{207m}Pb		796 ms	i.t.
^{194}Pb		10 min	β+, ec	^{207}Pb	22.1%		
^{195m}Pb		15 min	β+, ec	^{208}Pb	52.4%		
^{195}Pb		37 min	β+, ec	^{209}Pb		3.25 hr	β-
^{196}Pb		37 min	β+, ec	^{210}Pb		22.3 yr	β-
^{197m}Pb		43 min	β+, ec, i.t.	^{211}Pb		36.1 min	β-
^{197}Pb		8 min	β+, ec	^{212}Pb		10.64 hr	β-
^{198}Pb		2.4 hr	ec	^{213}Pb		10.2 min	β-
^{199m}Pb		12.2 min	β+, ec, i.t.	^{214}Pb		26.8 min	β-
^{199}Pb		1.5 hr	β+, ec				

82-1 Lead has isotopes with atomic weights between 184 and 214.

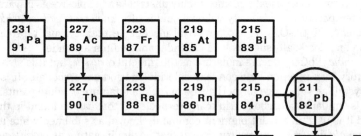

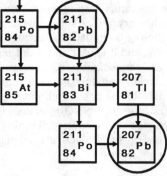

82-2 Radioactive lead – 211 appears in the actinium (Ac) radioactive decay series, and lead – 207 is the stable end product.

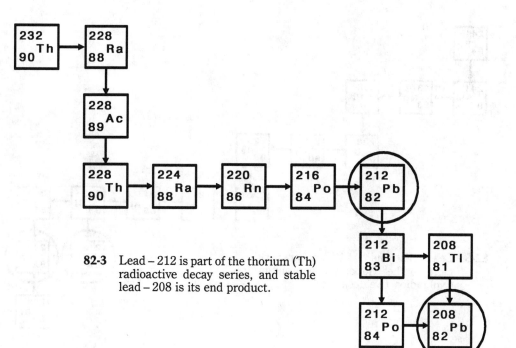

82-3 Lead – 212 is part of the thorium (Th) radioactive decay series, and stable lead – 208 is its end product.

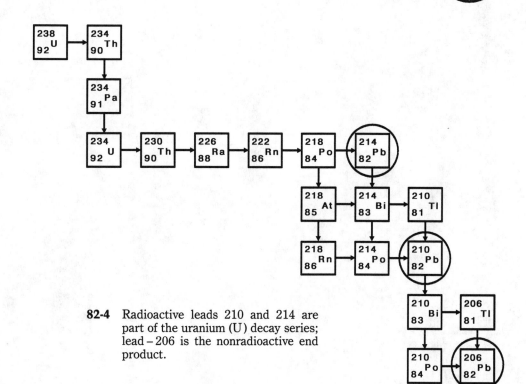

82-4 Radioactive leads 210 and 214 are part of the uranium (U) decay series; lead – 206 is the nonradioactive end product.

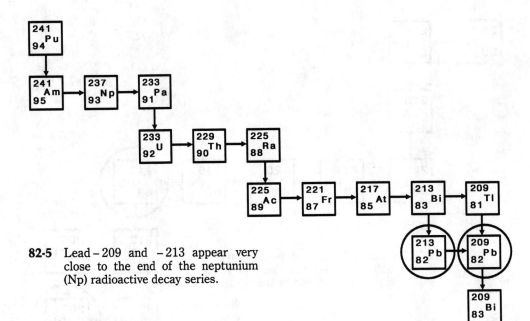

82-5 Lead – 209 and – 213 appear very close to the end of the neptunium (Np) radioactive decay series.

Element 83: Bismuth

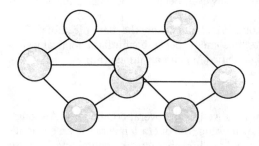

Name	Bismuth
Symbol	Bi
Atomic Number	83
Atomic Weight	208.98
Melting Point	271.3°C
Boiling Point	1560°C
Specific Gravity	9.8 (25°C)
Oxidation States	+3, +5
Electron Config.	(Xe) $4f^{14} 5d^{10} 6s^2 6p^3$

- Name pronounced as **BIZ-meth**
- Name from the German *bisemutum* (Now *wismut*)
- Isolated and described by Basil Valentine in 1450, but frequently confused with lead and tin until the 16th century
- Hard, brittle, steel-gray metal with a pinkish tinge

Alloys of bismuth, notably tin and lead alloys, have notably low melting temperatures. They are thus used in electrical fuse elements, special solders, automatic fire sprinkler heads, and release cables for heat-activated fire doors.

Historical background

References to bismuth metal began appearing in scientific and pseudo-scientific literature of the early 16th century. The following passage from *Heaven of the Philosophers*, by Philippus Aureolus Theophrastus Bombast Von Hohenheim (1493 – 1541, better known as Paracelsus), is interesting, not only because it mentions bismuth among a few other metals known at the time, but also because it reflects the mystical flavor of alchemy: "Two kinds of Antimony are found: one the common black, by which Sol [gold] is purified when liquefied therein. This has the closest affinity with Saturn [lead]. The other kind is the white, which is also called Magnesia and Bismuth. It has great affinity with Jupiter [tin], and when mixed with the other Antimony it augments Luna [silver]."

Since bismuth metal can be found in nature, there has never been any difficulty isolating it. The problem has been that of distinguishing it from lead and tin. Georgius Agricola (1494 – 1555) worked on the problem at about the same time as the mystically inclined Paracelsus. Agricola, however, takes a much more scientific view of the matter:". . . this which just now I said we called *bisemutum* cannot correctly be called *plumbum candidum* [tin] nor *nigrum* [lead], but is different from both and is a third one."

Bismuth, according to Agricola, is a metal that is quite different from tin and lead. The controversy continued, however. Even among those who could agree that bisemutum was neither tin nor lead, most believed it was a compound rather than an element in its own right. Caspar Neumann (1683 – 1737) was the first to make stick the idea that bismuth is a distinct element.

Properties of bismuth

Bismuth is a heavy, brittle metal. It can be polished to a lustrous, gray-white color with a slight tinge of pink. It is rarely seen in this form, however, because it is usually alloyed with other metals.

Bismuth is the last member of the Group-VA elements on the periodic table. This makes it the heaviest of the nitrogen elements. In some respects, bismuth is chemically similar to a couple of its fellow group members, arsenic (As) and antimony (Sb).

Production of bismuth

Bismuth exists in nature in its elemental form as well as in several compounds. Although bismuth can be directly extracted from ores by melting, the operation is rarely an economical one because the percentage of bismuth is so low. Fortunately, ores containing bismuth also contain relatively large amounts of lead or copper—two metals that are mined and refined profitably. Bismuth can then be extracted as a byproduct of an operation that has already paid for itself. At the present time, this is the only economical way to produce bismuth on a commercial scale.

Where bismuth trioxide is available, the metal can be reduced by roasting it with carbon:

$$Bi2O_3 + 3C \rightarrow 3CO + 2Bi$$
$$(bismuth\ trioxide\ +\ carbon\ \rightarrow\ carbon\ dioxide\ +\ bismuth)$$

Some compounds of bismuth

Bismuth is trivalent—most of its compounds include bismuth in its +3 oxidation state. For the most part, bismuth compounds have these general forms:

Bismuth fluoride, BiF_3

$$Bi^{3+} + 3F^- \rightarrow BiF_3$$

Bismuth sulfate, $Bi_2(SO_4)_3$

$$2Bi^{3+} + (3SO_4)^{2-} \rightarrow Bi_2(SO_4)_3$$

Bismuth oxide, Bi_2O_3, is a very popular yellow pigment for paints and cosmetics. It is also an important ingredient in the manufacture of other bismuth compounds. This oxide can be produced by heating bismuth metal, *bismuth hydroxide* ($Bi(OH)_3$) or *bismuth nitrate* ($Bi(NO_3)_3$).

Bismuth chloride, $BiCl_3$, is a white crystalline substance that can be produced by heating bismuth metal in chlorine gas or by reacting bismuth oxide with hydrochloric acid. The bismuth chloride reacts with ordinary water to produce a popular "bismuth white" pigment, *bismuth oxychloride*, $BiOCl$.

Isotopes of bismuth

Figure 83-1 shows the isotopes of bismuth. As shown in Fig. 83-2, bismuth-211 and -215 both belong to the actinium radioactive decay series. Bismuth-212 belongs to the thorium series (see Fig. 83-3), while bismuth-210 and -214 appear in the uranium series (Fig. 83-4). Bismuth isotopes 209 and 213 are members of the neptunium series—a series where bismuth-209 is the stable end-product (see Fig. 83-5).

Isotope	Natural Abundance	Half-Life	Decay Mode
^{190}Bi		5.4 sec	α, β+, ec
^{191}Bi		13 sec	α, β+, ec
^{192}Bi		42 sec	α, β+, ec
^{193m}Bi		3.5 sec	α, β+, ec
^{193}Bi		64 sec	α, β+, ec
^{194}Bi		1.8 min	α, β+, ec
^{195m}Bi		1.5 min	α, β+, ec
^{195}Bi		2.8 min	α, β+, ec
^{196}Bi		4.5 min	ec
^{197}Bi		10 min	β+, ec
^{198m}Bi		7.7 sec	i.t.
^{198}Bi			β+, ec
^{199m}Bi		24.7 min	β+, ec
^{199}Bi		27 min	β+, ec
^{200m}Bi		31 min	β+, ec
^{200}Bi		36 min	β+, ec
^{201m}Bi		59.1 min	i.t.
^{201}Bi		1.8 hr	ec

Isotope	Natural Abundance	Half-Life	Decay Mode
^{202}Bi		1.72 hr	β+, ec
^{203}Bi		11.76 hr	β+, ec
^{204}Bi		11.2 hr	ec
^{205}Bi		15.31 day	ec
^{206}Bi		6.24 day	ec
^{207}Bi		32.2 yr	ec
^{208}Bi		3.68x10^5 yr	ec
^{209}Bi	100%		
^{210m}Bi		3x10^6 yr	α
^{210}Bi		5 day	β-
^{211}Bi		2.14 min	α
^{212m2}Bi		9 min	β-
^{212m1}Bi		25 min	α, β-
^{212}Bi		1 hr	α, β-
^{211}Bi		45.6 min	α, β-
^{214}Bi		19.9 min	β-
^{215}Bi		7.4 min	β-

83-1 Bismuth has isotopes with atomic weights between 190 and 215.

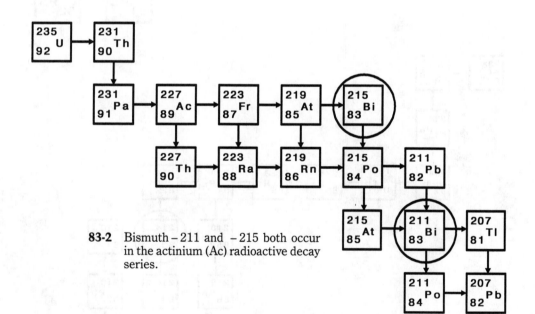

83-2 Bismuth – 211 and – 215 both occur in the actinium (Ac) radioactive decay series.

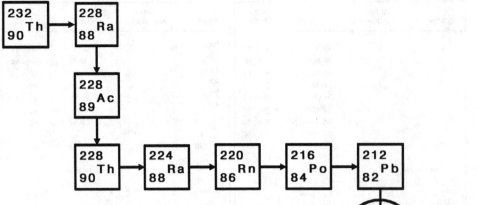

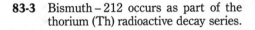

83-3 Bismuth – 212 occurs as part of the thorium (Th) radioactive decay series.

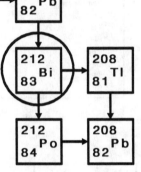

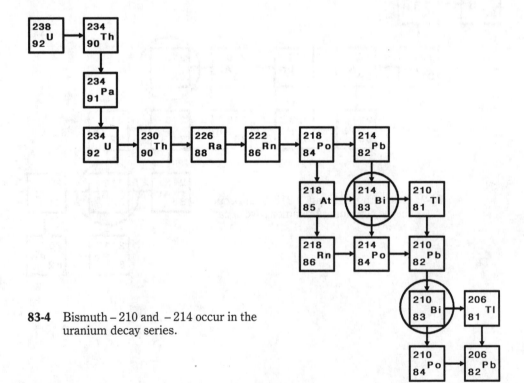

83-4 Bismuth – 210 and – 214 occur in the uranium decay series.

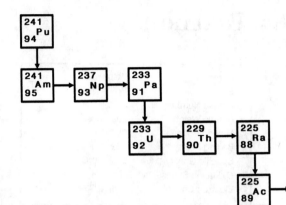

83-5 Stable bismuth – 209 is final product of the neptunium (Np) radioactive decay series.

Element 84: Polonium

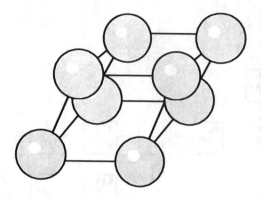

Name	Polonium
Symbol	Po
Atomic Number	84
Atomic Weight	209 Note
Melting Point	254°C
Boiling Point	962°C
Specific Gravity	9.32 (20°C)
Oxidation States	+2, +4
Electron Config.	(Xe) $4f^{14} 5d^{10} 6s^2 6p^4$

Note: Most stable isotope.

- Name pronounced as **peh-LOW-ni-em**
- Named for Poland, Mme. Curie's native country
- Discovered by Marie Curie in 1898
- Extremely rare, naturally radioactive element
- Silvery-gray metal

Although polonium occurs naturally in deposits of uranium ores, the yield is only on the order of 100 μg per ton of ore. Researchers and engineers interested in this metallic element must turn to artificial sources.

This metal is currently used in industrial equipment that eliminates static electricity caused by processes such as rolling paper, wire, and sheet metal.

Historical background

The story of polonium is intertwined with that of radium. The two were discovered at the same time in 1898 by Marie Sklodowska Curie (1867 – 1934). Shortly after finishing her thesis for a Ph.D., Mme. Curie noticed that samples of uranium-bearing pitchblende were far more radioactive than the uranium should make it. She surmised (and correctly so) that there was at least one additional radioactive substance in the mixture. This unknown substance must be extremely radioactive because it appeared in such minute amounts in her samples.

So Mme. Curie set about to obtain observable amounts of the new substance by refining it from several tons of pitchblende. She eventually succeeded, an ounce at a time, in isolating two new elements that were highly radioactive: polonium and radium (element 88).

Properties of polonium

Polonium is the final entry in the oxygen group of elements, Group VIA. Polonium is in a position on the periodic table where it could be a metal, metalloid, or nonmetal. It is officially classified as a metal, however, on the grounds that its electrical conductivity decreases with increasing temperature. Metalloids and nonmetals are either very poor conductors at any temperature or their conductivity increases with temperature.

Polonium readily dissolves in most acids, but only in a few alkalis. Generally it behaves chemically like tellurium and bismuth—elements located directly above and to the left, respectively, on the periodic chart.

Production of polonium

Although bismuth-210 occurs naturally in pitchblende, an ore of uranium, it is still quite rare. The common practice, then, is to produce bismuth-210 artificially from the element's more abundant natural form, bismuth-209. The milligram amounts of bismuth-210 thus produced are allowed to decay naturally to the desired end product, polonium-210. The reaction equation is:

$$^{209}Bi(n,\gamma)^{210}Bi \rightarrow {}^{210}Po + \beta-$$

Some compounds of polonium

There are no compounds of polonium that have any commercial significance, but a few are produced in the laboratory for research purposes. With oxidation states of $+2$ and $+4$, we can expect to find compounds having these general forms:

Polonium (II) chloride, $PoCl_2$

$$Po^{2+} + 2Cl^- \rightarrow PoCl_2$$

Polonium (IV) chloride, $PoCl_4$ (polonium tetrachloride)

$$Po^{4+} + 4Cl^- \rightarrow PoCl_4$$

Polonium (II) oxide, PoO

$$Po^{2+} + O^{2-} \rightarrow PoO$$

Polonium (IV) oxide, PoO_2

$$Po^{4+} + 2O^{2-} \rightarrow PoO_2$$

Small amounts of *polonium (II) sulfide*, PoS, can be found in pitchblende that has been treated with hydrochloric acid and hydrogen sulfide.

Isotopes of polonium

Figure 84-1 lists the known isotopes of polonium. A number of them belong to one of the radioactive decay series. Polonium-211 and -215, for example, belong to the actinium series (see Fig. 84-2), while polonium-212 and -216 belong to the thorium series (Fig. 84-3). As shown in Fig. 84-4, the uranium radioactive series includes polonium-210, -214, and -218.

Isotope	Natural Abundance	Half-Life	Decay Mode
^{194}Po		700 ms	α
^{195m}Po		2 sec	α
^{195}Po		4.5 sec	α
^{196}Po		5.5 sec	α, β+
^{197m}Po		26 sec	α, β+
^{197}Po		56 sec	α, β+
^{198}Po		1.76 min	α, β+
^{199m}Po		4.2 min	α, β+
^{199}Po		5.2 min	α, β+
^{200}Po		11.5 min	α, β+
^{201m}Po		8.9 min	β+, i.t.
^{201}Po		15.3 min	β+, ec
^{202}Po		44.7 min	β+, ec
^{203m}Po		1.2 min	i.t.
^{203}Po		34.8 min	β+, ec
^{204}Po		3.53 hr	ec
^{205}Po		1.7 hr	β+, ec

Isotope	Natural Abundance	Half-Life	Decay Mode
^{206}Po		8.3 day	ec
^{207m}Po		2.8 sec	i.t.
^{207}Po		5.83 hr	
^{208}Po		2.94 yr	α
^{209}Po		102 yr	α
^{210}Po	100%	138 day	α
^{211m}Po		25.5 sec	α
^{211}Po		520 ms	α
^{212m}Po		45.1 sec	α
^{212}Po		300 ns	α
^{213}Po		4.2 μs	α
^{214}Po		163 μs	α
^{215}Po		1.78 ms	α
^{216}Po		150 ms	α
^{217}Po		<10 sec	α
^{218}Po		3.11 min	α

84-1 Polonium has isotopes with atomic weights between 194 and 218.

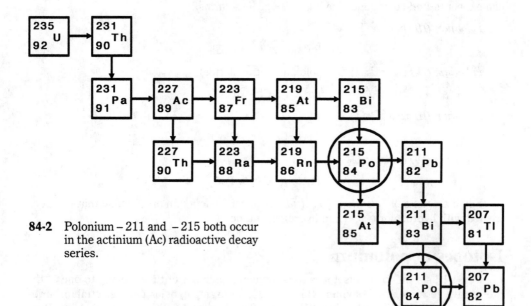

84-2 Polonium – 211 and – 215 both occur in the actinium (Ac) radioactive decay series.

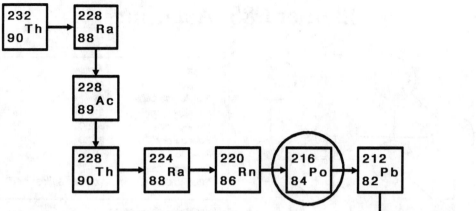

84-3 Polonium – 212 and – 216 both occur as part of the thorium (Th) radioactive decay series.

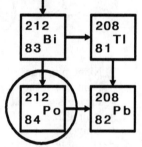

84-4 Polonium – 210, – 214 and – 218 occur in the uranium (U) decay series.

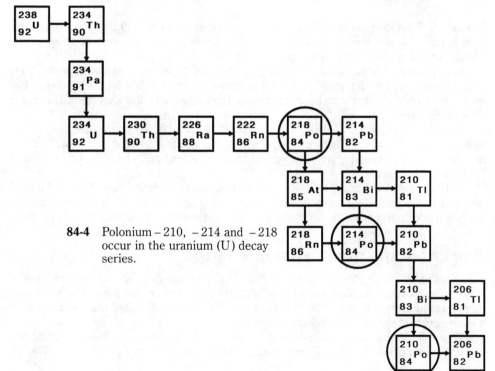

Element 85: Astatine

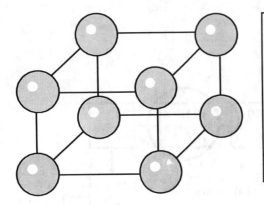

Name	Astatine
Symbol	At
Atomic Number	85
Atomic Weight	210 Note
Melting Point	302°C
Boiling Point	337°C
Specific Gravity	--?--
Oxidation States	--?--
Electron Config.	(Xe) $4f^{14}\,5d^{10}\,6s^2\,6p^5$

Note: Most stable isotope.

- Name pronounced as **AS-teh-teen** or **AS-teh-ten**
- Name from the Greek *astatos*, "unstable"
- Earlier suggested name was alabamine
- Synthesized in 1940 by Dale R. Corson, K.R. MacKenzie, and Emilio Segrè at the University of California
- Unstable, radioactive halogen

Through the first forty years of the twentieth century, chemists were busy trying to find real evidence for the existence of element 85. According to the nomenclature of Mendeleyev, this missing element was tentatively called *eka-iodine*.

Researchers knew it would be a halogen, resembling iodine in many respects. They were also prepared to find some metallic features. Because it would be a fairly heavy element with an odd number for its atomic number, the researchers also expected the element to be an extremely rare one.

During the first year of World War II, Dale R. Corson, K.R. MacKenzie, and Emilio Segrè at the University of California began looking for astatine in their cyclotron. The preliminary results appeared quite positive, but then the work had to be dropped because of America's war effort.

In 1945, the group completed their work and published their findings. They had indeed created astatine in the laboratory by firing high-energy alpha particles, or helium nuclei, at a target made of bismuth-209. Today's production method uses the same general approach.

Properties and production of astatine

The position of astatine on the periodic chart indicates that it should share a number of important properties with common iodine. Astatine, however, would tend to be somewhat more metallic in its behavior. It is difficult to describe anything in detail that exists for such a short period of time in such minute quantities.

When samples of astatine are needed for study, they are produced by bombarding bismuth-209 with alpha particles. The product is a pair of neutrons and astatine-211. The following expressions show this reaction in two different formats:

$$^{209}Bi(\alpha,2n)^{211}At$$

$$^{209}Bi_{83} + {}^{4}H_2 \rightarrow {}^{211}At_{85} + 2^{1}n_0$$

Compounds and isotopes of astatine

Astatine has very short half-lives and less than a gram has ever been produced for laboratory study. Obviously there are no commercially significant compounds of astatine; in fact,
experiments with astatine compounds provide more data by inference than by direct observation.

Figure 85-1 lists the known isotopes of astatine. All are radioactive and have short half-
lives. It is believed that traces of astatine-215, -218, and -219 might exist naturally in the
earth's crust; but if they do, the total amount weighs less than an ounce.

Isotope	Half-Life	Decay Mode	Isotope	Half-Life	Decay Mode
^{196}At	300 ms	α	^{207}At	1.81 hr	α, β+, ec
^{197}At	400 ms	α, β+, ec	^{208}At	1.63 hr	α, β+, ec
^{198m}At	1.5 sec	α, β+, ec	^{209}At	5.4 hr	α, β+, ec
^{198}At	4.9 sec	α, β+, ec	^{210}At	8.1 hr	α, ec
^{199}At	7 sec	α, β+, ec	^{211}At	7.2 hr	α, ec
^{200m}At	4.3 sec	α, β+, ec	^{212m}At	120 sec	α
^{200}At	43 sec	α, β+, ec	^{212}At	300 μs	α
^{201}At	1.48 sec	α, β+, ec	^{213}At	0.11 μs	α
^{202m}At	1.1 sec	i.t.	^{214m}At	0.7 μs	α
^{202}At	3 min	α, β+, ec	^{214}At	0.56 μs	α
^{203}At	7.4 min	α, β+, ec	^{215}At	100 μs	α
^{204}At	9.2 min	α, β+, ec	^{216}At	300 μs	α
^{205}At	26.2 min	α, β+, ec	^{217}At	32.3 μs	α
^{206}At	29.4 min	α, β+, ec	^{218}At	1.6 sec	α
			^{219}At	54 sec	α

85-1   Astatine has isotopes with atomic weights between 196 and 219.

Figure 85-2 shows that astatine-215 and -219 belong to the actinium radioactive decay
series. Astatine-218 belongs to the uranium decay series (Fig. 85-3), and astatine-217 to the
neptunium series (see Fig. 85-4).

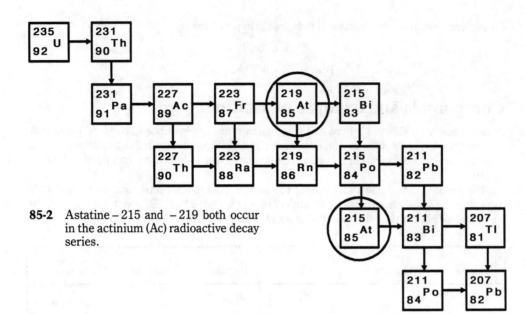

85-2 Astatine – 215 and – 219 both occur in the actinium (Ac) radioactive decay series.

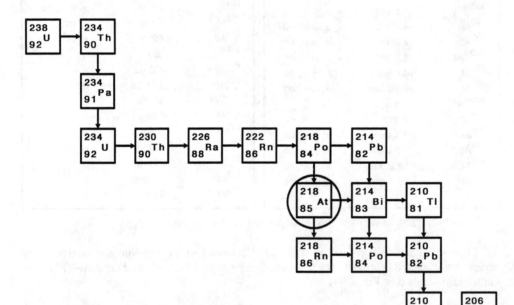

85-3 Astatine – 218 occurs as part of the uranium (U) radioactive decay series.

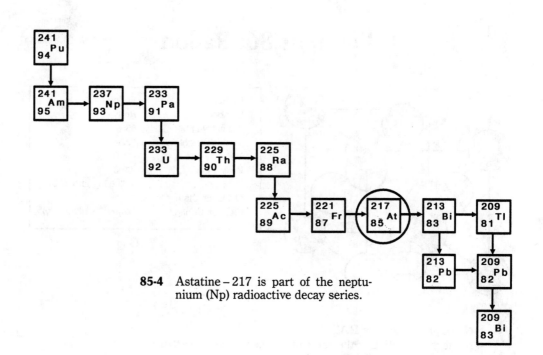

85-4 Astatine – 217 is part of the neptunium (Np) radioactive decay series.

Element 86: Radon

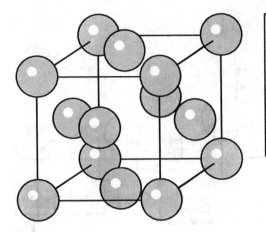

Name	Radon
Symbol	Rn
Atomic Number	86
Atomic Weight	222
Melting Point	-71°C
Boiling Point	-62°C
Density	9.73 g/l (1 atm, 0°C)
Oxidation State	0
Electron Config.	(Xe) $4f^{14}\,5d^{10}\,6s^2\ 6p^6$

- Name pronounced as **RAY-don**
- Name is a variation of the name of another element, **radium**
- Original name was *niton*, "shining"
- Discovered by Friedrich E. Dorn in 1900
- Heavy radioactive gas

Radioactive gas! It sounds like something from a B-grade science-fiction movie of the 1930s and 1940s. It really exists, though, as the element radon.

Radon gas cannot be detected by the human senses—it is odorless, colorless, and tasteless—but it can be detected by a Geiger counter. It was discovered by accident during the first year of the twentieth century, and it is now regarded as a potential health hazard in the air of basements in countless American homes. Its only commercial value is as a source of radioactivity for medical applications.

Radon is a gas under normal conditions. It is the heaviest of all the gassy elements, tipping the scales at 108 times the weight of hydrogen gas and about 7.5 times heavier than air. It is the only gas that is naturally radioactive, but its isotopes are all short lived. Radon is thus a rare element in nature. Most of it is found in small, scattered pockets of air several inches underground in regions having radium- and uranium-bearing rocks.

Historical background

In 1900, Friedrich Ernst Dorn (1848 – 1916) was studying the natural radioactive decay of radium. He was trying to put together details about what was happening to the mass when he detected the presence of a radioactive gas—Mme. Curie's "radioactive air." Dorn initially called his gas *niton*. The present name was not adopted until 1923.

Finding that radium decays to radon which, in turn, decays to polonium was a key element in the discovery that radioactive elements are transmuted into lighter elements.

Properties and production of radon

Radon is located at the bottom of the list of noble gasses in Group O of the periodic chart. Studies of this gas show that it fits the general mold for the so-called "inert" gasses.

Radon gas liquifies easily and changes to its solid state at just $-71\,°C$. As a solid, it glows with a yellow light that turns red-orange as the temperature is lowered further.

The only confirmed compound of radon is *radon fluoride*, RnF.

Isotopes of radon

Figure 86-1 lists the known isotopes of radon. Radon-219 belongs to the actinium radioactive decay series (Fig. 86-2), while radon-220 belongs to the thorium series (Fig. 86-3) and radon-218 and -222 to the uranium series (Fig. 86-4).

86-1 Radon has isotopes with atomic weights between 200 and 226.

Isotope	Half-Life	Decay Mode
^{200}Rn	1 sec	α, ec
^{201m}Rn	3.8 sec	α, ec
^{201}Rn	7 sec	α, ec
^{202}Rn	9.9 sec	α, ec
^{203m}Rn	28 sec	α, ec
^{203}Rn	45 sec	α, ec
^{204}Rn	1.24 min	α, ec
^{205}Rn	2.83 min	α, ec
^{206}Rn	5.67 min	α, ec
^{207}Rn	9.3 min	α, $\beta+$, ec
^{208}Rn	24.4 min	α, ec
^{209}Rn	28.5 min	α, $\beta+$
^{210}Rn	2.4 hr	α, ec
^{211}Rn	14.6 hr	α, $\beta+$, ec
^{212}Rn	24 hr	α
^{213}Rn	25 ms	α
^{214m}Rn	7.3 ns	α, i.t.
^{214}Rn	0.27 μs	α
^{215}Rn	2.3 μs	α
^{217}Rn		α
^{218}Rn	6 ms	α
^{219}Rn	3.96 sec	α
^{220}Rn	55.6 sec	α
^{221}Rn	25 min	α
^{222}Rn	3.82 day	α
^{223}Rn	43 min	β-
^{224}Rn	1.78 hrs	β-
^{225}Rn	4.5 min	β-
^{226}Rn	6 min	β-

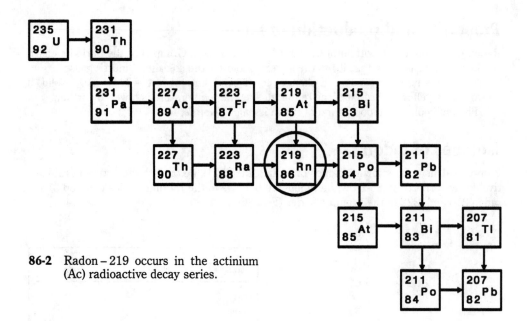

86-2 Radon – 219 occurs in the actinium (Ac) radioactive decay series.

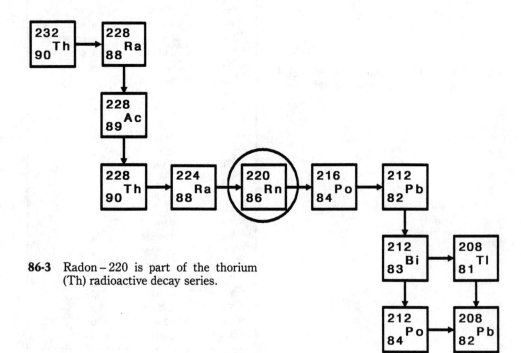

86-3 Radon – 220 is part of the thorium (Th) radioactive decay series.

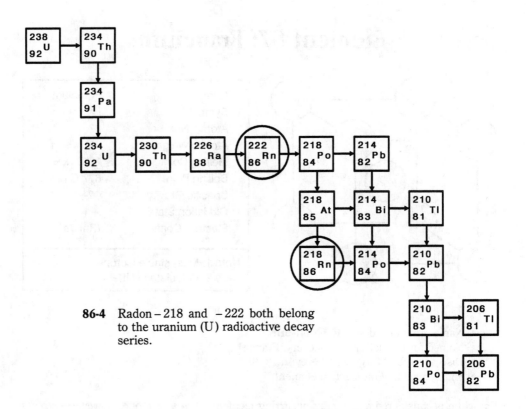

86-4 Radon – 218 and – 222 both belong to the uranium (U) radioactive decay series.

Notice that radon occurs naturally as a decay product of radium. This explains why early researchers saw a great similarity between radium and radon and, in fact, often confused the two. Radon always undergoes alpha-particle decay to polonium.

Radium is a common factor in the natural production of radon gas. The gas is also associated in nature with deposits of uranium ore, and this can be explained by noting the presence of uranium isotopes in the actinium and uranium decay series. Thorium isotopes also decay eventually to radium and radon.

Element 87: Francium

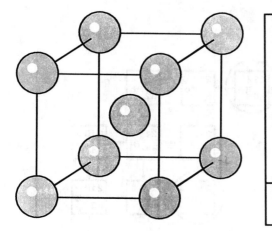

Name	Francium
Symbol	Fr
Atomic Number	87
Atomic Weight	223 Note 1
Melting Point	27°C Note 2
Boiling Point	677°C Note 2
Specific Gravity	--?--
Oxidation State	+1
Electron Config.	(Rn) $7s^1$

Note 1: Most stable isotope.
Note 2: Calculated value.

- Name pronounced as **FRAN-si-em**
- Named for the nation of discovery, France
- Discovered by Marguerite Perey in 1939
- Highly unstable radioactive element

Francium is considered a naturally occurring element. It is a rare one, however—experts estimate that there is no more than about one ounce of francium in all the materials that make up the earth's crust. One reason for its scarcity is that all of its isotopes are radioactive, and the longest half-life is less than 30 minutes.

Historical background

During the 1870s, Dimitri Mendeleyev, inventor of the periodic table of the elements, predicted the existence of element 87. Furthermore, he predicted it would have properties quite similar to those of cesium, so he named it *eka-cesium*. Based on Mendeleyev's excellent record for accurately predicting the existence and chemical nature of new elements, chemists around the world began searching frantically for convincing evidence of its existence. Whenever one of these people thought they had the new element isolated, they gave it a name. The scientific literature of the era shows people giving element 87 names such as *russium*, *virginium*, and *moldavium*. None of these claims of discovery passed the final tests, until 1939.

Marguerite Catherine Perey (1909 – 1975) was an assistant to the most successful and respected female scientist, Marie Curie, at the Radium Institute in Paris. Perey continued her work after Marie Curie died in 1934, unraveling the sequence of events we now know as the actinium radioactive decay series (*see* Element 89: Actinium).

Her initial view of the decay series was relatively sketchy. She knew about actinouranium, actinium-B, actinium-C, and actinium-D. However, as she attempted to confirm her results with more precise analyses, other elements began cropping up to spoil the systematic procedure for naming each of the species in the series. Francium – 223 was one of the final pieces of the puzzle. Finally, there it was! A new element sitting on the lab bench in front of Mlle. Perey. Half the sample disappeared by beta radiation every 21 minutes or so, but there was enough to confirm her discovery.

Properties and production of francium

Francium is the heaviest of the alkali metals in Group 1A on the periodic chart. It is also the most scarce of these metals. In fact there is only an ounce of natural francium scattered throughout the soil and rock of the earth; so no one has bothered to come up with a way to find it, let alone refine it. All francium samples that are available for study today are manufactured artificially. There are two different approaches to producing small quantities of francium. The more direct approach is to bombard thorium with protons. The second approach is less direct, but usually more practical. Radium is the parent element in this case. Once it is subjected to heavy neutron bombardment, it is converted to a species of actinium that decays naturally and quickly to thorium. Finally, the thorium decays naturally to francium.

Some compounds and the isotopes of francium

Figure 87-1 lists the known isotopes of francium. Francium-223 is part of the actinium radioactive decay series that was studied by Mlle. Perey (see Fig. 87-2). A second isotope, francium-221, was later found to be part of the neptunium decay series (Fig. 87-3).

Isotope	Half-Life	Decay Mode		Isotope	Half-Life	Decay Mode
^{201}Fr	48 ms	α		^{215}Fr	0.12 μs	α
^{202}Fr	340 ms	α		^{216}Fr	0.7 μs	α
^{203}Fr	550 ms	α		^{217}Fr	22 μs	α
^{204}Fr	2.1 sec	α		^{218}Fr	0.7 μs	α
^{205}Fr	3.9 sec	α		^{219}Fr	21 sec	α
^{206}Fr	16 sec	α		^{220}Fr	27.4 sec	α
^{207}Fr	14.8 sec	α		^{221}Fr	4.9 min	α
^{208}Fr	59 sec	α, ec		^{222}Fr	14.4 min	α
^{209}Fr	50 sec	α, ec		^{223}Fr	21.8 min	α, $\beta +$
^{210}Fr	3.2 min	α, ec		^{224}Fr	2.7 min	$\beta -$
^{211}Fr	3.1 min	α, ec		^{225}Fr	3.9 min	$\beta -$
^{212}Fr	20 min	α		^{226}Fr	48 sec	$\beta -$
^{213}Fr	34.6 sec	α		^{227}Fr	2.4 min	$\beta -$
^{214m}Fr	3.4 ms	α, i.t.		^{228}Fr	39 sec	$\beta -$
^{214}Fr	5.1 ms	α		^{229}Fr	50 sec	$\beta -$

87-1 Francium has isotopes with atomic weights between 201 and 229.

There are more isotopes of this element than confirmed compounds. If anyone ever finds enough francium to carry out the appropriate experiments, he will probably find that it has a single oxidation state of +1. Its metal ion would be Fr^+, so it would combine with common anions such as chlorine to form *francium chloride* (FrCl) and oxygen to form *francium oxide* (Fr_2O). If you could drop a sample of the metal into water, you would see an explosive reaction that would form *francium hydroxide* and hydrogen gas:

$$2Fr + 2H_2O \rightarrow 2FrOH + H_2$$
(francium + water → francium hydroxide + hydrogen gas)

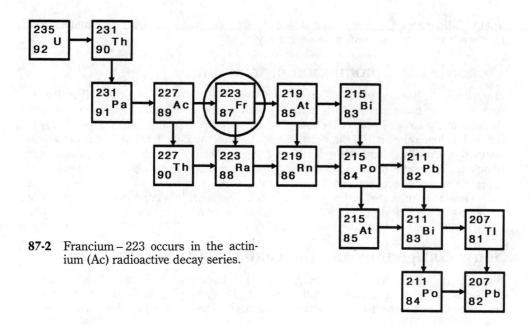

87-2 Francium – 223 occurs in the actinium (Ac) radioactive decay series.

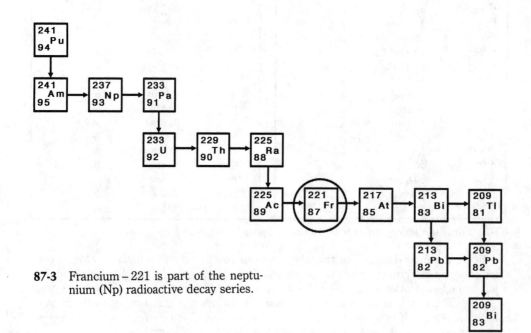

87-3 Francium – 221 is part of the neptunium (Np) radioactive decay series.

Element 88: Radium

Name	Radium
Symbol	Ra
Atomic Number	88
Atomic Weight	226
Melting Point	700°C
Boiling Point	1140°C
Specific Gravity	5 (20°C) Note
Oxidation State	+2
Electron Config.	(Rn) $7s^2$

Note: Approximate value.

- Name pronounced as **RAY-di-em**
- Name taken from the Latin, *radius*, "ray"
- Discovered by Pierre and Marie Curie in 1898
- Silvery white, radioactive metal

Radium is an active metal. It not only glows in the dark with an eerie bluish light, but also combines violently with water to produce the hydroxide. It is also intensely radioactive. The handwritten laboratory notes of the discoverers, M. and Mme. Curie, are still too radioactive today for safe handling.

Until the late 1950s, radium was mixed with a second phosphoresent material such as zinc sulfide to make luminous paint for wristwatches, clocks, and aircraft instrument dials. Recognition of the potential health hazards has recently forced companies to look for alternative materials for glow-in-the-dark paints.

Radium, sometimes mixed with beryllium, is used as a portable source of neutron radiation in medicine and industry. Radium is most often used in medical applications—particularly for the treatment of certain cancers.

Historical background

One woman, Marie Sklodowska Curie (1867 – 1934), experienced more excitement and accomplished more for science between the years of 1894 and 1911, than three or four people manage in a lifetime. In 1894, this daughter of a Polish physics professor and a high school principal, married a moderately well-known French researcher, Pierre Curie (1859 – 1906). In that same year, Marie began a series of research projects that would help her earn an advanced degree.

She found the subject of her great scientific passion in 1896 when Henri Becquerel announced his discovery of radioactivity in uranium. Marie did not have much to do with abstract theory, but she was an imaginative, careful, and tireless worker. She decided to test every element she could find for the presence of radioactivity. Her first discovery was the radioactive nature of thorium.

Then in 1898, she discovered that two common uranium ores, *pitchblende* and *chalcolite* were more radioactive than refined uranium. How could this be? There must be another element, one even more radioactive than uranium, mixed with these ores. Further work indicated the samples actually contained two new elements we now know as radium and polonium.

Now just four years into her career, Marie Curie had discovered radioactivity in thorium, showed that radioactivity is an essential character of certain elements, and discovered two new elements. But she was not done yet.

During the years between 1899 and 1902, Marie Curie dissolved, filtered, and repeatedly crystallized nearly three tons of pitchblende. She did not have a big staff to help her. She lifted every kilogram herself, working in a drafty makeshift laboratory that was sweltering hot in the summer and bone-chilling cold in the winter. (And this was in the days before health insurance and profit-sharing plans, sick days and two-weeks paid vacation each year!)

At the end of that working marathon, Marie reached her goal: $1/10$ of a gram of high-grade radium chloride. This was enough to confirm her discovery spectroscopically and determine the exact atomic weight of radium.

In 1903, Pierre and Marie were jointly awarded the Nobel Prize for chemistry. This was for their basic research in radioactivity. Marie's discovery of two new elements was not mentioned directly. That recognition came in 1911 when she was awarded her second Nobel Prize.

Properties and production of radium

Radium is the last element in Group IIA on the periodic chart. This means it is the heaviest of the alkaline-earth metals that comprise this group. Like the others in the group, radium is metallic and thus a good conductor of electricity. It appears to have a brilliant white color when freshly cut, but the intensity quickly lessens as a thin nitride coating develops. The chemical reaction in this instance is:

$$3Ra + N_2 \rightarrow Ra_3N_2$$
(radium metal + nitrogen gas → radium nitride)

Radium readily reacts with water to generate hydrogen gas and produce radium hydroxide:

$$Ra + 2H_2O \rightarrow Ra(OH)_2 + H_2$$
(radium metal + water → radium hydroxide + hydrogen gas)

Virtually all radium is derived from the byproducts of uranium refining operations as radium chloride and radium bromide.

Some compounds of radium

The most stable ion of radium is Ra^{2+}. Like most metals, it combines with the halogens to produce the chloride ($RaCl_2$) and bromide ($RaBr_2$). In fact, radium is most often sold, shipped, and stored as one of the halides.

Radium combines with the sulfate ion, SO_4^{2-}, to form the most insoluable sulfate known, radium sulfate:

$$Ra + H_2SO_4 \rightarrow RaSO_4 + H_2$$
(radium + sulfuric acid → radium sulfate + hydrogen gas)

Radium metal reacts with water to produce the most soluable of all the alkaline-earth hydroxides:

$$2Ra + 2H_2O \rightarrow 2RaOH + H_2$$
(radium + water → radium hydroxide + hydrogen gas)

Isotopes of radium

Figure 88-1 shows all the known isotopes of radium. Figure 88-2 shows that radium-223 is part of the actinium radioactive decay series. Radium-228 and -224 are in the thorium decay series (Fig. 88-3), radium-226 is part of the uranium decay series (Fig. 88-4), and radium-225 can be found in the neptunium decay series (Fig. 88-5).

88-1 Radium has isotopes with atomic weights between 206 and 230.

Isotope	Half-Life	Decay Mode
^{206}Ra	400 ms	α
^{207}Ra	1.3 sec	α
^{208}Ra	1.4 sec	α
^{209}Ra	4.6 sec	α
^{210}Ra	3.7 sec	α
^{211}Ra	13 sec	α, ec
^{212}Ra	13 sec	α, ec
^{213}Ra	2.7 min	α
^{214}Ra	2.46 sec	α
^{215}Ra	1.59 ms	α
^{216}Ra	0.18 μs	α
^{217}Ra	1.6 μs	α
^{218}Ra	14 μs	α
^{219}Ra		α
^{220}Ra	23 ms	α
^{221}Ra	28 sec	α
^{222}Ra	38 sec	α
^{223}Ra	11.43 day	α
^{224}Ra	3.66 day	α
^{225}Ra	14.8 day	β-
^{226}Ra	1600 yr	β-
^{227}Ra	42.2 min	β-
^{228}Ra	5.75 yr	β-
^{229}Ra	4.0 min	β-
^{230}Ra	1.55 hr	β-

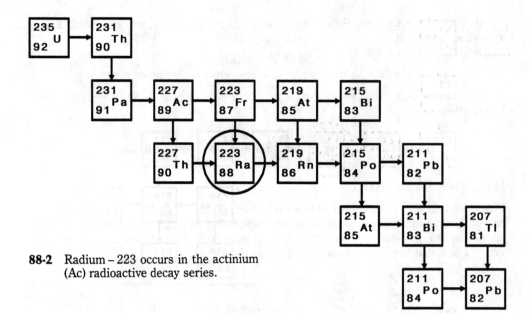

88-2 Radium – 223 occurs in the actinium (Ac) radioactive decay series.

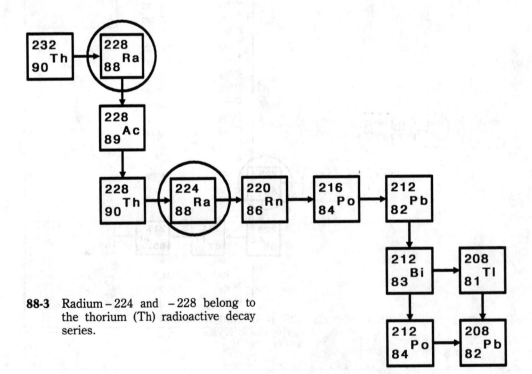

88-3 Radium – 224 and – 228 belong to the thorium (Th) radioactive decay series.

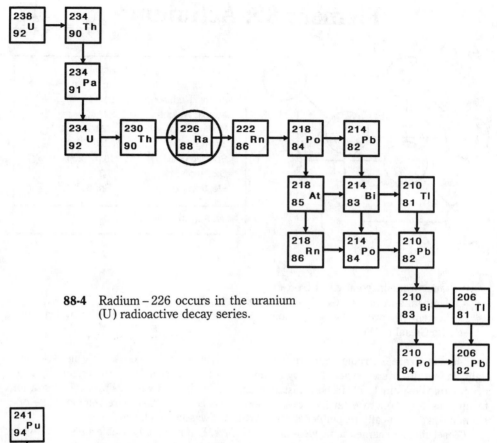

88-4 Radium – 226 occurs in the uranium (U) radioactive decay series.

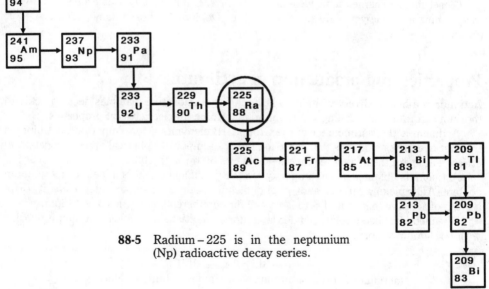

88-5 Radium – 225 is in the neptunium (Np) radioactive decay series.

Element 89: Actinium

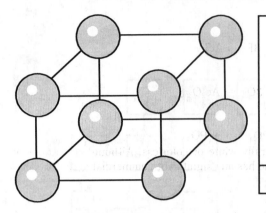

Name	Actinium
Symbol	Ac
Atomic Number	89
Atomic Weight	227.028
Melting Point	1050°C
Boiling Point	3200°C
Specific Gravity	10.07 (20°C) Note
Oxidation State	+3
Electron Config.	(Rn) $6d^1\ 7s^2$

Note: Approximate value.

- Name pronounced as **ak-TIN-i-em**
- Name taken from the Greek *aktis, aktinos,* "ray"
- Element discovered by André-Louis Debierne in 1899, independently by Friedrich Otto Giesel in 1902

Actinium is a rare, extremely radioactive metal that glows in the dark with an eerie blue light. It was discovered twice, first by André-Louis Debierne in 1899, then again by Friedrich Otto Giesel in 1902. In both instances, the investigators were using new separation techniques to sort out rare-earth oxides. In both instances, they discovered element 89—one element that chemically resembled a rare earth, but was far too heavy.

Giesel chose to name the new element *emanium*. Unfortunately, Debierne's paperwork was running a couple years ahead of Giesel's, so Debierne's chosen name, *actinium*, took priority.

Properties and production of actinium

Actinium is a heavy, silvery-white metal that is very radioactive. Samples decay quickly to thorium and francium, making it difficult to determine precise physical properties.

Actinium is the last member of the Group-IIIB elements. More important, actinium is the first of a series of metals that share a number of important physical and chemical properties. These are the *actinide* elements—elements 89 through 103.

Actinium is obtained as an "impurity" in the pitchblende that is mined for its uranium content. After picking through a ton of pitchblende, one can expect to squeeze about 1/10 of a gram of actinium out of it. There is no call for commercial quantities of actinium.

The metal has been isolated under laboratory conditions by reducing actinium fluoride with hot lithium vapor:

$$AcF_3 + 3Li \rightarrow Ac + 3LiF$$
(actinium fluoride + lithium → actinium + lithium fluoride)

Some compounds of actinium

Actinium has a single oxidation state of $+3$, so its metal ion is Ac^{3+}. This means its compounds have these general forms:

Actinium trifluoride, AcF_3

$$Ac^{3+} + 3F^- \rightarrow AcF_3$$

Actinium sesquioxide, Ac_2O_3

$$2Ac^{3+} + 3O^{2-} \rightarrow Ac_2O_3$$

Actinium phosphate, $AcPO_4$

$$Ac^{3+} + PO_4^{3-} \rightarrow AcPO_4$$

The compounds of actinium are generally white or colorless. Although a number of them have been prepared and studied, none has any significant commercial application.

Isotopes of actinium

Figure 89-1 shows all the isotopes of actinium. As shown in Figs. 89-2 and 89-3, actinium-227 is part of this element's own radioactive decay series. It is also the most common isotope and the one most often used in the compounds of actinium.

89-1 Actinium has isotopes with atomic weights between 210 and 232.

Isotope	Half-Life	Decay Mode
^{210}Ac	350 ms	α
^{211}Ac	250 ms	α
^{212}Ac	930 ms	α
^{213}Ac	800 ms	α
^{214}Ac	8.2 sec	α, ec
^{215}Ac	170 sec	α
^{216m}Ac	330 μs	α
^{216}Ac	330 μs	α
^{217m}Ac	0.4 μs	α
^{217}Ac	0.11 μs	α
^{218}Ac	0.27 μs	α
^{219}Ac	7 μs	α
^{220}Ac	26.1 ms	α
^{221}Ac	52 ms	α
^{222m}Ac	1.1 min	α, ec
^{222}Ac	4.2 sec	α
^{223}Ac	2.2 min	α, ec
^{224}Ac	2.9 hr	α, ec
^{225}Ac	10 day	α
^{226}Ac	1.2 day	α, β-, ec
^{227}Ac	21.77 yr	α, β-
^{228}Ac	6.13 hr	β-
^{229}Ac	1.05 hr	β-
^{230}Ac	2.03 min	β-
^{231}Ac	7.5 min	β-
^{232}Ac	35 sec	β-

You can find some actinium-228 in the thorium decay series (see Fig. 89-4); and as shown in Fig. 89-5, actinium-225 plays a role in the neptunium radioactive decay series.

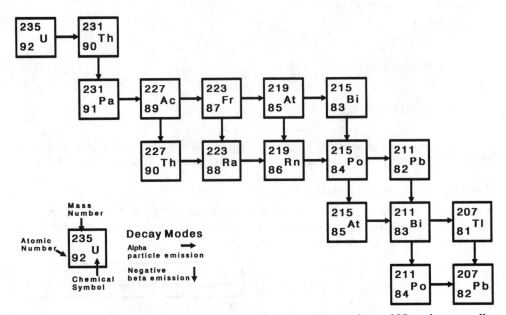

89-2 The actinium radioactive decay series begins with uranium – 235 and eventually comes to an end with stable lead – 207.

Isotope	Half-Life	Name	Earlier Name
^{235}U	7.15×10^8 yr	Uranium-235	Actinouranium (AcU)
^{231}Th	25.65 hr	Thorium-231	Uranium-Y (Uy)
^{231}Pa	3.25×10^4 yr	Protactinium-231	
^{227}Ac	21.6 yr	Actinium-227	
^{227}Th	18.2 day	Thorium-227	Radioactinium (RdAc)
^{223}Fr	21 min	Francium-223	Actinium-K (AcK)
^{223}Ra	11.68 day	Radium-223	Actinium-X (AcX)
^{219}At	54 min	Astatine-219	
^{219}Rn	3.92 sec	Radon-219	Actinon (An)
^{215}Bi	8.0 min	Bismuth-215	
^{215}Po	1.78 ms	Polonium-215	Actinium-A (AcA)
^{215}At	100 μs	Astatine-215	
^{211}Pb	36.1 min	Lead-211	Actinium-B (AcB)
^{211}Bi	2.16 min	Bismuth-211	Actinium-C (AcC)
^{211}Po	520 ms	Polonium-211	Actinium-C' (AcC')
^{207}Tl	4.79 min	Thallium-207	Actinium-C" (AcC")
^{207}Pb	stable	Lead-207	Actinium-D (AcD)

89-3 The actinium radioactive decay series includes some of the best known radioisotopes.

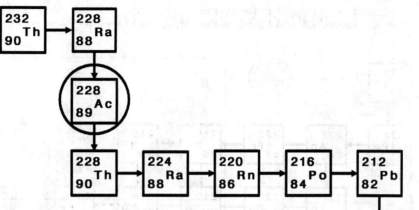

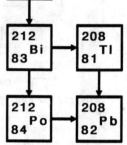

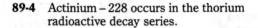

89-4 Actinium – 228 occurs in the thorium radioactive decay series.

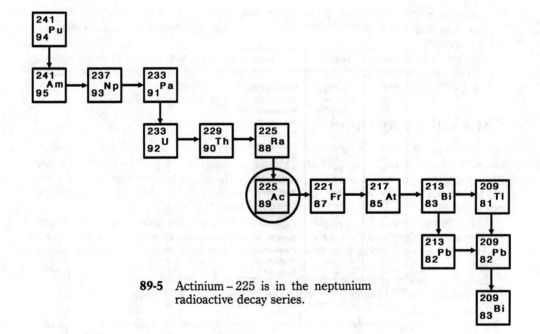

89-5 Actinium – 225 is in the neptunium radioactive decay series.

Element 90: Thorium

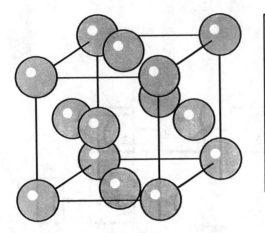

Name	Thorium
Symbol	Th
Atomic Number	90
Atomic Weight	232.038
Melting Point	1750°C
Boiling Point	3800°C Note 1
Specific Gravity	11.66 (17°C) Note 2
Oxidation State	+4
Electron Config	(Rn) $6d^2\ 7s^2$

Note 1: Calculated value.
Note 2: Approximate value.

- Name pronounced as **THOR-i-em** or **THO-ri-em**
- Named for Thor, the Norse god of thunder
- Discovered by Jöns Jacob Berzelius in 1828
- Gray, radioactive metal

At seven parts-per-million in the earth's crust, thorium is not regarded as a rare element. There is more than twice as much thorium as tin, for example—and tin is considered a common commodity.

Thorium is an important alloying agent for improving the high-temperature strength of metals such as magnesium. It also has applications in electronic photosensors, and the oxide is a common ingredient in high-quality lenses.

Historical background

The discovery of thorium begins with a curious mineral found by a skilled and enthusiastic amateur mineralogist, one Reverend Has Morten Thrane Esmark (1801–1882). The clergyman thought the mineral looked like gadolinite, but he suspected it was an earth of tantalum. He was not sure. It seemed too heavy to be either. So, as all good amateurs should do in such situations, he mailed a sample to the old pro himself, Jöns Jacob Berzelius.

Berzelius ran a few tests and determined that the sample was indeed an unknown mineral. Esmark was delighted with the news, and he proposed to name the new mineral *berzelite*. Berzelius was not anxious to have a mineral named for him, so he suggested *thorite* instead.

Berzelius noted that the new mineral was a silicon compound of a new element he named thorium. He confirmed his findings and announced the discovery and his preliminary descriptions in 1828.

Obscure little footnotes can be fascinating, especially when they illustrate the ordinary human qualities of some of the great figures of history. In 1815, a younger and less wise Berzelius claimed he had discovered the oxide of a new metal. And as such discoverers were encouraged to do, Berzelius submitted his claim to the authorities along with a name of his choosing—thorium, in this case. Unfortunately, the oxide of a "new element" turned out to be ordinary yttrium phosphate. A red-faced Berzelius had to withdraw his claim—but he saved the name for later use.

Properties and production of thorium

Thorium is a heavy gray metal that is soft, malleable, and ductile. It appears shiny when freshly cut, but gradually develops a dark gray or black oxide film. Other physical properties are not well established because they are so incredibly sensitive to minute amounts of impurities, including thorium oxide.

Thorium reacts slowly in water at room temperature, yet the only acid that readily attacks it is hydrochloric acid.

Thorium can be reduced directly from *thoranite*, or thorium oxide, with calcium:

$$ThO_2 + 2Ca \rightarrow Th + 2CaO$$
(thorium oxide + calcium → thorium + calcium oxide)

Thorium can also be reduced from its tetracfloride with just about any alkali metal:

$$ThF_4 + 4K \rightarrow Th + 4KF$$
(thorium tetracfloride + potassium → thorium + potassium fluoride)

The finest grades of thorium are produced by the electrolysis of a molten mixture of thorium, sodium, and potassium chlorides.

Some compounds of thorium

Thorium's principal oxidation state is $+4$; so its metal ion can be characterized as Th^{4+}. Representative examples of the compounds include:

Thorium chloride, $ThCl_4$

$$Th^{4+} + 4Cl^- \rightarrow ThCl_4$$

Thorium oxide, ThO_2 (the mineral *thorianite*)

$$Th^{4+} + 2O^{2-} \rightarrow ThO_2$$

Thorium nitride, Th_3N_4

$$3Th^{4+} + 4N^{3-} \rightarrow Th_3N_4$$

Isotopes of thorium

Figure 90-1 shows all of the known isotopes of thorium. All are radioactive, with thorium-232 having the longest half-life of 14,000,000,000 years.

Thorium-232 is also the parent isotope for a complete radioactive decay series that is appropriately called the *thorium decay series*. Figure 90-2 illustrates the series. The data in Fig. 90-3 provide additional information for each step in the series.

Thorium also appears in other radioactive decay series. Thorium-227 and -231 are both part of the actinium series (Fig. 90-4); thorium-230 and -234 are included in the uranium series (Fig. 90-5), and you can find thorium-229 in the neptunium decay series (Fig. 90-6).

Isotope	Half-Life	Decay Mode
^{212}Th	30 ms	α
^{213}Th	140 ms	α
^{214}Th	860 ms	α
^{215}Th	1.2 sec	α
^{216}Th	28 ms	α
^{217}Th	252 μs	α
^{218}Th	0.11 μs	α
^{219}Th	1.05 μs	α
^{220}Th	9.7 μs	α
^{221}Th	1.68 ms	α
^{222}Th	2.8 ms	α
^{223}Th	660 ms	α
^{224}Th	1.04 sec	α
^{225}Th	8 min	α, ec
^{226}Th	31 min	α
^{227}Th	18.72 day	α
^{228}Th	1.9 yr	α
^{229}Th	7.3 x10^3 yr	α
^{230}Th	7.54x10^4 yr	α
^{231}Th	25.2 hr	β-
^{232}Th	1.4x10^{10} yr	α
^{233}Th	22.3 min	β-
^{234}Th	24.1 day	β-
^{235}Th	6.9 min	β-
^{236}Th	37.1 min	β-

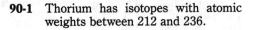

90-1 Thorium has isotopes with atomic weights between 212 and 236.

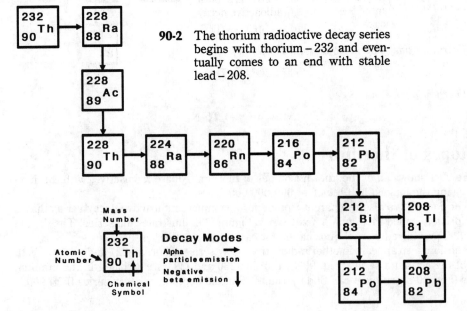

90-2 The thorium radioactive decay series begins with thorium – 232 and eventually comes to an end with stable lead – 208.

Isotope	Half-Life	Name	Earlier Name
^{232}Th	1.39x10^{10} yr	Thorium-232	
^{228}Ra	6.7 yr	Radium-228	Mesothorium-1 (MsTh1)
^{228}Ac	6.13 hr	Actinium-228	Mesothorium-2 (MsTh2)
^{228}Th	1.91 yr	Thorium-228	Radiothorium (RdAc)
^{224}Ra	3.64 day	Radium-224	Thorium-X (ThX)
^{220}Rn	5.15 sec	Radon-220	Thoron (Tn)
^{216}Po	160 ms	Polonium-216	Thorium-A (ThA)
^{212}Pb	10.6 hr	Lead-212	Thorium-B (ThB)
^{212}Bi	60.6 min	Bismuth-212	Thorium-C (ThC)
^{212}Po	30 μs	Polonium-212	Thorium-C' (ThC')
^{208}Tl	3.1 min	Thallium-208	Thorium-C" (ThC")

90-3 The thorium radioactive decay series includes some of the best known radioisotopes.

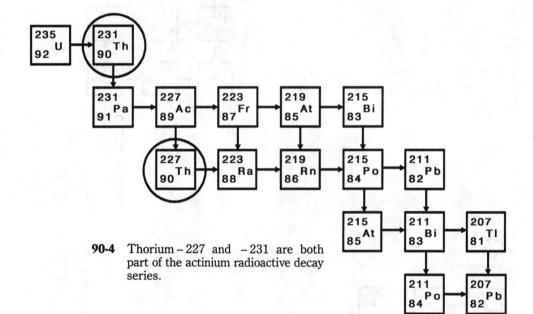

90-4 Thorium – 227 and – 231 are both part of the actinium radioactive decay series.

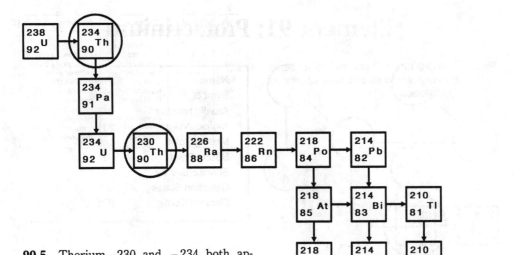

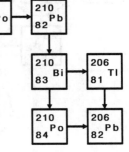

90-5 Thorium – 230 and – 234 both appear in the uranium radioactive decay series.

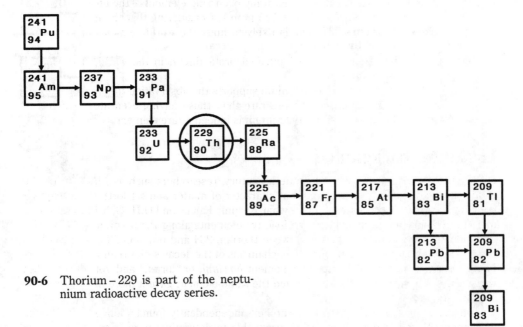

90-6 Thorium – 229 is part of the neptunium radioactive decay series.

Element 91: Protactinium

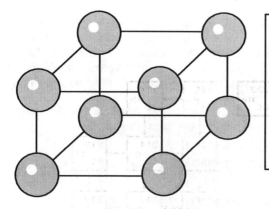

Name	Protactinium
Symbol	Pa
Atomic Number	91
Atomic Weight	231
Melting Point	1600°C
Boiling Point	--?--
Specific Gravity	--?--
Oxidation States	+4, +5
Electron Config.	(Rn) $5f^2 6d^1 7s^2$

- Name pronounced as **PRO-tak-TIN-eh-em**
- Name taken from the Greek, *proto* + *actinium*, "parent of actinium"
- Formerly known as *brevium* and *protoactinium*
- Discovered by Kasimir Fajans and O.H. Göhring in 1913; isolated by Aristid V. Grosse in 1934
- Silvery-white, radioactive metal

Protactinium is one of the rarest of all naturally occurring elements—the entire world supply of 99.9% protactinium is only about 125 grams. Considering that the element has no commercial application, this stockpile is likely to meet the world demand for decades to come.

It's a good thing there is so little purified protactinium in the world, because it is extremely radioactive and poisonous.

Incidentally, the scarcity of protactinium supports the observation that heavy elements having odd atomic numbers are far more rare than those having even atomic numbers. Ninety-one is an odd number, and protactinium is indeed a rare element.

Historical background

During the opening years of the twentieth century, researchers such as Marie Curie had established radioactivity as an important character of matter and set forth procedures for studying radioactive processes. This is what Kasimir Fajans and O.H. Göhring were doing in 1913. Tracing the transmutation radioactive elements along the uranium decay series, they noted a brief transition phase between thorium-234 and uranium-234 (look ahead to Fig. 91-3). More anxious to pursue the mechanisms of the decay series than fame and glory, Fajans and Göhring simply called the element *brevium*, or "brief," and got on with their work. Other researchers who later located the same element gave it more dramatic names such as uranium-X2.

During 1917 and 1918, several researchers independently found a longer-lived isotope of element 91. From this sample, they were able to determine more of the physical and chemical properties that are necessary for confirming the existence of a new element. Since the newer isotope proved far more meaningful to science than the one discovered by Fajans and Göhring, the name was changed to *protoactinium*. The name was shortened to the present one in 1949.

Although the existence of protactinium had been clearly established, the work was all done with oxygen and halogen compounds. No one had figured out how to isolate a sample of the metal, itself, until Aristid V. Grosse came up with two workable methods in 1934. Grosse's first method was to spray *protactinium pentoxide*, Pa_2O_5, with a stream of electrons in a vacuum. After several hours of this treatment, he found the oxide reduced to a shiny, metallic mass that he could prove to be the metal.

His second procedure was to subject *protactinium iodide*, PaI, to an electrically heated wire in a vacuum. He showed that this process reduced the metal this way:

$$2PaI_5 + heat \rightarrow 2Pa + 5I_2$$
(protactinium iodide + heat → protactinium + iodine)

Properties and production of protactinium

Protactinium is a heavy, silvery-white and shiny metal. It oxidizes very slowly in air. The metal, as well as all of its compounds, is radioactive and poisonous.

Protactinium follows thorium in the actinide series of elements. The actinides are all metals; the series begins with actinium (Ac, element 89) and ends with lawrencium (Lr, element 103).

The element is found mixed with uranium ores such as pitchblende. The proportions are on the order of one part in ten million, so it takes a trainload of ore to get some workable amounts of protactinium. To cite a true-to-life example, the atomic energy commission of Great Britian had to process 60 tons of ore to get that 125 grams of metal. The cost at the time was on the order of $500,000. You can see that there are no general trends in the protactinium refining industry.

Some compounds and isotopes of protactinium

Protactinium's most stable oxidation state is +5, although a +4 state is defined by an oxide:

Protactinium (IV) oxide, PaO_2

$$Pa^{4+} + 2O^{2-} \rightarrow PaO^2$$

Protactinium (V) oxide, Pa_2O_5

$$2Pa^{5+} + 5O^{2-} \rightarrow Pa_2O_5$$

Figure 91-1 shows all the known isotopes of protactinium. As shown in Fig. 91-2, protactinium-231 is part of the actinium radioactive decay series. Protactinium-234 is part of the uranium decay series (Fig. 91-3) and protactinium-233 is part of the neptunium series (Fig. 91-4).

Isotope	Half-Life	Decay Mode
^{216}Pa	200 ms	α
^{217m}Pa	1.6 ms	α
^{217}Pa	4.9 ms	α
^{218}Pa	120 μs	α
^{222}Pa	4.3 ms	α
^{223}Pa	6 ms	α
^{224}Pa	950 ms	α
^{225}Pa	1.8 sec	α
^{226}Pa	1.8 sec	α, ec
^{227}Pa	38.3 min	α, ec
^{228}Pa	22 hr	α, ec
^{229}Pa	1.4 day	α, ec
^{230}Pa	17.4 day	β-, ec
^{231}Pa	3.27x10^4 yr	α
^{232}Pa	1.31 day	β-
^{233}Pa	27 day	β-
^{234m}Pa	1.17 min	β-, i.t.
^{234}Pa	6.7 hr	β-
^{235}Pa	24.1 min	β-
^{236}Pa	9.1 min	β-
^{237}Pa	8.7 min	β-
^{238}Pa	2.3 min	β-

91-1 Protactinium has isotopes with atomic weights between 216 and 238.

91-2 Protactinium – 231 is part of the actinium radioactive decay series.

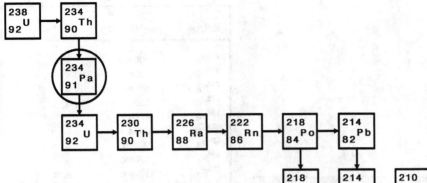

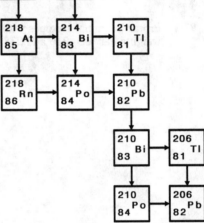

91-3 Protactinium – 234 appears in the uranium radioactive decay series.

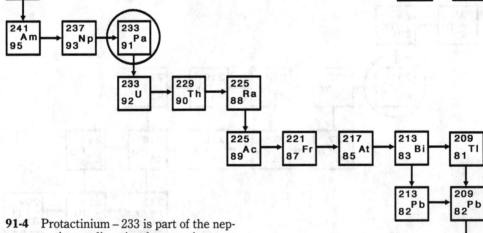

91-4 Protactinium – 233 is part of the neptunium radioactive decay series.

Element 92: Uranium

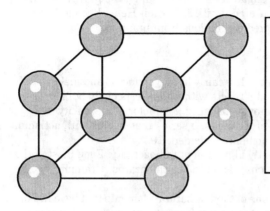

Name	Uranium
Symbol	U
Atomic Number	92
Atomic Weight	238.03
Melting Point	1132°C
Boiling Point	3818°C
Specific Gravity	19.05 (20°C)
Oxidation States	+3, +4, +5, +6
Electron Config.	(Rn) $5f^3\ 6d^1\ 7s^2$

- Name pronounced as **yoo-RAY-ni-em**
- Named for the planet Uranus
- Discovered by Martin Heinrich Klaproth in 1789; isolated by Eugène-Melchoir Péligot in 1841; found to be radioactive by Henri Becquerel in 1896
- Silvery-white, dense, ductile and malleable, radioactive metal

Uranium is no longer considered a rare element. The proportion of uranium is now reckoned to be two parts-per-million, making it more common in the earth's crust than tungsten, molybdenum, and beryllium.

Virtually all uranium and uranium compounds are used by the military and the nuclear power industry. Recent disasters and near-disasters at nuclear power facilities in the United States and Soviet Union have done much to cast a pall over commercial interest in nuclear power. It is difficult to say how long it will take our society to grow up enough to use uranium and its sister fuel, plutonium, in a responsible fashion.

Historical background

Until 1789, chemists and mineralogists believed that the mineral *pitchblende* was a mixture of zinc and iron compounds. Martin Heinrich Klaproth (1743 – 1817) changed all that when he demonstrated the existence of an unknown element in his samples. He named the new metal after the newly discovered planet, Uranus.

Although Klaproth is credited with the discovery of four elements throughout his career, he never managed to isolate any of them himself. (Producing compounds of an element is sufficient for establishing priority of discovery.) Klaproth thought he had isolated uranium metal after treating pitchblende with nitric acid and potash, then heating the substance in a charcoal crucible. He announced that the lustrous black crystals in the bottom of the crucible were bits of metallic uranium. This belief stood beyond Klaproth's lifetime.

It turns out that uranous oxide, UO_2, behaves more like a simple element than a compound, and this fooled a lot of experts for a long time. Finally in 1841, Eugène-Melchoir Péligot found his "pure uranium" reacting with uranium tetrachloride, UCl_4, in ways that made no sense at all. His only satisfactory explanation was that the stuff everyone thought was uranium metal was actually uranous oxide. Armed with this important fact, he isolated the true metal by heating it with potassium in a platinum crucible.

Even through all of this, no one had the slightest idea that uranium is highly radioactive. The property of radioactivity was not discovered until 1896 when Henri Becquerel developed an electrometer instrument that detected emanations from uranium.

Properties of uranium

Uranium is a heavy, silvery, and lustrous metal. It is fairly hard, yet ductile and malleable. It tarnishes in air with a thin oxide coating, and it reacts with water—especially boiling water. It dissolves in acids, but not in bases. It is not a very good conductor of electricity.

Uranium is part of the actinide series of elements, a series that begins with actinium (Ac, element 89) and concludes with lawrencium (Lr, element 103).

Uranium is best known for its consistently high level of radioactivity. Even most of the compounds, unless diluted to trace proportions, can pose health hazards. Uranium was the first substance known to be radioactive.

Uranium is also quite famous for being one of the few natural elements that have fissionable isotopes. You cannot make a nuclear reactor or atom bomb out of anything that is radioactive; the material must be able to undergo a fission process whereby the numbers of neutrons in motion can multiply, rather than remain fixed or diminish.

Production of uranium

Uranium metal is not refined directly from its ores, but rather is reduced with magnesium from uranium tetrafluoride. The reaction is a simple one to express:

$$UF_4 + 2Mg \rightarrow U + 2MgF_2$$
(uranium tetrafluoride + magnesium → uranium + magnesium fluoride)

This is not an easy reaction to do, however. The mixture has to be heated in an oxygen-free atmosphere. The temperature has to be high enough to melt both the magnesium and the uranium metals, and the chamber has to be filled with an inert gas such as argon. Molten uranium, being far more dense than any of the other participants in the reaction, settles to the bottom of the container where it can be drained off. Ingots weighing as much as 3000 pounds have been produced by this method.

There is actually little demand for uranium metal. Most uranium is packaged and distributed as sodium diuranate (also known as *yellow cake*) and a strangely formulated compound, *triuranium octoxide* (U_3O_8).

In a uranium refinery, ores such as pitchblende are finely ground and separated from a lot of different impurities by methods that take advantage of uranium's high density. Shaking and water-floatation equipment, for example, readily separate the heavier uranium compounds from the lighter impurities.

Once the ore is mechanically refined, it is subjected to a series of chemical operations that separate the uranium as *uranates*—compounds built around the UO_2^{2+} radical.

Some compounds of uranium

Uranium's most stable oxidation states are +4 and +6. These are demonstrated by compounds having the U^{4+} and U^{6+} ions:

Uranium (IV) chloride, UCl_4 (also called uranium tetrachloride)

$$U^{4+} + 4Cl^- \rightarrow UCl_4$$

Uranium (VI) chloride, UCl_6 (also called uranium hexachloride)

$$U^{6+} + 6Cl^- \rightarrow UCl_6$$

Uranium tends to form a uranyl ion, UO_2^{2+}. This is responsible for a family of uranium compounds. A couple of examples are:

Uranyl chloride, UO_2Cl_2

$$UO_2^{2+} + 2Cl^- \rightarrow UO_2Cl_2$$

Uranyl sulfide, UO_2S

$$UO_2^{2+} + S^{2-} \rightarrow UO_2S$$

Uranium tetrafluoride, UF_4, is a vital ingredient for the production of other uranium compounds as well as elemental uranium. It is produced by combining uranium dioxide and hydrofluoric acid at high temperatures:

$$UO_2 + 4HF \rightarrow UF_4 + 2H_2O$$
(uranium dioxide + hydrofluoric acid $\rightarrow$ uranium tetrafluoride + water)

Uranium dioxide, UO_2, is brown-black powder that can be produced by heating one of the higher uranium oxides in hydrogen or carbon monoxide. This oxide's formulation is rather peculiar: $UO_{2.0-2.6}$. Recall that this is the oxide that was once thought to be pure uranium metal. More questions than answers exist for this substance.

Uranium trioxide, UO_3, is a dense orange powder that is produced by heating *uranyl nitrate*, $UO_2(NO_3)_2$, to about 300 °C. Alternative names for this oxide are uranyl oxide and uranium (VI) oxide. Heating uranyl nitrate above 430 °C yields triuranium octoxide, U_3O_8.

Isotopes of uranium

Figure 92-1 lists the known isotopes of uranium. All are radioactive and many of them occur naturally. Uranium-238 is the most abundant because it decays so very slowly.

92-1 Uranium has isotopes with atomic weights between 226 and 242.

Isotope	Half-Life	Decay Mode
^{226}U	500 ms	α
^{227}U	300 ms	α
^{228}U	200 ms	α
^{229}U	3 min	α, ec
^{230}U	20.8 day	α
^{231}U	4.2 day	ec
^{232}U	68.9 yr	α
^{233}U	1.59×10^5 yr	α
^{234}U	2.45×10^5 yr	α
^{235m}U	26 min	i.t.
^{235}U	7.04×10^8 yr	α
^{236}U	2.34×10^7 yr	α
^{237}U	6.75 day	β-
^{238}U	4.46×10^9 yr	α
^{239}U	3 sec	β-
^{240}U	14.1 hr	β-
^{242}U	16.8 min	β-

Uranium is a key element in a radioactive decay series that bears its name. Figure 92-2 illustrates the steps in the uranium decay series and the data in Fig. 92-3 provide additional details.

Uranium also participates in two other decay series. (See the actinium series in Fig. 89-2 and the neptunium series Fig. 93-2.)

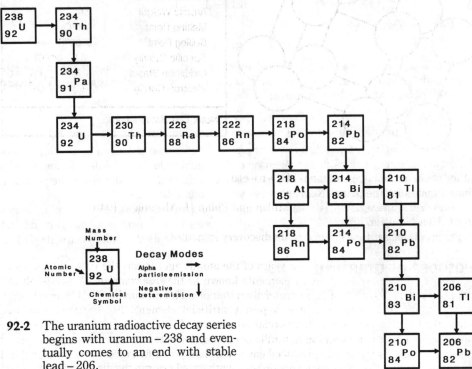

92-2 The uranium radioactive decay series begins with uranium – 238 and eventually comes to an end with stable lead – 206.

92-3 The uranium radioactive decay series includes some of the best known radioisotopes.

Isotope	Half-Life	Name	Earlier Name
^{238}U	4.5×10^9 yr	Uranium-238	Uranium-I (UI)
^{234}Th	24.1 day	Thorium-234	Uranium-X$_1$ (UX$_1$)
^{234}Pa	1.18 min	Protactinium-234	Uranium-X$_2$ (UX$_2$)
	6.7 hr		Uranium-Z (UZ)
^{234}U	2.47×10^5 yr	Uranium-234	Uranium-II (UII)
^{230}Th	8x104 yr	Thorium-230	Ionium
^{226}Ra	1602 yr	Radium-230	
^{222}Rn	3.82 day	Radon-230	
^{218}Po	3.05 min	Polonium-218	Radium-A (RaA)
^{218}At	1.6 sec	Astatine-218	
^{218}Rn	35 ms	Radon-218	
^{214}Pb	26.8 min	Lead-214	Radium-B (RaB)
^{214}Bi	19.7 min	Bismuth-214	Radium-C (RaC)
^{214}Po	16.4 ms	Polonium-214	Radium-C' (RaC')
^{210}Tl	1.32 min	Thallium-210	Radium-C" (RaC")
^{210}Pb	22 yr	Lead-210	Radium-D (RaD)
^{210}Bi	4.85 day	Bismuth-210	Radium-E (RaE)
^{210}Po	138.4 day	Polonium-210	Radium-F (RaF)
^{206}Tl	4.2 min	Thallium-206	
^{206}Pb	stable	Lead-206	Radium-G (RaG)

Element 93: Neptunium

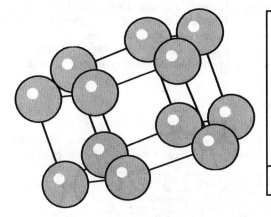

Name	Neptunium
Symbol	Nu
Atomic Number	93
Atomic Weight	237
Melting Point	640°C
Boiling Point	3902°C Note
Specific Gravity	20.25 (20°C)
Oxidation States	+3, +4, +5, +6
Electron Config.	(Rn) $5f^4 6d^1 7s^2$

Note: Calculated value.

- Name pronounced as **nep-TOO-ni-em**
- Named for the planet Neptune
- Discovered by Edwin M. McMillan and Philip H. Abelson in 1940
- Silvery metal
- Produced artificially prior to its discovery in nature

Neptunium is a product of the first years of the atomic age. It was the first element to be synthesized in the series of heavy elements known as the *transuranium elements*—all elements having an atomic number greater than that of uranium, number 92. Chemists originally thought that neptunium was a purely artificial element. Its discovery was well established and, in fact, some commercial production had started before researchers found minute amounts of neptunium in naturally occurring deposits of uranium ore. Although far more neptunium is artificially produced each year than probably ever existed in the natural state, the fact that the man-made version was synthesized prior to the discovery of the natural version makes the story an interesting footnote in the history of science.

Historical background

By the early part of 1940, Edwin M. McMillan (1907 –) believed he had found evidence of a new element, element 93, among some radioactive byproducts of uranium-235. Philip H. Abelson (1913 –), a former graduate student at McMillan's Berkeley laboratory, met with McMillan in the spring of that same year. They soon found they shared a special interest in element 93 and immediately decided to pool their efforts.

McMillan and Abelson created the element by bombarding uranium oxide with neutrons in the Berkeley cyclotron. They showed that the new element could exist with oxidation states 4 and 6, and that it demonstrated properties similar to uranium. The element was positively identified and officially presented to the scientific community later in 1940.

While considering an appropriate name for the new element, McMillan noted that it would directly follow uranium, atomic number 92, on the periodic chart. Then noting that uranium was named for the planet Uranus, he decided to name the new element for the planet that comes after Uranus in our solar system—Neptune.

The announcement of the discovery of neptunium managed to slip into the public arena just before United States national security requirements placed a ban on the publication of any information related to fission and atomic energy. Through 1940 and 1941, for example, Glenn T. Seaborg and others prepared a number of scientific papers describing their work producing pure compounds of neptunium. These findings, however, did not come to light until 1946, when the United States government lifted its security restrictions.

It was originally thought that neptunium was a purely artificial element. Although the amounts are incredibly small, researchers now know that neptunium exists in natural deposits of uranium ores.

Properties of neptunium

Neptunium is the first of the transuranium elements—elements having atomic numbers higher than that of uranium, number 92. Neptunium belongs to the actinide series of elements.

All isotopes of neptunium are radioactive. As shown in Fig. 93-1, however, neptunium-237 has a very long half-life—on the order of two million years. This long-lived isotope was the first to be created in measurable amounts and is the one that is commercially available today.

Isotope	Half-Life	Decay Mode
^{228}Np	1 min	sf
^{229}Np	4 min	α
^{230}Np	4.6 min	α, ec
^{231}Np	4.8 min	α, ec
^{232}Np	14.7 min	ec
^{233}Np	36 min	ec
^{234}Np	4.4 day	β+, ec
^{235}Np	1.1 yr	α, ec
^{236m}Np	22.5 hr	β-, ec
^{236}Np	1.2×10^5 yr	β-, ec
^{237}Np	2.14×10^6 yr	α
^{238}Np	2.1 day	β-
^{239}Np	2.4 day	β-
^{240m}Np	7.2 day	β-
^{240}Np	1.03 hr	β-
^{241}Np	14 min	β-
^{242m}Np	5.5 min	β-
^{242}Np	2.2 min	β-

93-1 Neptunium has isotopes with atomic weights between 228 and 242.

The discovery of neptunium was also important because it provided a missing link for a systematic group of radioactive decay processes. It was known that the thorium decay series has atomic mass numbers with values evenly divisible by 4. The uranium series featured atomic mass numbers divisible by 4 with a remainder of 2, and the actinium series had mass numbers divisible by 4 with a remainder of 3. It was frustrating to be unable to find a decay series where the mass numbers would be divisible by 4 with a remainder of 1. This frustration was finally relieved with the discovery of neptunium (see the neptunium decay series illustrated in Figs. 93-2 and 93-3).

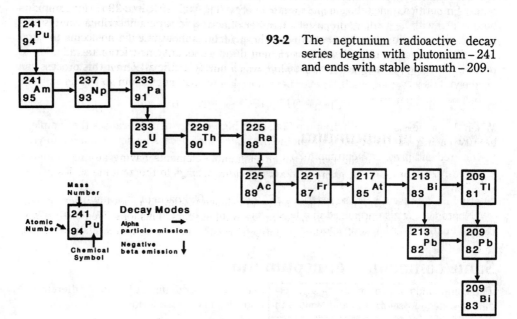

93-2 The neptunium radioactive decay series begins with plutonium – 241 and ends with stable bismuth – 209.

Isotope	Half-Life	Name
^{241}Pu	14 yr	Plutonium-241
^{241}Am	4.7 yr	Americium-241
^{233}Np	2.2×10^6 yr	Neptunium-233
^{233}Pa	27.4 day	Protactinium-233
^{233}U	1.62×10^5 yr	Uranium-233
^{229}Th	7340 yr	Thorium-229
^{225}Ra	14.8 day	Radium-225
^{225}Ac	10 day	Actinium-225
^{221}Fr	4.8 min	Francium-221
^{217}At	32.3 ms	Astatine-217
^{213}Bi	47 min	Bismuth-213
^{213}Pb	4.2 μs	Lead-213
^{209}Tl	2.2 min	Thallium-209
^{209}Pb	3.3 hr	Lead-209

93-3 Half-lives for members of the neptunium decay series range from 4.2 microseconds to 2,200,000 years.

Commercial production of neptunium

McMillan and Abelson prepared their earliest samples of neptunium-239 by striking atoms of uranium-238 with high-energy neutrons to create uranium-239 which, in turn, decays spontaneously by beta radiation to yield the neptunium isotope. The process is:

$$^{238}U(n,\gamma)^{239}U \rightarrow {}^{239}Np + \beta-$$

Today, elemental neptunium is produced in kilogram quantities as a byproduct of breeder reactors where either uranium-235 or uranium-238 is converted to plutonium and other "impurities," including neptunium-237. Starting with uranium-235, the sample is bombarded with high-energy neutrons. The target gains a neutron and emits a gamma particle to yield uranium-236. A second round of neutron bombardment transforms the uranium-236 to uranium-237. This material then decays spontaneously by beta radiation to produce only slightly radioactive neptunium-237. The nuclear equation for this process can be shown this way:

$$^{235}U(n,\gamma)^{236}U(n,\gamma)^{237}U \rightarrow {}^{237}N + \beta -$$

When the process starts with uranium-238, each high-energy neutron causes the sample to emit two neutrons. The result is uranium-237, which then decays by beta radiation to yield the desired end product, neptunium-237:

$$^{238}U(n,2n)^{237}U \rightarrow {}^{237}Np + \beta -$$

Neptunium is present in these reactions as 1 part per 1000 parts of plutonium.

Neptunium is also produced in a less-direct fashion by reducing neptunium trifluoride (NpF_3) in lithium or barium vapors.

Some compounds of neptunium

The compounds of neptunium closely resemble those of uranium. It has four different oxidation states, $+3$, $+4$, $+5$, and $+6$, so the fluorides take these forms:

Neptunium (III) fluoride, NpF_3 (also called neptunium trifluoride)

$$Np^{3+} + 3F^- \rightarrow NpF_3$$

Neptunium (IV) fluoride, NpF_4 (also called neptunium tetrafluoride)

$$Np^{4+} + 4F^- \rightarrow NpF_4$$

Neptunium (VI) fluoride, NpF_6 (also called neptunium hexafluoride)

$$Np^{6+} + 6F^- \rightarrow NpF_6$$

The principal oxide is *neptunium (IV) oxide*, NpO_2 (also called neptunium dioxide)

$$Np^{4+} + 2O^{2-} \rightarrow NpO_2$$

Element 94: Plutonium

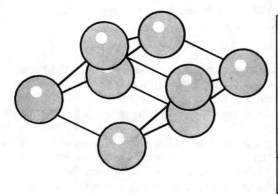

Name	Plutonium
Symbol	Pu
Atomic Number	94
Atomic Weight	242 Note 1
Melting Point	641°C
Boiling Point	3232°C
Specific Gravity	19.84 (25°C) Note 2
Oxidation States	+3, +4, +5, +6
Electron Config.	(Rn) $5f^6 7s^2$

Note 1: Most stable isotope.
Note 2: Alpha form.

- Name pronounced as **ploo-TOE-ni-em**
- Named for the planet Pluto
- Discovered by Glenn T. Seaborg in 1941
- Silvery-white, radioactive metal
- Byproduct of atomic power plants
- Main ingredient in atomic fission weapons

The element plutonium is a key player in the roller-coaster history of the atomic age. In the earliest years, it was an important ingredient in the development and production of the first atomic bombs. In later years, it became known as an environmentally hazardous radioactive waste from nuclear power plants, thus playing an important role in dimming the future of domestic atomic energy.

Historical background

Plutonium was unknown to the general scientific community until six years after its discovery. In fact, a small group of researchers determined the essential properties, identified some of the more important compounds, developed a way to produce elemental plutonium in kilogram lots, and built factories that produced masses of plutonium—all before most of the world even knew such a material existed.

During the first months of 1941, Glenn T. Seaborg (1912–) and his associates at Berkeley were putting the finishing touches on research aimed at identifying and isolating trace amounts of a new element, atomic number 94. They had found small amounts of the new element in samples of neptunium, and were beginning to identify the oxidation states. The paper announcing their discovery was written in the early part of 1941, but it was not published until 1946. Seaborg, like a few other select chemists, physicists, and mathematicians, were called from their university laboratories to participate in a project, conducted under an Illinois football stadium, known as the Manhattan Project.

Seaborg, and the United States security people watching over his shoulder, had found plutonium-239 to be a fissionable material at least theoretically satisfactory for building an atomic bomb. Seaborg's progress began with uranium-238, the most abundant naturally occurring form of uranium. The U-238 was then bombarded with high-energy neutrons to produce uranium-239. Once he got to U-239, Seaborg found that the rest takes care of itself. First, the U-239 decays by beta radiation to neptunium-239, then the neptunium-239 decays, also by beta radiation, to plutonium-239. The Seaborg process, represented by the following nuclear equation, changed the world forever:

$$^{238}U(n,\gamma)^{239}U \rightarrow {}^{239}Np + \beta^- \rightarrow {}^{239}Pu + \beta-$$

By the time it was possible to learn more about plutonium through the normal, uncensored channels of scientific journals, all the fun of initial exploration was over. Plutonium had already been well researched and worked over in secret government labs. Researchers who were left out of the early work with plutonium could only hope to use it as a springboard to the discovery of heavier elements.

One of Seaborg's colleagues at Berkeley, Edwin M. McMillan (1907 –), suggested the current name for element 94. He had recently named his own discovery, neptunium, after the planet Neptune. Since uranium and neptunium are side-by-side on the periodic table, he reasoned, and since their namesakes, Uranus and Neptune, are neighbors in our solar system, it follows that the next element in the sequence should be named after the next planet in the solar system: Pluto.

Incidentally, this was not the first time that plutonium had been suggested as a name for one of the chemical elements. In 1808, Sir Humphry Davy isolated the new element 56 and called it barium. Nearly a decade later, a professor at Cambridge University took issue with Davy's name for element 56 and petitioned it be changed from barium to plutonium. His thinking was that element 56 wasn't very heavy at all (barium is taken from the Greek *barys*, meaning "heavy"). Rather, since element 56 was being produced by a relatively new technique called *electrolysis*, the professor preferred a name that referred to the existence of fire. Plutonium would be a good name because it refers to Pluto, the Greek and Roman god of Hades. (The planet, Pluto, played absolutely no part in this dispute over the name of element 56—more than a century would pass before anyone would even know of the little planet's existence.)

Physical and chemical properties of plutonium

All isotopes of plutonium are radioactive. As shown in Fig. 94-1, the half-lives range from about 26 minutes for plutonium-235 to 82-million years for plutonium-244. The most widely produced isotopes, however are protonium-238 and -239.

There are six known allotropic, crystalline, metallic forms of plutonium. The alpha version is the one that exists at normal environmental temperatures, so it is the most widely recognized. The remaining allotropic forms exist at higher temperatures. A sample of α-plutonium has a silvery color that takes on a yellowish hue as it oxidizes in the air.

A softball-sized piece of plutonium would grow hot to the touch because of its high level of alpha radiation. A somewhat larger sample can boil a liter of water within a few minutes. A single kilogram of Pu-238 can release the equivalent of 22-million kilowatt-hours of heat energy.

Plutonium-238 is not fissionable; it cannot undergo a chain reaction. Plutonium-239, on the other hand, is fissionable and can undergo a chain reaction when compressed to its critical mass. In fact, the critical mass of plutonium-239 is only about one-third that of fissionable uranium-235. A kilogram of Pu-239 can release the explosive energy of 20,000 tons of TNT, making it the material of choice for fission weaponry.

Isotope	Half-Life	Decay Mode
^{232}Pu	34 min	α, ec
^{233}Pu		α, ec
^{234}Pu	8.8 hr	α, ec
^{235}Pu	26 min	α, ec
^{236}Pu	2.9 yr	α
^{237}Pu	45 day	α
^{238}Pu	87.7 yr	α
^{239}Pu	2.4×10^4 yr	α
^{240}Pu	6537 yr	α
^{241}Pu	14.4 yr	β-, α
^{242}Pu	3.8×10^5 yr	α
^{243}Pu	4.9 hr	β-
^{244}Pu	8.2×10^7 yr	α, sf
^{245}Pu	10.5 hr	β-
^{246}Pu	10.9 day	β-

94-1 Plutonium has isotopes with atomic weights between 232 and 246.

Commercial production of plutonium

Plutonium-238 and -239 are the only isotopes having applications outside the laboratory; plutonium-238 is used a source of heat energy for relatively small and portable power sources, and plutonium-239 is used in atomic weapons.

Plutonium-238 can be produced in much the same way Seaborg created the first identifiable samples of the element. Uranium-238 is bombarded with deuterons—the nuclei of deuterium, or heavy hydrogen. The nuclear equation for the process is:

$$^{238}\text{U}(d,2n)^{238}\text{Np} \rightarrow {}^{238}\text{Pu} + \beta -$$

This equation states that bombarding a U-238 atom with a deuteron produces two neutrons and neptunium-238. The latter decays spontaneously, emitting negative beta particles to yield plutonium-238.

There is no shortage of plutonium-239—quite the contrary. The problem is finding a suitable application for, or place to stash, the surplus plutonium from atomic reactors. The nuclear equation for producing this isotope is the same one used earlier in this chapter when describing the Seaborg process for transforming uranium-238 to plutonium-239.

Some compounds of plutonium

The principal oxidation states for plutonium are +3 and +4, although a few compounds having +5 and +6 are known. The Pu^{3+} ion shows up in a couple compounds:

Plutonium (III) fluoride, PuF_3 (also called plutonium trifluoride)

$$Pu^{3+} + 3F^- \rightarrow PuF_3$$

Plutonium nitride, PuN

$$Pu^{3+} + N^{3-} \rightarrow PuN$$

The Pu^{4+} ion appears in compounds such as:

Plutonium (IV) fluoride, PuF_4 (also called plutonium tetrafluoride)

$$Pu^{4+} + 4F^- \rightarrow PuF_4$$

Plutonium (IV) oxide, PuO_2 (also called plutonium dioxide)

$$Pu^{4+} + 2O^{2-} \rightarrow PuO_2$$

Plutonium compounds are usually derived from PuO_2 or *plutonium hydride*, PuH_3.

Plutonium-241 is the parent isotope for the neptunium radioactive decay series (see Fig. 93-2). This 14-year isotope decays naturally to americium-241 by way of β-radiation, or electron emission:

$$^{241}Pu_{94} \rightarrow {}^{241}Am_{95} + {}^0e_{-1}$$

Element 95: Americium

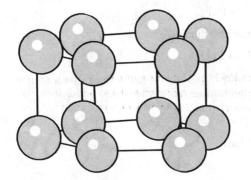

Name	Americium
Symbol	Am
Atomic Number	95
Atomic Weight	243
Melting Point	994°C
Boiling Point	2607°C
Specific Gravity	13.67 (20°C)
Oxidation States	+3, +4, +5, +6
Electron Config.	(Rn) $5f^7 7s^2$

- Name pronounced as **am-er-ISH-i-em**
- Named for the American continent
- Discovered by Glenn T. Seaborg, Ralph A. James, Leon O. Morgan, and Albert Ghiorso in 1944
- Silvery-white, radioactive metal

In spite of the terrible distractions of World War II, Glenn T. Seaborg (1912–) and his associates at the Argonne National Laboratory at the University of Chicago continued to exercise their talent for uncovering new and heavier chemical elements. Neptunium (element 93) and plutonium (element 94) had just emerged as vital new elements of both scientific and military importance. Seaborg and his group were convinced that elements 95 and 96 were just a few processes away. So, in 1944, this group of Manhattan Project workers began a serious search for evidence of the new elements.

The key to their impending success was that the heavier artificial elements, numbers 95 and 96, would have properties similar to those of the heavier rare earths. While the team worked along this line of thinking, element 96 popped up almost immediately, followed a few months later by element 95. The two new elements were discovered in reverse order, but even in the esoteric realm of transuranium research, you have to take it as it comes—especially when you are on a roll.

Finding evidence of new elements is one thing; identifying them according to official standards is a different matter. What was so simple at the initial discovery stage turned out to be a long and tedious procedure through the necessary identification stages. At least one of the workers suggested appropriate names for the two new elements: "pandemonium" and "delirium."

The name *americium* was chosen for element 95 because it turned out to be similar to the rare-earth element europium. And since the rare-earth analogue was named according to is continent of discovery, Europe, the new element should be likewise named. Americium is an actinide metal in Group VIII on the periodic table.

As shown in Fig. 95-1, all isotopes of americium are radioactive. Americium-241 was the one Seaborg and his coworkers found first. Today, americium-241 is produced in kilogram quantities and applied to high-precision measuring devices and gas (smoke) detectors. The reaction is the same one Seaborg used in his initial studies of americium. The reaction sequence begins by bombarding plutonium-239 with high-energy neutrons. The result is

Isotope	Half-Life	Decay Mode
^{237}Am	1.2 hr	α, ec
^{238}Am	1.6 hr	α, ec
^{239}Am	11.9 hr	α, ec
^{240}Am	50.9 hr	α, ec
^{241}Am	432.2 yr	α
^{242m}Am	141 yr	α, it
^{242}Am	16 hr	β-, ec
^{243}Am	7.4×10^3 yr	α
^{244m}Am	26 min	β-
^{244}Am	10.1 hr	β-
^{245}Am	2.1 hr	β-
^{246m}Am	25 min	β-
^{246}Am	39 min	β-
^{247}Am	3 min	β-

95-1 Americium has isotopes with atomic weights between 237 and 247.

gamma radiation and atoms of plutonium-240. The plutonium-240 is then subjected to neutron bombardment; this time the result is gamma radiation and atoms of plutonium-241. Nature takes care of the remaining reaction, in which natural beta decay transforms the plutonium-241 to americium-241. Symbolically, the sequence is:

$$^{239}\text{Pu}(n,\gamma)^{240}\text{Pu}(n,\gamma)^{241}\text{Pu} \rightarrow {}^{241}\text{Am} + \beta-$$

Only few notable compounds of americium exist. *Americium dioxide*, AmO_2 is the most important of the lot, if for no other reason than it is used for preparing the others. The halides, typical of this transuranium series, include *americium bromide* ($AmBr_3$), *americium chloride* ($AmCl_3$), *americium fluoride* (AmF_3), and *americium iodide* (AmI_3).

Americium-241 appears early in the neptunium radioactive decay series (see Fig. 93-2). In this instance, the isotope undergoes natural α-particle emission to yield neptunium-93. Viewing the α particle as a helium nucleus, the reaction is:

$$^{241}\text{Am}_{95} \rightarrow {}^{237}\text{Np}_{93} + {}^{4}\text{He}_2$$

Element 96: Curium

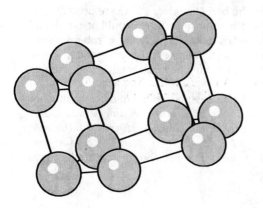

Name	Curium
Symbol	Cm
Atomic Number	96
Atomic Weight	247
Melting Point	1340°C
Boiling Point	-- ? --
Specific Gravity	13.51 (20°C) Note
Oxidation States	+3, +4
Electron Config.	(Rn) $5f^7 6d^1 7s^2$

Note: Calculated value.

- Name pronounced as **KYOOR-i-em**
- Named in honor of Pierre and Marie Curie
- Discovered by Glenn T. Seaborg, Ralph A. James, and Albert Ghiorso in 1944
- Silvery, malleable, synthetic radioactive metal

The Berkeley cyclotron had barely cooled down after Glenn T. Seaborg and his coworkers announced their discovery of plutonium (element 94), when they put it to work in search of elements 95 and 96. Seaborg correctly assumed that the new elements would have valences of + 3 and chemical properties similar to certain rare-earth elements, namely europium and gadolinium.

The group began thinking and working along these lines in 1944, and element 96 practically dropped into their laps—even before element 95 was found (*see* Element 95: Americium). They had produced isotope 242 of element 96 (Curiem—Cm) by bombarding plutonium-239 with alpha particles, or helium ions:

$$^{239}Pu(\alpha,n)^{242}Cm$$

The helium ion contributes two protons to the nucleus; thus, the jump of two places in atomic number—from number 94 (plutonium) to number 96 (curium). The helium ion also contributes two neutrons for a total increase in atomic mass of 4. One neutron is lost, however; so the net increase in atomic mass is only three—from 239 to 242.

It turned out that element 96 did indeed have chemical characteristics similar to the rare-earth element, gadolinium. And since gadolinium was named after a noted expert in rare-earth chemistry, Johan Gadolin, it seemed only fitting to name element 96 after another famous scientist (or a pair of scientists in this case): Pierre and Marie Curie.

Visible amounts of curium were isolated three years later, thus making it possible to confirm physical and chemical characteristics that had been suggested only in theory and by inference. The element was produced in this instance by a two-step process. The first step was to subject americium-241 to prolonged neutron radiation. The result was americium-242m. The second step was to allow spontaneous beta decay to transform the americium into curium-242. The overall atomic reaction is:

$$^{241}Am(n,\gamma)^{242m}Am \rightarrow {}^{242}Cm + \beta -$$

Curium is an actinide metal in Group VIII on the periodic table. There are presently no commercial applications for curium, although there is some hope that it could be developed into a fuel for a portable, lightweight thermoelectric power generator; a sub-miniature atomic power plant, so to speak. Scientists have put together some compounds of curium—a rather large number of them, considering they have no practical applications outside research laboratories.

As with most of the transuranium elements, the most stable compounds of curium are oxides and halides. The oxides are *curium dioxide* (CmO_2 and *curium trioxide* (Cm_2O_3). The halides include *curium bromide* ($CmBr_3$), *curium chloride* ($CmCl_3$), *curium tetrafluoride* (CmF_4) and *curium iodide* (CmI_3).

Figure 96-1 shows the known isotopes of curium. The list shows that at least two curium isotopes undergo spontaneous fission, *sf*.

Isotope	Half-Life	Decay Mode
^{238}Cm	2.4 hr	α, ec
^{239}Cm	3 hr	ec
^{240}Cm	27 day	α
^{241}Cm	32.8 day	α, ec
^{242}Cm	163 day	α
^{243}Cm	28.5 yr	α
^{244}Cm	18.1 yr	α
^{245}Cm	8.5×10^3 yr	α
^{246}Cm	4.78×10^3 yr	α
^{247}Cm	1.56×10^7 yr	α
^{248}Cm	3.4×10^5 yr	α, sf
^{249}Cm	64.2 min	β-
^{250}Cm	7.4×10^3 yr	α, sf
^{251}Cm	16.8 min	β-

96-1 Curium has isotopes with atomic weights between 238 and 251. Isotopes 248 and 250 undergo spontaneous fission, *sf*.

Element 97: Berkelium

Name	Berkelium
Symbol	Bk
Atomic Number	97
Atomic Weight	247 Note 1
Melting Point	--?--
Boiling Point	--?--
Specific Gravity	14 (20°C) Note 2
Oxidation States	+3, +4
Electron Config.	(Rn) $5f^9\,7s^2$

Note 1. Most stable isotope.
Note 2. Estimated value.

- Name pronounced as **BURK-li-em**
- Named for the city of discovery, Berkeley, California
- Discovered by Stanley G. Thompson, Albert Ghiorso, and Glenn T. Seaborg in 1949
- Radioactive synthetic metal

The cornucopia of synthetic heavy elements was still alive and well on the Berkeley campus of the University of California in 1950. Driven by the talent and energy of Glenn T. Seaborg, the Berkeley laboratory became the birthplace of three new synthetic elements in succession: plutonium (94), americium (95), and curium (96).

The fourth new element in a decade was ready by 1950, and it was about time someone thought about naming an element in honor of the Berkeley laboratory and the city of the same name. The choice of this name was not purely arbitrary, however. As Seaborg and his coworkers suspected, the new element did indeed possess chemical characteristics similar to the rare-earth metal, terbium. Terbium wa named for its city of discovery, Ytterby, Sweden. So it was altogether proper to suggest the name *Berkelium* for element 97. This element is an actinide metal in Group IB on the periodic table.

Figure 97-1 lists all the known isotopes of berkelium. Berkelium-243 was first produced by bombarding americium-241 with alpha particles (helium ions):

$$^{241}Am(\alpha,2n)^{243}Bk$$

As shown in Fig. 97-2, an alpha particle contributes two protons and two neutrons. The two protons advance the atomic number by 2, from 95 (americium) to 97 (berkelium). The reaction emits two neutrons, however, so the net gain in atomic mass is only two—from 241 to 243.

Today, berkelium-249 is produced in milligram amounts by successive neutron capture, beginning with curium-244, and beta decay of curium-249:

$$^{244}Cm(5n,\gamma)^{249}Cm \rightarrow {}^{249}Bk + \beta-$$

The first compound of berkelium was produced in 1962. It was a chloride, $BkCl_3$; the sample weighed only three billionths of a gram. Other compounds produced and identified since that time include *berkelium oxychloride* (BkOCl), *berkelium fluoride* (BkF$_3$), *berkelium dioxide* (BkO$_2$), and *berkelium trioxide* (BkO$_3$).

Berkelium and its compounds have no practical applications. Research applications are limited to studies of the heavier elements as well as further research into the nature of berkelium itself.

Isotope	Half-Life	Decay Mode
^{242}Bk	7.0 min	ec
^{243}Bk	4.5 hr	α, ec
^{244}Bk	4.4 hr	α, ec
^{245}Bk	4.9 day	α, ec
^{246}Bk	1.8 day	ec
^{247}Bk	1.4×10^3 yr	α
^{248}Bk	23.7 hr	β-, ec
^{249}Bk	320 day	α, β-
^{250}Bk	3.22 hr	β-
^{251}Bk	57 min	β-

97-1 Berkelium has isotopes with atomic weights between 242 and 251.

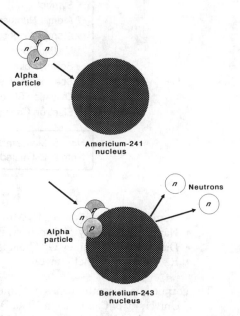

$$^{241}_{95}\text{Am} + ^4_2\text{He} \rightarrow ^{243}_{97}\text{Bk} + 2^1_0 n$$

97-2 Bombarding an americium – 241 nucleus with an alpha particle produces a berkelium – 243 nucleus and two neutrons.

Element 98: Californium

Name	Californium
Symbol	Cf
Atomic Number	98
Atomic Weight	251 Note
Melting Point	-- ? --
Boiling Point	-- ? --
Specific Gravity	-- ? --
Oxidation States	+3, +4
Electron Config.	(Rn) $5f^{10} 7s^2$

Note: Heaviest isotope.

- Name pronounced as **kal-eh-FOR-ni-em**
- Named for the State and University of California
- Discovered by Stanley G. Thompson; Kenneth Street, Jr.; Albert Ghiorso; and Glenn T. Seaborg in 1950
- Powerful neutron emitter

Californium is yet another alumnus—the fifth in succession—of the University of California Radiation Laboratory at Berkeley. In 1950, the group headed by Stanley Thompson converted a sample of curium-242 to californium-245 by bombarding the curium target with alpha particles (helium ions):

$$^{242}Cm(\alpha,n)^{245}Cf$$

The hardest part of the project seemed to be naming the new element. Through their most recent successes, the Berkeley group had been naming the new elements according to their rare-earth analogues; or, in other words, the element appearing directly above on the periodic table. Europium (element 63) was named for the continent of its discovery, so Americium was an appropriate name for element 95. Gadolinium (element 64) was named for a famous scientist, so it was appropriate to name element 96 for the Curies. Following the same line of reasoning, terbium (element 65) had been named for the city of its discovery, so element 97 was named berkelium. The problem with naming element 98 was that the origin of the name of its rare-earth analogue, Dysprosium (element 66) has no special significance. It was not named after a specific person, place or thing. *Dysprosium* literally means "hard to get at." The Berkeley group decided to ignore precedence altogether in this instance and name element 98 after the state of California. (Someone later suggested that *californium* was indeed an appropriate name because America's nineteenth-century settlers found California "hard to get at.") Californium is an actinide metal in Group II on the periodic table.

Figure 98-1 lists the isotopes of californium. The heavier isotopes are produced from berkelium-249 by a somewhat more complicated procedure. Bombarding berkelium-249 with neutrons yields berkelium-250 and some gamma radiation. Berkelium-250 has a short

Isotope	Half-Life	Decay Mode
^{240}Cf	1.06 min	α
^{241}Cf	3.8 min	α, ec
^{242}Cf	3.5 min	α
^{243}Cf	10.7 min	α, ec
^{244}Cf	19.4 min	α
^{245}Cf	43.6 min	α, ec
^{246}Cf	36 hr	α
^{247}Cf	3.11 hr	α, ec
^{248}Cf	334 day	α
^{249}Cf	351 yr	α
^{250}Cf	13.1 yr	α
^{251}Cf	890 yr	α
^{252}Cf	2.64 yr	α, sf
^{253}Cf	17.8 day	α, β-
^{254}Cf	60.5 day	α, sf
^{255}Cf	1.4 hr	β-

98-1 Californium has isotopes with atomic weights between 240 and 255.

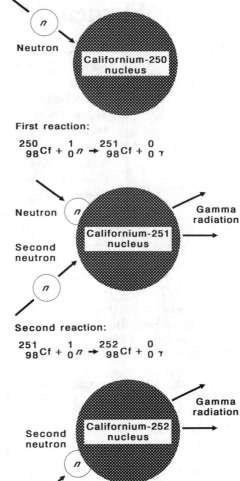

Neutron

Californium-250 nucleus

First reaction:

$$^{250}_{98}\text{Cf} + ^{1}_{0}n \rightarrow ^{251}_{98}\text{Cf} + ^{0}_{0}\gamma$$

Neutron

Second neutron

Californium-251 nucleus

Gamma radiation

Second reaction:

$$^{251}_{98}\text{Cf} + ^{1}_{0}n \rightarrow ^{252}_{98}\text{Cf} + ^{0}_{0}\gamma$$

Second neutron

Californium-252 nucleus

Gamma radiation

98-2 Bombarding californium with neutrons releases gamma radiation.

half-life (about three hours), so it readily decays by beta radiation to californium-250. The process, as described thus far, is noted as:

$$^{249}\text{Bk}(n,\gamma)^{250}\text{Bk} \rightarrow ^{250}\text{Cf} + \beta-$$

If californium-250 is then bombarded with neutrons, the process yields californium-251. Continued neutron irradiation then leads to californium-252. The nuclear notation for this part of the process is:

$$^{250}\text{Cf}(n,\gamma)^{251}\text{Cf}(n,\gamma)^{252}\text{Cf}$$

Figure 98-2 illustrates the entire procedure.

Very few compounds have been synthesized and properly identified: *californium oxide* (CfO_3), *californium trichloride* ($CfCl_3$), and *californium oxychloride* (CfOCl).

Element 99: Einsteinium

Name	Einsteinium
Symbol	En
Atomic Number	99
Atomic Weight	252 Note
Melting Point	-- ? --
Boiling Point	-- ? --
Specific Gravity	-- ? --
Oxidation States	+2, +3
Electron Config.	(Rn) $5f^{11}7s^2$

Note: Most stable isotope.

- Name pronounced as **ine-STINE-i-em**
- Named in honor of Albert Einstein
- Discovered by Albert Ghiorso and others in 1952
- Radioactive, synthetic metal

Element 99, now known as einsteinium, was discovered sometime between 1952 and 1954. Sketchy details about elements 99 and 100 appeared in scientific journals during the latter part of that period, but no one outside the Berkeley radiation group and Argonne Laboratories had a clear idea of what was going on. Certain security restrictions were finally lifted in 1955, and the details of elements 99 and 100 were announced to the scientific community.

Why would United States security restrictions apply to the discovery of these new chemical elements? The answer is simple: traces of the elements were discovered in the residue of the first thermonuclear (hydrogen bomb) explosion in November, 1952—an explosion that obliterated a small island in the Pacific Ocean. In such an explosion, some uranium-238 is converted by extremely intense neutron bombardment to uranium-253 and gamma radiation. Uranium-253 is then spontaneously transformed, by beta decay, to einsteinium-253. The nuclear equation for this process is:

$$^{238}U(15n,\gamma)^{253}U - 7\beta- \rightarrow ^{253}Es$$

Naturally, it is not feasible to blow up an island every time you want a new sample of einsteinium; so researchers worked out a somewhat more time-consuming, but less calamitous, alternative. The procedure begins with plutonium-239, a good choice, considering there is more than enough available today (*see* Element 94: Plutonium).

- Step 1. Plutonium-239 to americium-241:
  $$^{239}Pu(2n,\gamma)^{241}Pu \rightarrow ^{241}Am + \beta-$$

- Step 2. Americium-241 to curium-242:
  $$^{241}Am(n,\gamma)^{242}Am \rightarrow ^{242}Cm + \beta-$$

- Step 3. Curium-242 to berkelium-249:
$$^{242}Cm(7n,\gamma)^{249}Cm \rightarrow {}^{249}Bk + \beta-$$

- Step 4. Berkelium-249 to californium-250
$$^{249}Bk(n,\gamma)^{250}Bk \rightarrow {}^{250}Cf + \beta-$$

- Step 5. Californium-250 to einsteinium-253
$$^{250}Cf(3n,\gamma)^{253}Cf \rightarrow {}^{253}Es + \beta-$$

Of course, the element was named in honor of the legendary twentieth-century physicist, Albert Einstein.

Einsteinium is an actinide metal in Group IIIA and in the bottom row of the periodic table. Figure 99-1 shows all of the element's known isotopes.

The known compounds follow the same general pattern of oxides and halides that applies to most of the transuranium elements: *einsteinium trioxide* (Es_2O_3), *einsteinium trichloride* (EsCl_3), *einsteinium oxychloride* (EsOCl), *einsteinium dibromide* (EsBr_2), *einsteinium tribromide* (EsBr_3), *einsteinium diiodide*, (EsI_2) and *einsteinium triiodide*, (EsI_3).

Isotope	Half-Life	Decay Mode
^{243}Es	180 ms	α
^{244}Es	3.7 ms	sf
^{245}Es	4 sec	α
^{246}Es	1.1 sec	α, sf
^{247m}Es	9.2 sec	α
^{247}Es	35 sec	α
^{248}Es	36 sec	α, sf
^{249}Es	2.6 min	α, ec
^{250m}Es	1.8 sec	it
^{250}Es	30 min	α
^{251}Es	5.3 hr	α, ec
^{252}Es	25.4 hr	α
^{253}Es		ec
^{254}Es	3.24 hr	α, sf
^{255}Es	20.1 hr	α
^{256}Es	2.63 hr	α, sf
^{257}Es	100 day	α, sf
^{258}Es	380 μs	sf

99-1 Einsteinium has isotopes with atomic weights between 243 and 258.

Element 100: Fermium

Name	Fermium
Symbol	Fm
Atomic Number	100
Atomic Weight	257 Note
Melting Point	-- ? --
Boiling Point	-- ? --
Specific Gravity	-- ? --
Oxidation State	+3
Electron Config.	(Rn) $5f^{12} 7s^2$

Note: Calculated value.

- Name pronounced as **FER-mi-em**
- Named in honor of Enrico Fermi
- Discovered by Albert Ghiorso and others in 1952
- Radioactive, synthetic metal

Albert Ghiorso and his coworkers at Berkeley (University of California) detected fermium in the residue of the first thermonuclear, or hydrogen bomb, explosion in November, 1952, and so did researchers at the Argonne Laboratories in Idaho. There was a need to straighten out the order of discovery in order to give the earlier discoverer the proper recognition, including the right to name the element. The only problem was that a veil of secrecy surrounding the first thermonuclear explosions made it impossible for the groups to publish their results and thereby fix the official dates of their findings.

Both groups of researchers had to operate under the cloud of secrecy for nearly two years, and rest of the world was unaware that the periodic table was about to be extended once again. By the summer of 1955, however, the United States government lifted its ban on publishing the results. It was agreed that Dr. Ghiorso and his Berkeley group had discovered fermium first. This element is the heaviest Group IVA element.

Thermonuclear, or H-bomb, explosions create an incredibly dense, yet short lived, wave of neutrons. Within a few microseconds, a single atom of uranium-238 can pick up 17 neutrons from the wave, or flux. The immediate result is an atom of uranium-255 and a unit of gamma radiation. Uranium-255 then decays spontaneously by $\beta -$ radiation (electron emission, $^0e-1$) to form fermium-255. A nuclear equation for this process is:

$$^{238}U_{92}(17n,\gamma)^{255}U_{92} \rightarrow {}^{255}Fm_{100} + 8^0 \, {}^0e_{-1}$$

Today, fermium is produced only for research purposes. There is no commercial application of the element nor its compounds. Samples are produced by means of slow-neutron irradiation and a lengthy set of nuclear reactions. Each step consists of bombarding the target isotope with neutrons, followed by spontaneous beta-particle decay.

- Step 1. Plutonium-239 to americium-241:
  $$^{239}Pu(2n,\gamma)^{241}Pu_{94} \rightarrow {}^{241}Am_{95} + {}^0e_{-1}$$

- Step 2. Americium-241 to curium-242:
$$^{241}\text{Am}(n,\gamma)^{242}\text{Am}_{95} \rightarrow {}^{242}\text{Cm}_{96} + {}^{0}e_{-1}$$

- Step 3. Curium-242 to berkelium-249:
$$^{242}\text{Cm}(7n,\gamma)^{249}\text{Cm}_{96} \rightarrow {}^{249}\text{Bk}_{97} + {}^{0}e_{-1}$$

- Step 4. Berkelium-249 to californium-250:
$$^{249}\text{Bk}(7n,\gamma)^{250}\text{Bk}_{97} \rightarrow {}^{250}\text{Cf}_{98} + {}^{0}e_{-1}$$

- Step 5. Californium-250 to einsteinium-253:
$$^{250}\text{Cf}(3n,\gamma)^{253}\text{Cf}_{98} \rightarrow {}^{253}\text{Es}_{99} + {}^{0}e_{-1}$$

- Step 6. Einsteinium-253 to fermium-254:
$$^{253}\text{Es}(n,\gamma)^{254}\text{Es}_{99} \rightarrow {}^{254}\text{Fm}_{100} + {}^{0}e_{-1}$$

As shown in Fig. 100-1, fermium-257 has the longest half-life of all the isotopes. It can be produced in weighable amounts, and studies show that it has an oxidation state of $+3$ and possibly $+2$ as well. It can be produced by further neutron bombardment of fermium-254.

$$254\text{Fm}_{100} + 3{}^{1}n_{0} \rightarrow {}^{257}\text{Fm}_{100} + {}^{0}\gamma_{00}$$

With an oxidation state of $+3$, the metallic ion would be Fm^{3+}. The halides and oxides would thus take these forms:

Fermium chloride, FmCl_3

$$\text{Fm}^{3+} + 3\text{Cl}^- \rightarrow \text{FmCl}_3$$

Fermium oxide, Fm_2O_3

$$2\text{Fm}^{3+} + 3\text{O}^{2-} \rightarrow \text{Fm}_2\text{O}_3$$

Isotope	Half-Life	Decay Mode
^{243}Fm	180 ms	α
^{244}Fm	3.7 ms	sf
^{245}Fm	4 sec	α
^{246}Fm	1.1 sec	α, sf
^{247m}Fm	9.2 sec	α
^{247}Fm	35 sec	α
^{248}Fm	36 sec	α, sf
^{249}Fm	2.6 min	α, ec
^{250m}Fm	1.8 sec	it
^{250}Fm	30 min	α
^{251}Fm	5.3 hr	α, ec
^{252}Fm	25.4 hr	α
^{253}Fm		α, ec
^{254}Fm	3.24 hr	α, sf
^{255}Fm	20.1 hr	α
^{256}Fm	2.63 hr	α, sf
^{257}Fm	100 day	α, sf
^{258}Fm	380 μs	sf

100-1 Fermium has isotopes with mass numbers between 243 and 258.

Element 101: Mendelevium

Name	Mendelevium
Symbol	Md
Atomic Number	101
Atomic Weight	258 Note
Melting Point	-- ? --
Boiling Point	-- ? --
Specific Gravity	-- ? --
Oxidation States	+2, +3
Electron Config.	(Rn) $5f^{12} 7s^2$

Note: Estimated value.

- Name pronounced as **men-deh-LEE-vi-em**
- Named in honor of Dmitri Mendeleyev
- Discovered by Albert Ghiorso, Bernard G. Harvey, Gregory R. Choppin, Stanley G. Thompson, and Glenn T. Seaborg in 1955
- Radioactive, synthetic metal

Mendelevium is yet another product of the Berkeley lab at the University of California. Albert Ghiorso, Glenn T. Seaborg, and others had predicted the existence of element 101; because it would ultimately appear below thulium on the periodic table of elements, they called it *eka-thulium*.

Mendelevium-256 was first produced in 1955 by bombarding einsteinium-253 with alpha particles, or helium ions. A representative nuclear equation for this process is:

$$^{253}\text{Es}(\alpha,n)^{256}\text{Md}$$

Recalling that an alpha particle is a helium nucleus ($^4\text{He}_2$) and that a neutron has a mass of 1 but no charge ($_1n_0$), the "longhand" version of the equation is:

$$^{253}\text{Es}_{99} + {^4}\text{He}_2 \rightarrow {^{256}}\text{Md}_{101} + {^1}n_0$$

The alpha particle contributes two neutrons and two protons to the target atom. The collision, however, releases a neutron. So, the overall gain in particles, or atomic mass is $4 - 1 = 3$. The gain in atomic number is two—from 99 (Es) to 101 (Md).

Mendelevium is the first synthetic, or man-made, element that was assembled virtually one atom at a time.

As shown in Fig. 101-1, the most stable isotope of this element is mendelevium-258. The procedure for producing this isotope is identical to the procedure used for reacting the first atoms of mendelevium. The target in this instance, however, is einsteinium-255 instead of -253:

$$^{255}\text{Es}(\alpha,n)^{258}\text{Md}$$

or

$$^{255}\text{Es}_{99} + {^4}\text{He}_2 \rightarrow {^{258}}\text{Md}_{101} + {^1}n_0$$

Little is known about the nature of mendelevium compounds, but most chemists agree that the metal has a stable oxidation state of +3. This means it combines with halogen ions to form trihalides such as:

Mendelevium fluoride, MdF_3

$$Md^{3+} + 3F^- \rightarrow MdF_3$$

Mendelevium chloride, $MdCl_3$

$$Md^{3+} + 3Cl^- \rightarrow MdCl_3$$

The oxide would be:

Mendelevium oxide, Md_2O_3

$$2Md^{3+} + 3O^{2-} \rightarrow Md_2O_3$$

Isotope	Half-Life	Decay Mode
^{248}Md	7 sec	α, ec
^{249}Md	24 sec	α, e
^{250}Md	52 sec	α, ec
^{251}Md	4.0 min	α, ec
^{252}Md	2.3 min	α, ec
^{254m}Md	28 min	ec
^{254}Md	10 min	α, ec
^{255}Md	27 min	α, ec
^{256}Md	76 min	α, ec
^{257}Md	5.2 hr	α, ec
^{258m}Md	43 min	ec
^{258}Md	56 day	α
^{259}Md	1.6 hr	sf

101-1 Mendelevium has isotopes with mass numbers between 248 and 259.

Element 102: Nobelium

Name	Nobelium
Symbol	No
Atomic Number	102
Atomic Weight	259 Note
Melting Point	-- ? --
Boiling Point	-- ? --
Specific Gravity	-- ? --
Oxidation States	+2, +3
Electron Config.	(Rn) $5f^{13} 7s^2$

Note: Estimated value.

- Name pronounced as **no-BELL-i-em**
- Named in honor of Alfred Nobel, the discoverer of dynamite
- Discovered by Albert Ghiorso, T. Sikkeland, J.R. Walton, and Glenn T. Seaborg in 1958
- Radioactive, synthetic metal

In 1957, a team of researchers from the United States, Great Britain, and Sweden announced the discovery of element 102. It seemed that the string of successes attributed to Ghiorso, Seaborg, and others at the Berkeley lab was finally broken. The international group, working with an 85-MeV cyclotron at the Nobel Institute of Physics in Stockholm, bombarded a target of curium-244 with heavy carbon-13 ions. The researchers reported the creation of an isotope of element 102 having a half-life of 10 minutes. Everyone concerned seemed pleased with the work, and the group happily named the new element after Alfred Nobel.

Ghiorso and Seaborg and their coworkers were a tenacious lot, however; they set out to verify the results from the Nobel Institute. They tried bombarding curium-246 with carbon-12 ions, and found they could produce an isotope of the new element having an atomic mass of 254 and a half-life of 3 seconds. The nuclear equation for this process is:

$$^{246}\text{Cm}(^{12}\text{C},4n)^{254}\text{No}$$

Carbon, with its six neutrons and six protons, is accelerated to an energy level of about 80-million electron volts (MeV). Collision with the curium target drives four neutrons out of the curium atom. The net gain in atomic mass is eight, and the increase in atomic number is six. This work was conducted in 1958.

The Berkeley group could not reproduce the findings of the Nobel group, however. Furthermore, a Russian team at Dubna could reproduce the Berkeley results, but not the Nobel results. So the highly respected International Union of Pure and Applied Chemistry finally found itself with some egg on its face—it had been too hasty in accepting the claim of the group from the Nobel Institute. The claim to prior discovery was subsequently awarded to the Berkeley group. Not wishing to muddy the waters any further, the Berkeley group agreed to retain the original name of the element.

Nobelium is the heaviest of the Group VIA elements. It is very near the end of the transuranium portion of the actinide series. It is a *transuranium* element because it is an element heavier than uranium, and it is an *actinide* because it belongs to the series of elements between actinium (element 89) and lawrencium (element 103). As indicated in Fig. 102-1, all known isotopes of nobelium are radioactive, and all are synthetic. Most are alpha emitters, and a couple decay by means of spontaneous fission.

Isotope	Half-Life	Decay Mode
^{250}No	250 μs	sf
^{251}No	800 ms	α
^{252}No	2.3 sec	α, sf
^{253}No	1.7 min	α, it
^{254m}No	280 ms	α
^{254}No	55 sec	α, ec
^{255}No	3.1 min	α
^{256}No	3.2 sec	α
^{257}No	25 sec	α
^{258}No	1.2 ms	sf
^{259}No	58 min	α, ec

102-1 Nobelium has isotopes with mass numbers between 250 and 259.

Although no compounds of nobelium have been prepared yet, enough is known about the element to suggest that it would exhibit oxidation states of $+2$ and $+3$, with $+2$ being the more stable. Given this information, it is possible to speculate about compounds that might be found one day. The transuranium elements tend to form halides and oxides, so an ambitious chemist might set out to concoct the following:

Nobelium (II) fluoride, NoF_2

$$No^{2+} + 2F^- \rightarrow NoF_2$$

Nobelium (III) fluoride, NoF_3

$$No^{3+} + 3F^- \rightarrow NoF_3$$

Nobelium (II) oxide, NoO

$$No^{2+} + O^{2-} \rightarrow NoO$$

Nobelium (III) oxide, No_2O_3

$$2No^{3+} + 3O^{2-} \rightarrow No_2O_3$$

Element 103: Lawrencium

Name	Lawrencium
Symbol	Lr
Atomic Number	103
Atomic Weight	260 Note
Melting Point	-- ? --
Boiling Point	-- ? --
Specific Gravity	-- ? --
Oxidation States	+3
Electron Config.	(Rn) $5f^{14} 7s^2$

Note: Estimated value.

- Name pronounced as **lor-ENS-i-em**
- Named in honor of Ernest O. Lawrence, inventor of the cyclotron
- Discovered by Albert Ghiorso, T. Sikkeland, A.E. Larsh, and R.M. Latimer in 1961
- Radioactive, synthetic metal

By 1961, the Lawrence Radiation Laboratory at the Berkeley campus at the University of California was the birthplace of an unprecedented string of new elements; element 103 was just sitting there waiting to be next. Element 103 would be the last of the metals in the actinide series (a series that begins with element 89, actinium) and would be the heaviest of the halides. However, this was about to be only the second transuranium element that Glenn T. Seaborg would not be able to claim to some extent.

While Albert Ghiorso and his coworkers at Berkeley were cranking up the ion accelerator for another successful discovery, Seaborg was busy with his duties as chancellor of the University of California. The new element was originally produced by bombarding a mixture of three californium isotopes with heavy ions, boron-10 and boron-11. The reactions taking place were:

$$^{250}Cf(^{10}B,2n)^{258}Lr$$

$$^{250}Cf(^{11}B,3n)^{258}Lr$$

$$^{251}Cf(^{10}B,3n)^{258}Lr$$

$$^{251}Cf(^{11}B,4n)^{258}Lr$$

$$^{252}Cf(^{10}B,4n)^{258}Lr$$

$$^{252}Cf(^{11}B,5n)^{258}Lr$$

The target in this experiment weighed only about 2 μg, or 2-millionths of a gram.

Figure 103-1 shows that lawrencium-256 has the longest half-life of all known isotopes. In other words, this is the element's most stable isotope and, therefore, the one most useful

Isotope	Half-Life	Decay Mode
^{253}Lr	1.4 sec	α
^{254}Lr	20 sec	α
^{255}Lr	4 sec	α
^{256}Lr	28 sec	α, sf
^{257}Lr	650 ms	α
^{258}Lr	4.3 sec	α
^{259}Lr	5.4 sec	α
^{260}Lr	3 min	α

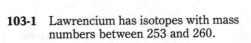

103-1   Lawrencium has isotopes with mass numbers between 253 and 260.

for confirming the chemical properties of it. Soviet scientists in 1965 used a heavy-ion accelerator to produce the relatively stable lawrencium-256, bombarding americium-243 with oxygen-18 ions:

$$^{243}\text{Am}(^{18}\text{O},5n)^{256}\text{Lr}$$

or

$$^{243}\text{Am}_{95} + {}^{18}\text{O}_8 \rightarrow {}^{256}\text{Lr}_{103} + 5\,{}^{1}n_0$$

A few atoms of *lawrencium oxide*, Lr_3O_2, have been studied—insofar as a few atoms of anything can be studied. For all practical purposes, no compounds of lawrencium exist, nor are there any prospects for producing any of them in the foreseeable future.

Element 104: Unnilquadium

Name	Element 104
Symbol	Rf or Unq
Atomic Number	104
Atomic Weight	261 Note
Melting Point	-- ? --
Boiling Point	-- ? --
Specific Gravity	-- ? --
Oxidation State	+4
Electron Config.	(Rn) $5f^{15} 7s^2$

Note: Estimated value.

- Temporary name is *unnilquadium*, pronounced as **oon-nil-QUAD-i-em**
- Suggested names and symbols are kurchatovium (Ku) and rutherfordium (Rf)
- Existence reported by Soviet Nuclear Research in 1964 and by the University of California at Berkeley in 1969
- Radioactive, synthetic metal

When the confirmed discovery at lawrencium, element 103, completed the actinide series of transuranium elements, researchers began looking for the heaviest of the Group IVB elements.

In 1964, Russian scientists at the Joint Institute for Nuclear Research at Dubna announced their discovery of element 104. They suggested the name *kurchatovium*, symbol Ku, in honor of the Soviet nuclear physicist, Igor Kurchatov. The claim was based on the production of an isotope of element 104 having an atomic mass of 260.

They managed the job by smashing a target of plutonium-242 with a very heavy ion of neon-22. Using the unbiased chemical name, unnilquadium (Unq), the nuclear reaction is:

$$^{242}Pu(^{22}Ne,4n)^{260}Unq$$

or

$$^{242}Pu_{94} + {}^{22}Ne_{10} \rightarrow {}^{260}Unq_{104} + 4^1n_0$$

The Lawrence Laboratory on the Berkeley campus of the University of California seems to have had difficulty reproducing the results of other would-be discoverers of new chemical elements. In this instance the equipment was simply unable to accelerate neon ions, so the American group had to resort to a different procedure—bombarding californium-239 with a mixture of two heavy-ion isotopes, carbon-12 and carbon-13. The reactions are:

$$^{249}Cf(^{12}B,4n)^{257}Unq$$
and
$$^{249}Cf(^{13}B,3n)^{259}Unq$$

There might have been some Unq-258 produced as well:

$$^{249}\text{Cf}(^{12}\text{B},3n)^{258}\text{Unq}$$

or

$$^{249}\text{Cf}(^{13}\text{B},4n)^{258}\text{Unq}$$

Finally, the Americans produced some Unq-261 by bombarding curium-248 with oxygen-18. The longhand version of the reaction is:

$$^{248}\text{Cm}_{96} + {}^{18}\text{O}_8 \rightarrow {}^{261}\text{Unq}_{104} + 5^1 n_0$$

Not only did the American group produce a wider variety of isotopes of element 104, but it produced larger quantities—thousands of atoms of each, instead of the Soviet's two or three. The Soviet group is thus challenged to produce more convincing evidence than they have done thus far. The only advantage they have is the earlier announcement; and although that is no small matter, being able to substantiate the claim in a convincing and responsible fashion is most important. It appears that the Americans will be taking the honors for this discovery one of these days. The American choice for a name, named after Enerst Rutherford, a physicist, is *rutherfordium*. This name is appearing in an ever-increasing amount of scientific literature.

Figure 104-1 shows the isotopes of rutherfordium that have been identified thus far.

Isotope	Half-Life	Decay Mode
^{257}Rf	4.8 sec	α
^{258}Rf	11 ms	sf
^{259}Rf	3.1 sec	α
^{260}Rf	20 ms	sf
^{261}Rf	65 sec	α
^{262}Rf	65 ms	α

104-1 Rutherfordium has isotopes with mass numbers between 257 and 262.

Element 105: Hahnium

Name	Element 105
Symbol	Ha or Unp
Atomic Number	105
Atomic Weight	262 Note
Melting Point	-- ? --
Boiling Point	-- ? --
Specific Gravity	-- ? --
Oxidation States	-- ? --
Electron Config.	(Rn) $5f^{16} 7s^2$

Note: Estimated value.

- Name pronounced as **HAH-ni-em**
- Temporary name is *unnilpentium*, symbol Unp
- Existence reported by Soviet Nuclear Research in 1967 and by the University of California at Berkeley in 1970
- Radioactive, synthetic metal

Hahnium is the heaviest of the Group VB metals. There is no longer any question that the element has been found; the only problem is one of placing the timing of discovery.

In 1967, a Soviet team at the Joint Institute for Nuclear Research claimed to have produced a few atoms of hahnium-260 and -261, supposedly accomplished by bombarding americium-24 with ions of neon-22:

$$^{243}Am_{95} + {}^{22}Ne_{10} \rightarrow {}^{260}Ha_{105} + 5^1n_0$$

and

$$^{243}Am_{95} + {}^{22}Ne_{10} \rightarrow {}^{261}Ha_{105} + 4^1n_0$$

In April, 1970, the Soviet group reported the results of exhaustive tests they had conducted on trace samples of element 105. For some reason, they did not suggest a name.

Later that same month, a United States group working at the radiation laboratory at Berkeley reported positive identification of the element and suggest the name *hahnium*, after a German chemist, Otto Hahn. Their method was to bombard californium-249 with ions of nitrogen-15:

$$^{249}Cf_{98} + {}^{15}N_7 \rightarrow {}^{260}Ha_{105} + 4^1n_0$$

The Berkeley group can show positive evidence that they actually accomplished the task on March 5, 1970; they are trying to show that it might have been done a year earlier as well. The group is not sitting still. In October, 1971, the same laboratory announced the positive synthesis of the rest of the isotopes of hahnium shown in Fig. 105-1.

Isotope	Half-Life	Decay Mode
^{257}Ha	1 sec	α
^{258}Ha	4 sec	α
^{259}Ha	1.2 sec	sf
^{260}Ha	1.5 sec	α, sf
^{261}Ha	1.8 sec	α
^{262}Ha	34 sec	α, sf

105-1 Hahnium has isotopes with mass numbers between 257 and 262.

Element 106: Unnilhexium

Name	Element 106
Symbol	Unh
Atomic Number	106
Atomic Weight	263 Note
Melting Point	-- ? --
Boiling Point	-- ? --
Specific Gravity	-- ? --
Oxidation States	-- ? --
Electron Config.	(Rn) $5f^{17} 7s^2$

Note: Estimated value.

- Temporary name is *unnilhexium*, pronounced as **oon-nil-HEX-i-em**
- Existence reported by Soviet Nuclear Research and by the University of California at Berkeley in 1974
- Radioactive, synthetic metal

The Soviet Joint Institute for Nuclear Research announced their discovery of element 106 in June, 1974. Three months later, the United States group at Berkeley claimed positive discovery of the same element. The claims have not been fully evaluated to establish priority, so the element is sitting in limbo for the time being. Neither group claiming discovery has offered a name, so element 106 goes by the neutral, generic name, *unnilhexium*. The temporary symbol is Unh (*see* Elements 108 and Up: The Superheavy Elements for an explanation of the neutral-name conventions).

Unh is the last and heaviest of the Group-VIB elements. Figure 106-1 lists the isotopes that have been found thus far.

106-1 Unnilhexium has isotopes with mass numbers between 259 and 263.

Isotope	Half-Life	Decay Mode
^{259}Unh	7 ms	sf
^{261}Unh	1 ms	sf
^{262}Unh	115 ms	α
^{263}Unh	800 ms	α

The American claim is based on a procedure that calls for bombarding a target of californium-249 with ions of oxygen – 18. The result is Unh-263 and four neutrons:

$$^{249}Cf_{98} + {}^{18}O_8 \rightarrow {}^{263}Unh_{106} + 4^1 n_0$$

The Soviet version describes how they bombarded three different isotopes of lead with high-energy ions of chromium-54.

Element 107: Unnilseptium

Name	Element 107
Symbol	Uns
Atomic Number	107
Atomic Weight	264 Note
Melting Point	-- ? --
Boiling Point	-- ? --
Specific Gravity	-- ? --
Oxidation States	-- ? --
Electron Config.	(Rn) $5f^{18} 7s^2$

Note: Estimated value.

- Temporary name is *unnilseptium*, pronounced as **oon-nil-SEPT-i-em**
- Existence reported by Soviet Nuclear Research in 1976
- Radioactive, synthetic metal

Soviet scientists reported they had produced an isotope of element 107 in 1976. Their claim has since been substantiated by German researchers. But for reasons that are difficult to understand, the Soviets are slow to suggest names for their elements—even where there seems to be positive evidence of priority of discovery. So element 107 is still going by its neutral, or generic name, unnilseptium. The corresponding symbol is Uns. (*See* Elements 108 and Up: The Superheavy Elements for an explanation of the neutral-name conventions.)

Uns is the last of the Group-VIIB elements.

Elements 108 and up:
The superheavy elements

The search for new elements continues today. The excitement of discovery is not over; maybe it is really just beginning. Figure 108-1 shows the periodic table of the elements as it might look in the distant future. The shaded blocks represent elements that have been discovered and confirmed to date. The rest of the blocks represent elements yet to be discovered or confirmed.

Until the existence of a new element is proven to the satisfaction of the International Union of Pure and Applied Chemistry (UPAC), the elements are to have names and symbols that are devised according to some very precise but simple rules.

The name is based on the digits in the element's atomic number:

0 nil	5 pent
1 un	6 hex
2 bi	7 sept
3 tri	8 oct
4 quad	9 enn

Example: Element 125

1 2 5
un-bi-pent-ium

The generic name for element 125 is *unbipentium*. The symbol is simply the first letter in each of the expressions from the table. The symbol for element 125 is Ubp. Only the first letter is capitalized.

The structure of this proposed periodic table is based on the notion that there will be a series of superheavy elements that correspond to the lanthanide and actinide series. Recall that the lanthanide series begins with lanthanum (element 57), picks up with cerium (element 58) near the bottom of the chart, and concludes with lutetium (element 71). The actinide series follows the same pattern. It begins with actinium (element 89), breaks away from the main body of the chart and resumes with thorium (element 90) along the bottom of the chart, then concludes with lawrencium (element 103). By analogy, then, there will be a series of superheavies that begin with Ubu (element 121), breaks away from the main body to Ubb (element 122), then concludes at the end of that row with Upt (element 153).

Unlike the lanthanum and actinium series, however, experts suggest there will be an additional extension of the series that includes elements 135 through 152. There is more uncertainty about details of this feature than any other shown on the proposed periodic table.

This table shows the elements up to atomic number 168. Why stop there? Because the arrangement of elements beyond that number would be purely speculative.

Can we possibly go beyond element 168? Yes, but the consensus is that we cannot go much farther. As atomic numbers approach 200, the forces required for holding the nuclei together and the electrons in orbit become immense.

IA	IIA	IIIB	IVB	VB	VIB	VIIB	VIII	VIII	VIII	IB	IIB	IIIA	IVA	VA	VIA	VIIA	0
1 H																	2 He
3 Li	4 Be											5 B	6 C	7 N	8 O	9 F	10 Ne
11 Na	12 Mg											13 Al	14 Si	15 P	16 S	17 Cl	18 Ar
19 K	20 Ca	21 Sc	22 Ti	23 V	24 Cr	25 Mn	26 Fe	27 Co	28 Ni	29 Cu	30 Zn	31 Ga	32 Ge	33 As	34 Se	35 Br	36 Kr
37 Rb	38 Sr	39 Y	40 Zr	41 Nb	42 Mo	43 Tc	44 Ru	45 Rh	46 Pd	47 Ag	48 Cd	49 In	50 Sn	51 Sb	52 Te	53 I	54 Xe
55 Cs	56 Ba	57 La	72 Hf	73 Ta	74 W	75 Re	76 Os	77 Ir	78 Pt	79 Au	80 Hg	81 Tl	82 Pb	83 Bi	84 Po	85 At	86 Rn
87 Fr	88 Ra	89 Ac	104 Rf	105 Ha	106 Unh	107 Uns	108 Uno	109 Une	110 Uun	111 Uuu	112 Uub	113 Uut	114 Uuq	115 Uup	116 Uuh	117 Uus	118 Uuo
119 Uue	120 Ubn	121 Ubu	154 Upq	155 Upp	156 Uph	157 Ups	158 Upo	159 Upe	160 Uhn	161 Uhu	162 Uhb	163 Uht	164 Uhq	165 Uhp	166 Uhh	167 Uhs	168 Uho

6	58 Ce	59 Pr	60 Nd	61 Pm	62 Sm	63 Eu	64 Gd	65 Tb	66 Dy	67 Ho	68 Er	69 Tm	70 Yb	71 Lu
7	90 Th	91 Pa	92 U	93 Np	94 Pu	95 Am	96 Cm	97 Bk	98 Cf	99 Es	100 Fm	101 Md	102 No	103 Lr
8	122 Ubb	123 Ubt	124 Ubq	125 Ubp	126 Ubh	127 Ubs	128 Ubo	129 Ube	130 Utn	131 Utu	132 Utb	133 Utt	134 Utq	153 Upt

8	135 Utp	136 Uth	137 Uts	138 Uto	139 Ute	140 Uqn	141 Uqu	142 Uqb	143 Uqt	144 Uqq	145 Uqp	146 Uqh	147 Uqs	148 Uqo	149 Uqe	150 Upn	151 Upu	152 Upb

108-1 A completed periodic chart of the elements will most likely include superheavy elements having atomic numbers 108 through 168.

Today's search for new elements

Researchers today are trying to track down new elements in areas of the periodic table that hold out the greatest hope for success. In some instances, a new element can be identified because elements with slightly lower atomic numbers have become well established. This is the principle behind the production of element 109 described later in this chapter. If elements 104, 105, and 107 had not been found before, it would be impossible to confirm the existence of 109.

On the other hand, some elements are more attractive candidates for discovery because they fit into groups that have distinctive patterns of characteristics. Such groups develop very systematically (hence, predictably) from top to bottom on the periodic chart. Here are the hottest examples:

Element 113, Uut, is a Group-IIIA boron element. It is also being called *eka-thallium* these days because it will be the analogue of the element directly above it on the periodic table (element 81, thallium).

Element 114, Uuq, is a Group-IVA carbon element that is also being called *eka-lead*.

Element 117, Uus, is a likely candidate for discovery in the near future because it belongs to the well-defined group of halogen elements, Group-VIIA.

Element 118, Uuo, will be a noble gas, which, like its predecessors in Group O, will resist reactions with other elements.

Element 119, Uue, will be a Group-IA alkali metal.

Element 120, Ubn, will be a superheavy alkali-earth metal.

Element 109

Element 109 was first detected in August 1982 by German researchers at the Heavy Ion Research Laboratory in Darmstadt. They managed the synthesis by bombarding a target of bismuth-209 with high-energy particules of iron-58. This produced a sample of element 109; more specifically, it produced the isotope unnilennium-266 and a free neutron. The reaction looks like this:

$$^{209}Bi_{83} + {}^{58}Fe_{26} \rightarrow {}^{266}Une_{109} + {}^{1}N_0$$

The German group supports their finding by carefully tracing the systematic sequence of decay products. About $^5/_{1000}$ of a second after it is created, Une-266 begins decaying to element 107, unnilseptium-262. The byproduct is a high-energy alpha particle, or helium nucleus:

$$^{266}Une_{109} \rightarrow {}^{262}Uns_{107} + {}^{4}He_2$$

The unnilseptium-262 then decays to hahnium-258:

$$^{272}Uns_{109} \rightarrow {}^{258}Ha_{105} + {}^{4}He_2$$

Then the Ha-105 transforms by electron capture to rutherfordium-258:

$$^{258}Ha_{105} + {}^{0}e_{-1} \rightarrow {}^{259}Rf_{104}$$

Further evidence is pending. The group has not formally proposed a name for this new element.

Index